MW01194114

STANDING IN THE
DARK

Struggle and Hope for Victims of Violent Crime

LaVARR McBRIDE

Penn State University

Kendall Hunt
publishing company

Cover image: © Shutterstock.com

www.kendallhunt.com
Send all inquiries to:
4050 Westmark Drive
Dubuque, IA 52004-1840

Copyright © 2020 by Kendall Hunt Publishing Company

ISBN 978-1-4652-4219-8

All rights reserved. No part of this publication may be reproduced,
stored in a retrieval system, or transmitted, in any form or by any means,
electronic, mechanical, photocopying, recording, or otherwise,
without the prior written permission of the copyright owner.

Published in the United States of America

Contents

Preface

For the past 35 years working in the field of criminal justice, I have had the privilege and honor to work with men and women who are victim survivors of crime.

Though the role of a victim survivor in a criminal act bares no personal responsibility for the ill-conceived behavior of a perpetrator, ironically I have found that both the offender and the victim of crime, experience trauma, sadness, despair, depression, anger, disgust, and so many other adjectives.

This book is a compilation of stories and events in my career that have introduced me to some of the bravest people I know in my life. Many of those that you will meet in this book have moved well beyond their victimization and have found a way to use their experience to better their own lives and affect countless others with their strength and their determination to not let what happened to them define who they are.

Survivors of crime often feel as though they are completely alone in their experience. We have learned through the many years of work with crime victims, that validation of the pain and trauma is one of the most important things we can do to assist those that have been affected by crime.

In talking to Survivors, they often speak of the memories of their pain resurfacing with what we refer to as normal human interaction, appearing in court, or seeing the perpetrator. If you were a victim of a kidnapping and every time you see a pick-up truck that looks like the truck driven by the person that abducted you then that will create a sense of helplessness, what we refer to as secondary victimization. According to the Office of Victims of Crime in Washington DC, they define Secondary Victimization with the following statement:

> After the trauma of a crime, many report being victimized by the very systems that were designed to help them. The media, health services and criminal justice system can respond to victims of crime in ways that make them feel traumatized again. A counselor can help to reduce the chances of secondary victimization by helping victims to understand their rights.

> http://www.ojp.usdoj.gov/ovc/new/victempow/student/student.txt

Secondary Victimization is real and affects every crime victim. Even though at different levels it still leaves many victims feeling vulnerable and unable to cope with what happened to them or a family member.

There are so many types of crimes and you would be surprised as to how many of us have been affected by the poor choices of another human being. I oftentimes

Portions of this Preface are written with permission of Dana Thomas. Portions of this Preface are written with permission of Carol McBride.

ask myself how could that person do that to another human being? For years we have researched, developed, and discussed theories as to why one person would intentionally harm another. Frankly, all the research in the world will not stop a person from making a poor choice. It is truly unclear how we will eliminate the threat of violence on our streets. However, that does not mean that we stop trying, or stop working tirelessly every day to help not only those affected by crime through victimization, but also finding ways to address with those who commit crime why they have made the choices to negatively impact the lives of others.

I believe that it starts with each individual and their commitment to positive change and addressing the concerns and the problems that seem to facilitate poor choices. I believe accountability is the most important concept to overcome an addiction, or other serious behavioral problems that affects countless lives. Before an individual can be accountable; they must first recognize the need for change in their lives and then act upon it. If somehow, we can affect this principle, we will be on the right road in our pursuit to help others.

I have also found that as an agent in public service I must be prepared and deal with all sides of crime, understand the organic nature of the relationship between the offender and the victim, and respect through listening and understanding each person's experience, in order for there to be real change, and meet the needs of both the victim survivor and the offender.

I have been privileged to work with many in addressing these questions I have posed. These individuals and of course countless others who I have worked with in my life in this field have influenced my life to always keep going and try harder in our help to others. These individuals have been successful in impacting countless lives in their work in our criminal justice system and have taught me many lessons that have clearly influenced my professional career and personal life.

The first two individuals I would like to thank are two wonderful people who have shared so much of their time and so much more in their successful launch of their non-profit organization called "Building Hope Today." Matt and Lynne Morgan live in Idaho Falls, Idaho. I first met Matt's mother Judy several years ago. Judy is close friend of my mother's and a woman of great compassion. I have grown to love and respect her so much.

I received a phone call from Matt in 2017. Matt had just won a civil lawsuit against his uncle for committing fraud. The fraud was the grooming and sexual abuse tactics that he inflicted on Matt. It was an unprecedented win in civil court. Matt shared with me his story of abuse. When he was an adolescent he was molested by his uncle over the course of a summer and then because of the shame he buried it for many years.

It did not surface again until he was in his 40s and he realized that he was experiencing difficulties with his relationships, with his drinking and just generally was not happy. Though he was a very successful and continues to be a successful commercial contractor in Idaho, he felt unhappy, and could not understand why. It was not until he reached out for help that he learned that he experienced trauma at a young age and had literally buried those emotions for over 30 years. Matt was diagnosed in 2010 with PTSD and Dissociated Amnesia (DA).

Matt explained to me that the PTSD and DA, locked up inside of him the secret for many years about his abuse. I will explain these diagnoses in Chapter 3. Matt wanted to start a nonprofit and help victims of sexual abuse. He said that they were trying but did not have a good footing and needed some help. I of course was more than happy to help Matt and Lynne.

Lynne is Matt's wife and one of the most kindhearted individuals you would ever meet. Lynne has been extremely supportive of her sweet husband and their children and to say the least it has been a journey for her. She has not faltered in her love for Matt and their relationship is truly inspiring.

Over the course of the last several years with the help of some amazing talented individuals their non-profit, "Building Hope Today," is now being marketed all over the country with police departments, district attorney's offices and many others, including moms and dads and schools.

Their non-profit looks at educating our criminal justice system and our communities on the dangers of pre-meditated grooming tactics of sexual offenders. Through the amazing work of many individuals working together tirelessly, this non-profit is now making a mark in the fight against sexual and physical abuse to our sweet children.

I am proud of Matt for not giving up, moving forward in his life, finding a positive way to deal with his abuse. I was one of the lucky ones to help Matt in his quest to influence this horrible disease in our society of sexual abuse. It was an honor for me to participate in the early stages of this non-profit's investiture. I was honored to get to know Matt and Lynne and to stand by their side as they unveiled this wonderful non-profit. I am confident that they will continue to see wonderful results of Matt stepping out of the dark of his abuse and not being afraid to tell his story.

I had the privilege to go with my dear wife Carol, Matt and Lynne, and Alethea Browning Cox to several prisons and several parts of the country learning from victims and inmates about the trauma of sexual abuse. Alethea is a good friend of Matt and Lynne and has done some incredible groundwork to support them with, "Building Hope Today."

On one occasion, as we visited one of many prisons, I stood next to Matt as he told his story in a Colorado State Prison. It was not to a typical audience; it was inmates in prison. With a great deal of anxiety and fear Matt valiantly stood and shared his story with hundreds of inmates. With tears running down all our cheeks, including inmates, Matt shared some of the most difficult days of his life when he was a victim. I was left in awe at his strength.

Matt clearly was standing in the dark for many years, and one day with the help and strength of his family, Lynne and their three awesome children Travis, Shante' and Blake he immerged from the darkness into the light. As my mind reflected on the title of this book, "Standing in the Dark: Struggle and Hope for Victims of Violent Crime," one of the stories and one of those who inspired me was Matt and his wife Lynne.

Matt, I honor you for not letting your abuser win. You truly are one of my dearest friends who I admire so very much. Thank you for your inspiration and never giving up. Thank you for what you are doing in our community in helping others understand the grooming techniques of sexual offenders and how we can not only recognize these signs but use them as evidence in a court or law. Your inspiration will have huge impact. Thank you, Matt, for not staying in the dark and immerging into the light.

Bill Lintz is a retired FBI agent who lives in Beaver, Pennsylvania. I met Bill nine years ago when I moved to Pennsylvania. He was hired under the direction of J. Edger Hoover and worked for the Bureau from 1968 to 1995. He entered the Bureau and was assigned to Jackson, Mississippi following the assassination of Martin Luther King Jr. Bill had an amazing career and saw and participated in many events in American History with the FBI.

Bill has seen some very difficult times in our nation's history working for the FBI. He has seen the fallout from racism and contention in the south, to many other famous crimes including an extensive history of work in Washington, DC.

What amazes me about this brilliant and kind man is that his heart and soul are fixed on helping others regardless of their issue. There has been many times when Bill has called me about his concern for others, including friendships with even some of those who he arrested that he now has contact with and tries to help even today. Bill has shared invaluable insight that has directly led to guest speakers in my classroom and insight that I continue to share in my classes.

Even today this wonderful man continues to impact our community with his knowledge and expertise. He has done several interviews with the media and participated in documentaries on individuals who have committed crime and he always seem to find time to talk to me. He truly has been a faithful friend.

Bill has introduced me to many professionals in the criminal justice field with his contacts, but what I have appreciated most about this wonderful human being is his love for others and his caring attitude for all people. I don't care who you are, when you leave a meeting with Bill Lintz, whether you have had a good or a bad day, he always makes you feel appreciated and respected. I will never take for granted the beautiful relationship I have established with Bill and I consider him one of my dearest friends. His influence in my life has clearly helped me in writing this book and being a better teacher. I will always be grateful for Bill in my life.

Another inspiring person to me is Dana Thomas, whom I have known for 10 years. Dana worked for the YCC Youth Crisis Center in Ogden, Utah as the Director of their Victim Advocacy program, and then for the state of Utah for The Office for Victims of Crime. I have trained and worked with Dana on many occasions and her sensitivity and care for others is exemplary to me—one who knows how to help others through some of the darkest hours of their lives. Dana is currently the Executive Director of the Wasatch Forensic Nurses in Utah. These nurses perform the sexual assault exams for the adults and children who have been sexually assaulted and abused. What an amazing service Dana provides as well as the special people who help victims soon after they have been victimized.

I have had many philosophical conversations with Dana through the years and I truly believe that if we had more individuals like Dana who can help survivors of crime, we would be much further ahead in finding ways to better support and care for these men and women.

Dana and I worked closely together on an initiative in Utah to help victim survivors find answers to their questions through the victim outreach program that I will talk about more in the book. Dana presented material to defense attorneys with me and truly has helped the field of criminal justice understand what it means to support victims of violent crime and find meaningful ways of supporting them.

I had a recent conversation with Dana where she shared with me how victim survivors have so much that happens to them from being a victim of a crime, having to go to court, harboring a deep feeling of inadequacy, and lack of self-esteem. Dana told me that as advocates for victim survivors, "We have to listen to the concerns of victims, and then help them by breaking it down for them." She shared with me that it is important for professionals who work with victim survivors that this process must be completed slowly to not overwhelm those impacted by crime.

She also shared with me that the process unfortunately will take some time for healing and that it really requires professionals to be patient and not follow their own timeline, but that of the victims. She explained that her role is to encourage them to do it for themselves and provide them the permission to go at their own pace and that the feelings they are having are normal. So many times, we want to relieve their pain not realizing that part of their healing is to experience pain and emotionally learn to how to cope with their difficulties.

In addition, she shared with me that in her opinion it will help them become stronger and they will learn to enjoy the little successes in their recovery, knowing they are progressing. This will begin to take them to new levels of understanding their success in their recovery as well as learning to live with their victimization. This is important, because it will help them to see and learn how to talk about their victimization in a positive way and help them to see that enduring their challenges have made them stronger and more confident.

Giving the victim survivor permission to feel the pain, the hurt, and anger can be therapeutic and will help relieve some of the emotional pain that they have suffered, not to mention the physical pain that they may have to overcome as well. There is a healing effect that comes from a person overcoming their challenges.

Dana shared with me that tragically in many cases of domestic violence for example, the offenders are often holding their family hostage. The more that we as professionals can help victims discover for themselves that breaking that cycle and experience little successes such as finding their own job, renting their own house, and getting counseling, will help the victim survivor to recognize that they are strong and they are capable.

She believes that it would be vital for us to continue our work in helping the defense attorneys to understand better what victims are going through and that prosecutors not only represent the state, but they represent the best interest of the victim survivor as well and that responsibility should be taken seriously.

She believes that many professionals need to recognize that if it were not for the victim coming forward they would have never had a case and that is why knowing how the victim feels about the case is vital to create justice for the victim survivor as well.

She provided me an example that when a family is in their darkest time during a domestic violent situation, many times the charges against the defendant for abusing in front of children is usually used as a bargaining chip in the plea negotiation instead of as validation to the victims that they are believed and that we a protecting them. By holding them accountable to their actions, especially to all the family members, sends a message to the offender that their abuse will not be tolerated.

Dana shared with me that what she has learned from over 15 years as one advocating for victims is that we never know the depth of the trauma in their lives. There may be something from their past and having to deal with being a victim and also having to possibly cope with other trauma can cause a great amount of distress in their lives. She said to me, "We really don't know and we have to listen and we cannot make judgment." I thought this was a beautiful example of the insight that Dana has as an advocate for victim survivors.

As I pay respect to these individuals who have impacted my life greatly in the work of criminal justice I believe that some of my own philosophies in working with victims comes from being taught by these individuals who have meant so much to me through the years.

Many offenders are released from prison. If they are not prepared, if they have no support system, and have no direction, their chances of re-offending will be inevitable. Since one of the real fears of most victims of crime is fear of retaliation from their offender or hurting someone else, we have a duty to address all of their needs, to help offenders address the addictive nature of their behavior as well as helping the victim survivor in their road to recovery. This is a complicated path, but one that must be taken for there to be real change.

Working in the field of criminal justice, one must realize that we do not have all the answers and that many times our best results come from listening and learning how we can best serve the populations we are privileged to work with. I have learned throughout my career that the more I listen the better I am able to see what I can do to serve not only those who have either committed crime or unfortunately became a victim of a crime.

We will never understand, unless we have been a victim of crime ourselves and know what it is like. Even if we ourselves have been a victim of a crime, everyone's experience is personal and no one person can duplicate the experience, especially when someone uses the term, "get over it?" That clearly tells me that they have no clue what a victim survivor has gone through. Educating the public is a crucial component in providing support to the survivor.

As a law enforcement officer, probation officer, corrections officer, an analyst, teacher, and consultant, I have had thousands of opportunities to be with people in many difficult times in their lives. I have cried, held-up physically and emotionally, listened too, and learned from these brave survivors of crime, how to be a survivor. They have taught me many valuable lessons. One lesson I would highlight that I have learned from survivors, is this lesson: It would be easy to give up, especially when a loved one is murdered, or one is raped, abused, or assaulted, but it is our human nature to survive, and I have learned personal valuable lessons that these strong individuals have not allowed the offender or the crime to keep them from being a survivor, and finding strength through their adversity!

Throughout this book, I will provide the reader with personal experiences of what it is like to work with victim survivors of crime and what I have learned in working with these brave men, women, and children. I write this book to honor their stories, to share their thoughts, through hours of interviews and being in the trenches with them learning and listening as to how I can become a better human being and a help agent in assisting them in their personal journeys.

I wrote this book as a tribute to these sweet people who have become my motivation for this work. They have been through so much, but they have not forgotten their individual worth and that regardless of what they have been subjected to, they have not lost their worth as a human being and certainly have gained my respect for their bravery, their inner strength, and their determination to learn from a very difficult situation what it means to survive.

Lastly, I honor my sweet eternal companion Carol and our four handsome boys, Mitchell, Justin, Nathan, and Nicholas. Carol is a survivor of a crime! She is my rock! Our children and I have witnessed the countless hours of crying, anger, and sadness that she has experienced as a survivor.

Though individuals who have offended may never know what she has been through, we as her immediate family have seen the pain she has experienced, and our boys have been stall worth men in their love and support to their mother. Our brave sons who are now men, have been subjected to altered relationships, confusion, and sadness for what has happened, but one thing I have learned from my sons, they too are survivors and they are strong men, and though they have seen some very difficult things, they have learned to treat their mother with respect, concern, and one-hundred percent support.

Our sons have all grown up now. Mitchell and his wife Jenny and Justin and his wife Hilary now have families of their own. Nathan recently got married to Sarah and have now started their own family. Nicholas will not be too far behind I am sure. As I watch all our children, it is amazing to see the compassion they have for others. I believe that their traits are a direct result of their relationship with their mother. We now have three beautiful daughter-in-laws, Jenny, Hilary, and Sarah. We also have five exceptional grandchildren. We might be partial, but Carol and I have the cutest grandchildren, Izabelle, Charley, Jack, Lucy, and Quinton. Our daughter-in-law Hilary is pregnant with our sixth grandchild.

I wanted to note that I am privileged to have Hilary, Justin's wife, as one of the editors for my book. She is a freelance editor for Kendall Hunt and has an amazing talent and I am grateful to her for helping me with this project. I have learned so much from all three of these brave, beautiful women and I am grateful that my son's have married these sweet women of courage and love for others.

As parents you always pray that your family will be healthy, happy, and safe throughout their lives. Carol and I have been blessed, but we also know that the reality is that we must in our world be vigilant to ensure our safety and happiness. Regardless of what may unfold in our future, I have learned one thing, we must always do our best to prepare ourselves and our families for the difficulties that come in life and to remember that strength through difficulties comes with faith, resilience, companionship, and perseverance.

My Carol is a survivor! There is no greater honor for me in this life then being by my wife's side and though I have my faults, it is my solemn duty to never have her doubt my respect for her and what she has been through in her life. I only pray that I will never add to my wife's grief she has felt from the betrayal she has experienced from others in her life. I can think of no person in this life that has been a better example of what it means to be a "Survivor!!!" Thank you, Carol, for your inner strength, you are **the amazing** part of our relationship.

In conclusion, I have always had a fascination of the analogy of light and darkness. When we are in darkness, we often seek a form of light to pave the way or provide comfort. I remember one time when I was a child my father showed me complete darkness when we went into a cave. He turned the flashlight off and I could see nothing. I panicked and said in an anxious voice, "Dad don't do that turn the lights on please!"

Though he was only doing it to show me how dark it was, I do remember my father also shared with me that light dissipates darkness and that when you are in need of light in your life, you will find it by reaching out and seeking light through communicating with God and through reaching out to others in my life for help. He said to me, "Don't ever be afraid of asking for help."

I have titled this book, "Standing in the Dark: Struggles and Hope for Victims of Violent Crime." I am using this title of course as a metaphor to life and my fascination with the concept of light and darkness.

Through the years when I have worked with crime and victims, I have seen some of the darkest hours in the lives of many of these victims. I have answered phone calls and spent many hours talking through with them and helping them navigate through our criminal justice process and the trauma of being a victim of a violent crime.

I would like to illustrate this simple concept of light dissipating darkness, through two short stories about our two oldest sons.

When my wife and I were young parents, we were camping with our four boys. We had the three younger boys, Justin, Nathan, and Nicholas in the camper with us. Our oldest son Mitchell wanted to be a "big man" and sleep in a tent with his cousin. They were about 11 years old, and we set up the tent right next to the camper.

About 2:00 am, I heard Mitchell screaming to the top of his lungs, "I can't see, I'm blind!" I jumped out of bed in my underwear and ran outside the camper into the campground.

I rushed to the tent and unzipped it as he continued to exclaim his dilemma. Now I know what you all are thinking and you are correct; there was a 99% chance that he was not blind, but it was a very dark night and you literally could not see your hand in front of your face. I shined the flashlight in his face and said, "Can you see the light?" With relief he said yes. I hugged Mitchell and told him that it was okay to be scared and not to be ashamed, that there will be times in your life when you are scared, but you will be fine.

In addition to Mitchell's story, Justin our second son served a service mission in a foreign country. He was faced with an imminent attack from members of the MS13 Gang in El Salvador, when they were trying to break into their apartment and attack them. These gang members would randomly attack homes in the middle of the night, and they attempted to break into their apartment by climbing through the windows that had no glass. Justin shared with us the absolute desolate and dark state that he and his friend felt at that moment and that their lives were in jeopardy.

Our son and his friend shared that they did not know what to do, except to drop to their knees and prayed for safety, and at that moment the garbage truck passed by their little apartment and scared the gang members off.

Both of our sons were faced with different types of darkness that created difficulty, unsurety, and desperation. However, in both of their situations they experienced relief from the darkness through reaching out for help that not only increased their understanding of how to survive and meet the challenges they face but brought comfort to their situations.

Without question, any victim survivor will share with you of the darkness they experienced at different times during their traumatic experiences. Some of them it was weeks, months, and even years that they experienced the darkness and feeling alone. Our challenges clearly require us to develop resilience, adaptability, and the knowledge that we can make it through those dark hours in our lives. Will it be a struggle? Yes. Will it be exhausting and emotionally draining? Yes. Will we sometimes feel like we are blind at our path ahead? Yes. However, with the help of each other and with understanding the strength we have within ourselves we will make it through the darkness and see light at the end of our tunnel.

Throughout this book you will hear the stories of their darkest hours, but you will also here of the triumph over their trials and how each one has found a better place after standing in the darkness.

Foreword

To begin this book, I would like to share the story of a family that I have been privileged to work with for the last seven years.

In 2012, I met Tim Ricard and his children Katie Smith, Joey Benson, JJ Benson, and Ben Ricard. I also have met Tim and Mary Ricard's grandchildren and extended family, including extended family in Ohio. Mary Ricard was murdered by an inmate in the Arkansas Valley Correctional Center in Colorado. She was a Sargent and Correctional Officer and helped inmates in the kitchen learn how to prepare food. She loved working with the inmates and helping them find a positive path for their future.

For many years Mary was a Pastry Chef at Copper Mountain Ski Resort. Soon after the release of her brother from prison, Mary shared with her family that she wanted to work in a prison and help inmates learn a skill in cooking so they not only have something to do when they get out, but help build their self-esteem and give them something positive to look forward to when they are released.

Mary worked at the prison for over nine years before she was murdered. I have received permission from their family to share my thoughts on their story and I have asked Katie Smith, the daughter of Mary Ricard to share some memories of her mother and how this has impacted her life and her family.

I met the Ricard family just weeks after Mary Ricard was murdered on September 24, 2012. I first was introduced to them at a correction officers union meeting in Pueblo, Colorado. The officers and their families gathered to talk about safety concerns inside the prisons for inmates and staff. This was the beginning of a relationship with the Ricard family that has been an amazing journey and an honor.

I remember them sharing that night that they were opposed to the death penalty. Their family does not believe it is right to ever take part in the ending of a human life whatsoever. They also shared with me that at some point they wanted to meet with the man who killed their mom.

I was not taken back by the request, but what I was surprised about was that they had taken this stand so early in the process. Over the course of the last 12 years I have assisted in this role in many death penalty cases and not once have I ever seen that commitment to forgiveness like I experienced working with the Ricard family.

Again, in my position as a bridge of communication between the victim's family and the defense teams, I have been privileged to work with many families that are for the death penalty and opposed to the death penalty. Regardless of the families position this work is important. Ethically it is not about changing the minds of the victims but

---

Portions of this Foreword are written with permission of Tim Ricard. Portions of this Foreword are written with permission of Katie Smith.

allowing them to participate more in the process and ask any question they may have for the defense attorneys. I am not part of the defense team but am hired by the defense teams as a liaison in communicating with the victims.

Victims do not feel the same way about a case and therefore it is critical to my role to be a good listener and see where I might help them with their needs. My role involves listening and finding answers. I ask them no leading questions about the case, I just assure them that I am there to listen and to find answers to their questions. I make no judgement on whether or not they support the death penalty, nor does it matter, this work is for all victims of violent crime.

Generally, defense attorneys will ask us to assist them in reaching out to the victims, but in the case of the Ricard family, they found out about what I do and specifically requested this service. It has been a pleasure to work with the Ricard family. I will always treasure the relationship that we forged and the opportunity I had to be not only a sounding block, but someone that could help them find answers to some very difficult questions they had as a family.

The title of my book, "Standing in the Dark" is a metaphor to the overwhelming feeling of darkness and loss that individuals feel after they have become a victim of a violent crime. Simply stated after experiencing that type of trauma, most victims do not know what to feel or who to turn to for help. This is overwhelming for them and very confusing. Their cycle of grief is challenging and really require a team effort in making sure their needs are met.

I have learned one important lesson in working with victims of violent crime, I have no agenda going into a case. It is virtually impossible for me to relieve them of their agony, as they struggle and experience emotional and physical pain.

I cannot tell a victim how to heal, they must discover their path for themselves. All we can do is help them by providing them access to the tools necessary to begin the healing process. Empowering victims to explore and create their own path of healing is the key. A victim specialist should do their best never to tell a victim how to feel or what they need. I will talk more about this program in Chapter Nine.

As for the Ricards, I have been privileged to work with this wonderful family for the last seven years helping them as they navigate through the criminal justice process. I always do my best to answer their questions to the best of my abilities. I also have attended court hearings and spent many hours talking to them, crying with them, and most importantly listening to them.

Mary and Tim were married on November 28, 1984, they were married 28 years before she was brutally murdered by Miguel Contreas-Perez. The Ricards are a blended family. Mary had three children with their father Jack. Their children are Katie, Joey, and JJ. Tim had one child from a previous marriage, Ben. I was privilege to get to know them all very well. I also have been privileged to meet other family members including relatives in Ohio and Florida.

My experience with them is nothing short of amazing. I cherish every moment I spend with the Ricard family not to mention the many other victim's families that I have been privileged to work with.

There has been a great deal of frustration over their case. This process has dragged on for seven years after many unfortunate but standard practices in a high-profile death penalty case. There have been changes to the defense and prosecution teams, the handling of evidence, the mental and physical state of the defendant, and the overwhelming amount of evidence to go over in a case like this. There have been thousands of pages of information and inquires as to how this could have happened in the kitchen to a female correctional officer.

The defendant is responsible for the death of Mary Ricard. On the morning of September 24, 2012, Miguel Contreas-Perez was working in the kitchen. He broke the tethering of the knife, hid the knife in his clothing and then asked Mary to escort him to the dry pack room to get some ingredients for making breakfast. When they were alone, he brutally attacked her. She fought with him, but eventually he cut her throat and she bled to death in that room in the prison.

He then left and went and approached another female correctional officer. He attempted to kill her but was stopped by another female correctional officer. Though she lived, the scars of that day will never go away physically or mentally.

The Prison staff did not know Mary had been killed until about an hour and a half later. A tragic ending to a beautiful woman who has such a wonderful family. In getting to know Mary through her family I am amazed at the impact she has had on so many. Mary was devoted mother, wife and most important a woman without guile.

There were many questions about what happened that day that the Ricards had hoped would be answered at a trial. Though they did not want the death penalty, they did want a trial to learn why and how this happened to their mom and wife. Many of the questions the Ricards had centered on how an inmate with a violent past would be working in a kitchen and have access to knives and to women. There were allegations of many problems with the protocols and the actions of the department of corrections, which seemed to be some of the biggest concerns for the Ricard family.

Again, though they were opposed to the death penalty they needed those questions answered. In the penalty phase of a trial, the prosecution must show evidence of aggravating factors that would give them enough facts to get the death penalty. In this case he had committed a rape and kidnapping of a 14-year-old girl. Though the conviction remained, his sentence was an illegal sentence and therefore could not be used as an aggravator for the death penalty case.

With that new evidence, the prosecution felt that they would not be able to get a death penalty conviction by a jury so they agreed to a settlement in the case that would leave the defendant in prison for the rest of his life without the possibility of parole.

This was troubling to the Ricard family because they wanted to hear the facts of the case in a trial. Now their hopes for understanding how this happened were dissipating. They had been assured by the defense team and the prosecution that they would provide them answers to their questions, however they still wanted to know how and why this happened and they knew that either a trial or the defendants own words would be the only way they would find out what truly happened that day.

On August 13, 2019, Miguel Contreas-Perez pleaded guilty and was sentenced to life without parole. One of the rare honors in my life happened that day. Katie Smith, Mary's daughter asked me to read her statement in open court during his sentencing.

As I shared her words in open court last week, she stood by my side and truly it was one of the highlights I experienced in working on this case.

Katie, her stepfather Tim and her brother Joey shared their beautiful thoughts and feelings in the courtroom that day. Just before he was sentenced, the defendant himself got up and made an open statement to the court. He turned and promised the Ricard family answers to their questions that only he himself knows the answers. According to his attorneys, after the defendant heard Mary's family's statements in court, he felt compelled to share with them that he would write them a letter and answer any of their questions in detail.

In October, Miguel followed through and sent the Ricards the letter that was promised. Though the contents of this letter are private, it helped the Ricards through his words in the letter that he provided to them.

After court as I met with the Ricard family, I could see some improvement in that great burden that they have carried these last almost eight years since Mary's murder. They also all commented on how much it helped for them to hear from Mr. Contreas-Perez say that he will answer their questions. Hearing him apologize was very helpful to them.

That relief will not bring back Mary, but it has provided them hope that through healing things will get better. The subtitle to my book "Struggle and Hope for Victims of Violent Crime," again is a metaphor to the fact that when we find hope for tomorrow, we begin to see light at the end of our tunnel of darkness.

Though the Ricards will remember this for the rest of their lives, with time, and with acknowledgement of their pain from the man who killed their wife and mother. This will most likely provide their family with another layer of hope for a "new normal" in their lives.

Though there is no way for me to fully appreciate what they have been through, I asked Katie, the daughter of Mary, who was killed, to share her thoughts more than seven years after the death of her mother, as the man who did this confessed and is now serving life without parole for killing Sargent Mary Ricard. I believe that her words are an appropriate beginning to my book. In her own words, Katie wrote:

I am Katie. I am a survivor of a murdered victim. In 2012 my mom was killed by an Inmate. My mom was a corrections officer. She was a sergeant. My mom chose to work as an officer, in hopes of teaching inmates' basic skills, in the kitchen. Skills that someday they could take with them once released from Prison to better their lives. Often time's inmates would converse with her, about the lives they had outside. She empathized with the inmates when they would share about the good & bad things that awaited them on the streets. She shares a few of the stories. One specific story she shared was of an inmate whose mother had passed away while he was imprisoned. She felt immense sorrow for him. So, she wrote uplifting messages on sticky notes to occasionally give away to those she felt needed a word of encouragement. Often, they were Bible verses. My mom was very caring and compassionate often times she said, "she was not there to be a judge that had already been dealt to them." I admired my mom for being an officer. I asked her often if she was ever afraid of the inmates, after all they are criminals. She always responded, NO.

I was very close to my mom. I would say we were best friends. I spoke with my mom on average of twice a day. Once at 11:30 am (the time her shift ended) and at 7pm (right before she would go to bed.) My mom had her own room in my home, because she visited so often. Almost every weekend. She wanted to watch her grandchildren grow up.

My mom & I had at least two extended weekends per year that we would go on a girl's weekends to just be mother and daughter. Those times grew our friendship even deeper. We resembled each other enough that people thought we were sisters. I shared everything with my mom even the simple details of everyday life.

The day before her death she had been at my home her last expression to me was a long hug and she whispered, "see you Thursday, I love you." She planned on returning to my house so we could attend our annual girl's weekend at a woman's conference. She was tired and I tried to convince her that 3 hours of travel home was too much and she should call in ill. She said she couldn't because she traded days off so we could go to the conference. I hold dear to the memory of that hug and the sincere whisper of "I Love You".

September 24th, 2012: The Day My Mom Was Killed at Work

My phone rang it was my husband who was at work. It was early in the morning so that in itself was strange. He told me to call my stepdad, immediately. I did and at that time the details were very vague. My stepdad stated something happened at moms work and she was being transported to the hospital. Well I then learned via text from the local news that in fact her prison was under lock down because an inmate had injured an officer still not knowing I began calling my brothers to just say "something has happened." I was scared and my brothers, both, came to my house. I called my husband back and requested he too come home.

Approximately 45 minutes later my dad called and said she had passed away. Thankfully my husband was almost home and my brothers weren't far behind. My stomach immediately became ill. Grief took over and there was no way I could stuff my feelings. My kids then became confused and scared. My kids, both my brothers and my nephew loaded up in my Durango. (The only vehicle that you can put 8 people in) We drove the three hours to the most desolate town I've ever been to. To this day I don't like going to the town she had once lived.

We went to a family friend's home where we were then greeted by the state governor and his entire entourage. There were several Department of Corrections People as well. They tried to express their compassion and empathy. My words to the governor were that my mom's murder would not be in vain but in some way, God would use her death to glorify him. 5 years later, I still don't know exactly how, but my mom's death will help others, somehow and show Christs Love for Humans. That day I felt every emotion that is humanly possible, Fear, Sorrow, Hopelessness, and Anger & Shock.

There were 10 days of constant people. We stayed in the town at a most gracious person's home that housed our whole family, so we could stay close and intimate. There we four memorial services during the first days following her murder then two national memorials that honored her line of Duty Death.

The Justice System or Lack Thereof:

About three months following her murder we had the first of too many to count court hearings. The first one entailed the charges being read then a family meeting with all the legal personnel. The # 1 person who was present was a person from the Attorney General's Office who basically was there to make it known the state was going to punish my mom's murderer by whatever means the state could. It will take almost 4 years until the DA announced their plan to pursue the Death Penalty. At nearly every meeting we as a family stated we did not want the DA to go that route. At the beginning we were given a victim's advocate who called often to check on us and to ask if we had questions and or needs. We were given free grief counseling for a little while. Once they realized we weren't wanting the same agenda they wanted, we lost any victims support. No calls no emails unless it was the bare minimum by law. The court room felt so lonely and I personally decided in 2015, I just could no longer go to all the hearing and court proceedings.

In either late 2012 or early 2013 the defense attorneys granted us our most valuable victims support. A D.V.O. (Defense Victim Outreach = Victim Specialist) our DVO created a non-biased liaison to the case. A person who was available to ask questions that pertain to the legalities that surrounded my mother's murder. A DVO is a person who is paid for by the defense's attorneys. This Liaison has no side to take other than the survivors. Our DVO gave me empowerment. I always felt safe in the courtroom when he attended the court proceedings. Following those courtroom experiences, we would go decompress. This was vital. I could ask questions immediately without forgetting. One of the hardest parts about murder is all the legal stuff. I had no understanding of the legal system prior to my mom's death. There were countless questions. There was also tons of confusion. I did not understand what a District Attorney was. DIVO lends a resource to you when you are likely so very vulnerable emotionally.

Moving Forward, Over 8 Years Later:

"A new normal". . . . I once read a book that talked about a new normal. I can tell you I am not the same person I was almost 5 years ago. I still have days of sorrow. I miss my mom each day. Prior to my mom's death I was a person who happily lived in the city. I was a businesswoman and enjoyed the City as a whole. That was no longer the case almost immediately I would hear sirens and immediately feel a lump in my throat. I would get startled by the slightest noise. I was living in fear. Today I live on a ranch / hobby farm. I continue my home-based career but now I spend most of my days outside with animals. It is a New Normal. Since moving from a city, I can think clearer and think mostly of happy memories of my mom. I get sad when I think of my kids not having their grandma. My mom loved her farm and I am honored to raise my kids to know how much she loved it. The farm is a legacy of sorts to her.

A common question I hear is: how do you go on? Honestly, I believe it is because of my Faith and the knowing that my mom would be proud of me. My new normal is missing my mom. My moving forward is honoring my mom each day through small acts and teach my children. Also, by sharing my story. There is silver lining all around if you just look around.

If you happen to be a victim, I encourage you to consider changing your thinking. Change it to be a Survivor. I highly recommend reaching out and talking about all your feelings. Your Thoughts do matter!

Copyright © Katie Smith. Reprinted by permission.

1

Rejuvenating the Human Spirit— Giving Voice through Story

When we here the phrase "Human Spirit," what comes to mind? There are many that have defined the term to be spiritual, while others look more to the term to mean maintaining or finding resilience when faced with difficult situations in one's life. I believe it incorporates both analogies.

Each of us can cope with everyday struggles. We recognize that no two individuals are alike and therefore we should never pre-judge how one individual versus another copes with stress, trauma, and many other feelings and emotions. All we can do is truly support and show love and concern through listening and providing service when needed and not needed. When they sense our sincerity and unconditional support, they begin to see the path ahead and find strength within themselves.

An individual who has suffered trauma and then finds the energy and begins to believe they can heal will emerge a victor over their tragedy and clearly possess resilience and perseverance. It is our charge as supporters to survivors to help through our service and being a listening ear. I love this quote from the author of the article, "Resilience and the Human Spirit." Kate Swaffer said, "People who could well choose to stay 'broken', but who never cease to astound me with their resilience and human spirit, their willingness to work hard as individuals to overcome their situations." https://kateswaffer.com/2013/01/07/resilience-and-the-human-spirit/

For me personally, I agree with Kate. I believe that each of us can find resilience and find a new path in our lives when we have been affected by trauma, which without question can break down the human spirit. However, we have found that most often we find the strength to combat those destructive thoughts through being gentle on ourselves and recognizing that we have the ability as human beings to cope, endure, and overcome.

Portions of this chapter are written with contributions by Tim Nielsen. Portions of this chapter are written with permission of Carol McBride. Portions of this chapter are written with permission of Nancy Wirkus. Portions of this chapter are written with contributions by Erin (last name omitted to protect privacy). Portions of this chapter are written with permission of Lisa Ferentz.

Often, when we read the newspaper, watch the news, or scan the Internet we may hear sound bites, pleas, and emotional outbursts from victims, but one thing we will never understand is how personally each person has dealt with their victimization. Some individuals have approached their trauma as a source of gaining personal growth, through healing. These individuals generally do not focus on the offender, but through their own experience and healing, they gain a better understanding that healing comes within themselves and finding the ability to reach down and find the strength to survive the horrible emotional and physical scars that come from being a victim of a crime.

Personally I have watched hundreds of survivors of crime go through the toll to the human spirit, to the point of them giving up and turning to depression, lack of motivation, alcohol, drugs, and many other remedies to cope with the toll to their ability to see past the harm that was inflicted on them.

I remember talking to Tim Nielsen. We will talk more about his story later in the book, but Tim's wife was murdered and their unborn son. She was 8½ months pregnant, and on June 14, 2007, Jenna Nielsen was murdered in a parking lot of a convenient store delivering newspapers to the kiosks in front of the store. Tim not only was dealing with the aftermath of his wife and son being murdered, but he was dealing with being a father of two sons, having to work, and on top of all of that not knowing who the killer was. Not to mention, for many weeks police considered Tim a suspect until they had completed their initial investigation.

If you think about it, that is a lot of emotional weight for one person to carry. Tim found himself, secluding himself to his home, not talking to anyone, he also found himself drinking alcohol more to self-medicate his depression and sadness. He felt overwhelmed in taking care of his children and would have his in-laws babysit the children often because he was having a difficult time coping with all of the stress of Jenna being murdered.

Recently I read that, "Crime victimization can impact an individual's ability to perform across a variety of roles, including those related to parenting, intimate relationships, and occupational and social functioning" (Impact of Crime Victimization on Quality of Life, Rochelle F. Hanson, https://www.ncbi.nlm.nih.gov/pmc/articles/PMC2910433/).

Tim was falling into a dark hole in his life and he had to find the strength to find himself again and continue his role as a father to his two sons, Schyler, and Kaiden. Later in the book we will discuss his case further, but Tim truly set the bar for recovering from such a horrific event and now is raising his sons in Utah, after getting his degree in Criminal Justice from Weber State University.

There are many aspects of being a survivor of a crime that unless you experience it yourself it is hard to conceive what a person really goes through. As a spectator to crime which pretty much includes all of us, we sometimes believe that we know what is best for someone who has just gone through a tragedy in their life. Even with our expertise sometimes we fail to remember that we are not the one that is going through a difficult time. We see what they are going through, through our eyes. We do not have all the same interpretation of how to best navigate through trauma, but somehow think we can render advice. For example, it is not unusual to hear from a person comforting one who has just gone through a traumatic event or a victim of a crime to say, "it is okay, you are going to be just fine, you are strong!" Those words offer little comfort to someone who is going through a tragic situation in their life.

I want to share a story that illustrates this point. Though this tragedy was not a victim of crime, it illustrates the toll to the human spirit when one experiences trauma. In June of 2018, my wife Carol and I had flown into Salt Lake City, the night before. We were in Utah visiting our children and grandchildren.

I received a text from my sister Nancy that her husband had been life flighted to Salt Lake City, Utah from Rexburg, Idaho. He had a laceration in his liver that we think he sustained in a four-wheeler accident that he had within the previous two weeks. We got to the hospital to find my sister alone in the hospital in the OR waiting area. Most of my immediate family lives in Idaho. At that moment we found out that some of our family were preparing to leave Idaho to come to Utah to be with my sister.

When we arrived, my heart was broken. I saw my sweet sister crying and huddled in a little room in the OR waiting room of the University of Utah Medical Center. We hugged and held my sister who was in complete distress over the events that had occurred in the last 24 hours. A few weeks prior to this, my Brother In-Law Brent, was riding a four-wheeler when he went over a big bump and jammed the handlebars into his side over his liver. Unknown to him or anyone else, he had a small laceration in his liver that was slowly bleeding and no one according to the doctor would have detected it without a thorough exam and x-ray. He thought he had just bruised his side. Nothing could have prepared my sister and family for what would happen over the next several days.

As we sat there in the waiting room with my sister, we were just talking and trying to comfort her during this emotional rollercoaster. Suddenly, the doctor entered the room less than a half hour after he had gone into surgery, 10 minutes after we arrived. My sister Nancy looked at him and she knew it was not good. With careful wording and tone, the Doctor said, "It did not go well." Nancy looked at him with sheer panic in her face and voice, pleading for answers. He then said, "Brent did not make it."

Hearing that put us all in a state of shock, it felt like a dream, like this was not real. Though I can share how I was feeling, I had no clue what Nancy was feeling. She kept saying to the doctor and to Carol and I, looking at each one of us she said over and over, "No, no, please, no, is this real, is this real?" She then kept saying to us, "it is my fault I am an OR nurse I should have known, I should have helped him sooner?" My sister has been a nurse for close to 30 years and she felt responsible for not knowing.

Many victims of crime and those that experience trauma, they often feel responsible, or feel that they could have done something to prevent a tragedy. Though this is a normal reaction to trauma, with time and healing, survivors begin to understand it was not their fault. However, it is very difficult and sometimes can linger the rest of someone's life that somehow, they are partially responsible or could have done something about it. She just kept repeating this over and over.

My sister is a beautiful petite woman, and we had to keep piling blankets on her because she was so cold. She was shaking beyond anything I had ever seen. She was hyperventilating, and her mouth was so dry when I would try to put the straw in her mouth, it would just fall out. I would gently have to remind her to suck the straw, to eat the granola bar we had for her, anything to keep her energy up as she was experiencing horrific trauma of being told your husband had died. I cannot remember her name, or what she even looked like, but the hospital social worker was telling me that physically when experiencing this type of trauma you need juice, water, food, or anything to keep your electrolytes elevated due to the trauma that occurs physically to the body. I also remember her saying it will prevent hyperventilating and passing out. They even at one point gave her a brown bag to breathe into. I thought that was folklore, but it is true, it truly helps from not hyperventilating.

I recall at one point; I was completely mortified as to what was happening to my sweet sister who has been through so much trauma in her life from previous relationships. My heart was breaking, and I felt helpless. The part of this that I want to make my point, that even though I have over 35 years' experience, and the fact that I work with crime victims all over the United States, I was finding myself at a loss of words as to what I could say to comfort my sister. In fact, I was thinking it would be good to encourage her and I said to her, "Nancy it is going to be okay, we are all around you and are here to help you." At the same time the social worker and my wife Carol looked at me, like why did you say that? Then Nancy said, "no it is not okay." I realized the mistake I made, for those experiencing trauma it is wrong for us to comfort anyone with words that are truly meaningless at the time. What I should have said is, "we are here for you, what can I do?" At a moment of loss no one wants to hear "it will be okay."

My point is that though I may be an expert, though I may have worked with and provided support to many victims of crime, at that moment when my own sister just needed a shoulder to cry on, I announced to her that it will be okay. It was not okay what happened, and victims of crime that experience trauma are not comforted by such phrases at that moment of their lives when everything is tumbling down around them. What they do need however is assurance that we will be with them and we will serve them and not judge or think for one moment that we know what they are going through. Even if someone has experienced the same type of trauma, they still do not have a clear picture as to what another individual is going through. Though we sometimes feel we can offer them good advice, even if we are experts, it is better to ask them how you can serve them or help them, and not judge what they need.

My sweet sister Nancy is doing great now, and I am so proud of her. She truly is resilient and one that I will always admire for her ability to adapt to life's challenges with a determination not to fail, and to show all of us through her exemplary way how to face our challenges. Thank you, Nancy, for your example to me, I will never forget the lesson I learned from you that day

There is a concept that we all have heard, "MONDAY-MORNING QUARTER-BACK." That is a figure of speech for someone who thinks they know what someone else is going through, or what a person or a team needs to do to be successful. Somehow, we become experts and know what to do or say because we think we know.

My point is that none of us have a clear understanding of what someone needs for healing after they have been traumatized. The main reason is we are not the victims and we were not there when it happened. We must refrain from second-guessing or what we think would work best. We are all different and interrupt and respond to life lessons much differently.

In the publication, "Trauma-Informed Care in Behavioral Health Services," we learn that, "How an event affects an individual depends on many factors, including characteristics of the individual, the type and characteristics of the event(s), developmental processes, the meaning of the trauma, and sociocultural factors." https://www.ncbi.nlm.nih.gov/books/NBK207191/

There are so many things to consider when working with those who have been traumatized and it would behoove each of us to consider our differences before we can judge someone for the way in which they are dealing with their trauma.

My experience provided me a better understanding of the symptoms of trauma, and how much of what one experiences during trauma is perfectly normal regardless. We cannot predict how trauma will affect each of us.

When I was 16 years old, our family home caught on fire. I remember running toward my house putting aside the danger of running into a burning house. I ran to the front door and luckily one of the firemen grabbed me before I could open the door. He explained that it would have caused an explosion (backdraft). I was acting on pure emotion and trauma.

As a young man I had earned my Eagle Scout award, and I was very proud of it. I was so upset by our house burning down, and being traumatized, all I could think about was that my Eagle Scout Badge was burning up. At first the fireman thought I had a real eagle in the house, but once he understood, he said, "you can get a new one!"

He of course probably saved my life by stopping me, but that is how trauma that day affected me. I thought my Eagle Scout Badge was more important than my safety. To this day my brothers and sisters remind me of that story and how I reacted to trauma.

One thing that is difficult for us to do is to predict how traumatization affects each one of us. Most reactions to trauma are considered normal, because each person is unique, they respond differently. However, we have learned through the years that there are red flags that we should be aware of with individuals who continue to suffer from the effects of trauma.

Initial reactions to trauma can include exhaustion, confusion, sadness, anxiety, agitation, numbness, dissociation, confusion, physical arousal, and blunted affect. Most responses are normal in that they affect most survivors and are socially acceptable, psychologically effective, and self-limited. Indicators of more severe responses include continuous distress without periods of relative calm or rest, severe dissociation symptoms, and intense intrusive recollections that continue despite a return to safety. https://www.ncbi.nlm.nih.gov/books/NBK207191/

As I have watched individuals go through the pain of being a victim of crime, who have demonstrated resilience, I could not go without mentioning my wife and all that she has been through, yet she has never given up and has always been there for me and for our children. Carol was a victim of childhood familial sexual abuse. Her abuse was not discussed until she finally went to her ecclesiastical leader who told her to lock her door. She suffered this problem alone for many years because those that she did tell, would not take it seriously, or were afraid of what would happen if the word got out that such behavior was happening.

When Carol and I were dating, she said to me, "there is something really important I need to tell you before we get married." I thought to myself, "Oh no does she have a terminal illness," or something else that will affect our future? Then she told me, "I was sexually abused when I was growing up for many years." My first thought was, thank goodness I thought it was something worse. Years later, I am a witness to the effect of sexual abuse on a small, innocent young girl, who suffered many nights in fear, not only from the abuse, but from the fact that no one would help her. Soon after we were married, my wife and I were in bed. I reached over just to hug my wife as we slept and she reared out of bed screaming uncontrollably and saying, "don't ever touch me like that while I am asleep!" I felt shame, disgust in my behavior like I had done something wrong. I kept saying I am sorry, I am sorry. Hours later she explained that it was not my fault, that it is a direct result of the abuse that happened to her and that just putting my arm around her in bed brought flashbacks to the many nights she was abused.

I thought to myself, how can she learn to cope with this, look at the effect it is having on her spirit? Carol was getting migraine after migraine headaches. I was so worried about her. However, we got her into counseling, kept communicating and went through some very difficult times, including her offender, victimizing another family member. Her offender continued his irresponsible behavior and was not taking responsibility for his actions. All Carol and I could do was to learn to protect ourselves and our children from further victimization. Even years later, another immediate family member tried to get her to engage in inappropriate behavior, even though she was married to me and we had four children.

We soon realized that even though we may at some point learn to forgive them for what they have done to Carol, we will not forget, and we will not put ourselves in any situation where they can take advantage again.

More importantly I want to talk about the resilience of my wife Carol and all that she has been through and her ability to not only cope with what has happened to her, but to have accomplished and continues to accomplish many great things in her life and our marriage. We have been married for 35 years. It has not been easy, but it has been worth it. I am grateful every day for Carol and her ability to see beyond her trauma and see her potential and self-worth.

Carol has chosen to take the higher road to her victimization. Rather than have it cripple her human spirit she has raised four young men who now are on their own. They have not only always respected their mother but also learned from their mother what it takes to endure, to be resilient, and to not let tragedy define who you are.

Carol recently started working with me in a program called Bridges to Life. We will talk more about this program later, but Carol has been a volunteer inside several penitentiary's telling her story and meeting with inmates to help them understand accountability to their victims. To see Carol sitting there with inmates, telling them that she cares for them truly is a sight to be seen.

Carol has experienced resilience so many times in our marriage. She has spent many nights suffering physically and emotionally from the effects of abuse, but continued to raise our boys, work part time, and provide service in our church. Her stamina amazes me, and I am so lucky to be married to a woman who truly understands what it means to overcome and to recognize her individual worth. I would also note that

Carol just finished her Master Gardner from Penn State University and I am so proud of her for not giving up and finishing her certification. I did not realize it was so hard to become a Master Gardner until I saw what she must go through. I am so proud of her and her accomplishments.

Carol has spoken with me at many conferences. She has spoken on her childhood abuse. I am always amazed at the individuals she impacts every time she speaks. She is not afraid to tell her story, to be vulnerable, and as a result lives have changed just hearing her story and feeling her human spirit. She is my modern-day hero who I love so much and honor and respect.

I have seen firsthand the toll on the spirit with Carol, but I have also witnessed her resilience. In this book I will bring up many stories of people who I have worked with, had the privilege of getting to know, and I can tell you that these individuals truly represent those who have not let their victimization overcome them, or define who they are. Has it been easy for them? No, it has not. In fact, many of them found themselves in darkness before they were able to overcome and not allow their experience to overcome them.

There are many victims of crime and those that experience trauma that struggle with depression, suicidal thoughts, and many other emotions and problems. There are many reasons why this may happen and why there are some that never find any relief from their grief.

The good news is for the majority of those that suffer trauma and victimization, they do find their path to healing and create a "new normal" in their life that can bring them satisfaction and a feeling of accomplishment for overcoming their adversity. As I stated earlier, there are many effects of trauma that are very acute after victimization or trauma. I have found that those who have gone through those horrific events in their lives have found a way to move past their grief and find their new path. They have found their own way of coping. No one can tell them; they must discover it on their own. It does not mean others cannot support and help, but in the end, they must make the decision to survive. Again, quoting from the publication, "Trauma-Informed Care in Behavioral Health Services," it describes this resilience of those who are victims of crime this way.

> Survivors' immediate reactions in the aftermath of trauma are quite complicated and are affected by their own experiences, the accessibility of natural supports and healers, their coping and life skills and those of immediate family, and the responses of the larger community in which they live. Although reactions range in severity, even the most acute responses are natural responses to manage trauma— they are not a sign of psychopathology. Coping styles vary from action oriented to reflective and from emotionally expressive to reticent. https://www.ncbi.nlm.nih.gov/books/NBK207191/

Effect of Storytelling on the Soul

Throughout this book, I will share the stories of many survivors of violent crime. It always amazes me when we I have the privilege to meet with valiant men and women who have met fear and trauma head-on and have been able to find their strength to carry on.

I have found that as others share their stories it creates what I call an ignition to their spirit and provides them the strength to move forward in their healing process. Each of us write our own narrative to our lives. When we look back what will we have written about, only the good things that happen to us? I would hope not. We learn and grow from all life experiences and I have found that as victim survivors tell their story, they create a healing pathway that if followed will help them cope with what happened to them for the rest of their lives.

The meaning of this story on storytelling is to give some thought to telling the whole and complete stories of our lives, communities, and nation. I recently read,

> In America there is a dominant narrative that succeeds in masking the true or complete narrative. America's story is one of kidnapping, triumph, injustice, economic exploitation, and bitter hatred, but the story that we privilege is one of triumph, victory, necessity. It is a story that masks the whole truth. It is a story that lists one group of people as the victims and the other as the offender. It is a story that has seeped into the cultural narratives of each group and is caused divide. This story has been perpetuated during the course of American history and a new chapter needs to be written, which tells the story in a way that does not privilege one truth over the other. This title should undoubtedly be named healing, because that is what will inevitably come from the writing of it. Everyone has a responsibility to add to this story. http://comingtothetable.org/stories/stories-healing-wounds/healing-power-storytelling/

As we begin to understand that the accumulation of our experiences is what creates our beautiful stories, we begin to discover our own resilience and will have the capacity to continue our journey and impact those around us with our story of triumph.

Erin's Path to a "Token Life"

Recently I met a young lady, who clearly demonstrates the characteristics of a survivor of physical, emotional, and sexual abuse. She grew up in a home where love was not shown the way love is supposed to be shown. For many years she did not know or understand what love truly meant.

Erin refers many times on her web site to a token life. Token can mean many things, but I found a meaning that I think helps me to understand the definition of Erin's description of a token life. Simply put token means, "Something serving as an indication, proof, or expression. . . . a sign" https://www.thefreedictionary.com/token

I am excited to share with you Erin's story. Her story and where she is presently, truly is a token or an expression of where she has been and where she has chosen to be today. Erin has accomplished many wonderful things in her life, and recently married the love of her life. Erin has helped many and carries with her a spirit of happiness and content. Though she has had some very dark days in her life, she is committed to living a life full of happiness and love. I have no doubt that Erin will always achieve that.

This sweet little innocent girl, Erin and her older sister were subjected to unimaginable trauma from early childhood. When I asked Erin what happy memories she remembers about her childhood, she said that there were a few occasions that she felt happy. Like most children, Christmas seemed to be a happy time in Erin's life. She also remembers having great memories of some of her activities in school when she was in elementary school.

However, when she thinks of how her life was at home, she does not have a great deal of memories that she could classify as happy memories. Her life is flooded of memories of many dark days at home while growing up.

Erin's father spent most of his time emotionally and physically abusing her mother. He would continually talk down to all of them and indicated that she never felt the love of a father while growing up. She does not remember spending any quality time with him. Both of these young innocent girls would dread coming home from school because they knew what it would be like at home. They lived in constant fear that their father would either yell at them or abuse their mother. They were both witnesses to the humiliation their father used against their mother through his abuse.

Erin described her father as an alcoholic, drug addict, bipolar, very depressed, and she said that he was generally "really awful to all of us." Her father also had a porn addiction, which she was exposed to in her home while growing up. She indicated that her father grew up in a home with mental illness, abuse, and neglect. She believes that he never had a really good example of what a family looks like. Her mother also grew up in a home where there was a lot of neglect. Her parents were immigrants and it was very difficult for her family. Erin's mother as a young girl kept to herself a lot, which is similar to how she acted as our mother. Erin said, "My Mother was paranoid that her husband would lash out and she wanted to make him happy so he would hurt her." So, Erin believes her mother was more focused on survival than really being a mother. She knows now that her mother always wanted to be a good mother but could not because of the trauma she was experiencing living with an abusive boyfriend. Both Erin and her sister were born out of wedlock.

Erin's abuse did not start until she was about 10 or 11, but prior to that they were exposed to the relentless physical and emotional abuse inflicted on their mother. Her sister has never really talked about her childhood or admits that she was ever physically or sexually abused from her father.

Erin explained how her father would come home intoxicated or high on drugs and demand money from her mother to pay for his drug and alcohol habit. Though he made good money, he would make her mother give him all her money. Erin cannot remember a time, except when he wasn't around that he was not yelling at someone. There was always screaming going on in our home. My mother had to defend herself from him many times. She kept a bat by the front door and would always have it close by in case she had to fight him off. The children grew up witnessing the constant fear.

Erin recalled one time coming home seeing her father with his hands around her mother's neck, strangling her and she was screaming. Oftentimes my father would leave for long periods, months at a time. Then he would show up again unannounced. She said that he had no consistency in his life and said that "we were there for his convenience." Erin said to me tearfully, "when he would come back, nothing would change, he would continue his tactics of yelling and abusing our mother, sister, and I."

Erin talked about the inconsistency in their home, and the constant yelling and abuse. She said that it has caused two major issues in her life. One, she said, "I really was not able to see what healthy family relationships looked like."

Erin said, "I was confused, I did not know if I should look at him as my dad who loves me or just a real scary man that I should be afraid of and stay away from."

Her father was a gift giver. He would groom his children and wife as part of his tactics to gain their trust back. She said that he would give her elaborate gifts and try to get her to trust him.

Soon after he started giving Erin gifts and treating her nicely is when the physical and sexual abuse began. First, he would just yell at us for just about anything and he was constantly yelling at her. He would order her to do things, calling her fat, or making fun of her for many reasons. She said to this day she still remembers those feelings she had when he would make fun of her or put her down.

The times that he was physical with them generally occurred when they would get in his way when he was going after their mother. He would push them out of his way. She feels that she has blocked out a great deal, but said she remembers one time he hit her in the face to get her out of his way.

Erin started asking her mother why she stayed with him. Erin said, "I was literally angry that I had to be exposed to this lifestyle, and I did not understand why no one was protecting me or my sister? I feel differently now, but then it was really hard."

Erin shared how she was arrested many times before she was 12. She was angry and felt that was the way one dealt with their problems. She said at the time, "I did not care, there were several girls that I literally put in the hospital. I was very protective of my sister and I would hurt anyone that would try to hurt her sister. I felt like no one could hurt me and I would not let them hurt me or my sister." Erin also was learning from her father that violence or beating is appropriate behavior when you are angry.

In addition to all the problems that she was having at home, Erin was not very good at schoolwork, and also realized that all of her friends came from the same type of background so there was not any real support. She said, "I felt like all that I was going through was normal and that this is the way life is." Erin attributes her poor education due to her living situation, and lack of motivation. She never really had a good experience in school, and she felt as though no one seemed to care.

She indicated that her father left for a long period of time and then all of sudden he was back at their house again. At the same time her father re-appeared into their lives, her mother was having a difficult time meeting their financial obligations. They were going to lose their home and so her mother decided that moving back in with their father was the only thing they could do and so they moved with their father to Florida.

Erin soon realized that his demeanor had not changed, but felt her mother had no choice because they were losing their home. Her mother was gone a lot working in Florida and her father would be at their home. She remembers sitting there watching TV and he would start fondling her and doing sexual touching that she had never experienced. She did not know what to do. This happened several times.

Then when she was around 12 years old, she was in her mother and father's room watching TV. Her mother was in the living room. Her father came in and he ended up taking all her clothes off and "totally molesting me." Though he never raped her he molested and fondled her excessively. She said, "He was doing things with me that confused me and I did not know what to do. I was not sure if I started screaming if he would hit me, or what he would do?"

When he finished, he got his cigarettes and went outside. Erin went to the bathroom and took a shower and cried and cried. She said, "I did not know what to do, I just started praying. I felt like my father would blame me and that it would all be my fault." Erin indicated that she got out of the shower and went out into the living room and told her mother that he had abused her and touched her sexually. Her mother looked at her with an expression of "this is totally my fault" and felt so ashamed that she had allowed this to happen. Her mother told her that she would not let that happen again.

Within a few weeks, Erin's mother moved Erin and her sister to Virginia. It was a really hard time for Erin. She felt that it was because of her that they had to move and that if she would not have said anything that it would not have put the pressure on her mother. Years later she realized the good that came from leaving her father. After that they never lived with him again.

Her father was never convicted for molesting her. Her father "got off" for what he did to her. She said, "He was never put in jail for this. The only thing that happened was that I received counseling in school." She also said that though her sister has never revealed anything to her, she believes that he might have done something to her as well. She also said that, "When we were in Florida my sister never really socialized with anyone, just stayed in our room. She also had a learning disability in school."

When Erin was a junior and senior in high school, she never really had any support at home with schoolwork, dealing with problems at school, or in life because her mother worked and she felt she did not have time for her problems. At school Erin was bullied all the time. She said, "I was overweight" and she recalled that when she was a junior that a boy called her "fatty" and then spit in her face. She was totally humiliated. She believed everyone felt that way about her when she would go to school and the teasing would continue.

As time passed, she still did not feel a lot of support from home, but she found that some of the kids at school were beginning to accept her into their crowd. She found herself spending a lot of time with those friends and staying at their homes over the weekend. She indicated that she tried marijuana and alcohol, but she got really sick, so she really did not get into drugs or alcohol.

After the abuse with her father she only went to counseling for about a year and realized later that she did not address a lot of the problems that came from her past. She had a real problem with what is referred to as the attachment disorder which was explained earlier. She was afraid of losing friends. She would do whatever she could to maintain friends. So many times, friends would use her and then would stop being her friend. She said, "I felt like I needed someone to love me in a good way, but I had a hard time finding that, or at the time did not understand it."

Erin believes that there were several things that happened in her life that were positive and helped her on her road to where she is today. She talked about joining her church when she was in high school. She said, "I was very active in my church because that is where I felt the most accepted." She believes it was her friends and leaders in her church that really kept her from going down the wrong path. She felt that if it were not for her church friends that she would probably have been more into the drugs, alcohol, and promiscuity.

After Erin graduated from high school she went to college in up-state New York. Erin felt that once in college she began to gain self-confidence. She was feeling more loved and accepted. She then transferred to another college in the west and continued feeling as though she was not being labeled by her past and that she was finally finding herself and finding her self-worth. She was seeing that she had the ability to cope with her past.

She decided to go on a mission to help communities for her church. She did this for 18 months, came home, and then got back into school out west. She loved school because she had so many friends around her and felt so much support and that "life was good." Because of her attachment issues, when she finished college, she felt a total loss because she was not around anyone, and she felt so alone.

This triggered her and she fell into a deep depression and felt totally out of control. At this point she got back into counseling to help her cope with the attachment disorder. She said, "going through the counseling and identifying the triggers has helped me realize I was still healing and needed to go through these experiences to keep me focused on my healing."

One thing she has discovered about herself is that through counseling she recognized that she was overcompensating with wanting to be loved or have friends. She felt if she made all these friends she would never have to experience being abandoned or feeling alone. She kept reminding herself that she could make it on her own and that she does not need others to see her individual worth.

Erin believes that she is so lucky. She now understands better how trauma can truly take over in your life. The one thing that has helped her more than anything is that she never emotionally buried what happened. That she was able to talk to her mother and continued to talk to others about what she had been through. She believes that this is what saved her. She said to me, "The more one speaks their own truth, the more they will understand how similar their story is to other people's stories." She also enjoys helping others to feel comfortable in telling their story. She shared with me that when she is helping others, she realizes how much it has blessed her life to learn to share her own story.

God does not make mistakes; he understands the pain and anguish we all experience. Erin believes that "people are afraid that others won't accept them or will hurt them" and that we have to become vulnerable in our lives and tell our story to change the rest of our lives. She said, "This is what gives me hope. I have to constantly remind myself of the strength that I have within myself. I am capable of loving and being loved and I know that others will accept me."

Everyone needs to hear that they are loved. If we realize we are all on our own journey that creates diversity. We need to accept each other for who we are, it will help us all better cope with what we are experiencing in life.

Erin now has a successful blog that she started to help others in their lives and to open doors to new friends and opportunities to help others. On her web site, tokenlife. com, Erin shares herself with others and provides them motivational thoughts and phrases to help others in their struggles in life.

On the opening page it has her name and the phrase, "Happiness is Contagious." I admire that a great deal because just reading that helps you to realize that we can always be unhappy, but we really have to work at being happy and when we associate with happy people it is contagious.

After going through her web site and blogs, I found two quotes of Erin's that I think are worth repeating in this book. The first one in my opinion is profound coming from a survivor of sexual and physical abuse. She said: "Sure, everyone's past is different, but we've all been exposed to something that has caused us to question who we really are, what our worth and abilities are, and where we're going in this life. We all need help in our own ways, and we need to help each other as best as we can." http://www.thetokenlife.com/2018/01/17/learning-to-love-myself-and-my-story/

I found this one as well that truly is the essence of this concept we have been addressing in this chapter of recognizing the importance of overcoming our challenges that take a toll on the Human Spirit. Erin said:

> Honestly it's the hardest thing I've ever had to do. I am learning to literally change the habits of the thinking processes that were instilled in me as a little child. They are habits that require work, study (both spiritual and scientific), fasting, prayer, and professional accountability to fight. But my mind, my heart, and my thinking can be changed. If I don't fight them completely in this life, I can learn how to at least manage them in a way where I don't have to be afraid anymore, and I can live free from the suffering they cause. God has helped people do it before, and I know it can happen for me. http://www.thetokenlife.com/2018/01/17/learning-to-love-myself-and-my-story/

Erin's story is not unique. Our society is latent with stories just like hers, the problem is that many of the women and men with similar stories have not found the courage that Erin has demonstrated. Erin said something that was significant to my whole reason for writing this book. We as a society must be willing to share our stories, to make sure we not only listen to the stories, but that we believe them. There are many who are afraid to share their story because they feel that they will not be believed or that it will just bring more negative light on themselves and someone will blame them for what happened to them and that is something that they just feel that they cannot endure.

We have a tendency in our society to hold within our anger, our abuse, and so many other negative aspects of our lives. This became a norm for our society many years ago. Up until the last several decades if you were a victim of familial sexual abuse or physical abuse you just did not tell anyone. A stigma was placed on society that if you tell, you are weak.

A good example of this came from an early sitcom to modern television called, "Leave it to Beaver." This series was about the depiction of a family that lived a perfect lifestyle. Mom was home with the kids, dad worked and each night when dad came home from a long day at work, mother would have a nice hot dinner on the table and the newspaper was on dad's favorite chair that no one sat in because that was dad's chair. The show always portrayed little gaffes that were quickly resolved. According to some experts the show attained an iconic status in the United States, with the Cleavers exemplifying the idealized suburban family of the mid-20th century. https://en.wikipedia.org/wiki/Leave_It_to_Beaver

Well many of us would watch this show and they never talked about the tough issues, so as a society this show was clearly a demonstration of what was really happening in our society. Don't talk about the hard things, or the abuse, neglect, alcoholism, drug addiction, and so on. If something was brought up in the home, it was quickly silenced and the "family secret" continued.

Erin had no one to turn to, she felt trapped in her home life. She was confused and did not know if what was happening to her was normal or not? She knew it felt wrong but did not know where to turn. Many who experience trauma feel as though they are all alone, that no one would believe them, and no one would understand what they are going through. We as a society built this imaginary wall in our lives through generations as the way to deal with the really tough topics.

A medical doctor by the name of Dr. Lissa Rankin wrote an article in Psychology Today. The name of her article was, "The Healing Power of Telling Your Story." It was a powerful article for me, because her understanding of this problem was centered on her own story. She talks about how telling your story can create a path of mental, emotional, and physical wellbeing. In her article she points out many of the harmful effects of not telling your story. She put it this way, she said:

> so many of us leave our stories untold, our songs unsung—and when this happens, we wind up feeling lonely, listless, out of touch with our life's purpose, plagued with a chronic sense that something is out of alignment. We may even wind up feeling unworthy, unloved, or sick. https://www.psychologytoday.com/us/blog/owning-pink/201211/the-healing-power-telling-your-story

For years my wife has suffered from the ill effects of her abuse. She has suffered from migraine headaches, sleep disorders, weight loss, and weight gain. Now she has been in two DUI accidents where drunk drivers hit her, one in a head-on collision. Both required medical care and long-term health issues, but there are many conditions she has suffered as a result from the ill effects of the toll of sexual abuse. I have watched her suffer, cry uncontrollably, and many times at the brink of completely breaking down and giving up.

The one thing that Carol is not lacking is the spirit she has within. Carol understands her worth. She understands that she is loved and that she is not alone. Carol and I celebrated our 35th wedding anniversary this past April, and I still consider myself the luckiest guy in the world to be married to such a strength to me and our four boys. She truly lives and shares with others what it means to endure and to rejuvenate the human spirit.

When my sweet wife started telling her story, overcame the fear of vulnerability over what had happened to her, I noticed a significant change in her demeanor and the way she looked at her past. Carol has been able to on her own finish her Master Gardner Certification, and for the last couple of years had a job working for a non-profit that supports the Division of Family Services in our County. She reached out to young people and helped them cope with life, school, whatever she could do to support the child and their parents. It is a transformation that she does not completely understand. Does that mean her bad days are behind her? Not at all.

What it has done for her is built her self-confidence, let her know that she is not alone, that she has significant worth, and that others have learned and been inspired by her bravery. This year she is coming with me to one of the biggest victim conferences in the United States and she is going to tell her story and how it has impacted her life to share her story. My sweet wife is my hero. She is the one that inspires me to help others. My life would be so insignificant if it were not for her. She gives me purpose; she allows me to make mistakes and forgives me. We are what she always refers to as the "MCBRIDE TEAM!"

Teams work together, they trust each other, and they endure the struggles that come from defeat and victory. They don't give up on each other. Teaching at Pennsylvania State University has been one of the highlights of my life. I have loved this campus and football team from when I was a small boy in Eastern Idaho. I always admired Penn State and especially Joe Paterno. I was reading quotes by Joe Paterno and I thought this was appropriate in describing this team concept. Our society must be a team against the ill effects of trauma. We have to work together to find solutions. He said, "When a team outgrows individual performance and learns team confidence, excellence becomes a reality." He also said this, "The name on the front of the jersey is what really matters, not the name on the back." https://www.brainyquote.com/authors/joe_paterno

If we are going to be successful in the challenges that we face, we must learn as human beings how to support survivors of crime and trauma, then we must understand that success requires us to work together to form solutions, to find more efficient ways of dealing with the offenders, find a better path of healing for the victim survivors and their families. It takes a concerted effort from all of us to determine how we deal with these issues within our society.

Recently I was reading a statement by Lisa Ferentz, LSCW-C DAPA. Ms. Ferentz is well known for her work in strengths-based, de-pathologized treatment of trauma and has been in private practice for over 33 years. Here is a description of what she has done. She has amazing experience and expertise in treating trauma.

She presents workshops and keynote addresses nationally and internationally and is a clinical consultant to practitioners and mental health agencies worldwide. She has been an Adjunct Faculty member at several Universities and is the Founder of The Ferentz Institute.

Lisa is the author of "Treating Self-Destructive Behaviors in Traumatized Clients: A Clinician's Guide," "Letting Go of Self-Destructive Behaviors: A Workbook of Hope and Healing," and "Finding Your Ruby Slippers: Transformative Life Lessons From the Therapist's Couch." She is also a contributing writer for mental health-related blogs and websites, including Psychologytoday.com. https://www.theferentzinstitute.com/2012/07/25/turning-tragedy-into-opportunity-resilience-of-the-human-spirit/

In her article "Turning Tragedy into Opportunity: Resilience of the human spirit," she discusses the examples of Hurricane Katrina in New Orleans, and the Fires in Chicago as examples to us about turning our tragedies into opportunities of personal growth. Ms. Lisa Ferentz said this:

I am writing this after returning from a wonderful and rejuvenating family vacation with my husband and our three grown sons. For many, many summers now, we have realized our goal of showing our boys the beauty of North America. We have walked countless magnificent trails and climbed incredible mountains in most of our National Parks, marveled at the pristine splendor of Alaska, and explored almost all of the majesty and charm of Canada. This summer, we wanted a more urban experience, so we spent time in wonderful downtown Chicago, and then fell in love with the amazing jazz of New Orleans. On the surface, these seem like disparate places to visit, but I soon discovered a fascinating and moving connection between our Mid-Western and Southern destinations.

Maybe the fact that I specialize in trauma and healing means that I see most of the world through a particular lens. But I was so struck by a theme that emerged both in the cities of Chicago and New Orleans. In both places, profound disasters threatened the very existence of the city and nearly led to their complete annihilation. The Great Chicago Fire of 1871 was one of the largest disasters of the 19th century, killing hundreds and destroying the very fabric of the city: the business district, hotels, department stores, City Hall, churches, the printing plants, theatres, and the opera house.

In 2005, Hurricane Katrina wreaked havoc on New Orleans and other neighboring states in the South. It was one of the five deadliest hurricanes and the costliest natural disaster in the history of the United States. Over 1800 people died, with total property damage estimated at $81 billion dollars. In New Orleans, 80% of the city and nearby parishes were flooded. Visiting the 9th Ward is a moving and sobering experience- the only way to begin to appreciate the depth of destruction and loss.

And yet, in both cities, these extraordinarily traumatic events actually led to rebirth, recovery, and rebuilding. Even with the magnitude of destruction, Chicago went on to become one of America's most economically important cities. And as New Orleans continues to rebuild, the palpable feeling of resiliency and gratitude is remarkable. Wherever we went, we were met with friendly, welcoming faces, and we were repeatedly thanked for supporting the city with our presence and much needed tourist dollars.

In both cities, I was moved by this idea of turning tragedy into an opportunity for regrowth. It made me think about our clients and the amazing courage and resiliency of the human spirit. It was a great reminder about our inherent capacity to heal, even in the face of devastating life events. I felt humbled and hopeful and was again reminded of what a privilege it is to bear witness to this process when we help our clients in their healing journeys. https://www.theferentzinstitute.com/2012/07/25/turning-tragedy-into-opportunity-resilience-of-the-human-spirit/

She talks about the "inherent capacity to heal." That is the amazing thing about us as human beings, our bodies and our minds are capable of healing. It does not always mean that we are back to normal. Some people of debilitating accidents leave them with a disability for the rest of their lives.

In a later chapter I will be discussing a woman who was raped by someone she knew. As a result of her rape she became pregnant. She had a decision to make, she had to fight through the emotions of being raped and decide for herself what she should do. Should she have this child, or should she abort this child? Many times, in life we are given moral decisions based only upon what others tell us to do and what we hear.

Each of us must find the strength within to make the decisions of our paths. She had a lot to think about. We often times make decisions and choices based on what others think, or to "save face" with those that we know, our friends and family. Victims of crime often will debate in their mind how they will cope with what has happened to them. They recognize that others may feel one way or the other, but the thing that we have to remind ourselves is that we must make our decisions based on what we know and understand what is within our heart. Others can give us advice, but ultimately, we are the ones that have to choose how we will digest the good and the bad that comes into our lives. Some remain bitter for the rest of their lives if someone else wrongs them.

As human beings we cannot let others control our decisions or how we feel or what direction in life we should go. Erin for many years was concerned more about what others thought of her and paid little attention to what she truly needed in her life. Until she realized her significance of her own life and realized her self-worth, she was always trying to gain more attention and affirmation from those around her. It is very easy for those who have been harmed to lose sight on their ability to control their own lives and that society or the person who harmed them have this temporary control over their lives. Erin recognized it, sought help, and now tells her story with great vulnerability. Being vulnerable and telling your story is strength not weakness.

Victim survivors of crime feel a sense of loss of themselves, meaning the person they were. Victimization tends to bring out the worst in a person because they feel used, broken, guilty, depressed, unwanted, and unloved. These feelings of inadequacy are very difficult to overcome if you have a sense within yourself that you will never open yourself up to being harmed again.

Many victims will seclude themselves both physically and emotionally. The fear of being harmed again takes precedence in their lives. Being vulnerable opens a person up to new experiences and understanding that they are not alone.

I have had the opportunity to bring victims together and as they talk, as they get to know one another they soon realize that they are not alone. They realize that there are others who have similar feelings and emotions and they recognize that this gives them a source of strength by knowing there are others to lean on that understand. This promotes healing and understanding, and truly helps them recognize that they can manage their pain through sharing their story and understanding better the significance of their worth.

Though we may at times put ourselves in situations where others can take advantage of us, crime victims never asked to be victimized, never asked to have a family member murdered. Poor choices do not mean that a person wants to be a victim. Though we can all learn to make good choices, we cannot be responsible for the poor choices of others, that is out of our control.

However, what we can control is how we deal with what life puts in front of us and make a choice to either let the trial we are going through define who we are, or overcome the trial in our lives by reaching out to one another and recognizing the strength from seeking help, but also more importantly we learn to be vulnerable and recognize our inner strength.

Take Your Garbage Out

I have often used the analogy of garbage disposal for my point about why it is important to share your story with your family, with a counselor, with the police, the court, and most importantly with yourself. The most important person to share your story with first is yourself. By acknowledging that it did happen you begin to heal and gain the strength to share with others.

I will ask a survivor why they take their garbage out of their house. They generally look at me with the "what?" look on their face. They then proceed to share with me that they take their garbage out so their house does not smell, and that they get rid of what they don't need. I love it when they look at me after they have said that and begin to understand my analogy.

In this life, some will have more emotional garbage than others. Some of us have been victims of crime; others of us have been through very tragic experiences, regardless of the reasons, if we do not talk about what has happened to us in our lives and work through those difficult times by sharing and learning from each other, it will fester in our souls. We will begin to experience more and more problems in our lives because we were not able to get rid of the emotional trash. We do not need it! So just like the garbage, those parts of our lives that have caused emotional and physical pain at the hands of another can become internalized and will start affecting who we are and our worth as a human being. By getting rid of that emotional garbage we are releasing ourselves from the bondage of those emotions and finding relief through not only sharing with others, but also recognizing we are not alone.

Many victims have described to me relief that comes from sharing with others what has happened to them and that begins the healing process. If it is not discussed and no effort is made to resolve that crisis in your life it will begin to create more problems that in some cases have consumed an individual's ability to cope and move forward in their lives.

In October 2017, Alyssa Milano posted on social media the importance of having a voice for all of those who have been sexually assaulted or abused. The movement's purpose, "Me Too," was first addressed by Tarana Burke. She was concerned and wanted to "empower women through empathy," "especially young and vulnerable women." (https://en.wikipedia.org/wiki/Me_Too_movement)

Whether you agree or disagree with their motives, the fact that this movement has affected millions is evidence enough that power comes from telling your story and being vulnerable. We as a society can take a lesson from this movement that this is a systemic problem in our society and that we need to start talking about it more.

The same concern is about all aspects of crime and victimization. We as a society must do a better job at holding the offender's accountable for their actions. We often think we are doing a favor by sending an offender away for many years, and though many of them need to go to prison, we have to remember that they are going to be back out on the streets and that we need to find a way as a system to hold them more accountable for their actions towards their victims and society in general.

What does accountability look like to an offender? Can offenders be rehabilitated and control their behavior? The answer is yes, they can. I have seen it. How do we achieve that level of accountability?

It requires the victims to speak up, to not be afraid to tell their story, to look the offenders in the eyes and hold them personally responsible for their actions.

Several years ago when Elizabeth Smart was at the sentencing of Brian David Mitchell for her abduction, and sexual assault that occurred for 9 months, I have to share with you that it was one of the most impactful victim statements that I have ever heard.

Elizabeth asked that the lectern be turned around and that she be able to look directly at the offender who was so brutal to this innocent young girl. It is incomprehensible how Elizabeth endured that behavior, but in the end, at the time of his sentencing she faced him again, only this time in a courtroom, being held accountable. Elizabeth shared her victim impact with him, word for word. I do not believe that I ever saw Elizabeth take her eyes off of Brian David Mitchell. With an eloquently prepared statement, Elizabeth read her statement and spoke with conviction, poised and determined to express to him that he will no longer be able to impact her life—an amazing way to share with the world. She was vulnerable, powerful, and successful at sharing her message.

Dr. Welner and forensic Psychologist who testified at the hearing on the Dr. Oz show made this observation of the strength of Elizabeth Smart to stand in front of her accuser and confront him. Dr. Welner said, "when you stand in court and you confront the perpetrator, the person who victimized you, you have the power, they are silenced, and they must listen to you holding them accountable . . . she is not only renewed, rejuvenated, resilient . . . but she has power." (https://www.linkedin.com/pulse/elizabeth-smart-window-kidnappers-mental-state-michael-welner-m-d-/)

Every time I see another person stand and tell their story, I honor them. They truly are rejuvenating the human spirit. A friend of mine who was a victim of sexual abuse once said to me that the hardest thing they have ever done is tell their story and they said that every time they tell their story, they said in their mind it would be the last time they tell their story. They said it is too hard and too painful, and then they said with conviction, that is why I need to do it. If I can help just one person then I believe that I am doing well by telling my story.

As I end this chapter, I want to pay tribute to all the survivors that were willing to be vulnerable to tell their story in this book. I am so grateful for the relationships that I have developed with them. It is empowering to me to be with empowered people who have been through so much in their lives.

I am in awe every time I hear another story or listen to the anguish of their souls as they poor their feelings out and truly begin the healing process and not remaining silent. We have to as professionals, as family and friends of survivors, to never think for one moment that we know what they are going through, because we don't. We do not understand unless we have been through it what it must feel like to be abused, or to have a loved one murdered. All we can do as I have said is be there for them and listen. I once asked a survivor of a homicide case how she was able to move forward and cope with the loss of her daughter. She said to me that even after all these years I still hurt, I still feel the pain, I just have learned to live with that pain and realize that it will never go away. Though a person never eliminates the pain, they learn to control their pain through telling their story and feeling strength through association with others.

In conclusion, I recently saw the movie "Hacksaw Ridge." This movie was one of the most inspiring movies I have ever seen.

He went into this battle with nothing to save himself with except his faith in God and his Bible he carried with him. Private Doss felt his civic duty to protect the freedom of our Country. He enlisted as a medic, but he refused to carry a rifle. Although he was ridiculed, he stayed true to his commitment.

The battle took place in April 1945. The battlefield, located on top of a vertical 400-foot cliff, was inundated with Japanese machine gun nests and booby traps, to make it even more difficult for the soldiers.

The ridge was called Hacksaw Ridge for the perilously steep cliff and was key to winning the battle of Okinawa. The mission they were on was near-impossible, and when Doss's battalion was ordered to retreat, the medic refused to leave his fallen comrades behind.

With facing heavy machine gun and artillery fire, Doss repeatedly ran alone into the kill zone, carrying wounded soldiers to the edge of the cliff and singlehandedly lowering them down to safety. Each time he saved a man's life, Doss cried out as loud as he could, "Lord, please help me get one more." By the end of the night he had rescued an estimated 75 men.

As I begin this important book to me, I want to say that we are in the battle every day to save lives and to assist those who are downtrodden and in anguish. We cannot let up in our fight for the rights of the innocent. We need to ensure that those who harm others are held accountable to their victims and ensure that as a society we do all in our power to make sure that we support those who have been victimized beyond our comprehension.

Again, I am grateful for those who have been willing to be vulnerable and to tell their stories. It is an honor and a privilege to know all of them.

2

Harmful Effects of a Sexualized Society

As I begin this chapter I have to confess that I am a realist. I am not afraid to tell the reader, society, or my classes at Penn State University what is really happening on our streets. I speak my mind. Some readers may find some of the material in this chapter very disturbing due to the nature of offenders and their abuse of their victims. Please know it is not for sensationalism but to help each person understand the extent of this problem and that we cannot afford as parents, teachers, men and women, to candy coat this topic or pretend that these things are not happening. Please know I share some of my experiences with the intentions of educating and helping the reader recognize the magnitude of this problem.

We now live in a society where the norm is that sex is openly discussed and being used as a commodity for television, movies, videos, musical lyrics, and on the Internet. Individuals are now open about their sex life, and Hollywood has taken it to a new level with the way we sell movie tickets and concert tickets. It is not uncommon to see women and men dressing more provocatively and that the inhibitions of sex in general has been taken to new levels that we have never seen, especially with the Internet.

I am not trying to sound prudish about sexuality, but as we all know sexuality is a huge part of our lives. It is the most powerful force for good that is healthy and accepted regardless of who you are and where you live. Sexuality is an important expression of love to someone we care deeply for and with whom we consensually want to express that love too through intimacy. Sexuality also allows us to create life, to bring little ones into our homes. I can think of no greater power on earth than to create life through this expression of love one to another. It brings a couple together and creates a bond like no other.

The next time you watch a sitcom on prime-time television, it is hard to watch a sitcom without hearing or seeing sexual innuendos throughout the entire program. It should be highly offensive to women to see how the media constantly uses the female form to sell products in magazines, television, at sporting events, and on the Internet.

There is no denying that the human body is a beautiful creation. We are inherently attracted to each other. The entertainment world understands this very well, however we now see that our bodies are being used to sell products, to entice viewers, and the sex industry is always pushing the limit as to what we see on the various forms of media.

A few years ago I took my boys to a stock car race in Salt Lake City. We were going to see cars race around the track, not be introduced to scantily dressed women. When we got there, it was "Playboy Racing Car Day," in the morning and the stock car race in the afternoon. So the first thing my kids were exposed to at a sporting event was Playboy bunnies (that is what they call women who pose nude for Playboy). These women were walking around in scantily dressed clothes signing autographs for men and their boys getting pictures with them, holding their thumbs up.

Again, not trying to sound like a prude, I took our boys to the race track that day to see cars racing not the displaying of these women as a commodity to racing cars. I was offended and could not believe that we are subjecting our children to this kind of attention to sexuality and the objectification of women.

The adult entertainment industry is exploding on the Internet and in adult establishments all over the United States and throughout the World. This industry is saying to the public that it is okay to objectify sexuality as titillating and a free expression of our First Amendment rights. As a result, we are seeing more and more people addicted to adult entertainment including pornography and increasing the chances of developing a sexual addiction that is as out of control as a drug or alcohol addiction in many people's lives. The addiction to pornography by science experts is now being compared to addictions to drugs and alcohol.

In a study conducted by Cambridge University, there is a significant resemblance of a brain of someone who is addicted to pornography and other sexual addictions and one who is addicted to drugs or alcohol. Here is one of the findings of Cambridge University, the name of the article is, "Your Brain on Porn." The article said:

> ...... the brains of those with the compulsive sexual behaviors "lit up" in a different way from those without such compulsions. Interestingly, the patterns of brain activation in these people mirrored those seen in the brains of drug addicts when they were exposed to drugs. (https://www.yourbrainonporn.com/cambridge-university-brain-scans-find-porn-addiction)

Several years ago, when I was supervising federal offenders on probation, I had a particular sex offender on my caseload. One day I asked him the extent of his addiction to pornography as part of his behavior when he sexually abused his daughter. He shared with me that he would literally spend all day everyday viewing pornography in multiple settings. He worked from home and his wife worked so he would spend intermittently 2-3 hours a day on company time viewing pornography.

At night he would find every excuse in the book to stay in his office and continue to view pornography and tell his wife he was working. He claims to have spent an average of 10-15 hours a day viewing pornography. He would go all night sometimes and not realize it until he would see the sun coming up. The pornography hypnotized him. When he was viewing pornography he could not concentrate on anything around him or the amount of time he was wasting. Eventually the fantasy of being with a teenage girl was too much and he acted out on his daughter. He said to me that pornography only satisfies the need for so long and then he found himself not being able to resist the temptation to act out his fantasies he was viewing on the Internet.

There was another offender who was using his daughters as sex objects. He would video tape his daughters having sex with animals and then he would sell the videos online. His claim was that at least he wasn't having sex with them! Now of course we get ill thinking about filming that, let alone with his daughters. It is repulsive, but it is also the reality of this systemic problem in our society. The unfortunate aspect of this behavior with this individual when looking into their life history, it started with pornography and progressed.

Another example of what we are talking about involved a mother and her daughter. The mother was a registered sex offender. She was exposed to pornography at a very early age with her father's magazines hidden under his bed. Her and her brother would go and sit under the bed and look at pornography for hours. They would act out what they saw on the pages of the magazines, which included intercourse, oral sex, and many other behaviors in the pages of the magazines.

Later on in life after she had left home and married, she had children. She found herself aroused by using her daughter in her fantasies. She would use objects to rape her daughters, at the same time arousing herself through masturbation. The most extreme was the use of knitting needles, inserting them in her daughter's body cavities. The authorities were notified when the mother brought her daughter into the ER because she punctured and ruined her daughter's uterus with her incestuous behavior. Her child would never be able to have children due to the mother's sexual addiction and pedophilic behavior.

This all was a result of behavior learned at an early age and continuing through her informative years. This complicates a person's life who is exposed at an early age. This type of behavior requires extensive intervention from the court system and extensive counseling. Though we know that the majority of those sexually abused do not go on to necessarily become an abuser, there is evidence to show that it does increase the chances. I recently read in an article called, "The Long Term Effect of Childhood Sexual Abuse," that:

> "In an extensive review and meta-analysis of the published research relevant to risk-factors for perpetration of child sexual abuse, Whitaker et al. (2008) found a strong relationship in the literature between being a victim of childhood sexual abuse and perpetrating child sexual abuse. Child sex offenders were found to be much more likely to have been victims of child sexual abuse than either non-sex offenders or non-offenders.

> It is important to note, however, that these findings indicate that *most* victims of child sexual abuse *do not* go on to offend sexually or in other ways, although the risks are higher than for those in the general population who were not sexually abused. Although the Ogloff et al. (2012) study clearly indicated that victims of child sexual abuse are at greater risk of subsequent offending behavior, most child sexual abuse victims (77%) did not have a criminal record." https://aifs.gov.au/cfca/publications/long-term-effects-child-sexual-abuse/interpersonal-outcomes

The last example of how pornography has disrupted lives involved a simple DUI probation case. We went to do a home visit check on an individual who was convicted of DUI and put on formal probation for two years. We always go and check out their homes to make sure that they are okay and that they do not have any alcohol in their home. It is always necessary when doing these home visits to go through and observe everything in the house.

As we entered their family room, they had several bookshelves with videos/DVDs by their TV. As I went closer I noticed that at least half the videos/DVDs included pornography movies. I turned to the man on supervision and I asked, "What are these doing here?" He was confused. He said, "Why does it matter where I put my videos? I am not restricted from looking at them."

I was somewhat frustrated already that he would have these out in plain site with four children in the home, ages 5-15. At this point I said to him, "You cannot have pornography that is accessible to children, do you know that?" He played innocent and said, "No I did not know that, I swear!" We then went around and observed closer and found stacks of hard core pornography magazines in his room, and the main bathroom of the house, stacked on the back of the toilet. At this point, the man was arrested for endangering children and taken to jail.

When interviewing the children, they informed us that there father would let them watch it all the time alone and with him. They also indicated that the children had acted out on each other mimicking what they saw on the videos. I am confident that if this issue had not been identified he would have advanced on them and possibly abused his children. We could find no evidence of abuse at that point, but there were strong indications that he was definitely grooming his children for other purposes than exposing them to pornography only.

Many victims of sexual abuse and assault indicate the use of pornography at some point when they were abused. So my impression of this individual by his attitude was that he was using the pornography as a grooming technique to advance on his children until it resulted in sexual abuse.

The concern that I have is every example I have given involved children and pornography. Exposing children to pornography at such a young age can have long lasting effects on their ability to see human intimacy as an expression of love versus satisfying the perpetrators lustful desire.

I do not believe I had one case of a sex offender who did not talk about their addiction to pornography before they acted out on a child.

Several years ago when the movie *Fifty Shades of Grey* was in movie theaters for the first time, I told my Penn State Criminal Justice class that this movie will entice someone to act out the behavior and will do it without consent of the victim, thinking that the victim will probably like it, just like in the movie. It was not but a few months later that there were several articles in major newspapers that stated a connection to new arrests on individuals who claimed to law enforcement that they were inspired by the movie *Fifty Shades of Grey*.

Recently, I spoke at a conference where I talked about the media and the impact on our society with respect to the use of pornography. I called the presentation, "Pornography: Russian roulette to Sexual Deviancy."

Though I do not believe that everyone who views pornography becomes a deviant person, like alcohol you never know if you will become an alcoholic until you actually are drinking alcohol, just like you will never know how pornography will impact your life, until it may be too late. My suggestion is that if you do find yourself viewing more and more pornography and that it is more enticing than actual intimacy it is probably time to get some help, because just like drugs or alcohol, once it has you hooked, it will be hard for you to let it go.

As I stated earlier, we should be very concerned as parents and those that have access to children that we are not leaving our children vulnerable and easily exposed to pornography.

On the web site American College of Pediatricians, there is a section called "The Position Statement of the College on the Impact of Pornography on Children," we read the following statement from doctors, psychologist and experts in this area:

> Grade school children are sometimes exposed to pornography accidentally when they view material on the Internet. They may also come into contact with a parent's or close adult's pornographic material. Sexual predators have purposefully exposed young children to pornography for the purpose of grooming the children for sexual exploitation. Pornography exposure at these young ages often results in anxiety for the child. Children also report feelings of disgust, shock, embarrassment, anger, fear, and sadness after viewing pornography.

> These children can suffer all of the symptoms of anxiety and depression. They may become obsessed with acting out adult sexual acts that they have seen, and this can be very disruptive and disturbing to the child's peers who witness or are victimized by this behavior. Children under twelve years old who have viewed pornography are statistically more likely to sexually assault their peers. In sum, children exposed to pornographic material are at risk for a broad range of maladaptive behaviors and psychopathology. https://www.acpeds.org/the-college-speaks/position-statements/the-impact-of-pornography-on-children

Our sweet children are innocent, there little minds and bodies are not ready for adult material at such young ages. We must do everything in our power to protect our children from exposure to these ideas, behaviors, and pictures that can possibly lead to addiction and other problems associated with sexuality.

Another alarming issue discussed in this statement by the American College of Pediatricians points out the impact that pornography has on the average person. It is obviously a deep concern when we see the kinds of statistics and data that shows a decrease in our respect for each other and base our interaction on our sexuality and the way we look. This portion of the article should raise our concern for better control of what is available to our young adults and to our children.

In the article it helps us understand the impact of pornography on older adolescents and young adults. The study involved finding young men from the surrounding area. Some of the young men were exposed to pornography for 6 weeks and the controlled group viewed normal programming on the television. The following results were collected after asking them a sequence of questions.

1. Male subjects demonstrated increased callousness toward women.
2. Subjects considered the crime of rape less serious.
3. Subjects were more accepting of non-marital sexual activity and non-coital sexual practices such as oral and anal sex.

4. Subjects became more interested in more extreme and deviant forms of pornography.
5. Subjects were more likely to say they were dissatisfied with their sexual partner.
6. Subjects were more accepting of sexual infidelity in a relationship.
7. Subjects valued marriage less and were twice as likely to believe marriage may become obsolete.
8. Men experienced a decreased desire for children, and women experienced a decreased desire to have a daughter.
9. Subjects showed a greater acceptance of female promiscuity.
   https://www.acpeds.org/the-college-speaks/position-statements/the-impact-of-pornography-on-children

Another area of concern as I mentioned earlier, is the impact that pornography and a sexualized society has on the sanctity of womanhood. Pornography degrades women more than anything I have ever seen. To put women in submissive situations by taking pictures, videos, putting them on a stage dancing in front of men, treating them like they are a menu item at a restaurant is disturbing.

Recently I was listening to two men in an airport talking about women that were walking by where we were sitting. I was shocked that they were talking so freely with others sitting around them (that in and of itself is an indication of where society is headed). Both men had a ring on their left ring finger, which indicates to me that they are married.

One of the men said to the other one, "That girl has a nice ass, I wish I could see her without those shorts on." Then the other one would say, "Oh look at that one, she has an amazing rack, love to see them naked!" I had to stand up and leave, I was disappointed in these married men.

One reason is for the way they were talking about women, but two, that they would do it so freely like it was okay. I think about the fact that those women could have been my wife, or my daughter they are talking about, and frankly it makes me sick that our wives and daughters have to walk around and have men openly make fun, or lust after women that we love and respect. I can think of no other way to be more disrespectful to another man's wife or daughter than to make light of their body parts or fantasize of what they look like without their clothes on.

I recently read an article by a student at the University of California Merced, Viviana Ojeda that supports my concern about the sexualized societal view of women. I think a note from her blog is worth mentioning at this point. She has a wonderful perspective on what she is seeing in the media and on social media. She said: "….it seems like I can't turn on the television without seeing a commercial sexualizing a cheeseburger or a can of soda…... Society in essence, is too obsessed with sex." (https://www.theodysseyonline.com/living-sexualized-society)

Reading what Ms. Ojeda has said about her view, should be a wake-up call for all of us to evaluate our own behavior. We cannot change the way society feels about this issue, but what we can do is change the way we individually look at this phenomenon that is objectifying the women we love and cherish, our wives and daughters.

Another part of the pornography industry in our sexualized society is the commodity of sex through strip clubs, prostitution, and human trafficking. Each of these issues brings another level and disheartening effect on women and men. We see the display of women and men in strip clubs as a product for individuals to be entertained by seeing women and men exposing their bodies for the mere pleasure of viewing sexual titillating behavior. This undoubtedly creates sexual desire that is more than likely relieved through self-gratification rather than sharing intimacy with a willing partner, which is an expression of true love and respect. The Internet now allows us to meet others online and engage in virtual sex or meet for sex with others.

This is very disturbing because many times it involves men acting as teenagers and meeting teenagers and sexually assaulting them. The Internet has become a powerful tool for the sex industry to meet and have sex virtually or in person with anyone who is willing to engage in these interactions on the Internet.

The scary thing is that many young people are innocently getting on websites, naïve to the dangers that are lurking on the Internet and are finding themselves in trouble and in many situations being exposed to abusive behavior and even death.

This industry which has flooded the Internet, with live adult models, and some web sites where you pick your model to your desire, and many other sites that match people together, and there are even sites that do not care how old you are, or what your preference is, they will match you with someone who will find you and use you for their own sexual desire. They do not care about what happens to you or how it affects you, only that you meet their preference for uninhibited sex and self-serving pleasure. It is like going to a restaurant and looking at a menu until you decide what you want to eat. Sometimes the choices are limited. It is disturbing that many of those choices involve the exposure and abuse of children.

One Victim's Story Derived from a Sexualized Society

A few years ago I met a young lady out west, her name was Anne. I met her through a mutual acquaintance. Her sister shared with me that a neighbor had recently sexually assaulted her younger sister Anne close to her family home.

The assailant was in his early twenties and she knew him, but they were not close. One day Anne was at home and he came over to her home and wanted to talk to her, he had just returned home from college. It was dusk and they went outside in their backyard. They spent a few hours talking. Eventually he asked her if she was a "virgin." She thought that was strange but reluctantly answered his question. Anne said that she was. He complimented her, but then as they continued to talk he kissed her and she at that point did not know what to do but went along with kissing him. He soon was fondling her and trying to take her clothes off, at this point she said, "No!" She specifically told him that she did not want to do this. He just kept going and said he wants to be her first and that many girls on their first experience are nervous and told her to try to relax. She kept insisting on him stopping, but he did not stop and held her down.

She was in shock and did not know what to do; it was like she was defenseless to what was happening. Her parents were literally right inside the house and she was close to where they would have heard her, but she felt defenseless to what was happening. He then said to her, "It is okay if your Dad comes out, he will see my bare butt and not yours." Before he had an orgasm he said to Anne, "Where can I finish?" At this point she said you cannot do that anywhere and asked him to leave. He was playing it off as no big deal and said to her as he was getting dressed "Hey maybe we can now become 'Fuck Buddies'?" When he left, she was not sure what had just happened, but felt responsible for what happened, but was confused about the whole event.

Weeks passed and she was full of different emotions, was it her fault? Should she report it? She just did not know what to do. Her mind was racing in so many different directions and she was just trying to cope with what had happened to her. Finally she talked to her sister and told her what had happened. Anne's sister told her that she needs to talk to someone and that is when she tried to introduce me to Anne. Anne did not really want to meet with me and resisted for a while but finally agreed to talk with me.

At this point Anne had not talked to anyone other than her sister. When we met, she just shared with me what had happened and how she was feeling. We ended up meeting several times and finally she felt ready to talk to her parents. I was very proud of her. Anne was a senior in high school and had a lot of different emotions and clearly was not prepared for the emotions that come with sexual assault.

Eventually after meeting with her parents and all of us talking, she shared with us that she was going to report the crime. Anne, her sister, and her mother went to the police department and reported the crime. This really created a lot of anxiety in Anne because reporting it made it real and that he would find out that she reported him to the police.

Soon after Anne reported the crime, the police visited with the perpetrator. He indicated that he did indeed have sex with her, but that she wanted to have sex. He played it off as consensual and took no accountability for what happened. He mentioned that they had had sex in the backyard right by her house, and said, "If she did not want to, why did she not yell out?"

He was told not to have any contact with her, a temporary protective order was completed and he was told what he could and could not do. He could not drive past her house and could not have any type of contact with her.

Anne's case was set to go before the grand jury. The DA prepared her for the case and Anne then testified. At the hearing she was asked questions that really confused her. For example, they asked her why she did not just leave if she was in her own backyard. The questions posed to her made it seem as though it was her fault or that she could have avoided it. They even questioned her about why she did not yell out if her parents were there in the house, and could hear her?

There are many victims who do not report sexual assaults. One of the main reasons is for what Anne went through with the grand jury. They feel helpless in a system that seems to believe that women put themselves in situations and precipitated their own assault. Though there are cases where women may have been intoxicated and were flirting, that does not mean that they were asking to be raped. That is the difference and you cannot, and I repeat you cannot place blame on a woman for being raped because she was drinking or dressed provocatively. It may put them at a greater risk of being assaulted, but you cannot blame them for someone committing a sexual assault. That puts responsibility on the victim and lessens the criminological act conducted by a perpetrator.

The concept of victim blaming is a theory discussed in victimology. Because of the sexualized society that we have been talking about, and also the fact that we view the world generally as a safe place, we tend to see those involved in sexual behavior as consenting to the act. We all have this belief that a person would not do such a vial act if they were not enticed by the victim in some way. Dr. David Feldman in the publication, "Psychology Today," provides a look at how we as a society came about in blaming victims for their victimization. He said:

> We wonder if he or she had done something to invite the tragedy. Maybe that survivor of sexual assault was wearing provocative clothing. Maybe that shooting victim was involved in gang activity. Maybe my neighbor had invited that burglary by associating with the wrong people. If this is the case, we tell ourselves, then it won't happen to me. After all, the world is a just place. https://www.psychologytoday.com/us/blog/supersurvivors/201803/why-do-people-blame-the-victim

Dr. Feldman is basically saying that we tend to blame the victim of sexual assault, because of the fact that no one would put themselves in that situation unless they wanted to have sex, or justify why this happened was both of their faults, and that we believe that way so we can protect our "rosy" view of the world and not entertain the belief that it could happen to me.

In addition to victim blaming, the average person does not understand unless you have been through such a tragic event, that many times we freeze when going through a traumatic event. Those questioning Anne do not realize that what she was going through was a coping mechanism in a traumatic event.

Many victims like Anne, when confronted with a stressful situation find themselves doing what is necessary to endure their trauma. We call this the "Fight or Flight" response to trauma. Anne literally shut down emotionally when she was being physically assaulted, not because she wanted to participate, but that it was her body's response to trauma. Recently when reading the Harvard Medical School Publication, I read an article called, "Understanding the Stress Response." In the article we learn that –

> A stressful incident can make the heart pound and breathing quicken. Muscles tense and beads of sweat appear....This combination of reactions to stress is also known as the "fight-or-flight" response because it evolved as a survival mechanism, enabling people and other mammals to react quickly to life-threatening situations. The carefully orchestrated yet near-instantaneous sequence of hormonal changes and physiological responses helps someone to fight the threat off or flee to safety. https://www.health.harvard.edu/staying-healthy/understanding-the-stress-response

The body is an amazing thing and clearly our body's responses to trauma are there to protect us from further harm. When individuals do not understand or believe this, then you get the kind of questions that were asked in the grand jury hearing in Anne's case. When others are not educated on these types of responses, and view the world as "rosy," then others assume that they were willing participants.

When Anne's assailant went before the grand jury he plead the Fifth Amendment, which is his right not to testify against himself. The grand jury came back with the decision not to file charges. Clearly the jury did not understand that in many sexual assault cases, victims generally freeze because that is a natural defense to trauma. In addition to their view of the world as safe, they blame the victim for their victimization.

This clearly tells us that it is vital that our communities are being educated on what happens when someone is faced with trauma and how a person psychologically and physiologically responds to trauma.

Now let's discuss the perpetrator. Anne's offender had built a reputation in school of being very lucid with his discussion of sex and making fun of sexuality through very crude sayings or crude placards on social media. One of the things that he was known for was his lack of respect for women, and it showed in his posts on social media. Her assailant was attempting to minimize and normalize his behavior by posting inappropriate pictures and phrases. Many individuals feel if you post it on social media it must not be that bad, or have the attitude, "Can't you take a joke?" Minimizing inappropriate pictures or phrases justifies his actions in his/her own mind.

In one particular picture, her assailant put a picture of a girl in a prison jump suit that had a caption that said "Lying about a rape will put you in jail." He put this picture on his facebook page the day before the grand jury. Her assailant was building a case against her on social media. No matter what he said to any friends, or posted on social media, she remained strong and followed through with the grand jury testimony.

Individuals like her assailant do not understand the imapct of their behavior. There is no accountability. When an individual has taken advantage of others, especially sexually, and they get away with the behavior, they feel there are no cosequences. This makes it easier to offend others because they have lost any emotion for caring what has been done.

If someone continues to get away with their behavior it will eventually create a false sense of security and they will become more self-righteous with their behavior and attitude.

The extent of the problem of men getting away with sexual assault has to do with the fact that there are many social conditioning aspects to their behavior. They truly believe that what they are doing is not wrong and also due to the excessive availability of sexual material from the Internet, they are becoming desenstized to their own behavior, and making it appear as normal or acceptable.

A university student conducting their dissertation wrote this in his paper,

> Sexual assault has become a serious social problem for our country. In the United States, one out of five women is raped in her lifetime (e.g., Koss, Gidycz, & Wisniewski, 1987; Tjaden & Thoennes, 2000), and over 50% of women have experienced some type of sexual assault (Koss et al., 1987). In 2007, there were 248,300 victims aged thirteen and older of rape, attempted rape, or sexual assault in the United States (Department of Justice, http://www.ojp.gov/bjs/abstract/saycrle.htm). In addition, nearly 25% of men admit to verbally or physically coercing a woman into unwanted sexual activity (Abbey, et al., 2002; Koss et al., 1987; White & Smith, 2004); and approximately 15% of men admit to having participated in behavior that meets the legal definition of rape or attempted rape (e.g., Abbey, McAuslan, & Ross, 1998; Koss, Gidycz, & Wisniewski, 1987; Loh, Gidycz, Lobo, & Luthra, 2005; White & Smith, 2004). Additionally, if guaranteed that they would not be

punished, nearly one third of men admit to at least some probability of forcing sexual activity on a woman in the future (e.g., Abbey et al., 1998; Check & Malamuth, 1983; Greendlinger & Byrne, 1987; Malamuth, 1981, 1989; Osland, Fitch, & Willis, 1996). These figures are staggering; especially when the high percentage of unreported sexual assault is considered. https://scholar.utc.edu/cgi/viewcontent.cgi?referer=https://www.google.com/&httpsredir=1&article=1444&context=theses

Many of these offenders believe that they can get away with it so it increases their chances of re-offending time and time again. They are not concerned with the system, and honestly feel that they are not responsible for a criminal act, and usually blame the victim or their past on their behavior. Again, this attitude is built over time of not being held accountable for their actions.

We have also learned that offenders have many more victims than what they generally get arrested for. Most sexual predators reveal that once they start committing offenses they cannot stop until they get caught. This is usually because they have created this pattern of addiction that controls their lives.

Once again, the true recidivism rates cannot be determined due to the under reporting of the crimes, and are most likely much higher. Marshall and Barbaree (1990) compared official records of a sample of sex offenders with "unofficial" sources of data such as polygraph examinations. The authors found that the number of subsequent sex offenses revealed through unofficial sources was 2.4 times higher than the number that was recorded in official reports. In addition, additional research using information gained through polygraph examinations, from a sample of imprisoned sex offenders with on average fewer than two known victims, found that these offenders actually had an average of 110 victims and 318 offenses (Ahlmeyer, Heil, McKee, and English, 2000). https://scholar.utc.edu/cgi/viewcontent.cgi?referer=https://www.google.com/&httpsredir=1&article=1444&context=theses

There is a great deal of complexity as to how someone can offend so many. Again working from the same pattern we have been developing, those who are over-sexualized and feel they get away with the promiscuity and sexual aggression towards women, tell themselves that what they are doing is acceptable and feel they can get away with it. Clearly, they are on a path that will affect so many lives, and objectify women like we have never seen, and sadly we are almost to that point.

So when individuals have created this pattern, how did it all start? There are many indicators, but one we definitely understand is that promiscuity can lead to this path. Those who are obsessed with sexual behavior can escalate and create havoc to others based upon narcissism and sexual addictions.

I recently read an article in the Science Daily that noted research from Mouilso and Calhoun that there are two general pathways that frequently lead to perpetration from male offenders, the first one being that of "promiscuity" and the second path would be "hostile masculinity." Mouilso and Calhoun conclude that, "people can be high or low on factors in both of those tracks, but if a person has both of them together, it makes that person much more likely to perpetrate a sexual assault, according to current theory." https://www.sciencedaily.com/releases/2016/03/160329184953.htm

Anne's assailant was more worried about his own reputation and did not mind sacrificing Anne's reputation in the process. His social media was full of posts that were degrading to women, which helps us conclude that this assailant is on a slippery slope, and until he understands accountability and respect of women, he will find himself in trouble.

Since Anne's case, there have now been several women who have contacted Anne and told her that he did the same thing to them. He is now developing this pattern.

One of the tragic effects of a sexualized society is the ease in which others can live out their sexual fantasies at the expense of many women, men, and children, who suffer as victims to such horrific selfish behavior.

Though we cannot blame pornography or a sexualized society for criminal offenders in every incident, I can generalize by saying it is obvious that in connection with other factors, a sexualized society is fuel to a fire that can impact so many lives.

In getting to know the strengths of Anne, I have been humbled many times by her ability to share her story, not in a demeaning way toward her assailant, but as an important lesson for all of us to watch our behavior, be accountable, and get help.

You would think that someone like Anne might be bitter. Though she is frustrated at our criminal justice system for not holding her assailant accountable, she also understands that this person did not get to this point without having major issues in his life. She has resolved that his only hope of change is accountability.

The amazing thing about Anne is that she is now getting involved in creating a new path for herself. For the last two years, Anne has been participating in a program within the walls of a prison. She has been participating in a program called "Bridges to Life." Anne spends 14 weeks with inmates as a facilitator where she works with inmates in this program to help them become more accountable to their victims and society. By being involved in this program and helping inmates, it has clearly helped her deal with her own victimization. I have heard her tell her story many times to inmates and she always tells them that the most important thing that she can do is help them to see that they don't have to commit crime and hurt others and that she believes in them and looks at them as human beings.

What amazes me is that attitude comes from being a victim of a crime and not letting it control her, but allows her to tell her story and hopefully affect their lives and help them to become more accountable and responsible.

Recently Anne attended a national conference for victim assistance and she has been telling her story in front of hundreds of people at conferences and in the classroom of a university. I am always amazed and proud of Anne. She has taken a very negative experience in her life and has affected hundreds of people with her strength and determination not to let it bring her down. She is truly what we call a "Survivor!"

How Do We Survive in a Sexualized Society?

Recently I was reading a blog called, "The Digital Parenting Blog." Tim Woda and Internet Safety Expert gave advice to parents of children who have access to the Internet and to the potential dangers of these type of websites, but also to very innocent websites such as blogs, Facebook, Instagram, and many others. Mr. Woda shared this on this particular topic.

> Microsoft reports that online predators contact kids in almost any online venue, including social networking, blogs, instant messaging, email and chat rooms. Once contacted, they use the following to establish a relationship and manipulate kids: (http://resources.uknowkids.com/blog/bid/334439/the-dangers-of-online-predators-and-how-to-protect-your-family)

Many women and men who have been through very difficult times in their lives, especially centered on this particular topic regarding pornography addictions or other types of addictions centered on mood altering behavior, their success in overcoming the odds and controlling their behavior must be centered on their perception of self. That this behavior does not define who they are. They must see the significance of their worth and recognize that behavior does not define self.

We learned from this chapter that many individuals who are trapped in this industry have some type of trauma earlier in their lives, especially in their childhood.

If we are going to have any impact on this problem it starts with one person at a time. We need to reach out to young people and help them see their individual worth. They need to know that adults will listen to them, whether it is a parent, teacher, or an adult they know and trust. They need to know that there are solutions to their problems and that they do not have to carry the burden of those problems alone.

Many young people and older people both have a lot of self-doubt when they have been hurt or traumatized. Many of these folks will resort to behavior that will help them cope. Many women and men in the sex industry find that their way of coping within the sex industry is to use drugs, because of the lack of self-esteem and the lack of alternatives. Many within the sex industry believe that all others want is sex and that at least those within the industry can control what is happening to them by being involved. However, in order for them to adapt is to self-medicate because of the degrading behavior and the lack of others having any concern for them.

That is why drug and alcohol use is so high with those in this industry. It takes away the pain of degrading behavior and many times these people think they deserve this. We must better equip ourselves with the knowledge to support those who are hurting and help them recognize that there are people around them that will listen, support, and help them in their lives. No one is exempt from problems, but that also means that we have the ability to solve any problem we are faced with.

The industry looks at people, especially women, as a means to an end. As a society we must find a solution to this problem by seeing this problem through the eyes of those affected and finding solutions that will help them in making better choices and recognizing their individual worth as a human being.

There is no way that we could ever slow down or rid our society of the insatiable drive of the sex industry. The only way we can ultimately affect this problem is not to be afraid to confront the problem and bring it to the attention of others.

Several years ago, living in Harpers Ferry, West Virginia, I had the opportunity to help our community and county to restructure the ordinances centered on adult businesses.

The problem that we were facing involved a business owner that wanted to put an adult entertainment establishment in the front of our subdivision of our home. This was a very bad idea for many reasons, but two of the most prominent reasons involved the degrading and ill effects that would cause many different types of problems, including but not limited to, sexual addictions, abuse, and drug and alcohol problems, as well as the de-valuing of our property by putting a strip club in our subdivision.

There are so many examples of the impact of the sex industry in our society, which represents that exposure to sexualized media and the effect on society. This was the reason that I was so concerned about what was happening in our community in West Virginia.

I put together an action plan and presented it to the County Commissioners. They were receptive because I shared with them statistics and personal experiences in my professional life that help them see the magnitude of the problem and the need to establish a place for them, but not where it would affect the communities. Though there were many that thought it was ridiculous for me to make an issue of this problem, we were successful in changing the ordinances to keep it out of the subdivision that included a church and an elementary school. They had no ordinances protecting small communities and had we not pursued these changes, then they would have put one of those adult dance clubs right in our backyard.

I wanted to note that at the initial meeting my oldest son Mitchell, who at the time was a senior in high school shared with the county commissioners that there was a girl in his high school that was looking forward to graduating and going to work as a "stripper." She indicated that she could make more money stripping than working at a fast food restaurant. I was proud of Mitchell for being willing as a teenager to share his thoughts on this topic. Carol and I were so impressed that he felt so strongly about the sanctity of womanhood.

We as a society must realize that though there may be a place for those types of establishments due to the first amendment rights, I have seen the ill effect on society when we introduce these vices into our community that only bring an element that we do not want.

We cannot stop this industry continuing to grow, but we can influence those around us, most importantly our children. Though there are some things we cannot predict, there is one thing for sure, we have a rare opportunity for a few years to raise our children to be good people, who love and respect others, and put the needs of others before themselves.

I have been blessed to have a wife and children who understand that we do all that we do for each other. As we work together and help our children feel accepted and wanted, they will trust us and we will trust them. We can help each other as we face these problems knowing that we have the power together to overcome anything that we are faced with in our society, and more importantly in our families.

3

Ending Sexual Abuse—Protecting Innocence

The problem in our society of sexual abuse is a difficult topic to discuss and to even think about. However, it is time to address this problem head on, not be afraid to discuss, help those who have been affected by this crime find their new normal, and hopefully find avenues through our discussion on how to reduce the problem of sexual abuse. We have made so many positive strides addressing this problem of sexual abuse and we need to continue this movement to protect individuals and families from the trauma associated with sexual abuse.

We can all agree that there are still many issues to resolve and one issue that I have found absolutely critical through my consulting work is allowing victims to ask questions and hold the wrongdoer to a higher level of accountability than ever before. Men and women who commit these crimes need to answer the difficult questions and learn how their behavior has impacted their victims. The offender must understand and learn what it means to be truly accountable through learning for themselves what lead to their abusing their victims.

The Need for Offender Accountability

When we talk about sexual offenders they are basically categorized into two groups, intra-familial and extra-familial abusers. Abuse by a family member (biological and non-biological, stepparent, or relative) that generally occurs in the home. These offenders are considered Intra-Familial sexual offenders. Abuse by an offender outside the family including a friend, teacher, or a stranger is considered an Extra-Familial sexual offender. https://www.omicsonline.org/open-access/differences-in-risk-scores-among-intrafa-milial-and-extrafamilial-sexual-offenders-1522-4821-1000326.php?aid=76577

Portions of this chapter are written with contributions by Riley (name changed to protect privacy). Portions of this chapter are written with contributions by Andrea (name changed to protect privacy). Portions of this chapter are written with permission of Carol McBride. Portions of this chapter are written with contributions by Theo (name changed to protect privacy).

I want to talk about intra-familial abusers first. The real problem with abuse, which I have learned from countless hours with offenders, reading reports and talking to victims, family members of victims, and offenders, is that regardless of how much the offender may love or care for their victims in intra-familial abuse their desire for sexual satisfaction and meeting their own needs takes precedence in their lives. Much of the same problem affects the extra-familial offender. Many as we talked about, justify their actions and minimize the impact of their victims. I have had offenders say to me that "if they had not worn just a t-shirt and panties it would not have caused me to abuse them." That is an excuse that Mr. Joe Sullivan, M.A., described in defining "Spiral Theory." He pointed out the stages of the spiral theory. He said that, "It moves from the initial motivation, through the internal struggle, to the decision to offend and follows the steps taken to facilitate the abuse and dealing with the aftermath."

It has been my experience that generally, most offenders use excuses to deal with the aftermath of their actions. This makes it very difficult for victim survivors to comprehend why when someone commits a crime how can they make excuses and not accept accountability?

The extra-familial abuser sees opportunities within society to find their victims. This could be a student, someone that they meet on the Internet, an acquaintance, or children. It does not matter; they will find a source other than their own family to target.

In one case I had there was an offender who lived in a small community and was known as the neighborhood babysitter. He would often watch neighbor's children so they could go out on dates, to parties, etc. He had built a rapport with these parents, had gained their trust, and took advantage of the opportunity to abuse children. When we finished with that case there were many, many victims. This was one of the most difficult sexual abuse cases I worked on because of the extent of this man's pain he inflicted on hundreds of people.

The only way we as a society can fully grasp the impact is by listening and learning from those that have endured this pain, but also what we can do as a society to recognize what we can and must do to better address this issue of sexual abuse.

If we are going to adequately address this problem, we have to look at the offenders of sexual abuse. Oftentimes we hear from the media that the offenders must pay for what they have done and punish them to the full extent of the law. Though I do not disagree with the fact that we must hold these individuals accountable and responsible for their behavior, we must recognize that, "At least 95% of all state prisoners will be released from prison at some point; nearly 80% will be released to parole supervision." bjs.ojp.usdoj.gov/content/pub/pdf/reentry.pdf.

Since 95% of the prison population will be released, we must find a way to ensure that those who are released have the proper transitional plan to improve the chance of them not re-offending to protect society. We must have a vigilant society that is not afraid to report, and to follow their instinctual emotions that something does not feel right. There are so many ways we can protect each other, just by listening, observing, and reporting.

As we discussed in chapter two, Sexuality is a human instinct, which unfortunately is being used as a commodity by sexual offenders. We must as a society learn innovative ways in addressing this problem from a preventative standpoint, but also helping those that unfortunately have already been infected with this pandemic plague in our society, and also help others navigate the difficult road they have been forced to endure.

In addition, with the advancements of social media, we must address how this problem has been complicated by providing to the perpetrators new methods in exploring sexuality and has increased the ways and ideas of perpetuating their illness. We live in a time when it is absolutely necessary to become completely transparent with this problem in our homes, schools, communities, and globally.

I have found through my work in criminal justice that the only way for an offender to be truly accountable is to accept full responsibility for their actions, make no excuses, and must incorporate boundaries on him/herself for the rest of their lives. There is no compromise on this, in order for them to improve their chances of not re-offending; they must have boundaries for themselves.

A Sex Offender's Story

I had a sex offender and his wife come to my class and share their story with students at Penn State Beaver and New Kensington. I had the opportunity to work with their family and extended family in this very difficult case as part of my consulting work. I really enjoy when I have offenders come in and share their stories. It not only helps the students understand and appreciate the perspective of these offenders, but also holds the offender to a higher level of accountability. This offender does this by not only telling his story, but how he plans to control his behavior, so he does not harm another child. In addition, the students ask them questions that allow them to review what went wrong in their lives and provide the offender a glimpse as to how their behavior not only impacts their victims, but society as well.

Again, my consulting work helps bring relief to victims by providing them access and answers to those difficult questions as to why this happened and provides them answers to those very difficult questions that plague the mind of victims for years. That is one of the main reasons I do this work is to provide relief to victims. I have now worked with hundreds of victims, survivors, and family members, and I can tell you that there is no greater work in this field than helping others recognize and find relief from their pain and suffering and help them on their road to healing. No one can heal a victim but themselves, but we have the distinct privilege of guiding them and providing the tools for their individual experience of healing.

I made it clear to the offender's family that when he is released from jail, he must have boundaries the remainder of his life and fully accept and appreciate the harm that he has specifically caused to his victims. Those factors were a must for him to learn how to control his behavior.

Years ago, the offender and his wife were tasked with babysitting her younger cousins. Her aunt and uncle had to go overseas for an extended period of time. So the offender and his wife moved into her aunt and uncles home. They had one girl that was in her teens.

In the offender's own confession, he admitted that when the teenage cousin would ask him to scratch her back that he was beginning to enjoy this and it was not too long before he was seeking out opportunities to rub her back, which eventually led to opportunities to go further and further. He eventually fondled her extensively. He made it clear that he never had intercourse with her. The young girl corroborated his story, however that is relative to the fact that regardless of the actual behavior, he still had violated that relationship and her innocence by sexually abusing her.

The young girl finally revealed to her parents that her cousin's husband had touched her inappropriately. Because this was a close knit family, they were not sure how to handle it, but they decided to go to their minster. The minister said that he needs to repent of his wrongdoings and nothing else was done at that point. The family of course was very mixed on their feelings about him not going through the justice process. This happened at a time in our society where there were not the reporting laws that we have today. This surely would have been handled differently in 2019.

However, after many years, the offender was eventually held accountable through the criminal justice process for his actions years earlier. Due to the new law within the state where he offended the young girl, the statute of limitation was lifted and they could now prosecute him for behavior that occurred years earlier. He plead guilty for the abuse of his wife's cousin. He went to prison for 5 years, completed sex offender treatment, and was released from prison to serve several years on parole, and he had to register with the sex offender registration.

Obviously, what he did was wrong, and he needed to be held accountable for what he did. He admits that he is solely responsible for what he did and that the only way for him to show he is sorry is by the way he lives the rest of his life and to be fully accountable for his actions.

Though it has caused discontent in the family, he understands and recognizes the need for full disclosure and accountability for his behavior. He also realizes that his extended family and his wife's cousin may never forgive him for what he has done, nor want to be around him. He recognizes that it is understandable, and he accepts that fate knowing he was the cause of this horrible tragedy in the family.

This offender's wife has stayed by his side the entire time. Though some may not agree with her, she has chosen to stay with him because she has had several children with him, they have lived together for almost 30 years, and she recognizes the goodness that he has, aside from what he did. For a long period of time after the offense she had to move away from him and work through her own anger and frustration. With time, she realized that she still loved him and that as long as he kept making progress and communicating, that she would try to preserve their relationship. Many have chastised her for staying with him even within her own family, but she remains resolved to make it work.

I have heard her tell her husband many times of his obligation for complete fidelity in their marriage, honesty, and adhering to the boundaries that they have established in their marriage.

Though there are many that think she should have left him, he has maintained his commitment since the event to her and their family. He has been clean for over 20 years and continues to keep those boundaries in place to protect others and himself from re-offending.

He had an opportunity to hear from his cousin and what their questions were to answer why he did what he did. Though there will probably never be a relationship with them, he was able to provide them answers to their questions. Though this does not of course bring 100% relief, it definitely helps victims to know that the offender is willing to answer difficult questions and accept accountability for his actions.

He recognizes that he took complete advantage of this young innocent girl for his own satisfaction and justified his behavior by saying to himself, "It's not that bad," and "she wanted me to rub her back?" The offender told me that when you are fully engaged in the abuse, you justify and minimize in order to continue this behavior that had taken over his life.

He still has a long road ahead of him, and he must be open in his relationship with his wife, and family, and absolutely must respect and honor the boundaries that the rest of the family has placed on him. This offender's wife is a "rock." I have to say I am not sure if I could do what she has done, but it shows him and others her level of commitment. If the offender was to jeopardize the faith, she has put in him, it would devastate so many. The challenge will be for this family to support the victim survivor and not assume they know what she needs, but truly listen and honor her requests.

Healing and forgiving for victims does not mean that they have to enter back into a toxic relationship with their abuser. Forcing a relationship can often lead to triggers such as unwanted emotions or flashbacks from the victims. This grossly impacts proper opportunities for healing. Victim survivors must be in complete control of their journey and no one can walk that road for them or tell them where to go. This work is about listening and helping them with what they, as the victim survivor, feel they need.

Many sex offenders have described it to me that they would get tunnel vision to the behavior and that they did not have the ability to resist, or at least they thought they did not have the ability.

This story is not unique, I can tell you many other stories with almost the same circumstances that have taken many roads. If an offender does not take responsibility and is not accountable, they are a danger to society and to themselves. We as a society must be vigilant because of the offender who takes no accountability for their actions. It is not prudent to be naïve in today's world. Even with those we know, we must be vigilant and teach our children so that they will be vigilant in their own lives and not be afraid to share with us, in the unfortunate event that they become a victim of this horrific and debilitating crime in our society.

Why Do Men and Women Sexually Abuse?

Clearly, we learn that those who take advantage of these sweet children are obviously apathetic of how their self-interested behavior has impacted others. They are only thinking of their own pleasure and meeting their own needs and have little or no concern for their victims.

That is not to say that they do not have feelings, it just means that they have completely repressed those feelings in order to justify or live with their poor decision making that has caused their behavior. We know from research that no two offenders are the same. There are so many factors that go into why a person offends.

Sexual offenders will do all they can to go undetected and sexual grooming clearly develops a pathway for offenders to abuse their victims. There have been many examples in my career of offenders using tactics to entice their victims and to also develop a rapport with their parents in order to get access to the children. In fact, some sex offenders have told me that their first target is actually the parent; to develop a rapport with them so they can gain the access they need to get to the children. Coaches, relatives, teachers, and many others have become successful at their tactics of preying on the victim's families as well as the victim of the abuse.

Recently, I spent several hours speaking with Georgia Winters and Elizabeth Jeglic about the stages of sexual grooming. They are leading experts in this area, and it has been very informative and helpful to speak with them on many occasions. I have always been impressed with their knowledge about the importance of prevention of sexual abuse. They discussed six stages of grooming that I would briefly like to discuss.

In their article they discussed six stages of grooming that seem to be common with respect to the behavior of predators. As I have worked with sex offenders through the years, I can tell you that they have developed these patterns of behavior to choose their victims and to prey upon their innocence. In the article they discussed the six stages of grooming.

Stage one involves the offender selecting their victim. There are many ways they select their victims whether it involves their looks or the fact that they are appealing to the perpetrator. Stage two, according to the authors, involves the offender gaining more access to the victim and finding opportunities to isolate the victim. Stage three involves what the authors call "emotional recruiting." This is where the perpetrator gains trust and creates normalcy in their relationship. Stage four involves the perpetrator experimenting with "sexual conversations and increasing sexual touching." According to the authors, if the victim responds then they can easily go to stage five which increase the physical sexual contact with the victim to further desensitize them to the behavior. Stage six is basically maintaining the control on the victim. This time can vary. For many victims it can go on for years without any relief to the victim. Georgia M. Winters & Elizabeth L. Jeglic (2017) Stages of Sexual Grooming: Recognizing Potentially Predatory Behaviors of Child Molesters, Deviant Behavior, 38:6, 724-733, DOI: 10.1080/01639625.2016.1197656

The authors to this article point out that there is a great deal of research showing that educating the public brings awareness and helps to identify patterns of behavior before the event occurs. However, the authors, provide a glimpse of understanding that there are huge hurdles to overcome to provide the proper information to the public to increase awareness without compromising an individual's innocent behavior that does not involve the perpetration of children.

A few years ago, I met a family here in the United States. As part of this discussion on the spiral model, or grooming, I wanted to share their story as illustration to the complexity of this problem and how the selfish actions of others can have a lasting impact.

Riley's Story of Adversity and Finding Strength

I want to share the story of Riley. Riley was 13 years old when her junior high school substitute teacher sexually assaulted her.

Before I share her story, I want the readers to know that I have interviewed hundreds of victims of various crimes, including many, many of sexual abuse. There are many victims who waited years to come forward and share what happened to them. That is typical in many abuse cases. Of course there are many that do report as well, but it is always amazing to me when a young girl of 13 recognizes that what was happening to her was not normal and made her feel uncomfortable and understood that she needed to tell someone what was happening to her and her friends.

I wanted to pay my deepest appreciation for Riley. I watched in awe as she has shared her story in front of the court of law, and in front of college classes at Penn State University. It literally brings tears to my eyes when I had the privilege to sit with Riley and her family in court when she had to face her offender. I think about that moment in the courtroom, when Riley gave one of the most beautiful victim impact statements I have ever heard. Riley, I honor you through sharing your story.

When I first met Riley's mother Andrea, it was actually over the phone. I met Andrea through her cousin and they were wondering if I could give some advice to them on how to handle some difficulties that they are having holding her accuser responsible in this situation where their daughter Riley who was sexually abused by a junior high school teacher. Andrea was very distraught on our phone call. She shared with me that the district attorney's office had their case and that they had not made a decision on the case and it had been over a year. They were really feeling frustrated and confused.

Many victims I have worked with have shared how cold and calculated the system has been. Many times victim survivors feel little or no support for what they are going through from the system. As professionals, we have to recognize that for many, this is the first time they have encountered our criminal justice system. No one really knows how difficult that is until you have to go through it yourself. I can't even try to put myself in Riley, Andrea, or Riley's dad Ken's shoes on how they must have felt during this entire process.

I told them that of course I cannot give them legal advice, but I shared with them that the "squeaky wheel gets the grease." I told them to keep on the DA and go in and see them and make sure they do not forget your faces. They reported the case in March of 2016 and they did not receive relief on this case until July 2017. The original offense took place in early 2016.

Fortunately within a short period of time the case was moved to a resolution. The original offense was a felony sexual battery charge, but through negotiation, he plead guilty to two counts of misdemeanor battery toward a minor. This will stay on his record and the next time he commits this offense it will be evidence of his behavior and the sickness that he has.

Riley's Grooming and Abuse

The following details have been altered slightly to protect the victim and her family. Riley reported with three other girls to the principal at their junior high that a substitute teacher in their English class had touched them in their genitalia and their breasts in the classroom. These girls were all around 13 years of age.

Riley shared with me that the very first day he was there that he started paying attention to her that made her uncomfortable. She went to the front of the class to ask him a question and he answered her question, but called her "babe," and "lover." He also in a joking and flirtatious way grabbed the back of her bra strap and flipped it slightly and laughed when he did, as though it was no big deal.

Riley remembers going back to her seat saying to herself, "did that just happen?" did he call me those names and really flip my bra strap? It bothered her, but she did not seem to think at that point that it was worth repeating to anyone. She thought, well, maybe he is just playing.

At first he was just being nice and calling her those names, and then after three days of similar behavior, she went to the front of the class again to ask him a question about her assignment.

This time was different. With her standing close to the desk facing the chalkboard, without the class being able to see, he took his hand and rubbed over her clothing down across her breasts and down her stomach and ended with his hand between her legs. She was shocked, confused, and quickly walked back to her seat. He did not say anything to her, but gave her a smile that compounded her emotion and she described his smile as very strange and made her feel very uncomfortable.

As class ended, he walked up to several students, gave them some candy, and when he came to her, he patted her directly onto her buttocks. He then smiled at her at said, "Have a good day." She left the room confused, scared, and not really sure what to do.

Riley's Strength to Report

She soon heard from other students in the hallway, that there were other girls that experienced the same thing. These girls got together, and Riley said, "We need to go to the principal's office and tell them what the substitute teacher did."

When they got there, they told the principal what had happened, he set them in a room, and got one of the teachers who has a good rapport with the girls and asked her to come in and ask them questions. They shared with their female teacher what the substitute teacher had done and the principal called all the parents. The girls were asked to make statements and were released to the custody of their parents.

The substitute teacher was suspended immediately. However, it was discovered that about a year before the incident he had another complaint against him for an inappropriate text that he sent a student at the same school. On that incident he was fired.

Less than a year later he was rehired by the superintendent as a substitute teacher. This did not sit well with the families once they found out that he had been let go previously for similar behavior. They also found out that he was involved in another incident with a minor female several years before that, which never resulted in prosecution. He had built a reputation in the area as someone who liked young teenage girls. It is amazing that the school district would hire this man back after the first incident at the school with the knowledge of a previous relationship, which resulted in him being fired the first time.

That day when Riley and the other girls reported it to the principal, Andrea received a phone call from the school. She was living in another state. When they told her over the phone, she described it as one of those moments when time stands still and you feel like you are not even there. She quickly got a hold of Riley and both Riley and her mother were crying and very upset. Andrea quickly got an airline ticket and headed to the small town to be with her daughter.

The girls were taken to a children justice center in a larger city in the county and a forensic interview was conducted as well as physical exams. It was a difficult time for their entire family. As a mother and father, you cannot fathom the pain when one of your children is hurting. Ken and Andrea were at a loss as to how to help their daughter through this tragic event in her life.

Overcoming the Difficulty of Court – The Strength of Riley to Share Her Story

Her parents made sure that Riley had the support she needed soon after the incident. The two other girls were not allowed to be part of the case for very odd reasons. One of the girls was told by law enforcement that because the defendant's actions were a misdemeanor and not a felony, she would not be part of the case. This was very confusing to them. The other girl, her parents refused to have her testify and were not part of the case.

The case sat for several months, in fact they had to put pressure on the DA to expedite the case. Andrea, Ken, and Riley went several months with no communication or resolution in their daughter's case. This happened in small town America, which sadly may result in delayed prosecution or provide misguided information to the victim and their family. As I shared earlier, after they contacted the DA, the case started to pick up momentum and in July of 2017 the case was finally adjudicated.

Because the other girls would not testify in the case, the entire validity of the case fell on the shoulders of Riley, having to be the only witness in her case. Though this put so much pressure on her, Riley knew she had to do it. Riley was so nervous going through this process and having to sit in the same room with him on two different occasions for several hours.

As I shared earlier, he was charged with two felonies, sexual battery, and ended pleading to two misdemeanors charges of battery of a minor. Andrea, Ken, and Riley invited me to come to the hearing, which was such a privilege to be with them.

So in late July 2017, I attended the hearing with this family. This town is so small that it made Riley nervous because several times in the court process they ran into the defendant in a restaurant or a store. Also everyone knows everybody, so it takes away the anonymity of a court process. For example, one time after she had testified against him in an earlier proceeding, soon after that hearing, he was walking into the same restaurant and gave her that same smile he had given when he molested her. This was a difficult time for her since she was in such close proximity to the offender almost everywhere they went in that small town.

A few weeks previous to this hearing, they both prepared their statements for court. They had learned a lot about grooming, his behavior, and Riley clearly recognized that it was not her fault. I had the privilege of helping them write their victim impact statement. My intentions of course were not to change their meaning, but maybe help them with wording.

The day arrived for the sentencing hearing. We met prior to court, Riley, Ken, Andrea, grandparents, cousins, and several others. The mood was quiet and full of nervousness and uncertain anticipation. You could tell that this sweet young lady was picturing having to share her statement in front of family, friends, and the defendant. It was important to Riley and her parents to have that much support. Both were scheduled to testify in the defendants sentencing hearing.

As both Andrea and Riley read their statements you could feel their sincerity, their need for resolution, and holding the offender accountable for his actions. Here are both of their statements in court at the sentencing hearing that they both read to the man who molested Riley.

Andrea's Statement (Victim's Mother)

Thank you, your honor, and all those here today for your support, and for allowing me to make my personal address on this distressing case. Before I speak about our daughter, I would like you to put yourself in her shoes, those of a 13-year-old girl, who has been sexually violated by a person she was supposed to trust, her teacher.

The principal of our daughter's school called to inform me that our daughter had been sexually abused by her teacher. A heavy sadness filled my heart, and I began to cry, thinking this is every parent's worst nightmare. Then I called our daughter, and all that she could do was cry, and I wished that it could have been me, instead of her. Our daughter is a very happy and well-balanced girl. She gets good grades, and excels at everything she does. We taught her to be confident, and to standup against things that are not right; she demonstrated her courage to come forward, and have her voice be heard, and we are so proud of her for making that decision. Sexual abuse is one thing that every parent prays, that their child will never have to endure, and one of the most difficult things, is to try and put my feelings into words, all the anger, hurt, and humiliation that this man has put our child through.

As a parent, you tell your child that they will be safe at school, and because of you and your unethical and unprofessional misconduct, she will always question the trust and safety of her schools. Defendant, I am going to define and provide step by step how you groomed our daughter for sexual abuse. Grooming is an insidious predatory set of behaviors to manipulate a child into a position that makes them more isolated, dependent, likely to trust, and more vulnerable to abusive behavior.

Step One: Groom the environment and identify the victim. You abused your role as a teacher to gain false trust and connect with the students and the victim at their level by being, the "hip & cool", "high energy" teacher, who tells jokes.

Step two: Target and lure the victim. You would handout candy to the classroom for doing a "good job" but you would target our daughter with calibrated and special attention by giving her two pieces of candy and giving her the answers to math problems. You attempted to lure our daughter, by using verbal seductive and special name calling such as "lover."

Step three: Test the boundaries: First, you started small by putting your hand on our daughter's shoulder and flicking her bra strap as you walked through the classroom, or if she raised her hand for a question. Then you moved to the next level, by slapping her bottom as she left the classroom.

And finally, you touch her private parts to see how she reacts. Defendant, what gives you the right to steal the innocence of a child? You turned what should be a nurturing role, into an opportunity for abuse and psychological harm to our daughter. Again, there is no doubt that an intent to gratify yourself, is the one and only reason that you, Defendant, would touched our child, in the sexual manner that you did.

She paid a tremendous price for your actions, emotionally, psychologically, and spiritually. She has flashbacks and paranoia, regardless of where she may be; she is nervous to go to school, because she sits in that same classroom, and she relives what you did to her. She fears seeing you at the grocery store, or at the local pizza restaurant. She walks downtown with her friends, and she feels like you are leering at her, and she hopes that she does not see you in the cars that pass by. She waits at the bus stop, and feels like you are watching her. She can't even go hangout at the mall, because she sees men that resemble you.

Defendant, you left an indelible scar in her soul that created a sacred wound, an intrusion into her deepest, and most delicate parts as a human being. We have no doubt in our mind, that your action is a felony, and that you should be required to register as a sex offender, because that "is" who you "are", regardless of whether you acknowledge it or not. We did everything that we could to prove our side, but we are not the law, therefore you should consider yourself a very lucky man. You take that luck, and you pay it forward, in a positive way, and become a better man, because if you don't, next time luck will not be on your side.

The focus of this case, was based on the "intent" of Defendant, the perpetrator, and you "minimize" the impact that is immoral, crafty, sexual behavior has had on our daughter and others. Victimization has a ripple effect, spreading the damage in waves to family, friends and the community. Trying to heal the wounds, and talking about the abuse, will never be enough, for the ripple effects are endless.

I want to remind you, Defendant, that the internet never forgets; all the parents, and everyone who reads the newspaper, and subscribes to social media, know what you are, and what you did to our innocent children, and you will never step foot in a school as a teacher again. Although my daughter will never forget what you have stolen from her, I will always pray, that she will not carry the shame and disgust that truly belongs to "you." My heart goes out to your children, for them having to know, the deepest harm that you have created.

Defendant needs to be penalized for his inappropriate behavior, and damaging actions, at a minimum thru community service, and proper counseling for rehabilitation, in order not to be a threat to other innocent children; in addition, a mandatory monetary contribution should be donated, to an organization devoted to helping abused children. Defendant should complete a full psycho sexual evaluation, and participate in a treatment program deemed necessary for his sickness. Furthermore, there must be follow-up, to ensure completion of the treatment. Otherwise, how do we know that he is getting the help that he desperately needs, to never gain abuse children in the future, and learn to control his illness. Without proper evaluation, abusers that get caught, learn from their mistakes, and refine their techniques to abuse again.

(SPEAKING TO THE JUDGE) Your Honor: In our last meeting on March 20, 2017, you made a statement that disturbed me, and I would like to address it and why I feel it is important. You stated that as a father yourself, you find that any sexual touching would be very difficult for you to stomach or accept, but as you step back and put on your robe, you must adhere to the rules of the state. I understand your position as a figure of authority, but the laws dealing with children, should be subject to a different standard, because children are defenseless. The way I understood your statement, was that your children have a minimal impact on your decision, and that one side is black, and one side is white, but my question is, "shouldn't your reasoning be gray"? I ask that you take into consideration, how proliferative sexual abuse, is ruining the lives of the present and future generations of our children. Also, consider very carefully your own children, as well as the innocent children of the community, when determining the proper sentencing for Defendant. In conclusion your honor, I would again respectfully recommend, that you order him, to complete a Psycho Sexual Evaluation. Thank you, your honor, for allowing me to speak. (Statement from Mother Andrea)

Copyright © Andrea (name changed to protect privacy). Reprinted by permission.

During Andrea's statement you could tell that it was from her heart. I can't imagine what it has been like for Andrea and Ken. Though they are not living together and are divorced, they both deeply care for Riley. Andrea and Ken have stayed by their daughter and supported her ever since.

Andrea said something that I thought was significant. She worried about her daughter not feeling believed and holding this in and not dealing with it properly. It was clear of the admiration she has towards Riley for coming forward, testifying in court, and sharing her statement, all in front of the person who caused this disruption in her life.

Ken and Andrea are amazing parents who raised a wonderful daughter. She is a rock and truly has parents that support her and all that she needs as she starts facing more and more difficult challenges in life. Riley has said that this has made her a stronger person, and I could not agree more.

After her mother had read her statement, Riley proceeded to share her victim impact. Below is Riley's Victim Impact Statement that she read in court to the defendant.

Riley's Victim Impact Statement

Thank you, your honor, for allowing me to voice my opinion before you sentence the Defendant, the man that hurt me.

No Kid, should ever have to go through what I have gone through and what I am going through right now. Because of you I have lived in fear for over a year now. You took something from me that you will never be able to give back. I still have flashbacks of what you did to me and what you did was wrong and disgusting. What you have put me through and what you have done to me I will never forget. I will never forget the way that you touched me, and the names that you called me.

I shouldn't have to be scared at my own house or when I am with my friends. Because of you, for the longest time I could not hangout with my friends outside of school because I was scared that you would hurt me, stalk me, and do what you did to me all over again. Because of you, I lost all trust in men outside my family. You have put me and my family through hell but today, all that hell and all my pain now belong to you.

You hurt four girls and although I am the only one here today, I feel like my words would also be theirs. I know that coming forward and having my voice be heard was the right thing to do because it only takes one voice to make a difference.

Although, my flashbacks remain, I want you to know that I am not scared of you and you do not intimidate me. You will never hurt me again and I will not let what you have done to me determine who I am and who I will become. I know that one day I will learn to trust again. My battle scars may not show on the outside, but on the inside they will always be with me.

Copyright © Riley (name changed to protect privacy). Reprinted by permission.

As I was listening to her share this in court, I sat there in awe, wishing the world could hear this statement, from a 14-year-old girl. Riley is stronger today, more determined to always be a fighter and not let anyone control her happiness. She is a beacon, a survivor, an example for all. Thank you Riley for sharing your story.

The Effect of Abuse on our Children

There is so much evidence that abuse not dealt with correctly results in a life of shame, confusion, and feeling alone in the world.

The key to helping survivors of sexual abuse understand that it is not their fault, comes with our ability as a society to help them feel safe and in helping them to identify what has happened. We need to allow them to share what has happened so that we can help them process and fulfill their needs of recognizing that they are not alone in their abuse.We have learned that listening and communicating with victims is one of the best resources for victims of sexual abuse.

However, from experience, this can only happen if we create trust with victims and help parents and children understand that it is safe for them to talk about their feelings, their past, and their abuse. Many in our society do not understand this problem. We often hear family and friends of victims ask, "Why didn't you say something earlier and not come forward with this earlier?" This can be debilitating to victims because it will increase their sensitivity to the shame, which says to them that they are to blame for their abuse.

In addition, eating disorders, and overall body image issues are often associated with this phenomenon that we do not necessarily always attribute to sexual abuse. However, we have learned from victims and experts that this not only is true, but sexual abuse can be a major contributor to body image issues as well.

Many who have been abused resort to behavior that is self-destructive because they already feel they are "used goods" and that the only way they can survive is to participate in very destructive or dangerous behavior. Many victims have shared with me that drugs, alcohol, careless avenues of dealing with body image, and sexual behavior (consensual and incautious) have become their means of self-medicating themselves to survive.

Unless you have been a victim of sexual abuse, you cannot fathom the emotions attributed to sexual abuse. Survivors of sexual abuse experience post-traumatic stress disorder (PTSD), similar to what those in time of war or victims of other tragic events experience.

Posttraumatic stress disorder is defined as, ". . . trauma and stress related disorder that may develop after exposure to an event or ordeal in which death, severe physical harm or violence occurred or was threatened. Traumatic events that may trigger PTSD include violent personal assaults, natural or unnatural disasters, accidents, or military combat." https://www.psychologytoday.com/us/conditions/post-traumatic-stress-disorder

They are triggered by events, emotions, sexual experiences, smells, tastes, etc. When they experience those symptoms it can exhibit in their behavior, through anger, self-harm, destructive, and criminal behavior. Oftentimes, victims are unsure of where this displaced anger is coming from not realizing the connection to their abuse. Through counseling and transparency, victims begin to realize what is causing the PTSD in their lives and can trace it back to their abuse when they were a child.

This is a debilitating force that survivors must confront and learn to live with. Survivors can learn to control their emotions, behavior, and needs, by not only sharing what they have been through, but also finding help and support from their families and those around them.

There is strong evidence that if a child who has been sexually abused never discloses their abuse and tries to address the issues themselves through different means of surviving that I have discussed, they are very likely to experience PTSD as an adult, many times without really understanding why they are acting out until they actually have a chance to deal with their abuse and come to terms with what happened.

I would like to share with you one victim's struggle with post-traumatic stress disorder and how he has dealt with this since his abuse when he was 16-years-old. Theo gives a detailed description of what he has been through since he was abused.

About Me

"My name is Theo, and I am a graduate student now. I graduated in five years with a Bachelor's degree each in Information Science and in Psychology from a top university, and a Master's Degree in Data Science now. I also published in an international journal and travelled across the country to present my work. I also served as the student body president while in college, and I was awarded the two top awards for my sustained leadership to the university.

In my personal life, I have attained my Eagle Scout badge in the Boy Scouts of America and still volunteer as an adult leader six years later. I also serve my nation in the USAF Auxiliary, Civil Air Patrol, and I have attained the grade of First

Lieutenant (O-2) there. If that isn't enough, I volunteer in the local prison helping coach inmates to reduce recidivism, and I've been a moderator on a car review website for nine years.

The Incident

As I write this, I am 23 years old, male, completely heterosexual. When I was 16, I was sexually assaulted while I was sleeping in a cabin while on a campout. I woke up in the middle of the attack. Two of my so-called friends were the perpetrators, and they thought it was hysterical, making jokes about it even years later until I eventually lost touch with both of them.

I was asleep in my sleeping bag, on my stomach, wearing sweat pants, a t-shirt, and a sweatshirt. When I woke up, my pants had been almost completely removed, and I heard uncontrollable laughter. There was a pressure on my back and penetration in my anus, which I had not initiated.

I remember seeing a citronella light on, over on the next building's rafter. It was dark outside; I estimate that I was sexually assaulted sometime between 11:00 p.m. Friday night and 2:00 a.m. Saturday morning. The perpetrators had been watching a video. I heard the theme music in the background, but I have no idea what movie was playing. The cabin had a fireplace, although I don't know if there was a fire or not. My head was toward the wall, my feet toward the aisle, and I remember feeling a draft from where the floor met the wall, and from a door that had been left ajar.

I remember reaching for a long broom handle to try to defend myself, but I ended up just being cornered, nervous, defenseless, weak, and afraid.

In all, there were approximately six people in the cabin at the time, all male, ranging in age from 16 (me) to 23. The other three (or so) had absolutely nothing to do with the attack, but I don't recall them trying to halt the affair.

I want to point out, also, that I was in a car accident when I was 21. I was rear-ended by a ladder truck and I lost some memory, but everything related to my sexual abuse I can recall as crisply today as I could six years ago.

Life after the Abuse

If there were one change to me after being sexually abused, I'd definitely say that it left me as being more afraid. Afraid of not being able to defend myself. Afraid of sex offenders. Afraid of walking alone. Afraid of going to sleep. Afraid of what people would think of me. Afraid to see who I would become. Afraid of everything.

Without even knowing it, I had begun by suffering from flashbacks and hyper-vigilance, both prevalent characteristics of PTSD. I would look at the Megan's Law website for my home, work, and school zip codes religiously, every day, because feeling aware of the sex offenders made me feel less afraid. Any time I would travel to a new zip code, I would need to query the Megan's Law database of the offenders in the given area for me to be physically comfortable with entering a new zip code.

I watched my PTSD turn into OCD. Being a "little hypervigilant" is probably okay, but what started as checking the site for a few minutes each day turned into straight compulsion. I needed to do it to put my mind at ease. The Megan's Law checking happened virtually every day for at least five years. I'd say that I had the names, heights, weights, addresses, car models and license plates, offense, and last check-in date of any offender in a ten-mile radius of my house, work, or school address memorized at one point. I could probably count on my two hands the number of days in the first five years after my trauma that I didn't open up the Megan's Law website.

I watched my OCD turn into paranoia. I was okay in the beginning with compulsively checking the Megan's Law website, but after a while, looking back on it now, it eventually began doing more harm than good. I became so engulfed in checking the site that it ate into family time and doing homework. I became so paranoid that one semester I ended up having a 1.2 GPA because I was spending hours up at night looking at the website, trying to protect myself from run-ins with sex offenders.

I didn't do a single homework assignment for my Chemistry class that semester, because I would come home from school tired, and I would still need to check out the Megan's Law website to see if any of the sex offenders near my house had gotten a new car or had become noncompliant with their registration requirements. Checking the website was more crucial to me than finishing my homework or studying for an exam.

I didn't have the sex offenders list affect my mind, but it also affected my schedule. If I knew that a sex offender lived on a certain street, I would have to re-route myself not to drive on that particular street. I wouldn't go anywhere near a sex offender's house if I knew they lived there.

I watched my paranoia turn into an eating disorder. As if being afraid of leaving my own house was not enough, eating became my crack. I would binge eat, constantly, on anything I could find. Oreos, the kind with a double dose of frosting, were my favorite indulgence and my go-to crutch. I would take gift cards that I found lying around the house and use them to buy Oreos, so my parents couldn't track where I was swiping my credit card at. I would rather they see that I withdrew $10 from an ATM than to see that I spent $3 at the grocery store. My father kept track of every transaction my credit card made, so I made concerted efforts to use cash and/or gift cards when possible.

I would eat a large package of Oreos every single day (the kind with three sleeves of Oreos), in addition to numerous meals and unnecessary snacks. I was constantly eating, and I couldn't go much more than 20 minutes without feeling compelled to eat. I'd sneak food into class all the time just to keep my mind at bay. Everyone noticed that I was gaining weight at an alarming rate, but I didn't want to admit that I had a problem. I would hide trays of cookies under the seats in my car, so no one would know they were there. To top that, I would purposely take the "long way" to get places. My college campus and my home are 13 miles apart, but I found a way to get to school that was 40 miles, just so I had time to eat more Oreos in solitude.

Flashbacks and Sleeping

I tell myself that the abuse isn't what tore me down and rebuilt me; it's all in how I dealt with the cards I had to play. I knew PTSD existed in military veterans, but I didn't realize I could be diagnosed with PTSD, but I was almost exactly three years after being sexually assaulted. I figured that my life was pretty good; I was studying at a top institution, I had a car, I still lived with my parents, and I was volunteering in my down time. I couldn't be diagnosed with PTSD because I was on top of the world.

Some people dream when they sleep, and some don't. In my slumber, I dream and I dream vividly. Very vividly. I used to wake up with flashbacks four or six times a night- not four to six per week, but four to six flashbacks every night. Every single night. I couldn't go much more than an hour of sleeping before I saw myself being raped in my dreams. I still get flashback memories, but with a far lower frequency. I'd say that I have one or two flashbacks weekly now; down from at least four nightly.

The scariest part of my PTSD, by far, is waking up with flashbacks of the trauma. Hands down, I fear the flashbacks the most. They're all so real, it's uncanny! I've learned to do some grounding exercises if I ever wake up with a flashback.

Another variation of flashback is that the same people who raped me will rape me in my sleep, but instead of a backcountry cabin, I'm being compromised in a grocery store, on a cruise ship, in a public bathroom, at a volunteer event, at college, on my ex-girlfriend's couch, in a dark alley, in class, or at my workplace. The extrapolation of the abuse at work was particularly scary; that office had very few private areas, and the vast majority of the private areas had at least one transparent glass pane in their construction.

For many months, years after I was raped, I was legitimately afraid to go to sleep at night. I didn't want to be raped in my dreams; I didn't want to wake up screaming from the sights, sounds, and feelings I had endured. Every time I woke up with a flashback, even to this day, all I ever wanted to do was hit something or bite myself. I didn't want to meet my perpetrators in my dreams, and I certainly didn't want to revisit the cabin where I experienced this trauma in while dreaming. I figured, the way I was the safest, was to get as little sleep as I possibly could in an effort to avoid the dreaming stage of sleep. If I sleep in any bed other than my own, I need to have a night light because I am afraid of the dark after what happened. I'm a 25-year old male, with a graduate degree, and I'm afraid of the dark.

My parents don't lock the house at night- or ever, really. We live in a suburb north of Pittsburgh, Pennsylvania. While it is a reasonably safe community, one can never be too careful. My father works the night shift and gets home at about 6:30 in the morning. Why my parents don't lock the doors, I don't know. Their answer is always along the lines of "well, we don't need to." I asked my father why he insists on locking the car in the driveway, but not the entryways to my house, and I was met with a stare and a reprimand.

PTSD: Labeling Myself

In the summer of 2013, I began to ask myself if I would have flashbacks multiple times per night, every night for the rest of my life. I went to see the career counselor on campus to explain to her what I had been through, and how I thought it was affecting my life negatively. She said that she "had a very strong suspicion that [I was] suffering from post-traumatic stress disorder." She had told me that I had buried my fears and emotions, and they were coming to the surface with every flashback.

I remember the day I was formally diagnosed with post-traumatic stress disorder (PTSD), and that day was Friday, September 20, 2013, in my junior year of college. I had an appointment on my college campus at noon, where I met with a social worker to undergo a complete psychiatric evaluation.

On that same day, I was going to meet with my Accounting study group at 6:00 p.m. in a computer lab on campus; around 4:00, I went to Wal-Mart to buy a pair of scissors. I just needed the one item, so I was planning for a quick trip in and out, followed by a quick stop at Subway across the street, so I could bring the sandwich back to the computer lab with me and do some preparation before the study group. Talk about feeling watched! I felt like everyone was staring at me as I hustled through Wal-Mart, like I weighed 3,000 pounds.

I moved very hurriedly through the store, not running but doing that speed walk thing, just doing my best not to look at anyone or draw attention to myself. I felt this great weight on my shoulders, like I had been crushed by tons of bricks. I didn't strike up a conversation with the cashier as I normally do, and I felt like a spotlight was following me around, like a lead singer in a Broadway musical. I felt so out of place; I thought the paparazzi was following me like the People magazine follows Jennifer Aniston. I didn't look through the Hot Wheels display like I usually do.

Guilt and Shame

*Even years later, I feel guilty for being sexually abused. I know that the affair wasn't my fault, and that I could have done nothing to prevent what I went through; excepting not going on that particular outing. Even then, the media taught me that you could still be raped at home. I know that seven years later, **I can't go back and rewind what happened, but the shame of being a victim has been imprinted on my mind.***

I would do things continuously to punish myself for being sexually abused. I never tried drugs; I've never even smoked a cigarette. But, the thought of using illicit drugs crossed my mind more times than I care to remember. I didn't drink alcohol, either. My parents drink liquor at the rate of a six-pack annually. Quite frankly, I'm also afraid of becoming an abuser of alcohol. I don't want to depend on alcohol to provide me happiness, so I just avoid it all together and hope for the best.

I turned to less visible punishment methods. I would bang my head against the wall (literally), and I'd try cutting myself with pens, safety scissors, and nail clippers. The pain felt good, and I could not get enough pain to punish myself for being sexually abused. I would wrap various electrical cords around my neck, making it difficult, but not impossible, to breathe. I had worried about leaving marks visibly exposed skin (for example, your hands show unless you wear gloves and your lower forearms show unless you have long sleeves on). Fortunately, no one had ever noticed any of these marks on my neck or on hands, or if they did, they were too nice to say anything.

I'd also hit myself with anything I could find. A hard-cover textbook worked great. I liked to use thick dowel rods because they were heavy. I loved to hear the bloodcurdling "smack" as my flesh met the wood. I also used a car detailing wire brush (I originally had it because it was my backscratcher), and the leather belt I found first on a given day. I'd swing at myself with a lamp. I haven't hit myself in a number of months, but my chest, buttocks, and thighs still have welts and bruises on them from when I'd whip myself fifty times a day, or more. I don't think they'll ever heal one hundred percent. They're my battle scars. I still get the urge to hit myself every so often, but I don't.

After all that, my diet also turned to complete shit. I would eat 6000+ calories a day, and I gained 40 pounds in my darkest two months. I'd also do things like build my blood sugar sky-high just to have the crash so I could "punish" myself not just for eating the wrong thing, but also for enduring the migraines I would suffer from the sugar crash. I wasn't watching which foods I was eating, the calories I was taking in, or how frequently I was eating, because eating was the only thing I could do to get my mind off of being sexually abused as a teen.

Telling Friends – Losing Friends

Telling people any of the details of how I've survived this trauma, or how I've lived since is no easy task. It seems to be getting more "normal" to me- it's like saying that I'm wearing a blue sweater and you're wearing a red dress blouse; it's just a simple fact. That's how I look at being a survivor: it doesn't define me as an individual, but it is a piece of the Theo assembly.

There was a girl at school I liked. I explained to her very tenderly about what I had been through. This was before I ever went to therapy, so I had a hunch that something was wrong in the fact that I had flashbacks multiple times a night and that I was spending multiple hours a day looking at the Megan's Law website. I had a work-study job in a computer lab, and Jane actually walked in one morning and saw me poking around the lists of sex offenders. She asked me not to talk to her again, and one of her friends messaged me on social media telling me that Jane didn't like me.

A few days later, I saw Jane in the cafeteria at school and I approached her. Without me saying a word, she said something to the effect of: "go away. You make me feel uncomfortable, and I don't like you. I don't want to see you. I don't want to talk to you. I don't want to think about you, and I certainly, certainly do not want you thinking about me. Don't ever talk to me again."

It's kind of strange to see how my "friends" all seem to leave once I tell them I've been raped.

Reporting the Crime

I ultimately didn't report the sexual abuse until I was months out of being abused. I had watched a lot of TV shows such as Cops and Law and Order and NCIS I knew that, being a minor, a report of child sexual abuse would open an investigation with the police, my parents, and my school, so I didn't go that route. I didn't want all the attention. I wasn't about to let child case workers into my home and interviewing both my friends who committed the offense and the ones who didn't prevent it.

Therapy

I've seen a few different therapists to combat my PTSD and other diagnoses. The first time I saw a therapist, I was extraordinarily nervous. The campus's faculty arranged the very first appointment (where I was diagnosed on campus) with Jack. After that, I was on my own to schedule my appointments and drive to the medical center (which was only a few miles from campus). I remember taking the call when I was in my Psychology class, so I stepped outside to take the call. I was pacing up and down the sidewalk, hoping that no one would recognize me or hear the conversation. On the other line, Jack's receptionist kept asking me for some very personal information, such as my social security number, credit card number, my health insurance, and the symptoms I was having. I really didn't want to give the receptionist any information because I was afraid of my father finding out where I was swiping my bank card at, and then asking me why I was spending so much money at the hospital near campus.

I went through three rounds of treatment before I found a therapist that was helpful for me. She has me write about my trauma, and then do talk therapy by reading the prose I wrote, which felt great. I was unloading, and it felt so good to release that internal struggle that I was dealing with. I continue to go to counseling to help me to continue to deal with my PTSD.

"Magic Power"

I thought that writing about my PTSD and battles associated with being sexually abused would be a royal bitch. I was afraid of what people would think as they read my words, and I still had my doubts about people believing what they were seeing; that PTSD could turn into an eating disorder, or that avoiding driving down given streets was raw truth.

In the fall of 2012, I would say I reached my ultimate low. I had stopped studying for class, and was only going to school for my job in the computer lab, and to sit in class but not absorb anything. My mind revolved around only on a few things, my courses, girlfriend, my job, my food addiction, how I would fall asleep, and excessive use of Meagan's Law.

It was a complete waste of energy and tuition for me to study Chemistry that term. In the Chemistry labs, I was utterly lost. I was also taking a Western Civilization course, but I wasn't retaining anything we learned. The professor's teaching method clashed with my learning method, and it just wasn't a pretty picture for me to begin with.

As my mind was racing about sex offenders and where they live, I can tell you exactly which parking space I had parked my Ford Focus was in; and I got in. I turned the key, and the stereo grabs me in with big arms and doesn't let me go. I look to the display, and I see that the performer was Triumph; the piece "Magic Power." I caught the song at the very beginning, and it wouldn't let me go. Even before Rik Emmett began singing the words, I had the stereo turned up, the windows down as far as they would, and the stereo just as loud as a Ford Focus would go.

Wow! This is a great song; it immediately became my favorite. By the second chorus, I felt like the song was an old friend of mine. "I'm young, I'm wild, and I'm free. Got the magic power of the music in me!" Rik Emmett tells the story (please note that this is my interpretation, and not Triumph's official word, or Rik Emmett's verification) of a woman who is in bed, listening to the stereo. As such, "music does the talkin'; says the things you want to hear" and this unidentified woman is in her own world where no one can judge what battles she is fighting when she turns on the music.

That's exactly what I needed to hear! Even through my exhausting lifestyle, including but not limited to my extensive use of the Megan's Law website, my paranoia, my daily diet, the fact I didn't have family support, my flashbacks multiple times each night, and my 1.2 semester grade point average, no one can judge me. I had to hit rock bottom and then have "Magic Power" be my rescue helicopter on the way up.

Something about that first note Triumph plays grabs me each and every time, and the song is as vibrant to me today as it was that first time I heard it. In my mind, "Magic Power" is a reminder that even if the world is judging you, really you are your own boss. You make your own choices; sometimes they're easy and sometimes they're hard. You ride the wave when the tide is high and you smack your face on the ground when you fall. In Triumph's "Magic Power," I think the music is a metaphor for the actions we take. "I've got the magic power of the MUSIC in me," what's MAGIC is when we SUCCEED. For me, success would be when I start passing Chemistry quizzes again; when I get my check from the car dealership.

As individuals, we use the tools we've been given to SUCCEED, but not everyone knows these tools are there. I didn't think about using Microsoft Excel to track my caloric intake (this was back when I still had a flip phone). I had thought about getting Calculus tutoring, but didn't move my pawn on the chessboard. "Magic Power" taught me that maybe we round corners at times, maybe we get lucky sometimes, maybe we're unprepared sometimes, and maybe all the planets line up. But, we're FREE to tap into that "MAGIC POWER" at any time.

My favorite couplet of "Magic Power" is "so turn me on, turn me up, it's your turn to dream. A little magic power makes it better than it seems." This couplet speaks to me because we all have dreams, and it's up to each of us to embrace that. It doesn't matter if your dream is to be a chef, an interpreter, a car dashboard designer, or a social worker; everyone has their dream and it's up to them to pursue it. I was letting my PTSD (undiagnosed at the time) eat me alive, and I was letting my diet consume my every fiber of motivation. I'll never forget the first time I heard that song, and it's been my favorite ever since.

How I Have Been Preserved

My sexual assault saga is coming shortly to a close. As I've written this narrative, I've done a lot of pausing and reflecting. I've listened to a lot of motivational songs (what I would consider motivational, anyway). I've done some soul searching. I've had conversations with God. While I still can't quite grip this bulky package, I've come to terms with what I've been through and where I've come from. I tell people that this journey is about 10% what I endured in the sexual assault that night. The other 90% is all in how I handled it after the fact.

All things considered, I don't think I would change any of the ways I handled my PTSD. I needed to be broken down and rebuilt, and I think that being a victim of sexual assault can tear anybody down. It's in the rebuild that you learn who you're supposed to be, and what makes you who you are. Sure, I didn't like gaining 40 pounds, but it showed me that when we aren't disciplined, we reap the consequence. "Magic Power" saved my bacon when I realized that I was falling victim to my guilt and shame, and Triumph really helped me to break out of that hard shell. I hated walking through Wal-Mart in a defensive, angry state. I don't like to admit that, even years after the fact, that I know certain license plates belong to a given sex offender (even if they've transferred the old tag to a new vehicle).

I've said some dumb things to people. I've scared others away. I'm pretty numb emotionally now, but that showed me to empathize with others.

Here's the revelation in my eyes: none of that matters. It doesn't matter that I did three internships, or that I was feature in a news article about landing an internship at a Fortune 500 firm. It doesn't matter to be that I had attained Honors in high school. It doesn't matter that my girlfriend didn't give me a chance.

Here's what matters: I know who I am and what I'm made of. I am a victim of statutory sexual assault. It's over. It happened. It helped mold me as a person. It's like saying that I like red velvet cake, and you like confetti cake. There's nothing wrong with that; it just demonstrates that we have undergone different experiences. I am a victim of statutory sexual assault; there's no going back, there's no changing that fact, and there's no way life will ever be the same.

I'm here. I'm alive. I have a fire burning inside of me. Instead of using that fire to memorize the offenders' residences where my grandmother lives (five states away), I can use that fire to improve me. I can use it to get fit. Some days, the fire needs more help than others to burn brightly. Some days, you need to put a log on the fire. Other days, you need to cut down a tree to keep the fire going. Even then, there are days that you chop down an entire forest to keep the flames burning. Other days, you can pull your pickup truck up backward to the fire, lay down in the bed, and roast marshmallows.

Don't fall victim to a label. You can get help, and you can live a regular life. If I wanted to relay one message in this, here it is: sometimes shitty things happen to good people. You can let it eat you alive like a bunch of mosquitos, or you can face your deepest fears and become a stronger individual for it. Find YOUR "Magic Power." Maybe it is the same "Magic Power" for you that it is for me, maybe not. That's okay. You're a better person for surviving a trauma.

Contributed by Theo (name changed to protect privacy). Copyright © Kendall Hunt Publishing Company.

I met Theo while teaching at Penn State University. Theo has spoken in my classes and has helped in a prison program where victims can tell their story and work with inmates for 14 weeks to help the inmates understand accountability and responsibility.

We learn a great deal from Theo's story. Theo has suffered a lot and continues to struggle even today, but one thing he is sure of is that he is stronger than he has ever been and has shown that he can survive. Being sexually assaulted as a male is difficult. It is definitely a bigger problem than we think.

I want to pay my deep respect to Theo. He has been through so much in his life and he does not give up. He still struggles with many of his phobias and dreams, but he is always positive when I talk to him and he has the will to survive. He is an amazing young man that I admire so much. He is one of my modern day heroes. Thank you Theo for sharing your story.

Recently I was reading on the website about an organization called "1in 6." This organization was established to support men who are sexually abused. On their website we read:

> Male victims of child sexual abuse often do not speak of their abuse or seek help. They are frequently alone with their experiences and feel deep shame. If you are a man, over the age of 18, who was the victim of child sexual abuse prior to age 13, you can help us help the many boys and men who sit alone with their victimization. https://1in6.org/get-information/1in6-trainings-and-presentations/research-on-male-survivors/

In the Preface of my book I talk about Matt Morgan and his abuse. He realized after going through treatment for his alcohol abuse that he was suffering from Dissociated or Psychogenic Amnesia, as a result of childhood sexual abuse he suffered from his uncle. A term that is not familiar with a lot of people, including victims of sexual abuse. Until these innocent children become adults, sometimes they do not fully understand and process what happened to them and come to the realization that it really did happen, it was not just a nightmare, that they are not crazy or making it up. In the article, "Betrayal Trauma: Traumatic Amnesia as an Adaptive Response to Childhood Abuse" it explains this effect very well. It states:

> Betrayal trauma theory suggests that psychogenic amnesia is an adaptive response to childhood abuse. When a parent or other powerful figure violates a fundamental ethic of human relationships, victims may need to remain unaware of the trauma not to reduce suffering but rather to promote survival. Amnesia enables the child to maintain an attachment with a figure vital to survival, development, and thriving. Analysis of evolutionary pressures, mental modules, social cognitions, and developmental needs suggests that the degree to which the most fundamental human ethics are violated can influence the nature, form, and processes of trauma and responses to trauma. ETHICS & BEHAVIOR, 4(4), 307-329; Copyright © 1994,

Lawrence Erlbaum Associates, Inc.; Betrayal Trauma: Traumatic Amnesia as an Adaptive Response to Childhood Abuse, Jennifer J. Freyd, University of Orego

Through research we recognize the realization that we are doing a lot of good in our communities. But we also recognize through our research and community interaction that we need to do better in helping our communities through interaction with each other and the sharing of resources. The research demonstrates the need to identify the paths in which we as a society must pursue.

> ....empirical research has clearly shown the negative impact of child sexual abuse on social, psychological, and sexual functioning later in life, it has also been reported that some individuals remain asymptomatic despite a history of experiencing child sexual abuse. This implies that negative outcomes later in life are not inevitable and illustrates the critical need to elucidate how resilience may moderate the negative impacts of child sexual abuse. In addition to emphasizing the role of resilience, this review also underscores the important role that cultural context plays in understanding child sexual abuse, as there are known risk factors and protective factors specific to different cultures. Similarly, one's culture may also influence whether abuse is reported and addressed, and the topic is given special attention in this paper because it is not widely discussed within the existing literature. The impact of child sexual abuse on mental health, sexual health, and social functioning is also discussed. A Review of Child Sexual Abuse: Impact, Risk, and Resilience in the Context of Culture, Journal of Child Sexual Abuse. Aug/Sep2018, Vol. 27 Issue 6, p622-641. 20p. http://web.b .ebscohost.com.ezaccess.libraries.psu.edu/ehost/detail/detail?vid=13&sid=723ef594-4505-42d0-b9e9-ec05484d6988%40pdc-v-sessmgr03&bdata=JnNpdGU9ZWhvc3QtbGl2ZSZzY29wZT1zaXRl#db=c-ja&AN=131371942

Carol's "My Buddy's" Story

As I conclude this chapter, I would like to share some additional insight from the preface of the book when I talked about Carol's experience. I would like to share a little of why I am passionate about finding solutions to combat this pandemic in our world.

My own family to this day struggles with the effects of the insensitive and selfish behavior that has forever forged divides and sadness that I hope will one day be realized. I can tell you that it has not only affected Carol, but also myself and our four boys and their families. Trying to explain to our children why they cannot go and stay overnight with their relatives or friends because of the lack of confidence that they will be safe, due to the actions of my wife's abusers that have forever changed the dynamics of our relationships with family and friends. It is hard to put restrictions on all family and friends with respect to the safety of our children, but if you look at the statistics, 80 % of victims of sexual abuse under the age of twelve knew their offender." https://www.sdcda.org/preventing/sex-offenders/facts-about-sex-offenders.pdf

The problem of sexual abuse has affected in one way or another most of our society. It has personally impacted my own family, which was one of my main motivations to get involved in this work. All I have wanted to do throughout my married life is protect my wife and children from becoming victims of this horrible crime.

My wife was a victim of sexual abuse during her informative years. She is not sure how old she was when it started, but the abuse was centered on meeting the sexual needs of those who offended her and disregarding the impact that it was having on my wife Carol.

I remember those weeks before our marriage Carol telling me of her abuse. I was uneducated and did not clearly understand the complexity of sexual abuse and the psychological and physiological effect of abuse on an innocent child.

We have now been married for 35 years, we have battled withdrawal from family members, emotional setbacks, illnesses, questions from family and friends, and just about every imaginable emotion and set back from sexual abuse. The one thing that has never happened is that it has never separated us, we have never allowed it to control us, and we have not been silent.

As I previously shared, I have watched my sweet wife stand in front of hundreds of inmates in prisons and tell her story. She has also shared her story with many other audiences. With courage and valor, she has stood before others and shared that this has not broken her spirit to keep going. Two of Carol's friends who died of suicide and drug overdose were sexually abused, and though there have been weak moments in her life she has endured, she has shown the courage beyond any courage I have ever been able to show in my own life, and the determination to be the best that she can be.

My beautiful wife and I have raised four sons that have in their own ways been successful and understand from an intimate point of view the effects of abuse. They have created a path for their families that will not let this illness continue in their own families. They have learned what healthy boundaries look like, they have seen their mother and father struggle, they know what it means to be vulnerable and not be afraid to be open and share their difficult times and find resolutions to their own struggles.

Many times, Carol has said, "What good have I done in my life?" Sexual abuse, and for that matter any type of abuse, destroys self-respect and self-esteem. As we have grown closer together each year of our marriage, those feelings are less of course, but when she does feel that way, I remind her of the valiant way in which she raised four boys during some of the most difficult times in her life. I remind her of the countless lives she has influenced with not being afraid to tell her story, to hold her abusers accountable for their actions. Though they never faced criminal prosecution for what they did to her, they have been reminded time and time again through boundaries and openness that it is not forgotten.

I remember on one occasion as Carol was in a very dark place emotionally, she looked at me and said, "Why did you marry me?" That statement took me by surprise, I could not understand why she would say that. I asked her why she asked me that question. She said that I would have probably been happier with someone else who was not a victim of abuse and who does not have all these problems. I thought for a moment how I could answer my wife, who lay in a hospital bed, in pain, and in absolute desperation for relief both physically and emotionally. I thought to myself, how can I answer her to help her truly know of her worth? I shared with her the story I often have told youth who are struggling with their identity and self-worth. I said to her that there is no one, no problem that can take away your self-worth to yourself, your children, and your God. I then reminded her of the metaphor of a 20-dollar bill. I can rub that bill in the dirt, spit on it, call it names, I can treat it disrespectful, but then I can take the abused bill to the store and still use it to purchase goods or services. Why? Because abusing a bill does not diminish its worth. Just like the $20 dollar bill, regardless of the way a person is treated, in the eyes of God and those that truly care about that individual they will never ever lose their worth.

Going back to Carol's analogy of a team that I talked about in the preface, a team supports each other, and a team overcomes together. Carol will be my team captain for eternity. I never leave my wing woman!!!!

I am so proud of my "Buddy!" Nothing I have ever done in my life is more important than being a husband and father. I hope that I will never let my Carol down, that I will always be there for her, and remind her the rest of our lives that she is my strength. I am nothing without her; I will never do anything more important in this life than to be her husband and a father to our four boys. God has granted me the privilege to be married to a survivor, and I will always thank God every day for "my Buddy!"

4

Acquaintance Rape—
Hearing, Respecting and Believing

What I have personally learned in my career from interviewing women of acquaintance rape is that many of the offenders get away with their behavior because of two underlying factors. First, women are shamed not only by the rape itself but the humiliation they feel when they report it. They believe through what they have seen and heard from women who have been raped is that others will be questioning their motives or participation, especially in the court system, and they just can't emotionally deal with being told they are partially responsible for their rape.

Secondly, it is my opinion that these male offenders believe that because sex is something we are all engaged in that they can manipulate not only the women that they offended but can create a ploy with society, and influence others into thinking that the woman was a willing participant. This in my opinion is all part of the sexualized society that I spoke about in chapter two. We have crossed so many lines that the line between respect for each other and proper use of sexuality has been manipulated and used for others own selfish desires and not for true intimacy.

I once read this statement about intimacy that truly shines light on the dark aspect of acquaintance rape. The author, Dr. Marie Hartwell-Walker, in her article, "The What and How of True Intimacy," she talks about what constitutes true intimacy. We often think that it is something that happens overnight or after sex. No, she gives a good explanation of what intimacy involves:

> It doesn't develop when one person nurtures a relationship more than the other. No. Intimacy, like fine wine takes time to deepen and mellow. It takes gentle handling and patience by all involved. It takes the willingness to make mistakes and to forgive them in the name of learning. https://psychcentral.com/lib/the-what-and-how-of-true-intimacy/

Portions of this chapter are written with permission of Savannah (name changed to protect identity). Portions of this chapter are written with permission of Liz (name changed to protect identity). Portions of this chapter are written with permission of Leslie (name changed to protect identity).

In this chapter I will share stories of courage that these women portray in their lives. I will also discuss how selfish attitudes and selfish acts of others has cheapened intimacy in these women's lives and in many situations evolve into women truly believing they could have done something to stop the assailant from raping them. Basically, they believe they are responsible for their own rape when it is someone they know.

The numbers of acquaintance rapes each year is staggering. A few of those statistics I believe are worth mentioning at the beginning of this chapter. These statistics were taken from the National Sexual Violence Resource Center (NSVRC) web page. Here are just a few of the statistics that I thought were noteworthy and help us see the big picture of this type of crime that is saturated throughout the world.

In their report they indicate that, "51.1% of female victims of rape reported being raped by an intimate partner and 40.8% by an acquaintance, over 92 percent of rapes occur by someone the victim knows." And that "Rape is the most under-reported crime; 63% of sexual assaults are not reported to police." https://www.nsvrc.org/statistics

We learn from the first statistic that the majority of rapes occur by individuals that the victim is acquainted with, whether it is a partner, boyfriend, or a new acquaintance. There are so many reports that go unreported and these statistics are just a glimpse at the impact of sexual assaults occurring within our society.

I am grateful for these women who are willing to share their stories. Working with victims, for me, has been one of the most rewarding activities that I have been involved with. I can't even imagine what these women have been through. All I know is they are incredibly brave for not only sharing their stories, but for their ability to find their path in their journey despite the adversity from such a horrific experience.

Many of these women describe their experience in our criminal justice system as more traumatic than the actual rape. This is not a new phenomenon that women experience, it has continually been an issue as to why we have had such a difficult time encouraging woman to report. According to the one study I noted above, 63% of sexual assaults do not get reported. I personally believe that there is evidence that the percentages of rapes not reported are much higher. https://www.nsvrc.org/statistics

Referring to the stories that I will share in this chapter, there are women who have not reported, and those that have reported. You will see that there are arguments from these women for both views, but the bottom line is that we must give women and men a voice to be heard, believed, feel safe, and support them with their own specific needs.

Reporting acquaintance rape does not necessarily always result in prosecution, but truly reporting the rape is an individual choice for each victim survivor to make and to find their own safe place and take back the control that was taken from them. From my experience, we can never tell a victim survivor what to do; we can only encourage them and assist them through active listening and respect.

Sadly, the first group of victims I would like to discuss are teenage and young adult victims of acquaintance sexual assault and rape. Many of these young women carry the burden of what happened to them because they are afraid or embarrassed about what happened to them. Whether they were drinking or being careless in their behavior, many of them have a difficult time living with the shame that they feel after they have been taken advantage of by an acquaintance. I have personally heard victims say, "If I had just not gone to that party!" or "I should have known better!" One that truly concerns me is when I hear them say this, "I probably deserved it, I was so careless."

We know that this is not true, but still it is an emotion that we must not ignore. Now this does not mean that we still do not do a proper and thorough investigation, it just means that we accept the fact that most women will not report if they have been sexually assaulted unless it has actually happened. False reporting is actually overstated and that there are less than 10% of cases that are actually false reports. This is a myth that has a tendency to keep victims in the woodwork and are not able to report or share their story. They basically adapt and learn to hide their shame and accept accountability for their own rape.

Interestingly, I found three sources of statistics that shows a consistent pattern that the majority of rape cases are not false reports. Most women would never report this crime, unless they knew that the offender would not get away with it. The statistics said:

A multi-site study of eight U.S. communities including 2,059 cases of sexual assault found a 7.1 percent rate of false reports (Lonsway, Archambault, & Lisak, 2009).

A study of 136 sexual assault cases in Boston from 1998-2007 found a 5.9 percent rate of false reports (Lisak et al., 2010).

Using qualitative and quantitative analysis, researchers studied 812 reports of sexual assault from 2000-2003 and found a 2.1 percent rate of false reports (Heenan & Murray 2006). https://www.nsvrc.org/sites/default/files/Publications_NSVRC_Overview_False-Reporting.pdf

Later in the book I will be outlining a program in the chapter on Restorative Justice. This program was started by a dear friend of mine, Dwayne Peace. The company that sponsors this program is his company, "Life Synergy for Youth."

Dwayne addresses the topic of sexual assault in his program for young adults in middle schools, high schools, and colleges. He speaks to youth and young adults about the truth regarding the difficulties of life, builds a rapport with them, and helps them to see the value within themselves. He also talks about parenting in these difficult times and the importance of believing our children and supporting them through difficult times.

Part of gaining their trust to speak freely, he builds a rapport with the students through holding small group discussions with youth and young adults. Dwayne talks about how many of the children in his programs talk to him about the very issues that he talks about in his book that we need to have with our children.

It is scary to think of the situations that our young people experience and the difficult scenarios when they are in school. The peer pressure, the pain, the embarrassment, all of these things cause great stress in our youth and young adult's lives.

We need to ask ourselves, "What are we doing to build our relationship with our young people?" Dwayne shares his experience with the youth and young adults in his program. In Dwayne's book, "Parenting with Eyes Wide Open," he says:

Your children are telling me things they should be telling you but do not feel safe doing so for whatever reason. Fortunately, whenever I contact a parent over this, the response is overwhelmingly supportive for their child and what I am doing. If your child has been sexually assaulted, seek professional help. Sexual assault should never be swept under the rug; it's harmful to your child, who will interpret secrecy and shame as evidence of their own failure, and it's harmful to other people out there who might be targeted next and aren't as strong as your child was when they came to you in confidence. (Parenting Eyes Wide Open, Dwayne Peace, Page 96).

Our youth and young adults who feel unsafe to share with their parents the difficult things they are going through is unfortunate, and we need to work on helping our children recognize that sharing and building trust with their parents will provide the children options and they do not need to feel alone in their struggles. We can help both the young adults and their parents see the need for building trust and respect in their individual homes. Parents need to recognize that building trust does not necessarily mean chastising or deliberately shaming them with prudish ideas and thoughts. Parents must listen and respond to their individual children's needs that they do care. They do care and we need to intervene constantly. This does not mean that parents should not hold their children accountable for the things they do wrong. Balance and active listening are crucial to the parent/child relationship.

The next two stories that I would like to share involve two examples that show the difficulties that teenagers go through being sexually assaulted, and also point out how differently the victim survivors handled their acquaintance rape.

As we all know, no two cases are alike. Each survivor has unique circumstances and especially at these ages it is critical that they get the support they need to navigate the aftermath of sexual assault.

Our first story is of a young woman in high school. There are so many pressures put on our youth in school. Leslie's story is a very powerful example of what those pressures look like with respect to sexual assault. We don't want to think about our youth being victims of sexual abuse, but it is happening more than we know.

Many youth are quiet about what is happening and feel trapped in these relationships due to peer pressure and lack understanding and fear of the outcome of reporting what happened to them or telling their parents.

I am so proud of Leslie and her strength and her willingness to tell her story. She has made some amazing changes in her life, but the thing that has impressed me the most is that Leslie is a survivor and not a victim. She now is working toward her college degree and hopes to help other survivors. Her strength is exemplary to me. Here is her story.

Leslie's Story

I was 16-years-old, a cheerleader, and just started out my junior year. I was looking forward to moving past the rough time that I had my sophomore year with a senior boy who had just graduated and starting this year fresh. The first day of school I realized I had gotten a new neighbor who I later was introduced to later that week by mutual friends. He became close friends with one of my best friend's boyfriend. He was the new star on the football team, the reason we won games, and everyone loved him because of it. He was shy and sweet to everyone at the school for those first couple months. Him and I started talking and began dating. I was one of the head cheerleaders, we were neighbors, and it seemed like a movie storyline where he became the boy next door. He met my family, I met his, and we would walk our dogs together, and would go on double dates. It started slow and sweet, until one day it wasn't that at all.

It was a Sunday in October; my parents took my little sister out somewhere and I was grounded and couldn't leave the house so, I invited him over. He knew I was a virgin, that was one of the things that made him so attracted to me. It was the way I would hold my head high knowing I was still a virgin, when around my school was not very common among the high schoolers, especially my junior class. It was something that gave me more confidence in myself. He and I were sexually active in other ways we just didn't have intercourse. He would always ask if we could have sex, but I was used to being asked that by guys who I have dated and turned down, so I didn't have any red flags up by him asking all the time. It seemed almost normal to me because everyone else was having sex at our age.

When he came over we started becoming physical with one another like we have before when suddenly, he stopped and looked at me. He said, "We're going to have sex." I told him no, that he knew I was a virgin and I wasn't ready to take that step, which is when he responded with "well you can just lose it now." That's when it happened, I lost my virginity. Well actually I was robbed of it. It was weird. I couldn't move. I felt nothing. I couldn't speak. I was numb during the whole process of it all. Everyone always asks victims, why didn't you fight him off or why didn't you scream, I never knew what complete shock was like until that very moment. I lost all control of my body and voice because well, that is what he wanted to take from me anyway isn't it? He wanted to take that control over me.

When he was done, he started getting dressed and I finally came to, it was then that I started realizing what had just happened to me. I started shaking and I was absolutely terrified. I got dressed, walked him to my door, walked him to my gate and he kissed me goodbye like everything was normal. Once he was on the other side of the gate and I was able to shut it, I said to him do not ever talk to me again and a few other words and I ran inside and locked my doors. I rushed into the shower feeling absolutely disgusted and just tried to wash away him, the memory, and any skin he touched. The memories of it, kept replaying over and over in my head and it was so vivid like a movie clip playing on a TV right in front of me. All I could see was what my viewpoint was when it happened. Him on top of me and my whole body just stiff and frozen like an ice sculpture. It felt like my body was no longer mine, just like a shell. I couldn't stop the panic attacks; the shower didn't help that at all. All that confidence I had was gone as soon as I got out of the shower. I could feel myself shrinking. It was like someone took my insides and just started pressing them down. I was proud of myself for having my virtue, and when it was taken from me, I never got that height back. I feel like I've been smaller ever since. I don't walk with my head held high anymore and it all started that day.

After I got out of the shower, I called my friend Maggie, no answer. I called my friend Laura, thank god she answered. I just started screaming and crying and physically shaking like a leaf. She couldn't understand a word coming out of my mouth. I don't even remember if I said words until I choked out his name, Jason. Right then she knew, and she said, "Leslie did you have sex with him?" and all I could say was yes followed by more sobs. Hearing that, shook something in me and I told her exactly how everything happened, and I remember thinking no I didn't have sex with him, I was raped, but I wasn't a virgin anymore. She comforted me in the way she would have thought I needed comforted, the way she would have wanted comforted after her first sexual experience.

Laura was also raped her first time she had sex. It was an older guy, they were all drunk and her best friend told the guy that Laura would be down to have sex just so her friend Michelle could hook up with the guys' friend. Laura didn't really know what happened to her until the morning and she had a really hard time coping with it. She started seeing guys left and right and hooking up with them, I believe to try to reenact her first time. You see when something you hold dear is taken from you you want to try to get it back to fill that void. Obviously, when it comes to your virginity there is no getting that back, but you can try to trick yourself into being okay with the fact that you had sex by continuing to have sex, on your terms. She and I were the only girls in our friend circle that weren't having sex so she and I bonded on a different level. We had the same feelings on waiting for the one who was going to be our high school sweetheart, you know the fairytale movie plot most teenagers want.

Maggie called me back after I got off the phone with Laura. I told her what happened, a little calmer than I told Laura because I became numb again. Maggie was raped when she was just 14 by a guy just a couple years older than her. She knew him all through elementary school and went to go hangout with him at his friend's house to get her belly button pierced. When she got there, his friend left the room and the guy started trying to do stuff with Maggie. She wasn't a virgin at this point, but she said no to him because she had to get back to coaching her KVL cheerleaders, she was already running late and was just there for the piercing. He pinned her down after hitting her in the face and said we can do this the easy way, or the hard way. After that, Maggie just never said no to a guy again which led to her sleeping with 30+ guys by the time she graduated high school. She said that she knew how hard it would be for me to hold resentment in my heart to Jason and that it would tear me apart like it did to her if I let it so that the best thing I could do would be to just let it go. In her mind, since he had my virginity and was my first that it would be better if I kept him in my life so that way the memory of my first time wouldn't be so tarnished.

I took the advice from both my friends in a way. I kind of did what Laura did. I started looking for a way to "reenact" my first time by filling the void with guys I had deeper feelings with that I turned down from having sex with before I ever met Jason. I remember my second time, was with Joey. Joey and I had dated at the end of my sophomore year, but it didn't last too long, very briefly. I didn't exactly want to, but since I already had sex I didn't think I could say no now because he knew I had sex with Jason. In my mind, having sex for the second time with Joey, someone who

I cared about and knew was safe from our past, was like my redemption. I took it as my do-over. In my mind, I was giving it away this time, so it was going to be the time I counted as my actual "first time." It of course did not work as I hoped and that of course did not take away the memory or pain that I experienced from Jason. I was just going off how my friends had dealt with it and trying to cope in my own way.

With Maggie's advice, I let Jason slide and even though I broke up with him I remained friends with him and wouldn't allow myself to hate him. This resulted in us having sex at random times because, well, after all he was my first, right? We would randomly hook up if we both happened to be single, I never said no to him unless I was talking to someone else because I knew it didn't matter, that no didn't matter. It wasn't until I started hearing stories that he tried to force himself on other girls, as he had done to me, that I realized he was dangerous. I realized that our sex wasn't an accident, it wasn't that he got too excited and couldn't contain himself as he said, but that he had a problem and he thought he was able to do whatever he wanted to anyone he wanted.

This went on for me until about March, until I started dating Troy again, a guy from my past. At this point of my life I was rebellious. I would lie to my parents about where I was going or what I was doing, I became someone who smoked weed every single day, and I would drink here and there. Troy and I were not allowed to date so I hid it very well from my family what exactly I was doing. We went to a party one night with a lot of older people. I was still only 16 at the time, he was 18, and our friend Greg was also 18 and about to leave for the air force so were hanging out with his older sister and her fiancé and their friends. The first time we went to the house party, everything seemed fine. I was surprised that all these 25 or older people were okay with me drinking at their house though.

The next weekend, Troy, our friend Greg, and I went back to the house party. This time, everything was not fine. Greg's sister Linda's fiancé Bart, had zero boundaries. He started asking if Troy and I would have a threesome with him, he started asking for videos of Troy and I having sex together, he asked for naked pictures of me and that he would pay for them, and he also followed Troy and I to a back room when we left the party to have sex. I caught him opening doors looking for us trying to catch us being with each other and I thought it was very weird. Then after, Troy went to the bathroom and Bart cornered me and tried to force himself on me to kiss me. I just blew it off as he was drunk, especially since he was engaged and friends with my boyfriend. So I tried to not make a big deal about it and let it go.

Later after the party, Troy and I went with Greg to his sister's house, so we could sleep there. Troy and I were asleep on a couch when suddenly, I felt tugging on me feet. It woke me up and I saw Bart sitting there. Not only was he sitting there but he was messing around with someone on the other end of the couch. I tried to stop it by getting up and walking into the kitchen to get some water because I knew it wasn't Linda, Greg's sister that Bart was with, since she went upstairs to her room to go to sleep. Bart knew I was awake, he saw me getting up but he didn't care to stop what he was doing.

When I came back to lay down with Troy, the sexual stuff going on the other end of the couch continued and I tried to wake Troy up, but he was too drunk. I *looked up, right at the bottom of my feet, because Bart stood up with his pants off and started having sex with someone who was laying on the other end of the couch. I looked over and I realized that the person he was having sex with was a man, not just a man but Greg who was sleeping on his stomach. He was raping his brother in-law inches from me and there wasn't anything I could have done to stop it. I was scared, scared that if I stopped what was happening with Greg, that Bart would turn around and rape me instead, like Jason had and I never wanted to experience that again.*

When it was the morning, Linda came downstairs and started making break-fast and Bart was sleeping at my feet. Troy woke up and tried to wake up Greg by ripping his blanket from him. That's when everyone saw that he was completely na-ked, Greg ripped the blanket back over top of him and just hid his face in the pillows and wouldn't move or talk. I looked up at Bart who was still sitting on the couch and he was staring right at me with an evil, devious look in his eyes, I stared back real-izing he was testing me in that moment. To see what I would do with the information of what I saw him doing, little did he know I was not going to be silenced about it.

Bart became persistent at texting Troy asking him to come over and bring me or make plans with him in some way. He would offer for him to do side work as pay-ment, a couple times he would text him asking for pictures or videos of me. That's when I took Troy's phone and told Bart off. I told him that he was a predator and that he needed to leave us alone or the truth would come out. He attempted to call my bluff, so I realized I had to tell Troy what I saw and why I never wanted to hear or see about Bart again. When I finally told Troy what happened and what I saw, he broke up with me. Linda, Greg's sister told Troy that if he loved me at all that he would get me out of all of this or my world was going to fall apart, she knew about how strict my dad was.

Shortly after, Greg's dad found out that Bart was having sex with Greg's lit-tle brother, by taking his phone as punishment, who was only 13 at the time. He groomed Colton for a long time and then started paying him for completing sex acts with him or for naked pictures of him. The family sent their proof into the police, and Bart was put in jail. The entire time he kept bringing my name up in his court hear-ings or when he first spoke to the police. Even though Troy and I weren't together he kept saying my name. He knew I was the one that started him being caught, I told about what happened with Greg. I was one he couldn't groom into submission.

Looking back now, I realize that in high school when it comes to dealing with this kind of stuff, it is the blind leading the blind. I of course was not going to go to my family about what happened to me because when it happened, I was supposed to be grounded so in a way it felt like my fault enough. I went to my friends who I knew had similar experiences and I wanted to see how they dealt with their situ-ation. I never even thought about going to the police over my sexual assault. The only time I did was when I realized by not saying anything, I let him go on and do that to other girls too. There were more girls I knew in high school that were raped than just Jackie and Amanda, 4 of them were raped the first time they had sex just as I had been.

Communication needs to happen. There is such a fear in kids to go to adults about these kinds of issues. The stigma alone in high school among your peers is hard enough. If you're not having sex, you think you're better than anyone and above them since you won't let anyone share your body with you that way. If you are having sex, you're a whore or one of the cool guys when actually you're just terrified of ever saying no again because one time, you did, and you were forced to do something you didn't want to do. Parents put so much pressure on kids to not be doing what their body may be telling them to do. In high schools most kids got into a frenzy over sex and their significant others. Some kids stay away as long as they can but even then, their decision is not respected and is criticized which makes it even harder to go against the grain. The average school day is filled with friend's peer pressuring friends and jokes about people's sex lives are the talk at lunch tables. Guys sweet talking girls to put them into a vulnerable state where their guards are down and then they can take advantage of them, and girls allowing guys to do what they want from past life experiences. It is all sorts of screwed up. Teachers see and hear what is going on but no one cares to say anything so again, we go back to what I said before, the blind leading the blind. Kids are going to go and get worldly immature advice from their friends who they think will give them the advice they may be looking for. I could have gone to other friends who may have told me tell your parents and tell the police, but I didn't. I wanted to hear the advice that I was ready to hear, not the advice I needed to hear.

Copyright © Leslie (name changed to protect identity). Reprinted by permission.

What We Learn From Leslie's Story

Leslie's advice is amazing. Here is a young girl who was faced with so many decisions and pressures from her friends at school. Leslie recognizes that she is not to blame for what happened to her. The difficult thing about this type of assault is that it happens with those you know and care about. If her boyfriend would have recognized what it means to have self-control and respect her, she would have never had to go through this experience.

The alarming aspect of sexual assault we learned from Leslie is that there are young women who believe that sexual encounters like Leslie's is almost like a "Right of Passage" that young people experience in high school and that it is readily acceptable, yet in the eyes of the law is criminal. This results in a great deal of pressure and confusion on what is acceptable and what is not acceptable.

Leslie shared with me that her average school day involved discussions with her peers during lunch about everyone's sex lives and making jokes about it. She also shared that guys sweet talk girls into putting themselves in what she referred to as "vulnerable states," where the young lady's guard is down, and they take advantage of them.

It truly is hard to comprehend that many of our young adults are experiencing this and do not even realize until it is too late that they have been a victim of sexual assault. This is why it is so critical that we as parents find a way to reach out to our children and help them navigate through their teenage years. It is also critical that our schools reach out to young people that are showing signs of trauma or changes in personality. Generally, they are directly related to behavior that is occurring in their lives, whether it is happening at school, at home, or with peers.

The second story I would like to share is a story of a young adult, 18-years-old who was working toward her EMT certification. I am so proud of Savannah telling her story and coping with what she has been through the last two years. She recognizes now that regardless of what happens to the offender, she knows what happened and knows that it is not her fault. Here is Savannah's story.

Meeting Her Offender Online

The day started warm and sunny, moving on to a lunch cookout with family and friends. Later in the day, I was invited to watch a basketball game at the apartment of a guy I had been chatting with online. We had been chatting online for a while and I let him know that I was only interested in a friendship, nothing more. He was cool with that although he had mentioned us getting together for more and I said no. I let him know that I had a boyfriend and I wanted to meet people and make friends, nothing more. Since we had never met in person, I was nervous about hanging out with him and some of his friends.

Meeting in Person

That evening around 7:00pm I drove to Martinsburg, WV to the address he had given me. When I got there, I met his roommate. There was no one else there. Things felt odd and my nervousness grew but I thought to myself "everything will be al-right." After a short time of watching the game, he told me to come with him to his room because he wanted to show me something. In his room, the TV is on and he says we can watch the game in there.

Sitting on the bed, he starts kissing me. I turn away and tell him no, let's just watch the game. He continues to kiss on me and starts putting his hands on me. I push at him to stop but he pushes me on the bed and gets on top of me. Three times I told him to stop! He didn't.

I was SCARED. I didn't know what to do. He was bigger than me and stronger than me. My heart was racing, I couldn't breathe, and I was panicking. I wanted to scream but nothing came out; I froze. I wanted to run; I couldn't move. So I just lay there. Afraid.

He touched my neck, moved down to my breasts and squeezed them, he moved his hands down my stomach and into my shorts. I didn't want this to happen! This couldn't happen. I tried to get out from under him but he held me down. He took off my shorts and that's when I started to shut down. He wasn't easy, he hurt me in more ways than one. He wouldn't stop, no matter how many times I said to. I didn't scream out for help because I didn't know what he would do to me if I did. I didn't know this person. My mind went off somewhere and it didn't feel real. And I just thought to myself, "Just kill me." I didn't want this to happen, but it did. When he was done, he got off me and left the room so I could clean up. I felt gross and I wanted to cry. I stayed in the room for a while trying to get the courage to run out of the apartment. I went into the living room but the roommate was sitting by the door. I felt trapped again and afraid. Not knowing what to do I sat on the arm of the sofa and tried to act normal. Tried to think of a way out.

He Raped Me Again

I guess it had been a half hour. He stands up, grabs my hand, and pulls me after him to his room. My mind is screaming that I should run. He pulls down my pants, his fingers jamming in me. Again he pushes me down and he is on me. He is in me. I can't get out. I can't scream. Just kill me.

The Aftermath

When he was done, he told me to leave. He didn't care who I was or what just happened. I know I left as fast as I could. I drove away. Crying and scared. I didn't know what to do. I didn't know where to go. I had a friend that lived close by so I went there. She was home. I was crying. I told her what happened, and she instantly called the police and then my parents. I was hesitant when she wanted to call my parents because I had lied to them about where I was going and I was scared about what they would do. The police showed up, an EMS crew showed up, at that moment, that's when I knew it was real. The police were all men, tall, big. The ones you wouldn't want to mess with. The police and EMS were asking me questions, "What happened?" "Do you know him?," "Where does he live?," "Are you hurt?." I couldn't answer any of their questions due to being so upset. The EMS crew took me to the hospital and my friend came along.

At the hospital two police officers, two nurses, and a Women's Advocate came into my room. The nurses were taking my vitals, the police officers were asking me questions that I still couldn't answer for being so upset, and the advocate was sitting next to me, holding my hand. I have never met this lady before, but she made me feel safer. They made my friend leave the room. I was wondering where my parents were. I felt like it had been a very long time. I was cold and shaking and scared. It's about 9pm now. The police had stepped outside due to the nurse's orders, the nurses are running tests. They give me plan B just as a precaution. They also gave me some other medication and they wouldn't tell me what it was. The nurses were not very nice to me. They took my shorts; they saw blood on them. They did a rape kit on me. They used cotton swabs and used them all over me to collect DNA. All of this made me feel uncomfortable, sick, and made me cry again. Once they were done, an officer came in to talk to me. He was nice. He was patient. I told him what happened and where the guy lived. They left.

After about an hour of them being gone and the police officer came back with a State Trooper. This time, they weren't nice. They made the nurses and the advocate leave. They had found him and spoke with him. They seemed angry and were asking me about my personal life . . . if I had a boyfriend and how often I see him. They asked, "Did you do this to get back at him?" When the police officer said that, I KNEW they didn't believe me. They said they were going to make me take a lie detector test because they knew I was lying. They told me they would have a warrant out for my arrest. They said I wasn't "answering the questions correctly." They said they would prove I was a liar. At that time the nurses had doped me up on meds and from all the crying, I just felt numb. They took my phone for evidence.

My parents were here. The advocate gave me time with each of my parents, one at a time. My mom came in first, crying. I felt so ashamed. I was shaking uncontrollably. And crying. Then my dad came in. That was the first time I've ever seen my dad cry. He held me and told me everything was going to be okay. The nurses told me I could go home.

When I got home, it felt like I slept for a few days; didn't want to do anything, didn't want to see anyone, didn't want to eat or drink. I just wanted to stay in bed all day, by myself. On day 3 of sleeping, my mom wanted to talk about what happened; but I didn't. It was still so painful and I was ashamed. I took a shower but couldn't scrub the grossness off no matter how hot the water or how hard I scrubbed. It was sickening.

My parents hired a lawyer and upon giving him the name of my rapist, the lawyer said he probably wouldn't be convicted because it appeared that he has parents who may be police officers. My heart sank even lower and I felt even sicker. He's going to get away with it.

Finding Strength Moving Forward

Days would go by and my thoughts and nightmares were eating at me. I told my mom several times that I was going to take all the pills in the medicine cabinet, cut my wrists with my pocket knife, or drive my car off the road. She instantly took all of that away. My mom held me and talked with me and helped me through each day. Mom and Dad reminded me that this was not my fault, no means no, and I am the victim. Mom reminded me not to take responsibility for his crime!

But I had the good fortune to have a family friend who is an amazing man! His extensive background and experience dealing with situations like mine gave him the ability to understand and counsel me and help me through the toughest time in my life. His love and kindness, his faith and encouragement has helped lift me and helped to know that I could get through this. Thank you LaVarr for being there for me and helping me not give up!

I decided to start working on me and trying to feel better and get better. My mom told me to be strong, be brave, and be courageous. She kept telling me that. She reminded me that I was loved and needed here. On days that I didn't want to go on, she was there with love, encouragement and her arms around me. She was strong for me and I couldn't have gotten through this nightmare without her. A year went by and I got a tattoo on my right forearm with a big lion face and wording around it saying, "Be Strong and Courageous," as a reminder every day of who I am. And to see that every day, has made me stronger and reminds me to be brave and be the person I want to be and to fight for what I want. Some days are still hard but I am moving forward and growing and learning each day. I am an Emergency Medical Technician now and I want to help others get through the worst day of THEIR life.

Copyright © Savannah (name changed to protect identity). Reprinted by permission.

Thoughts on Savannah's Story

The first time I spoke with Savannah I could sense her lack of self-esteem and shame that went with what happened to her. The way she was treated by law enforcement was unacceptable. They basically became her judge and jury without proper vetting of her case. Though we do not have all the thoughts of law enforcement it is unfair to place blame alone on the police officers, but this is one concern in small jurisdictions. Many departments do not have qualified forensic interviewers that can properly discern based on the evidence what information is needed to ensure that the correct charges are filed, that it is not false reporting, provide service, and support to the victim.

Though there were many aspects of Savannah's case that could have protected her rights and her ability to hold her offender accountable, the more important aspect of her case was that Savannah has found her road to take care of herself and find the path to healing which she found through her relationship with her parents.

Her parents stayed by her side and showed her through their love, acceptance, and believing her. Regardless of what happens in the criminal justice system, we have to help our victim survivors know that first they are not at fault, second, that true healing is within and if they can preserve their self-worth as we have talked about, then they will find their path to healing and acceptance of the new normal.

Like Savannah's parents, I remember as a young father that I told my children when they were old enough to start dating and going out with their friends that if they ever felt trapped, to use me as an excuse and say, "I can't, I told my Dad I would go to the movies with him."

On one occasion my son came up to me on a Friday night and asked if I wanted to go to a movie. I said, sure. We went to the movie and before it started, I said to him, why did you want to go to the movie with me? He looked at me and said, "You told us if we were ever in a situation that we were uncomfortable with, to make the excuse of your family going to a movie." He said that he was getting pressure to have sex with a girl and that they wanted him to go to a party where he could have sex with her."

That night as I laid in my bed, got a little emotional and then I got scared. I was thinking to myself about the pressure he must have felt, and he reached out to me instead. I am so glad that my wife and I had that kind of a relationship with our four boys. Were we perfect parents? No, but that night I felt like had the perfect son!

We learn through the story of Savannah that her parents played a critical role in their daughters' recovery. Savannah reached out to her Mom and Dad and as a result she has constantly had their support and love. It has been wonderful to watch.

Acquaintance Rape and Pregnancy: Now What?

I would like to share two additional stories in this section. Many times, we as experts are asked, can a woman who is dating be raped? We often hear that there are women who have been raped that became pregnant and had to make a decision whether or not to keep their child. This first story is about Beth who was involved for many months in a relationship. However, her boyfriend only seemed to care about control and having her available for sex. Many times, she said she was not ready, but he paid no attention to her pleas. Here is Beth's Story.

Beth's Road to Recovery

This first story involves a young woman who I met many years ago, and I will call her Beth. Beth was a vibrant student who was an accomplished dancer and had so many wonderful things going for her as she started her college experience.

During her second year, she met Ben. He was a student at the same school and was on the football team for the college. He also was in Beth's church group that met once a week for activities. This church group has leaders and Beth was one of the leaders.

Beth noticed that he was paying a great deal of attention to her and eventually he became more and more interested in her. Most of the interludes were associated with church and school, but on one occasion she found herself with him alone at her apartment where she lived.

While he was at her apartment, he became aggressive with her and Beth got scared and he physically tried to force her to have sex with him. She resisted and he became even more aggressive. It was then that he raped her for the first time.

Beth being away at college and not knowing the best way to handle it, she tried reaching out to her church leaders and saying that she wanted to be released from her responsibilities as one of the leaders of this group, hoping that would discourage him from coming around her. She even talked to the football coaches and asked not to be around or associated with Ben anymore. She would not come right out and tell others what he was doing, but just said she did not want to be around him. She was afraid of what he would do to her if she really told others what he was doing.

However, nothing changed and his behavior towards her turned into a complete nightmare most of her second year. She told her parents that she wanted to leave, and though they left it up to her, they still put pressure on her to stay and finish. She was so confused on what to do and tried to stop his behavior but did not know what to do aside from telling others what was really going on because of the fear she felt from him.

At the end of her second year, she graduated from this two-year school and moved to another state to finish her last two years of school. Ben followed her to the new school and continued his control and manipulation in her life. She felt trapped and did not know how to end the relationship. He raped her multiple times and she could not get away from his emotional grip that he had placed on her, with rhetoric that he loved her and his continual manipulation and control. He became progressively worse. She considered herself naïve to his behavior and did not realize how much control he had over her. She was allowing him to maintain control by not sharing with others what was really happening to her.

Prior to leaving the first school he had not only yelled at her, hit her, and raped her, but he also demanded respect through his narcissism and his manipulation. He continued his behavior not caring how it affected Beth. Many times, Beth told him no, but he did not listen and did not care. Beth felt so much shame. She came from a very religious background and was taught that pre-marital sex was wrong and before Ben, she had never had sexual relations with anyone. She knew what he was doing was not only morally wrong in her eyes but felt as though she was responsible because she was not stopping him. However, she was petrified as to what he would do if she really told others what was going on.

There are many victims who feel a great deal of shame for their behavior, especially when it is someone they know, are dating, and for many of them, they feel completely responsible for what is happening to them. I cannot even imagine the internal struggle that was going on with Beth, trying to navigate through an abusive relationship, make sense of his behavior, and try to survive.

After several months at the new university, he continued to rape her. She then became pregnant with his child. Beth was ashamed and she felt responsible for her actions because she felt as though she allowed him by not resisting and not telling others what he was doing.

When she told him, she was pregnant he wanted to marry her and wanted to take care of her and the baby, but she refused to marry him. When she told her parents that she was pregnant, though they did not force her to place the baby up for adoption, she felt that would be the only way to end her relationship with Ben by not having their child. Even though it was very difficult for her, she did end up making the choice to put her child up for adoption.

Beth shared with me that her parents were very controlling and that there was physical abuse going on in her home from her father, and that she believes that she had learned from a very early age to not tell and to put up with behavior going on around her.

Beth did not know what to do, she was at a very conservative privately-owned school and they had a strict honor code. Because she could not discuss this with others—his control—she never shared with anyone that she became pregnant from an abusive, controlling, and sexually assaultive relationship.

Beth dropped out of school, spent the next several months pregnant, and was forced by her parents to give the baby up for adoption. She felt very strongly that her parents were embarrassed of her behavior and were more concerned with the way it appeared than for her to keep her child. So, after the baby was born it was given up for adoption. To this day, Beth regrets not being able to raise her child.

Beth became paranoid about men in her life because of her father's behavior and the way Ben was treating her.

Beth of course, after having her baby and feeling completely controlled and manipulated by not only Ben but her parents, she found that she was having a very difficult time finding her path. She has been married, divorced, and feels many times like she has never been able to plant herself into a relationship or situation in her life where she has felt content. Though she has been successful in many aspects of her life, including acting and other projects and wonderful job opportunities, she has never been able to feel completely content with the direction in her life.

Until the last several years, she has felt that others have controlled her paths and feels that for many years she has had a difficult time in relationships and in life in general.

In the last several years, Beth has taken back the control in her life. Beth was adopted and she recently reached out to her biological family and has rejuvenated her relationship with her family. She has even changed her name and has completely changed her attitude.

Though she is now in her 50s, she has truly begun a new chapter of her life that has brought her to this point, where she now feels that no one controls or manipulates how she lives her life or what she does for herself.

I know Beth very well, and with all that she has been through in her life, for her to now take these bold moves by changing her name, her attitude, and finding joy in her journey she has truly created an amazing resilience. A resilience, that for many years, she felt she was in the dark in her relationships, and in her ability to be in control in her life.

Though her adoptive family does not feel her decisions are appropriate, the fact that she feels in control now in her life is so important for each of us to do. It is important to take control and recognize that we have the ability to see the good within ourselves, and that regardless of our past and the length of time that it takes to get to this point in our lives, that we can be successful and live a good life. That is what impresses me about Beth is that she has never, ever given up in her struggles and triumphs of gaining control in her life even after experiencing abuse in many forms, from her adoptive father, her boyfriend, and giving up her child for adoption.

Personally, I cannot imagine the emotions that someone goes through who is physically attacked through sexual assault, from someone they know. It is unthinkable and terrifying to think that there are those in our society who have absolutely no honor for the sanctity of womanhood and manhood and use human sexuality to have power and control over others. Sexuality is a gift from God and when used properly, is such a beautiful expression of love. However, when used for selfish desires, it becomes a symbol to the victim of flashbacks, nightmares, pain, and shame.

Now after a woman has gone through the humiliation of a rape, now compound that trauma with the news that you are pregnant from being raped. It would be hard to conceptualize what that must be like for a woman to be confronted with both emotions. Not only experiencing trauma from being raped, but trying to comprehend the dilemma of being pregnant and knowing that she will now be confronted with the choice of whether or not to keep her child, give it up for adoption, or justify in their mind the option of an abortion. No one can make that decision for any woman. They must confront that challenge themselves. Though she will have others that will be there for her, she will ultimately have to make that decision. It is tragic that a woman would have to make those types of decisions.

How frequent is this phenomenon of a woman becoming pregnant from a rape? In the professional journal, Jacobs Institute of Women's Health, I found that it happens more than you would think. The article in part reads:

> Results of a population-based survey indicated that approximately 5% of women who experienced rape became pregnant as a result of the assault (Holmes, Resnick, Kilpatrick, & Best, 1996), and were more likely to terminate those pregnancies than to continue them. One percent of women in a cross-sectional study of women's reasons for choosing abortion reported that their pregnancy had resulted from rape (Finer, Frohwirth, Dauphinee, Singh, & Moore, 2005). For women who choose to terminate rape-related pregnancies, abortion care can be an opportunity to disclose the assault to their medical providers and be provided with health care, emotional support, and referrals pertaining to the assault, in addition to the abortion procedure.

Practices Regarding Rape-related Pregnancy in U.S. Abortion Care Settings Rachel Perry MD, MPH, Molly Murphy MPH, Kristin M. Rankin PhD, Allison Cowett MD, MPH and Bryna Harwood MD, MS Women's Health Issues, 2016-01-01, Volume 26, Issue 1, Pages 67-73, Copyright © 2016 Jacobs Institute of Women's Health.

I am proud of Beth and her decisions. It is not easy having to face those challenges so young in a person's life. However, the way in which Beth has chosen to survive and live her life is exemplary in her ability to see that she is the only one that can control her life, that she has the ability to succeed, and be the person she wants to be. It is a constant battle that faces Beth to focus on her future and keep the trauma that she has been through in perspective.

However, I have no doubt that Beth now sees her potential and understands that though a person can manipulate and control others, we can maintain control in our own lives and become the person we have always wanted to be. I am proud of you Beth!

Liz's Story of Rape and Pregnancy

I would like to share another true story of one of the bravest women I have ever met. I became acquainted with Liz several years ago. When I met Liz, she had a beautiful baby named Grace. As I got to know Liz, her husband Jeremy, and the daughter Grace, Liz shared very personal information about her little family with me.

Liz shared with me that several years ago she was raped, and as a result of the rape, she became pregnant. I was in my early twenties and was taken back by her news. I was not sure how to react, it was an awkward moment, but one I will cherish for the rest of my life. To have Liz and Jeremy feel safe to confide in me and share that was such an honor and a privilege.

Years later, I was well into my career and was working with many victims of violent crime including rape. On an occasion I had the chance to ask Liz if she would mind sharing with me her story. As I was anticipating her answer, I felt nervous like maybe I should not have asked her. With amazing dignity, she said that she would share her story with me. With deep respect, I now share Liz's story.

That Night Changed my Life Forever

Both Liz and her assailant Hank worked close together in the small town where they lived. They began just talking at first. She was impressed with him. He was polite, easy to talk to, and seemed genuinely interested in her. They talked on several occasions before Hank asked her out on a date. She agreed to a date and was looking forward to going out with him.

They went on a date and then he asked her if she wanted to come back to his apartment to just chat. She agreed to go with him. As they went to his apartment they began to talk and as they kept talking, she remembers him getting her a Diet Coke.

Everything to that point seemed harmless. As they were talking, drinking their Diet Coke, he out of the blue told her that he was going to have sex with her. She remembers telling him no, that she did not want to have sex. That was the last thing that she really remembers until the next morning.

Awkwardly she woke up the next morning, confused, and at first did not know where she was. She was undressed and he then said, "How did you sleep?" Like it was no big deal. She left frightened, confused, and not sure what had happened that night. She just knew that something happened and felt uncomfortable with the casual attitude he had, and that was the last time she would go out with him.

She tried very hard to forget the whole incident and did not know how to handle the situation because she truly could not remember anything that had happened. There is a very good chance that Hank used a date rape substance in her drink. Statistically, this happens in about 4.5 % of rape cases, where a person is drugged involuntarily. https://www.ncjrs.gov/pdffiles1/nij/grants/212000.pdf

What Should I Do "God?"

Liz truly did not fully comprehend or know how far he had gone until about two months after the incident; she started to experience morning sickness. She at first could not figure out why she was getting sick in the mornings. She soon became fearful that she was pregnant from the incident because the night when she woke up, she was completely undressed, and she felt as though something had happened but was unsure and definitely unclear.

She went to the doctor and he confirmed her fear, she was pregnant. She had no sexual relations with anyone during the timeline of her pregnancy except for her encounter with Hank. It was clear now in her mind that he had raped her.

At this point, being confused on what she should now do, she thought about reporting to the authorities what happened. She thought about the fact that they may blame her or put some responsibility on her because she was pregnant, and it happened several months previous. She worried they would wonder why did she not come forward sooner. She also did not want to be confronted if her behavior provoked him to do this to her. All of these emotions were swimming around in her head and she truly was at a complete loss on what to do.

Liz's Decision – Unconditional Love

With all that bottled up emotion, and the fact that she was now pregnant, she decided not to report the rape. She had not told anyone, but at this point felt compelled to tell her parents and some close friends. She was overwhelmed with emotion and felt alone in this decision on what she should do.

Because of her beliefs she said that abortion was never an option for her. She indicated that it was between keeping her child and giving the baby up for adoption. She actually went back and forth for many months until she finally decided to keep her child. She had gone so far as fill all the paperwork out and actually have a couple picked out to have her child. But close to the time of having her baby she decided that she would keep her baby. I asked her once, that because she had made the decision to have her baby, did she ever regret her decision? She said that she absolutely never questioned her decision.

Liz never reached out to Hank for any support or to inform him that she had become pregnant. She said that the main reason was that she did not want to take a chance that he would somehow try to take their baby away or want joint custody. She could not fathom having to share her daughter with the man that raped her.

During her pregnancy she met her husband Jeremy. When they started dating, she of course had to share with him that she was pregnant. She told him that it was because of an acquaintance rape. I can't even imagine the emotion that he felt when she shared that with him. He of course supported her, and throughout his life until his passing, he loved her and treated her as his own daughter. He recently passed away and their daughter Grace was there with him until the end when he passed away. She took care of him and loved him as her real father. I can only imagine that type of unconditional love. It is a beautiful relationship, one that truly humbles me to think about and appreciate the selfless actions of Liz and Jeremy as they accepted this sweet child into their home and raised her as their own.

Jeremy and Liz Facing the Questions

Liz shared with me that when she was pregnant that it was of course awkward for her and Jeremy, especially when she started showing. She was in a very religious community and felt very much alone in her journey with others judging her for being pregnant before her marriage to Jeremy. She received a lot of obstinate looks from others. Though she was comfortable with her situation it still was very uncomfortable for her.

Even when she met with her ecclesiastical leader, he mentioned to her about the pregnancy, and asked her what her plans were and that she would not be able to get married in their church because the baby was out of wedlock. She informed him at that point, that she had been raped and that the pregnancy was a result of the rape. She explained that she met Jeremy after she had been raped and that he had agreed to adopt the baby and be her father. Of course the minister had to backtrack and felt sheepish about what he had insinuated with his comment. Jeremy and Liz did get married in their church with the blessing of her minister.

It is hard to believe that there are people that treat others with such a judgmental attitude without really understanding the circumstances and treating each other with respect. We live in a society where others are quick to judge and that was one more awkward and difficult result of this man taking advantage of Liz in such a selfish manor.

It was not always easy for Liz and Jeremy to deal with what had happened to her. Of course there are memories and issues centered on intimacy that were very difficult times for her and her husband. She said that you cannot have something like that happen to you that does not affect you at some point and cause some emotional trauma. She told me that there were many times that prayer and faith in her God were the only things that saw her through.

The Results of Her Decision to Keep Her Baby

It has been over 30 years since the rape. Grace is now a mother and grew up in a loving home with two wonderful parents who taught her how to treat others, with respect and unconditional love. I followed Grace and her two brothers through letters and occasional visits while they were growing up. Every time I gave Grace a hug or talked to her, I would think to myself, what if Liz had given her up for adoption, or had aborted this sweet beautiful little girl?

Now that Grace is in her thirties, she has five children of her own. Liz is now remarried, and she and her husband now enjoy five beautiful grandchildren as a result of the life of Grace. She does not look at Grace any different than she does her two other children, two boys. Grace had two brothers to protect her.

I asked Liz why she wants to tell her story, and she shared with me that if she can help one woman that is struggling with her same struggles and help her find her way, then it would all be worth it. She does not look at what happened to her as a curse or as something that has broken her spirit.

Of course, there are some that would look at Liz's story and say, "How could she keep that child, I would think about what her father did all the time." We can only imagine the awful things that others may say. That is why Liz chose not to share what happened to her with all of her friends. She realizes that there are some that would never understand.

Liz's Unconditional Love

Liz said something to me that I will never forget. She said that even though the circumstances that brought her daughter Grace to her life were unfavorable, she has never regretted her decision or has ever really thought about what life would be like without her. Liz told me that this was God's plan for their daughter to come into the world. That it did not matter then, nor does it matter now. Grace is her daughter for eternity, and no one can take that away from Liz or her family.

As I have contemplated this story in my own mind, I am in awe every time I think of the selfless love and compassion that Liz and Jeremy have shown to each other and to their daughter Grace. The other day I was looking at the family picture on the Internet of Grace and her husband and their five beautiful children and said to myself, Liz you absolutely made the right decision, you truly are a gift from God to and an example to all of us of unconditional love. I only hope that all of us will learn from this beautiful story and comprehend the absolute need to support those who have been traumatized and help them discover their own path of healing.

Liz found her path with her family and the world is a better place because of the decisions that she made in her life. When I think of her story I am reminded of the phrase about lemons. "When life gives you lemons, make lemonade." I read a woman's story about what this phrase means to her. I likened what she said to Liz's story.

A women by the name of Patty Jackson said:

"When life sent lemons my way, I decided not to make lemonade. I made an entire lemonade stand. I built this stand not just for myself, but for anyone who might need something sweet to chase the bitterness away. My lemonade stand was not built overnight. It took some very hard decisions and a lot of sweat and tears." https://onlinelibrary.wiley.com/doi/pdf/10.1002/dat.20529

Liz, I honor you with your lemonade stand that you have built because of your decision to have Grace and raise her as your own. I can only imagine what you have been through in your life. I am in awe at your love for your sweet family and for your selfless service to them. I hope that I can have the ability in my life to learn from you about what it means to love unconditionally.

Can you imagine if we as a society could comprehend the depth of unconditional love that Liz has shown not only to her daughter, but her family, extended family, friends, and society. I believe we would be well served to learn from this brave woman and see through her eyes what it means to love completely. Thank you, Liz, for your selfless act and for your strength and courage, it is truly humbling.

Conclusion

In this chapter I have shared the stories of incredibly brave women who have been faced with some of the most difficult times in their lives. All of these women have found the strength to move past their sexual assault and have recognized the path of true healing is within themselves.

Of course the victim wants their offenders to be accountable for their abuse to them. There is the aspect of justice that we cannot ignore. Offenders can be very manipulating and can turn the tides of a case by their demeanor, their tactics, and their lack of taking responsibility.

After hearing from many victims and spending time with each of these women in their cases, I can tell you of the need for our law enforcement officers to find the necessary resources to provide thorough, fair, and objective ways to collect the evidence to present to prosecutors that will "paint the picture," as to what lead up to this crime, who is responsible, and who is the victim. Prosecutor's cases are to go by an objective and not subjective report to determine who is at fault. As I have said, trained individuals who understand all the dynamics in a sexual assault case takes a great deal of effort, time, and money. Though departments do not always necessarily have the funds nor the volume of cases to provide forensic interviews in their cases, they definitely have access to professionals who can lend support to these small jurisdictions to help them in obtaining accurate and fair information to find justice for the wrong committed.

Recently I read an article about what forensic interviewing is and I thought it would be worth mentioning. First, how do we define this type of interviewing?

> Forensic interviewing is a means of gathering information from a victim or witness for use in a legal setting, such as a court hearing. It is a key component of many child protective services investigations. The purpose of these interviews is to gather factual information in a legally defensible and developmentally appropriate manner about whether a child (or other person) has been abused (Newlin et al., 2015). Forensic interviews are conducted by trained professionals, including child welfare caseworkers, law enforcement, and specialized forensic interviewers at children's advocacy centers (CACs). These interviewers are frequently part of a multidisciplinary team investigating the case. https://www.childwelfare.gov/pubPDFs/forensicinterviewing.pdf

Having a trained individual in this type of interviewing gives both the victim and the offender the confidence that there case is being looked at objectively and that the best possible course of action will follow to provide justice in these very difficult and emotional cases.

So, we know that our system definitely needs to improve. I have talked with law enforcement officers all over our country and many of them have talked about the need for better training and understanding of these sensitive types of cases, and either learn or turn their investigations over to these expert interviewers to provide them with an objective view of a case. We owe it to the offender and the victim.

I believe that the most important thing that we can do in our system is hold the offender accountable to their victims. It will help the victim to appreciate that they are believed, and that the offender must be accountable for what he has done. When an offender does not have that opportunity to be accountable, they see no real good reason to change their behavior.

Dr. Judith Herman in her book, "Trauma and Recovery," shares her belief with respect to the behavior of an offender who does not take responsibility for his crime. She said, "In order to escape accountability for his crimes, the perpetrator does everything in his power to promote forgetting. If secrecy fails, the perpetrator attacks the credibility of his victim. If he cannot silence her absolutely, he tries to make sure no one listens." https://www.goodreads.com/work/quotes/530025-trauma-and-recovery

Offenders are in absolute need of extensive treatment in order to deal with what they have done and understand the importance of accountability for their actions. In chapter nine I will discuss restorative justice and its impact on the offender and victims of crime.

However, where a victim does not have the opportunity to face her offender in court and for him to be held accountable, this can be very devastating for victims.

We must work together in large and small jurisdictions to support law enforcement and our communities in not only better detection of perpetrators but improving the way we investigate and bring to justice those who have committed such heinous acts of violence.

Many of our victims have made it clear that their road to recovery came through self-discovery through treatment and support from others. That with this help from others; counselors, family, and friends, the survivors found their inner strength.

It is my experience that truly helping the victims of this type of offense takes a great deal of strength from the victim survivor to know that healing is personal and that they are the only ones that can truly control their purpose and self-respect. To know that they are completely innocent of wrongdoing and to understand that what they went through did not break them but gave them strength to meet adversity in this life.

Truly the best thing that we can show the offenders who escape prosecution is that they did not destroy the victim. That the victim is in control of their lives and found their path of healing and no longer sees the need to worry, seek revenge, or demand justice in order to heal.

I have learned so much from these men and women who have gone through such horrible circumstances and I hope that we truly listen and try to understand from them what we can do to support them through such horrifying experiences.

5

⤳

Surviving Domestic Violence— Stories of Courage and Bravery

Women and men who suffer from domestic violence live in silence, enduring years of their abuse because they are terrified to tell their family or to leave their partner because they are afraid of what they might do. No one can deny that those feelings are real for them.

We hear the term all the time, "The fear of the unknown." I recently read this definition of "fear of the unknown." It reads, "These negative feelings and thoughts create mental blocks. It is these mental blocks that influence the way in which we live our life and if let loose can have a detrimental impact on us living our lives to the fullest. . . . Essentially it is the fear of anything that is beyond their comfort zone." https://www.lifehack.org/347868/why-fear-the-unknown

When we choose to allow fear to control our lives, the choices we make do not serve us well. Any decision we make based on this fear will not be a decision that will move us forward in life and create a safer journey for ourselves and those around us.

The "fear of the unknown" is an emotion we feel when we fixate our fear on what we don't know what lies in front of us. So women and men who are being abused will wonder what will happen if they leave. Will the abuser find them and/or kill them? Will they lose their children? How will I take care of the children and myself? This emotion is very real to victim survivors. As a society we have got to do more in our support to those who are abused, help take the guess work of their future out of the scenario and trust those around them, but also hold the offender's accountable for their behavior, and create safer environments for everyone.

Portions of this chapter are written with permission of Kathy Carlston. Portions of this chapter are written with permission of Nicole (last name omitted to protect privacy). Portions of this chapter are written with permission of Dana (name changed to protect identity).

However, fear can also be a wake-up call and motivate us to improve our situation or to take risks in order to achieve a goal, or in the case of domestic violence, free oneself from the chains of emotional and physical abuse and control. We see some that triumph over their fear and find that there is a way to overcome and to find oneself on a new path that will bring joy and happiness.

I look at it this way; fear has a way for creating the roadblock to happiness. I love this saying from author Sarah Parish, "Living with fear stops us taking risks, and if you don't go out on the branch, you're never going to get the best fruit." https://www.success.com/19-quotes-about-facing-your-fears/

Those that face the fears and the pain of domestic violence deserve happiness and contentment. The best way to achieve that is to find the strength to get out on the limb and find your fruit. I always tell victims when giving them this quote, think of telling your story and seeking help as a ladder. Think of victim advocates as those that can help you onto the ladder. We can't pick your fruit, but we can sure help you find a way.

The bottom line, it sounds easy to us, but to victims, reaching for the fruit of happiness is sometimes an uncontrollable fear. As individuals we see people probably every day that are suffering from abuse, let's do our best to look out for them and find a way for them to obtain their fruit.

Years ago, I helped a mother who will refer to as Sarah. She was being physically abused by her husband. She had three children lived in a rural community and she was kept away from her friends. She was trying to finish college when they got married but he refused to let her finish once they got married.

At first, he was charming, he always treated her well when they were dating while they both finished college.

However, in time after their marriage he began to control everywhere she went and who she could be with. Eventually it got to the point where he would beat his wife severely and when he was through he would urinate on her, to humiliate her even further. No matter what she did he would not stop his behavior. He would beat her in front of the children and did not care. He would abuse his children through emotional abuse. Always putting them down, telling them not to side with their mother, and threatening to kick them out of the house.

There were a few times that she would contact the police, they would arrest him and within 48 hours she would drop the charges against him and even pay his bail. Finally, we decided with her consent, to move her out of her house, relocate her, and find the resources in that area to support her.

We took her and her children through seven different modes of transportation, and 200 miles. When we got her settled into her apartment, within a few hours he came to the door with a gun and marched her and the children back home. He had tracked her with a GPS locator on her phone. No matter what she did she could not get out of his life or his abuse.

On several occasions he beat her severely, then would take her to the hospital and she gave them a typical story of falling, hitting her head, and many other excuses. It is amazing the improvement that is occurring in emergency rooms in educating staff on detection of abuse, but still we have many cases that are missed by professional staff in hospitals and law enforcement.

This is clearly due to the sheer number of cases that come through the emergency room as an accident and not asking the right questions or ignoring instinct. It also comes from not going to the hospital and victims living with severe injuries that many times do not heal properly.

Even her family was not aware of what was happening because she was afraid, he would go after her own family. She felt completely trapped with nowhere to go and felt little hope of surviving. The worst part was that there house was so filthy that no one would ever come and visit and she had no family close by, so she felt trapped, alone, and isolated from the rest of the world.

Tragically, Sharon is still in her abusive relationship. It's been over 20 years and she has not felt safe enough yet to leave him. Her hope is that she can leave now that her children are in college.

Sharon described how her faith that things would improve would diminish less and less each passing month. Many of her family now is aware of the abuse and they cannot understand why she stays in this relationship. This is the tragic story of abuse; it becomes much more difficult for them to face the "fear of the unknown" and leave their abusive relationship. They would rather stay in the relationship where at least they know what is coming. "The fear of the unknown" is much more powerful than we all recognize, and it would behoove us to be more sensitive to that emotion of those being abused. We must see through their eyes in order to know how to best support and assist them in changing their circumstances.

Shockingly, I share with you some of the general statistics of the difficulty that we face in combating this problem. According to the National Coalition Against Domestic Violence (NCADV), "nearly 20 people per minute are physically abused by an intimate partner in the United States." In addition, "1 in 3 women and 1 in 4 men have experienced some form of physical violence by an intimate partner." https://ncadv.org/statistics

There is no dispute that we are faced with very complicated family and relationship issues even in our own families. Domestic violence and other similar crimes are difficult to detect, many times because these types of crimes have so many variables that create this type of chaos in the lives of others. Just by the sheer number of cases, it tells us that this issue is a "Pandora's Box" in our society because it is so hard to control what happens in each individual home and with human behavior in general.

Thank goodness we do recognize the need for progressive reform that can decrease the problem that we face in our society. I am not what you call a pessimist, but I am a realist. We cannot keep up with the volume of victims and secondary victims, including men, women, and children in our current state as a society. The numbers as you read above are staggering, outlining the complexity of this issue.

Many adults who are participants in domestic violence, whether it is the abuser or the victim, oftentimes do not see or want to see the damage that is happening with their children and in their own lives. Many children who either witness abuse or are being abused are learning very early in their lives that problems are handled with violence, yelling, and belittlement. Thus you create a path of shame in our young people that follows them into their adult life, unless they either have someone intervene in their lives, or they are strong enough to see the path they are on and change their path by their own will to survive. There are many young people who never abuse when they become adults because they simply chose not to continue the behavior they witnessed.

Impact of Domestic Violence Through a Child's Eyes

The safeguarding of our children in my opinion is the single most important role that we have as human beings. To raise children that can be productive members of our society, can accomplish their inner most desires, and feel the support and guidance of loving parents is of course the path that we want all of our children to have in their young lives. Now to many, that sounds impossible to raise children in a perfect scenario and to always be productive members of society.

With that said, I believe we as a society need to take the role of a parent more serious in combating the problems within our society. The more children see resilience in their lives, the better chance they have to manage the difficult road of growing up in today's society.

I was recently reading some literature on this very issue and I found the following passage that I feel best explains my concern for raising children in a non-abusive home.

> Children exposed to DV are considered to have experienced psychological abuse (British Psychological Society, 2007) and are more likely to experience difficulty with peer relationships, low self-esteem, anxiety, depression and trauma symptoms (Carlson, 2000). . . .
>
> *(Educational & Child Psychology; Vol. 36 No. 1; Domestic violence in teenage intimate relationships: Young people's views on awareness, prevention, intervention and regaining one's sense of wellbeing, Angela Griffiths).*

There is enough pressure on youth and young adults nowadays and we need to do all we can to preserve the next generation to be productive members of society and teach them how to navigate through the difficulties laid out before them in our world today.

Children that need this love and support are greatly impacted by the selfishness of a perpetrator. The difficult aspect of this problem is that many of these kids do not see their father as a bad person, but someone who needs help. Families struggle on how to best support their family member, hold them accountable, and ensure the safety of others, if the abuser is on the street.

Those who commit these crimes either against little children or in front of children, are clearly dealing with a deep seated problem that in many cases these individuals have no interest in changing because first they would have to face their family member or friend and answer to their behavior. And secondly, there is little or no motivation to change due to the lack of accountability by the system. There are many that do not care but for those who do, it is an eye opener to them when family members hold them accountable and set boundaries that we discussed in Chapter hree.

I would like to share with you Dana's story. Dana is now in her twenties and working toward her college degree. Though Dana is handling her situation much better and recognizes the fact that it is not any ones fault except the perpetrators decision to act out and cause harm to their mother and the children.

I want to say how much I appreciate Dana for telling her story. It is not easy to tell a story where you are a victim at such a young age. No child should have to experience emotional, physical and sexual abuse ever!

Here is Dana's story about what she experienced and to this day continues to face. As a teenager growing up she witnesses her mother's boyfriend disrespect her mother, Dana, and her brother. It is incredibly brave for Dana to tell her story. The following is her story told in her own words.

We Loved Him, Even I Loved Him

My name is Dana and I have been a victim of domestic violence for more than half of my life. It all started in May 2008 when my parents decided to separate. My mom purchased her home and on the day we moved in her "friend" helped her with all the heavy lifting. I later discovered that this friend was her new boyfriend. He seemed like a really great guy at first; he made my mom happy, played catch with my brother in the street, and even built a clubhouse in the backyard for me and my friends to spend our days in the summer. The family loved him; I even loved him. He was perfect. Absolutely perfect.

The Abuse Begins

On one warm summer afternoon that perfect man showed his true colors. My mom needed new brakes in her car and he offered to replace them in his dad's garage. I'm not exactly sure what started the argument because I was too young at the time to pay attention, but my mom and him were fighting. At one point he threatened my mom that if she would leave the garage he would kill her, me, and my brother. So of course, out of fear my mom stayed in the garage.

He locked us in this garage with no way of getting out except through a basement door he failed to secure. Eventually, he left the garage to go upstairs for some reason, and at that moment my mom knew this was her only chance. We escaped through the basement door and we began speed walking up the street. I say speed walking because I'm pretty sure my mom didn't want to scare us by telling us to run; especially my brother who was only about 4 or 5 at the time. We made it to a four-way intersection where there was an abandoned Walgreens Pharmacy located on the corner. I remember standing in the parking lot begging my mom not to go back to the garage; I told her we could just walk home it'll be fine. We were about a half an hour drive from our house so to walk home it would have taken us hours. Clearly my emotions were clouding my judgement.

However, while we were standing in the parking lot of Walgreens a patrol car stopped at the red light. My mom then flagged the officer down and told him the whole situation. The officer drove us back to the garage so my mom could retrieve her car and we could go home. When the officer confronted him on what had happened, he denied everything and told the officer my mother was crazy and to not believe her. The officer proceeded to take each of their statements, and afterwards we went home never to speak of the day again.

Manipulating His Way Back in Our Home and Lives

We didn't see him for a few months after the whole ordeal, however, slowly but surely he began stopping over for dinner, or swinging by to grab a few things. In other words, he was just inching his way back into our lives. Before long, he was back living in our house full-time. Everything seemed normal again, or at least what I thought was considered normal. My mom and he would argue from time to time, but nothing ever escalated like the day in the garage. I couldn't tell you if that was the case when my brother and I were staying at my dad's for the weekend. I like to think that was the case, because I would hate to think my mom went through such ordeals alone.

Doesn't End

Fast-forward to January 2018. My mom came home from having major abdominal surgery, so as you could imagine she was in a lot of pain. I was woken up in the middle of the night to my mom screaming and crying. Every time this sort of thing would occur I would always get out of bed and try to find my mom to figure out what was wrong. I walk into my mom's bedroom to her begging him to leave her alone. He was drunk and trying to force himself on my mom. Clearly, my mom was in no mood to be doing any of that after having surgery and having a drain placed on the side of her stomach. I proceeded to tell him that he either needed to leave or to go sleep downstairs away from my mom.

He refused to listen to me and continued to lay in her bed. When I repeated myself, he got out of bed and started to yell at me. He said my mom was "taunting him" with her pain medication and that she was shaking the bottle, upsetting him on purpose. He had/has a bad drug problem so clearly my mom being prescribed pain killers was a huge trigger for his violent outburst.

Once he started getting in my face, my mom got out of bed to put herself in between us. He started to get physical with her, pushing her back onto the bed, so I forced myself back in between the two of them. One thing led to another and I ended up at the top of the steps with him begging him to just leave. At that moment, he shoved me down the stairs. I caught myself after about five steps; at this point, my mom is hysteric.

Called the Police, Again

I locked myself in the bathroom and called 911. The operator stayed on the phone with me until the officers were outside of my home. She asked me if I felt safe enough to go down stairs and to let the officers into the house, I responded with "Not at all but I have to do this." I then ended the call. I ran down the stairs, through the living room, and out the front door to the middle of the street where I dropped to the ground surrounded by five police officers. Might I remind you, it is January so there is snow on the ground and it couldn't be more than 30 degrees outside. Yet, I ran out of my house in a t-shirt and I had no shoes or socks on. I guess you could blame the adrenaline running through my body for me not even being phased by the cold weather.

The police took our statements, but because there were no physical marks on either my body or my mom's they were not able to arrest him or even tell him to leave. They told my mom to go to the courthouse and file for a PFA (protection from abuse) so they would have the authority to escort him out of our house. At this point, it was 4:00 am and my mom really did not want to get into a car and drive downtown to night court, so the police officers left and we tried to go back to bed while he was downstairs in the basement doing only God knows what. We woke up the next morning and I drove my mom down to the courthouse and she filed for the PFA.

After the order was in place, we drove straight to the local police department so an officer would follow us back home and to escort him out of the house. The department is well aware of how dangerous he can be at times, so they told us to park down the street and let them handle it. As we were sitting in my car waiting for the officers to tell us it's okay to come home, he drives past us and mouths the words "you're dead" to my mom. He clearly just violated the order and the officer watched him do that, therefore he was arrested immediately and put into the county jail. That didn't last long; my mom never renewed the PFA and she even paid his bail.

These two instances are only some of the awful things this man has done to my mom and my family the past eleven years. He has physically, mentally, emotionally, and financially abused my mom for so long, but if you would meet him in public, he acts like he is the most amazing man and treats her like a queen. That fact alone is probably what drives me up a wall the most, because people wonder why I refuse to speak to him or why I just don't like him as a person. He is a completely different person in public, but if anyone would see how he is behind the closed door they would understand where I came from and why my family is the way that they are.

Facing Reality

I have come to the realization, at the age of only 20, that the only way this man will ever be out of my life is if he dies of an overdose, or if he kills my mom and goes to prison for the rest of his life. No child should ever have to think of their mom being taken away from them in that way; it's just not right.

My Mom Was Not the Only Victim

My mom is not his only victim. My brother and I have fallen victim to this terrible man. Just in the last year my brother was diagnosed with severe depression and anxiety, forcing my mom to pull him out of school. Luckily, he has been going to therapy and has been prescribed medication which has helped tremendously. My mom does not see a correlation between my brother's diagnosis and her boyfriend's abuse. She believes my brother's diagnosis has something to do with my dad not being around as much once they separated.

I thoroughly believe that he has everything to do with my brother's diagnosis. I at least remember a time when this man wasn't in our lives, however my brother was too young to remember. Therefore, all he knows is this abuse. My mental health has taken a turn for the worst in the past six months. I am sad all the time, have absolutely no motivation to go out with friends and have fun, sometimes I get so anxious at home that I have to leave and go for a drive (no matter the time of day), and I cannot remember the last time I had a good night of sleep.

I try to handle everything on my own, and I really hate talking to anyone about what is going, but I have realized I cannot continue to do that. I have put everyone else before myself, and in return, my mental health has severely declined. I put on a good front where no one would ever expect what I go through on a daily basis. I have just recently started counseling, and I believe it will help extremely. The saying "you can't judge a book by its cover" cannot be any truer than to me and my situation.

Copyright © Dana (name changed to protect identity). Reprinted by permission.

What We Learn From Dana's Story

I have known Dana for several years now and I can say without exception that she is one of the bravest young ladies I have ever met. She has a confidence that will sustain her for any aspirations that she has after college. She has a very strong desire to help others who have gone through the same thing she has experienced.

Dana is very understanding of the impact that her mother's boyfriend has had on her life, but she refuses to let him control her life and will stand against him in protecting her family.

Recently Dana spoke at an event bringing awareness to domestic violence. As she spoke, I could see many in the audience being physically moved by her story. Dana's strength in sharing her story is exemplary. She has blossomed into a strong woman who knows her path and refuses to allow this man in her mother's life to control her any longer.

Intimate Partner Violence in College

This story is very typical for Intimate Partner Violence and manipulation that occur on college campuses. Many young women are away from their parents. Friends that they make while at school are generally those, they associate with the most in college. Oftentimes, there are those that have taken advantage of young college men and women that are on a campus for their first time. I could tell you story after story that I have heard from victims and from my investigations with my work, preparing reports for the courts on sexual assault cases. Sometimes the stories start to sound like a scene from the movie "Ground Hog Day." Where someone lives the same day over and over. Many times, we as professionals hear these stories and we say to our co-workers, or ourselves it seems like I have heard that story before.

In Chapter Three we talked about grooming. College men that take advantage of others, often will use their grooming tactics to lure women in and use them for selfish purposes. They create trust, then they keep moving them into a position where they can have sex with them and become possessive of them.

Kathy was one of those young college girls that I met while I was teaching school in Utah. Kathy was a student in the Psychology program but was minoring in criminal justice. She was taking a victimology course from me and I was talking about the importance of reporting crimes against men and women on college campuses so that we can not only hold the perpetrator accountable, but also help the victim survivors with their journey of healing. I brought in a guest speaker who shared her story of abuse on a college campus.

After the presenter had come and spoke, Kathy approached me and said that she was experiencing something similar and needed some help and did not know what to do. I of course put her in touch with the school counselors and they took it from there in getting her some help. She lived about 7 hours from her parents. She visited them about once a month but did not have a great deal of contact with them. She was close to them, but what was happening to her on campus she felt responsible for.

Kathy began a relationship with a young man from California. His father was a successful businessman and was very wealthy and they lived in a large home in Southern California. Alex grew up privileged and felt a lot of power and control because he had learned that from his father in business and by the way he treated his own mother.

Alex grew up accustomed to women not working, but staying at home, cooking, cleaning, and taking the kids to the soccer games. The man is the only one who works in the home and the wife basically is at their beckon call. Alex's mom was very passive and just did what his dad would tell her to do. She would not complain because she had everything she wanted, a nice house, etc.

Alex's sister was going to college in Utah and he wanted to venture out, so he moved to Utah to be close to his sister and check out the college scene. He claimed to Kathy that he was thinking about college and soon after he met Kathy he enrolled in school.

Kathy shared with me that she was scared of her shadow and did not know what to do. To this day from time to time I have talked with Kathy. She will call me occasionally and share news of her life with me. She is now married and has two children. She has a part-time job at a law firm as a paralegal and hopes to use her Psychology Degree. I have not seen her for several years, but recently in talking to her, I asked her if I could share her story. She agreed.

I first want to say how proud I am of Kathy. She is amazing. She met her husband after college back in 2011 and got married soon after that. She indicated to me how appreciative she is of everyone that helped her during one of the most difficult times in her life. Here is her story in her own words.

Kathy Meets Alex

College was not the typical experience for me like it is for most people. It was a living hell. It all started out good. I made friends quickly, had a boyfriend, and was learning a lot. I met a girl named Felicia my very first semester, in my very first class, Anatomy. Felicia was from Paris, France and still had a very heavy accent. English was her second language so I "took her under my wing." Helping Felicia understand the material was helping me to learn the material as well. I often would go with her to her apartment and that's where this story begins.

There, she lived with four roommates all from the United States; she was the only foreign student in that apartment. One of her roommates had an older brother that would hang out at their apartment. Since I was there all the time helping Felicia, we all became friends. Felicia and her roommate Emma and I became friends. We would go to different places together and I would hang out with them all the time. Alex was Emma's brother. He would come along with us. As time progressed Alex told me one day when I was over at Felicia's apartment that he decided that he was going to go to school and wanted me to go with him to enroll. I went with him. Eventually Felicia and Emma started getting very busy with their schedules and Alex would ask me if I wanted to go and hang out with him and study now that he was going to school. I would go and hangout with some of his friends and their girl-friends. We would all just hang out. We all liked dancing so we would go to a local club a lot and dance.

First Signs That Something Was Wrong

Within the next 2 years I would experience things so hard for me that I still remember them vividly. This is the first. One night, Alex and I had gone to the basketball game at the rival university in an adjacent city. I left my car on campus and I drove with Alex to the game. He drove me back to campus to retrieve my car after the game, I lived a few blocks off campus, and it was winter and really cold outside. I remember it was snowing and really cold that night. When we got to my car, I went over and turned my car on and came back to his car so my car could be warming up.

Once we got to my car we were just small talking in his car. We were talking about the game and the rival between the two universities. It was then that I heard the *click* of the doors re-locking. I can still hear the lock clicking in my mind. He got this inappropriate sneer on his face and said, "I want to kiss you." I kind of had a boyfriend, so feeling some loyalty and the fact he locked the doors, I retorted "NO!" I was trying to open the door; but to no avail. My back was flat against the door with my right hand behind me still trying to work the lock on the door. He was persistent that he wanted a kiss. Again, I angrily retorted "NO!" It was at that time that he told me that I wasn't getting out of the car without kissing him. Still fiddling with the lock, I told him that he would have to take it from me because I sure wasn't going to give it to him. He slunk across that front seat to the passenger side and kissed me. Very slowly. He slunk back over to the drivers' side of the car and FI-NALLY unlocked the doors, and did not say anything else to me, other than, "good night?" The drive back to my apartment was horrible. I was hysterical, scraping my mouth, and calling my boyfriend. My boyfriend was pissed; not at me, but with him.

The Manipulation and Control Continue

I did not see him for a while. Sometime later, my boyfriend and I split up mutually due to distance. One thing led to another and before I recognized it, I was in a relationship with Alex and began to realize that I was essentially becoming Alex's property.

He was so very controlling, manipulative, and paranoid. He would make fake Facebook accounts and constantly stalk my friends and me on social media. He contacted my old boyfriend even posing as a girl and in a private message would ask *my old boyfriend if I did anything sexually with him? My old boyfriend felt trapped in his questions and made up stuff as to not "look like less of a man." And I can't blame him for it since we were together for two years. Alex would then take that information and berate me as a liar, whore, and every other deplorable adjective. He used social media to destroy me.*

Alex would make everything my fault. I remember one time I met a student who I became friends with. We were not interested in a relationship but were just friends. I had invited him over to my apartment to do some studying and just talk. This student was having a really hard time with just the bad hand that life had dealt him. He was very reserved to an alarming level. I worked with him to finally gain his trust. This is where my next vivid memory comes into play.

This student was finally opening up about the horrific tragedies that he had experienced as a child, his upbringing, and how it got him to where he was at now. I gave him my complete and undivided attention. This included the silencing of my cell phone and turning it over so that I would not get distracted. We were talking in my apartment. All my roommates were in the apartment in the kitchen or room, but we were not alone in the apartment.

Well, apparently, Alex was trying to get ahold of me and I wasn't responding and he was pissed. He came to my apartment, just walked in and started screaming at me for not answering him. I immediately told the student it might be better if he would leave. He left my apartment and walked back to the campus.

His Behavior Was Escalating

After the student left, Alex was on the south side of the room and I, yet again was with my back to the north wall of the living room. He was screaming in my face; my roommates did not know what to do and stayed away from us. He was so close that I can still smell the spices on his breath. I took a few steps away from him to create a space between us. He picked up a chair and threw it at me from across the room. I dodged the chair and that infuriated him. He flew across the room and had me pinned up against the north wall with his body. He hit the wall next to either side of my face a few times while continuing to yell in my face. I was stuck. Once he finally felt satisfied, he stepped back and said "You can never say that I ever hit you. . . . I never physically hit you"; then left my apartment. My roommates were stunned and did not know what to say.

His anger was out of control. There were times he would get so angry that he would punch anything. One time in our apartment he punched the side window and cracked the window. He also broke the mirror on my car because I would not go study with him.

Physical and Emotional Abuse to Sexual Assault

I will never forget this night, he told me that we were going to hang out at the dance club. When I got into the car and we were driving I said, "We are not going to the club, where are you going?" He said, "I am taking you somewhere special a place different than our normal places." I was on high alert because I needed to be prepared for whatever demented thing he was planning. This day will forever haunt me and I wish I never had to relive it in my mind. He drove and told me that he got a HOTEL ROOM. I was a virgin, saving myself for marriage. I didn't want to have sex, especially with him. I made that abundantly clear to him. He said, with the same awful sneer on his face, "You want to bet? He said, "We will have sex, understand?"

As you can guess, he went into a store, and I know he picked up some condoms. I can still remember that CVS Pharmacy he stopped at. We got to the room. It literally looked like something straight out of the movie Psycho. I literally thought that someone probably had died in that room before. It was in the middle of nowhere! We got some Mexican food and brought it with us to the hotel. We ate while watching TV. I am normally a very fast eater, I inhale food. But I ate very slowly trying to buy myself some time. I thought I was in the clear; but I was very wrong.

He then went to the bathroom, and came out of the bathroom naked and said, "Are you ready for me?" I said "NO." He asked again, and I was silent this time. He got this look in his eyes as if he was looking straight through my soul and it shook me to my core. He made me say the word "yes" all by itself out loud. After I said it, I asked why. He said that since I just said "yes" that I had just consented to what was about to happen. He got that look again and it scared me to my very core.

I just kept telling myself to "just endure for now. . . . It will be over soon. . . . I don't want to know the capable actions behind that horrific gaze. Thankfully, for me, it didn't last but a few moments and yet again, that was my fault. I didn't bleed because it was shallow and only a few moments before he finished so again, I was called every deplorable name that one can be called for "lying about being a virgin."

Trapped

That was the start of 1 ½ years of living hell. Filled with forced consent sexual encounters, and an unending amount of verbal abuse. My parents started asking me if I was okay when I would call. I knew that lying to my parents would take time to repair the lost trust that I was about to inflict upon myself. But lying to Alex, I didn't know what would happen to me and I wasn't about to find out. I would rather take initially lying to my roommates and parents and having to put in the work to regain their trust in order to stay safe enough to eventually make it up to them. I was in full blown survival mode.

Two times, in particular, I can remember us being in a parking lot and having police officers roll up on us. Again, that was my fault. One police officer repeatedly asked me if I was being held against my own free will. Inside I was SCREAMING! But my now distant demeanor kept reassuring the officer that I was here on my own free will out of blatant fear. I never thought that I would be "that girl."

We fought all the time. During one of our fights, I told him I was turning off my phone. Well, since he is controlling, that was not an acceptable response because that meant that he didn't have control. Once I turned off my phone, he lost that control. So, he did what he could to try to take that control back. He contacted my roommates and told them that he had not heard from me and that I had said something to him about leaving college and going off on my own and leaving town. For obvious reasons, my roommates were concerned and called my parents trying to get ahold of me. He wanted his control back. A couple hours later I turned my phone back on and had multiple missed calls and messages from my roommates and parents. He lied to them to try to regain that control.

During another fight I was on my way to work from school and I told him that I couldn't talk. I worked in our local movie theater. I hated the job because I was always in fear I would see him. That night, I walked into work and one of my managers noticed that I was "off" that day. She asked what was wrong and I said that I was fine. She didn't buy it and asked again. I told her what was going on and she told me to let Alex know that they are cracking down on friends visiting and that I could get fired. She assured me that I wouldn't actually get in trouble, so I told him what she said. To hopefully have him leave me alone . . . even if it was for a few mere hours of my shift. My phone buzzed with a response and I instantly started sobbing big crocodile tears.

I flipped my phone around to show my manager his response. It read, "I don't care what they say, see you soon!" My manager kept me in the office and called our loss prevention associate into the office to show a picture of him. They kept an eye out for him to arrive. I was with a male coworker at all times that shift. When he showed up, our loss prevention staff let us know and my coworker instantly took me to the dock of the store where only associates were allowed. They couldn't kick him out since he hadn't done anything on property, so I was to stay where I was until he left. He stayed around for a while and finally left. He would leave notes on my car and would have friends follow my every movement.

Another time, he went with his friends on a weekend trip for a couple of days and when he returned, he said to me, "So you fucked around on me while I was gone!? He called me a fucking whore in front of his friends!" Unaware of what he was talking about in the slightest, he showed me a picture. The picture, at a quick glance, looked like me. But upon closer inspection (that no one would do) you could tell it wasn't me. She was missing a scar on her forehead, a mole on her neck, her breasts were the wrong size, and her stomach was fatter, amongst other discrepancies. He said that he would send the photo to everyone on social media to show that I was a whore and that no one would look at it like I had. They would have "photo proof."

He was an emotional abuser. He would tell me that I was worthless, a disappointment to my family, I would never amount to anything, and every single nasty adjective that one can think of. He said that I would never graduate college and that I was a complete joke of a human being and a total waste of space.

Enough – I had to Stop This Relationship

When I finally got out, I knew it could get worse. But in all honesty, I was fed up, and quite frankly I didn't care. I was tired, sexually, mentally, and emotionally. I just wanted to feel again. I wanted to feel something other than the numbness and fear that had overcome me for one and a half years. My anger and hatred were feelings that I finally felt other than being numb. I started swearing a lot once I found my voice against him. I refused to be silenced anymore. Although I don't like how much I swear now, it has a subliminal message to me. My voice. I will never be silenced again.

Alex said I was too lazy and dumb to finish school. Ironically, Alex ended up dropping out of college and never finished school, but I was still there! I was convinced that he only went to college to control me, he never really wanted to go to school, at least his behavior showed me that until he had met me at his sister's apartment on campus.

After I broke off my dysfunctional relationship with him and he left college, he was still getting desperate for control over me. On one occasion, after campus had closed, one of my friends walked me to my vehicle to make sure that I was safe. While at my car, I was facing my vehicle and my back was to the road while my friend was giving me a hug goodnight. A vehicle drove down the street and made a U-turn to head back in our direction. That was not uncommon on that portion of the side street. I thought it was the campus police officer, but I wasn't that lucky—it was Alex. Since he didn't get the last word with me, this was what he was looking for—me. He slowed down by my car and yelled out, "So, who did you fuck tonight?" and with that same sick smile and horrific laugh, he drove off all proud of himself as he sped off. The next day, I filed a restraining order against him downtown and on campus.

My final semester of college, I went to a play on campus. While at dinner before the play, I looked to my left and there he was. I could never get away from him. I instantly felt ill and fled to the nearest restroom. My mother who was with me chased in after me since I had turned completely ghost white. He destroyed me. My mom knew it and I knew my dad knew it.

When I graduated, we went to my favorite restaurant to eat. There he was again eating at the restaurant with that same snickering look on his face. I thought to myself, I am decked out with my multiple honors, my graduation robe, cords, and pins. It was ironic since he said that I would never graduate.

For a while I was unable to look at certain colors because I would always see "Alex" and have an anxiety attack. If I heard certain songs, I would hear Alex. It was like he hijacked my mind and was still tormenting me. I would lie to my family about the stupidest things because that's all I knew for almost two years. I was put on depression medications for a year and a half after everything.

I REFUSE to let him control any more of me. He gave me the backbone that I thought I always had. I will NEVER be silenced or suppressed ever again.

Copyright © Kathy Carlston. Reprinted by permission.

Perpetrators Use of Revenge Porn

We hear this term, but what does it mean? I wanted to point this out because of what we learned from Kathy's story. Kathy shared with us that Alex threatened to release a picture to his friends showing someone that looked similar to her as a way of showing what a "slut" she was.

"Revenge porn is a form of cyber sexual harassment or, in some cases, cyber-bullying, and should be taken very seriously, particularly if minors (those under the age of 18 years old) are the subject of the revenge porn." https://criminal.findlaw.com/criminal-charges/revenge-porn-laws-by-state.html

Offenders use this all the time to control, manipulate, humiliate, and destroy the reputation of young men and women using porn. Alex used this to control Kathy and thought nothing of it. Social media as we discussed in Chapter Two is a tool that is being used by predators, abusers and those that have little or no social values in the respect of human beings and all sense of decency.

In Kathy's situation, he was attempting to use this photo to control her and manipulate her in being forced to stay in the relationship. This is used by many to not only show control, but as a way of objectifying the person and threatening them to ruin their relationship by releasing the photo.

There have been some victims of revenge porn who have been so humiliated with the photographs that were released on social media that they felt there was no other option and committed suicide.

Evidence that this is a problem was found in this article on a young woman that was threatened by her boyfriend and he eventually released some sexually explicit photos on the Internet showing her performing a sexual act on him. https://www.foxnews.com/world/man-whose-girlfriend-committed-suicide-after-he-threatened-to-send-revenge-porn-to-her-family-may-face-manslaughter-charges.print

This problem is real, and we as a society must understand that there are many methods to control and manipulate victims of intimate partner violence. Revenge porn is just one of those ways where victims are controlled by their abuser with the threat or actual release of material to embarrass or humiliate their victims.

What an opportunity we have as members of our society to stand up against this type of manipulation and control of offenders. Part of our responsibility is if we see this happening we must speak out, protect, and report this type of abuse to the authorities.

Because of the emotional trauma associated with the release of such material, we need to make sure we concentrate on helping the victims of this type of abuse recognize that it was not their fault. We need to help them on their road to recovery and to understand that they can heal and do not have to let it control the rest of their lives through low self-esteem, embarrassment, or shame.

Kathy's Healing

Though Kathy still suffers from the memories of her assailant, she has found her journey of survival. Kathy's path is now one of having her family supporting her and being sure of herself and knowing that although this remains a memory, she also recognizes that she was able to find her way out of a manipulative and controlling relationship and that she is a survivor!

I want to thank Kathy for the beautiful example she is of a strong woman that did not let her victimization keep her a victim, it taught her how to be a survivor. She tells me whenever we speak that she wants others to know her story, to know that if they are trapped, they are not alone and that there are others that can help. Each woman in this world is strong enough to find their path to healing and truly hold their head up high as a survivor and know that no one will ever control them again!

Recently I asked Kathy to speak at a domestic violence event. She was so excited and agreed to do so. As I listened to her speak, the confidence she has developed within herself is inspiring and gives me continued hope that those survivors that are not held back by those that have offended them and have found their way forward, clearly are examples of those who chose not to be a victim, but a survivor!!! Thank you for your example Kathy!

Nicole's Story: "If I Can't Have You No One Can."

This last story in this chapter comes from Nicole. I met Nicole many years ago. She openly shared her story with me and I was so moved by her willingness to tell her story, knowing that she had gone through a very traumatic experience with a man that she had met. Here is Nicole's story.

Through My Eyes, by Nicole:

A friend of mine introduced me to Robert; he was kind, charming, and fun to be around. We started seeing each other and within a few months we were spending a lot of time together. I would stay at his house or he would stay at mine since we lived almost an hour away from each other. In this stage of the relationship things were great we had a good time, things looked like they were going in the right direction. Robert gave me a ring and we discussed long term plans for our relationship.

After we had been dating for about six months or so, on Friday 13th of October in 2000 we had made lunch plans. I was going to drive to his work, and we would go to lunch together since I was not working that day. It was raining when I was driving and on the way my car hydroplaned and smashed into the wall on the freeway. I was terrified and shaken by the event but grateful I was not hurt, and my car was still drivable. At this point in my life I did not have a cell phone but a good Samaritan stopped and allowed me to use their phone to call the police and Robert to let him know what had happened and that I would be later than we had planned. Once I finally arrived at to his work I was still shaken, he met me in the parking lot came out and asked "Am I going to kill you for the damage you did to the car?" This struck me as odd, but he played it off as if he were joking around. I recall this being the first time I began feeling at all uncomfortable around Robert.

A couple weeks later Robert asked me about moving in with him, I told him I owned my house, it was close to my job, my family, and my friends, I had no desire to sell it and move. After asking a few times he began making a joke and would say, "What do I need to do to get you to move in with me, burn down your house?" I didn't think much of it at the time but a few weeks later, I came home at midnight from work and my back door was wide open. I walked in that door to figure out what was going on and noticed a terrible odor. My roommate must have heard me because she opened the door to the kitchen and said, "Don't turn on the light switch, there was a fire earlier, the fire department was here and put it out, they said things should be ok now but let's not chance it."

My roommate and I went to stay in a hotel while the restoration company did repairs at my home. Robert came to the hotel for a few nights and things were fine while we were at the hotel. Finally after about a week we were able to return to my house, the first night we were back at the house Robert and his cousin Justin came over. Robert began acting weird and I decided to ask him to go back home the next day and told him I just couldn't do this anymore. Meaning I wanted to be done with the relationship. The next day when I returned home from work, I noticed he had taken all of his belongings and was gone, I was relieved. When my roommate got home, she informed me she was moving out because things were too weird at my house and she felt like we (Robert and I) were both just crazy. I was confused but could not change her mind about moving.

About a week later I got home from work and had a voicemail on my house phone from Robert, I still did not have a cell phone at this time. The voicemail sounded urgent and as if something was wrong, so I called Robert back. When he answered he said, "Why are you calling me we are over, stop calling me." I said ok and hung up, I was very confused because I was returning his call. Less than five minutes later my phone rang, and it was Robert, it sounded as if he were in a tunnel and I assume he was in the bathroom. He said to me "Who have you been talking to? Who have you been seeing?" I responded and said I am not doing this and asked him to hold on because my other line was ringing. My phone was not ringing but I figured I needed to record the conversation to show my friend what was going on, I clicked over to my other line and called my phone number on 3-way calling, of course my voicemail picked up and after it beeped I linked the calls. I told Robert we were over and to stop calling me, he then said, "They are after you, they put a green light out on you and I can protect you." I told him we couldn't be together and asked who is coming after me? He said, "They want to kill you." I ended the conversation by saying please leave me alone and don't call me anymore.

A week went by and I did not hear anything from Robert until one night some friends were at my house visiting when my phone rang, it was Robert. I again told him I had nothing to say to him, he asked who was at my house. I ended the call and my female friend had gotten a call on her cell phone and needed to leave and asked if I could drive my other friend home, I agreed and she left. As we were getting ready to go there was a knock on my door, when I opened it, Robert was standing there looking frazzled. I asked if he was ok and said we are just leaving, he said he just needed to get a drink of water and he would go. I agreed he could come in and reminded him we were heading out the door. Robert went into my kitchen and got a drink while I grabbed my coat and we all walked out at the same time and left my house.

When I returned from taking my friend home, I had a missed call from the friend I had just dropped off, so I returned his call thinking he was going to tell me that he had left something at my house. I was wrong, he said, "Why did you give him my number?" I was confused and asked who? "Robert," he said. I responded, "I did not give him your number." We got off the phone and I started getting ready for bed. Then there was a knock on my door, I was not expecting anyone, it was late and I wanted to go to bed. I walked over and looked out the window on my door, it was Robert. I said "What do you want? I do not want to talk to you." Robert replied, "Please let me in, I just want to talk then I will leave. I promise."

I said okay, but only if you promise to go after and I opened the door. We talked for a while and he was kind and acting like his old sweet self. We talked for over an hour and it was late, and he asked if he could sleep on my couch, I agreed and went to bed in my room. When I woke up in the morning Robert was gone and nothing was out of place. After I got off work that day I was in my kitchen and noticed a small cold breeze, so I checked my window and it was unlocked and open a crack. This was especially strange because I always kept my windows locked, it was December so there was no reason I would have had it unlocked or open. I knew at that moment that he had unlocked it while he was "getting a drink of water" and must have climbed in while I was gone taking my friend home. He had checked my caller ID and that's how he got my friends number and who knows what else he did while he was alone in my house. I called my friend and told him what I discovered and that I was worried, then I asked him to call Robert and tell him to please leave me alone and that I did not want anything to do with him any longer.

A few weeks went by and I had not heard from Robert, I was relieved. It was New Years and a new beginning. On New Year's Day 2001, I worked the night shift and got off work at midnight just as I had many other nights, nothing out of the ordinary. When I got home, I wanted to check on one of my friends that was in the hospital, so I called the nurse station and they put me on hold. While I was waiting, I heard a knock at my door, which was odd because it was late, so I hung up and walked over to look out the window on the door, it was Robert. I said, "Go away we have nothing left to talk about, we are over." Robert responded, "I just want to get my rings and I will go." I said "No, who is with you?" He responded, "Nobody, I am alone, I just want my rings, if you ever loved me you would let me in." My heart sank because I had loved him, so then I said, "Okay, but only to get your rings and then you need to leave."

I opened the door; he came in and almost immediately began asking me "Did you call the cops on me?" I responded, "No, why would I?" Just as I said that there was another knock on my door, I said I am not excepting anyone, don't answer it. Robert walked over and opened the door anyway; it was his cousin Justin. Just as I saw him a scared feeling came over me, I was unsure of what was going on, confused because he said he was alone. Justin stood against the wall with his hands behind his back, but I noticed he had gloves on. I then said, "Here I'll grab your ring, it is in my bedroom"; I hurried into my bedroom and grabbed his ring and took it to him in the living room. I noticed Justin was no longer in my house and my phone was missing.

I handed Robert the ring and he asked where his other ring was, I said it was in my car, I would get it for him, and I grabbed my coat and keys. On the way out of the house I locked my door not wanting them back in my house. I got into the passenger side of my car and grabbed the other ring and handed it to Robert. Robert motioned for Justin who was sitting in Robert's truck parked on the street, Justin walked through my yard to my house carrying a big black gun. I remember thinking what is going on, what am I going to do, my thoughts were interrupted by Robert saying, "If you scream, he will shoot you, if you try to run he will shoot you. You are going with us, and if you don't, he will shoot you." I looked around at my neighbors' houses hoping someone would come out but nothing, complete silence in my neighborhood, as if the world was standing still.

At this point I felt I had no choice but to get into his truck. Robert asked me about my friend that was in the hospital, I figured if I could get him to go there, I could get away from them and whatever they were planning. He began to drive towards the hospital then turned and went to opposite way and got onto the freeway and headed south. Robert asked me if I wanted a beer, I said no and he said, "You should have a beer, it will be your last, you're not going to make it through the night." After this comment, I decided that I was going to smoke a cigarette and when I was finished, I stuffed the butt far into the seat behind me, so that if something did happen the police might be able to find my DNA. I hid several cigarette butts in the seat of his truck.

Robert drove for over an hour as he continued to make comments about me being dead or me not making it through the night, Justin did not say much the whole time we were driving. Robert then said to Justin, "We need gas, I need to get off the freeway and find a gas station." When we pulled up to a gas station Justin got out of the truck and said he would put the gas in. I said that I had to go to the bathroom, but Robert grabbed my arm and would not let me out of the truck and said we would stop somewhere else so I could use the bathroom. We were the only vehicle at the gas station. I noticed a man inside the gas station working and I tried to honk the horn to get his attention, but Robert saw what I was trying to do and grabbed both of my hands and held them close to him. Justin finished putting in the gas and said to Robert, "I put $20 in, I just used my card, so we don't have to go inside." Justin got back into the truck and Robert pulled out of the gas station.

We drove through the little town and up a dark road until he found a pullout, he backed his truck into it. He got out and pulled me towards the driver's door and said, "You can pee here." He walked me to the back of his truck and I just looked at him, honestly, I didn't even really have to pee so I said, "Well can you at least turn around," so he walked back to the truck and got in. I looked around as I pretended to go to the bathroom trying to figure out how I could get away. I recall seeing a little house across the street a little way down the street in front of his truck and behind the truck there was a large field with cows or horses in it with a large house up a hill on the other side of the field. I remember thinking as I looked into the field, I wonder how far I would get before they would shoot me in the back. Just as I was trying to figure out how to get through the fence, I saw headlights from a car coming up the road. Unfortunately, Robert saw it too and ran back where I was and grabbed me pulling me to my feet, pulling me to his door, and pushed me into the truck as he jumped in as well. Just as he closed the door the car drove in front of us, it was a police car, I tried to push the horn again, but he grabbed my arms and pinned them against me this time until the car passed.

Robert waited a moment until the cop was way past us and heading the hill and he pulled out and drove the opposite direction then quickly got back on the freeway going south again. At this point we were almost 65 miles south of my house, I was terrified and had no idea what they were planning, but I knew I needed to *figure out how I was going to get away. Robert drove another 30 miles south before he exited the freeway and drove down a dark road that I recognized from when we were dating. His friends had their horses on this road; they had a stable and a barn on this property.*

Robert stopped in the middle of the road in front of a horse property that I recognized as belonging to his friend Karen where we had come here once before when things were good. Both Robert and Justin got out of the truck. As they were getting out Robert said to Justin, "Don't shoot her until she is in the well, the well is over there" Justin disappeared somewhere behind where I couldn't see. I noticed Robert had left the keys in the ignition. I knew this was my last opportunity to try to get away and I slid myself over into the driver's seat. I saw Robert began unzipping his pants to relieve himself on the side of his truck near his door, so I kicked him away and pulled the door closed. I held the door with my left hand because I did not know how to lock it and it all happened so quickly. I then started the truck with my right hand and put the truck in gear. I was trying to hold the door closed with my left hand and Robert was pulling on it from the outside. Just as I pushed the gas pedal Robert got the door open and jumped in, I had the gas pedal floored, I heard a gunshot, and the truck stopped all at the same time. I did not realize Robert was stepping on the brake until later when the break overpowered the gas.

Robert then got out of the truck taking the keys this time to see what happened to his truck. As both Justin and Robert were out of the truck, I remembered they had put their cell phones in the glove box, so I opened it and grabbed one of the cell phones and locked the passenger's door where they were standing. Robert ran around the truck jumped in the driver's door and grabbed me by my throat pushing me down to the seat and he began to strangle me. Justin started yelling at Robert "We have to get out of here, someone had to of heard that." Just as I felt like I was going to pass out Robert released his grip on my neck, he grabbed the phone away from me, unlocked the passenger's door, then got off of me and sat in the driver's seat again. I sat up and Justin got into the truck, Robert started to drive away.

I was desperate, I now knew they were serious, and they wanted to kill me, not just scare me. I told them I had money and I could pay to fix the damage from the gunshot if they just let me go. Robert did not believe me, so I said he could call my bank and the automated system would tell him how much is in my account. I had just received the check from the insurance company to pay for the fire damage. Justin got his phone out and I told him the number to call for my bank and I entered my account access info into the phone. Justin verified I had a significant amount of money in my account and told Robert, "Let's just get the money."

Robert drove through the small town and we ended up at Karen's trailer court, we had been there before as well months before. Robert had started dating Karen after we broke up. Robert got out of the truck and told Justin to wait there, so Justin and I stayed in the truck. Justin apologized to me saying, "I'm so sorry, I did not want anyone to get hurt." I begged Justin to let me go while Robert was inside. I said, "Just tell him I got away, I will run and figure out how to get home." Justin refused saying, "I can't but I really am sorry." Just then Robert opened his door to the truck and got back in but he was not alone, Karen was right behind him.

I begged Karen to help and asked her to tell him to just let me go. Those words fell on deaf ears as Karen without missing a beat, said, "This is your shit, you have to deal with it." Karen talked to Robert for a few more minutes and we left her house heading back north on the freeway. Robert continued to come up with ideas to try to cover up what he had done, one was to take the truck to Deer Creek Reservoir and put the truck and me into the water. I again begged him, pleading that I would give him the money if he would just let me go. At this point Justin said he was done and wanted to go home, so Robert drove to his house which was about an hour north of where we were and was also just over halfway to my house.

When we arrived at Justin's house only Justin got out and he took the big gun with him, I felt relieved and I felt that Robert had deescalated and was going to take me home and let me go. We drove north towards my house and Robert wanted me to call my friend that was at my house the night he stopped by and tell him I did not want anything to do with him. It was very early in the morning and I did not want to call and wake him, but he insisted. Robert dialed the number and began talking to him, he said, "Nicole is with me and she has something to tell you," then he held the phone towards me and I was able to get out, "He took me and won't let me go." Robert pulled the phone away from me at that point and said something to my friend that I don't remember and hung up. Robert then warned me he had another gun in his bag.

When we finally got back to my house it was about 4:30 or 5:00 am in the morning. I was happy to be home alive and quickly got out of the truck hoping to get into the house before he could get to the door. It didn't work, he was on my heels as I opened the door and we went inside. I said, "The bank opens at nine," and I sat on the couch. Robert came over and laid on top of me on the couch so I couldn't get away and we both fell asleep. I woke to the sound of my alarm playing music in my bedroom only a couple hours later. Robert rolled a little and I was able to sneak out from beneath him and go turn off the alarm before it woke him, as I did, I noticed he had brought a bag inside and my phone was sitting on top of it.

Knowing I was scheduled to be at work in only a few hours I hooked the phone back up and took it into the stairway. I called a co-worker to cover my shift and told him a little about what was happening and told him I just needed him to cover my shift so I could get things figured out, he agreed and we hung up the phone. Then I called my friend in the hospital and told her what was going on and she told me to call the police and I begged her not to because I was so afraid of what might happen if the police showed up. She said she would not call them, but I better check back in with her in an hour or she would call, I promised. As I walked back into the kitchen Robert woke up and jumped off the couch asking, "Did you call the police?" I told him that I had not, that I had called a co-worker to cover my shift and he seemed to believe me.

Robert then demanded I take all of my clothes off and he began questioning every bruise, scratch, and mark on my body. Just then the phone rang, and I ran to answer it. My friend that was in the hospital had called her mother and she was calling me to check on me. She asked if I was alone and I responded no, she then said, "If you are not alone . . ." Robert grabbed my other phone out of his bag and quickly plugged it in ". . . in an hour . . ." (She must of heard him pick up the line) and she ended with ". . . we will go to lunch." I agreed and hung up the phone. Robert hung up as well frantic, saying "She is coming over, we have to get out of here." I reminded him that the bank would be open soon so we can wait and just go to the bank at 9 when they open. He threw clothes at me and told me to get dressed because we are leaving.

I put clothes on but did not intend to leave with him. He pulled me outside and then I saw my friends mom drive up my road, I was afraid he would hurt her if she were to stop so I jumped into his truck and said to go to my bank to get his money then he could go. He began driving and I told him to turn right at the end of my street, instead he turned left, and I told him he was going the wrong way and he needed to pull over so I could get out. He began driving faster and got onto the freeway, this time heading east. I began thinking if I jump, I might survive and I wondered how fast we were going, I grabbed the door handle and was thinking about jumping out. We were going about 70 mph; I was scared and did not know what to do or where he was taking me. The miles increased between my home, he was driving up the canyon and I knew if I jumped, it would take too long for help to come if they were able to find me in time. So, I decided against jumping and decided when he stopped I would get out and run, I would get away. Robert had no intentions of taking me to my bank, he had other plans.

We ended up about 65 miles east of my home before he finally stopped at another gas station. As soon as he stopped, I said I have to use the bathroom and I jumped out of the truck and walked as fast as I could into the gas station. When I got inside, I looked around and saw the restrooms, I walked past some truck drivers sitting at the tables and mouthed, "Help me" but I do not think they noticed. I went into the bathroom and my heart hit the floor there was no window for me to crawl out, I had no choice but to walk out the same door I walked in knowing he would be standing there waiting. I took as long as I could, but eventually came out and as I predicted he was standing there waiting for me.

We walked into the main area of the gas station where there were shelves, he began talking to me as if I was just being a grumpy girlfriend. Robert said, "Oh come on honey, it will be ok, lets just go." I noticed there was a stairway behind him in the opposite direction as the door to outside. I knew this would be my last chance to get away if I was going to be able to so I said, "Ok, I will follow you." He began walking towards the door and I ran as fast as I could up the stairs not having a clue what could be up there. When I reached the top, I saw a lady and some doors with numbers on them, I asked can I go in one of those doors. She said of course and I ran to the door and went in locking the door behind me.

It was pitch black in the room after I closed the door, I left the light off and tried my hardest to be quiet but my breath was heavy from running up the stairs and my heart was pounding like a drum. I listened at the door but all I could hear is the thump of my heart. It felt like ten or fifteen minutes had passed before I slowly opened the door and peeked out. Nobody was out there so I walked over to a window and looked outside. I saw Roberts truck pull into a parking spot in front of the store, so I ran back into the door that had saved me and quietly closed the door. Listening again my heart was a little quieter but was still the only sound I heard. This time it felt like forever before I opened the door again, when I checked the window this time, I saw Roberts truck driving away from the gas station towards the highway.

Relieved, I let out a deep breath and walked back to the door that saved me, turned on the light, and found that it was a shower for truck drivers. I started for the stairs, I walked down slowly and peeked around the corner, I heard a woman's voice from the counter say, "He's gone, we told him we didn't know where you went." When my eyes got to the counter, I noticed it was the lady that had let me go into the shower room upstairs and tears filled my eyes, it was over. I finally got away after twelve and a half hours.

The Sheriff arrived and took me to the Sheriff's office for questioning about what happened. I did not want to talk to the police out of fear that he would come after me again. Then an advocate came in and sat with me until a friend came to pick me up. Later, the advocate testified at his trial saying that when she came in the room that I was in the fetal position, rocking back and forth, crying, and very scared. I don't recall that at all, but I will never forget her testimony. I remember how frightened I was that he would find me or come after me again if I talked with police, so I gave them minimal information, I just wanted this to all be over.

When my friend arrived, she drove me to my house to get some clothes and my car. I went to stay at her house; I ended up staying with her for at least a week only going home if someone was with me to grab clothes. One day after work I did not have anyone to go to my house and I needed to grab something fast. I only planned to be there for a minute, just run in and run out. A couple seconds after I was inside, someone knocked on the door, my heart dropped and so did I. I crawled into the kitchen to look out the window to see who was knocking, fearful it was Robert. Relieved to see my parents, I quickly stood up and walked to the front room and opened the door, I told them I was on my way out and that I had somewhere I was supposed to be. They said, "Okay, we will finish what we came to do and lock the door on our way out."

I was very hypervigilant and terrified he would come back and kill me the next time. I had told my mom what had happened before they came over so she understood me needing to get out of the house. I never did find my courage to tell my stepfather before he died five years ago. My mom had told me that my stepdad had said to her that day, "What's wrong with Nicole, she looks like she saw a ghost?"

The next day, I decided the only way I would be safe is to go to the court and file for a Protective Order. The judge came out to talk to me and said he would sign the order, but when I come back for court if I had not filed a police officer report, he would dismiss the protective order. I felt like I had no other choice to keep me safe, so I left the court and drove to the police department and asked to speak to someone to make a report. A detective came to the lobby and we sat down, and I told him everything that had happened, it took well over an hour. Then in my opinion he said the worst thing an officer could say to someone who has gone through anything traumatic. He said, "Can you write that down for me?" I completely understand that he was just doing his job, but I just couldn't do it. He said you can take it home and call me when you are finished, I agreed and took the papers, his number, and left the police station. I wrote about a page of what had happened then I put it away and decided I would finish later, maybe. The judge told me I had to report it, I had done my part in my mind.

A few days later, my friend told me that she wanted me to go and speak with one of her friends, an FBI agent, about what had happened. I wasn't sure I wanted to or if I even trusted her completely, I still was not going to my house alone. After a while of talking, I agreed and she we arranged a time with the FBI agent. That morning I got up early and planned to leave before she came to get me, I did not plan on going with her, but she must have sensed this because she was early as well. I told her I did not want to go, at this time I trusted nobody including my friends. She said, "I will let you drive, and I will go with you and I will stay the whole time." I agreed to go but I told her I needed to go to work before I could meet with him. My friend came and sat in her car in the parking lot the entire time while I worked for a few hours. When I was finished working, I asked one of my co-workers to drive around to the back door and pick me up and take me home. He said, "I will drive you home, but you have to tell your friend, you cannot leave her out there, otherwise I won't drive you."

I was scared as I walked to the parking lot and told my friend I did not want to go meet her friend and that my co-worker was going to drive me home. My friend said, "I understand, we don't have to go, I will call him and tell him we are not coming, you can drive my car back, whatever makes you comfortable." I agreed and let my co-worker know the plan, I drove her car back and she was so kind and so understanding. She called her friend and he asked if he would talk to me over the phone, he asked if I would meet up with him somewhere that was comfortable for me. I said the only way I am meeting you is at the police station near my house, he agreed, and we arranged a time.

The time came for me to meet the FBI agent so I drove to the police station, my friend was waiting for me in the parking lot when I arrived, looking around I got out of my car and walked to my friend. We walked into the station and met with Detective Tony, he was a city detective assigned to the FBI He took us up some stairs and I remember seeing an officer I knew walking down the stairs, I was so nervous and scared all I could do was smile, like a big smile. I can't explain it, but I remember the other officer saying to me, "You look so happy," that was the farthest thing from what was going on inside me at that moment.

We got upstairs and I sat with Tony telling him what had happened, the same thing I had told the other detective a week before. When I finished this time, he asked me if I was willing to tell him again so he could type it up, this was better for me then having to write the entire thing, so I agreed. We finished up and left the police station, Tony told me he would see what he could do, but he was going on vacation the next week so it might be a couple weeks, I left with no hope they would do anything. One of the first things I did after I was safe was get me a cell phone and about a week and a half after I had meet with Tony I was driving, and my phone rang. I still remember exactly where I was when my phone rang, and I pulled over to take the call. It was Tony, calling to let me know they had arrested Robert and he was on his way to jail. I can't explain the feeling that came over me at that moment.

A few weeks later, I had to go to a meeting for work when I was driving home on the freeway and I saw a tow truck, didn't think much of it until I got closer and realized it was Robert's truck on the bed of the tow truck. I sped up and passed it not looking back, then my phone rang, it was Tony asking where I was and apologizing when he realized it was me in the little MR2 that had just flown past the tow truck he was riding in.

I went to court for the protective order and also the initial kidnapping charge the same day. They put in the permanent protective order in place, which is still currently in place today, 18.5 years later. This is about the time I first met Camille the prosecutor, she was great, and she was so kind through the entire court process, keeping me informed of what was going on, explaining everything, and making sure I was doing okay. About six months into the court process, Camille called me and told me that Justin and his attorney had met with her and Tony the day before. Justin told them his version of what had happened, there were only two small discrepancies in our version of events, one was the color of the gloves Justin was wearing and the other was which freeway we drove on, neither of those were issues for the case. Camille discussed my thoughts about them giving Justin a plea bargain for testifying against Robert, I felt like Robert instigated the entire thing and pulled Justin into it, so I agreed. When Justin went before the court, the judge decided not to follow the plea agreement because he had discharged the firearm, he decided to hold him more accountable, and gave him jail time but allowed the charge to be lowered.

It took almost two years before we had a trial date for Robert because he went through several attorneys. They would either quit or he would fire them when they would not do what he asked them to because his requests were unethical. Finally, in September 2002 we were ready for trial, Robert showed up without an attorney and the judge told him he had been given every opportunity to hire an attorney, so the trail was going to happen without Robert having an attorney. I testified and tried my best not to look in Robert's direction, however since he did not have an attorney, he was allowed to cross-examine me himself. I was terrified, but I found I knew I needed to stay strong and get through this.

The rest of the trial I could be in the courtroom, and it was very hard to listen to the testimony throughout the trial. I heard testimony on evidence in the truck that the bullet missed me by a quarter of an inch, it could have gone right through my back if I had been sitting an inch farther over. I think I cried most the way through the testimony from Justin, the advocate, Roberts's friend who he had planned this with.

Robert was found guilty at trial and was sentenced to 10 years to life for aggravated kidnapping. After he was sentenced, Tony drove me back to my car from the court, he told me "I don't know if I should tell you this or not, but when you first came and saw me I didn't believe you. I thought there is no way, but as I started the investigation the evidence proved what you said happened. I want you to know I apologize for not believing you." I said back to him "Tony, you did your job even though you had doubts and that is what makes you a good cop and a good guy, Thank you."

After sentencing, Robert appealed on the grounds of not having an attorney, he won the appeal, and the court said he did not knowingly and intelligently give up his right to counsel. It had been another couple year by this point and Camille had gone into private practice so we had to basically start over with new attorneys. Robert was in prison at this time even though he had won the appeal they kept him in custody.

It was about four years after the that day in January 2001 when Tony called me and asked if I would be willing to go with him to the locations of that night, I was nervous, but trusted Tony completely so I agreed. That morning he showed up to pick me up with Brenda and Bill, the new prosecution team. We drove to each of the locations only backward from the night this all happened, I think they were trying to decrease retraumatizing me, but they wanted to see firsthand the locations in preparation for the second trial. The first place we stopped was the gas station I escaped at, it looked the same to me despite a little remodel, but nothing big. Then we went to the other gas station we had stopped for gas. Then they asked me to guide them to the little road Robert stopped on so I could use the bathroom. I did not think I was going to be able to find it because the small town had grown and looked very different, but I just told them to turn as I remembered and we were able to locate the road and spot. It looked exactly as I had explained it to Tony all those years ago, he told me he was surprised I remembered.

The second trial resulted in Robert being found guilty once again. He was again sentenced to 10 years to life in prison for the kidnapping charge. During his incarceration, I was able to attend and speak at two parole hearings, even though the first was twelve years after that night. My voice still shook when I spoke and I was scared, but I felt like the parole board heard me at the first hearing.

The worst part of attending the parole hearings was the people who were there in support of Robert who were sitting a few rows behind my advocates and me. They kept making comments after I testified that I had to sit and listen to and the fear of running into them in the parking lot before or after the hearing. The entire time they were talking behind me saying that he would never do this, and I was such a liar. I contacted the board afterwards and told them what had happened. To my understanding, the board now handles these situations so that victims are not exposed to harassment from family members of the inmate, I just hope nobody has to ever go through that in the future when they attend a parole hearing and find their voice to testify there.

Last January, a year and a half ago, I was notified Robert had received a release date of June 2018 he would be on a monitor that would track his movement for six months and then he would be on straight parole. I knew this day would come but it was earlier than I hoped, I checked with the courts about my protective order to ensure it was still in place. I was a little nervous when the date came in June of 2018. The farther away from that date it gets the less I worry, I am still vigilant and always keep my house locked, pay attention if I am being followed, and take regular safety precautions. Overall, I think I am good, I am not a victim, I survived all of this and have found that by helping others helps me continue to grow stronger.

Since 2001 when this happened, I decided to change my life, I finished my ed-ucation, I completed my bachelor's and Masters in Criminal Justice, and I became a victim advocate myself. I love the work I do and the people I get to help every day, so they do not have to go through their journey alone.

Copyright © Nicole (last name omitted to protect privacy). Reprinted by permission.

I am amazed at the strength of Nicole. I have seen her accomplish some amazing things, including her current work as a domestic violent advocate. Truly her strength is derived from her ability to see past her victimization and see herself as a thriver. I remember when I was interviewing her for this book she called herself a thriver not a survivor. I thought it would be appropriate to use that term as I conclude this chapter.

Victim to Survivor to Thriver!

As I interviewed and put together this chapter of the courageous stories of these women who have gone through such difficult times of their lives, I am reminded of what Nicole told me when I referred to her as a survivor. She said, "I am not a survivor, I am a thriver." Nicole has taken a traumatic event in her life and has learned to cope with what happened to her, by helping others.

After Nicole's case, she turned her fear into a positive in her life. She went back to school and not only obtained her Bachelor's Degree in Criminal Justice, but went further and received her Master's Degree in Criminal Justice. She now is a victim ad-vocate working with victims of domestic violence.

When we look at what happens to the lives of those who are victims of crime, we generally see two paths that they may take. One path is one of shame and fear and the other is strength and determination to no longer be controlled by their offender.

We see so many wonderful people in our system become emotionally controlled by their offender's the rest of their lives. They cannot let go of the anger, of the fear that was caused by the offender, and as a result they continue to provide power to the offender to even control them years after the offender victimized them.

Clearly Nicole found a way to survive and thrive by reaching out to those who are suffering themselves or going through very similar emotions and fear that she experi-enced. She is helping them to find their path to healing and creating their new normal.

Nicole's passion is inspiring. She has spoken with me at National Conferences and in my classes at Weber State University, and never ceases to amaze me with her strength to survive and to thrive.

I recently found a quote that really is the essence of what Nicole has done in her life. The things that she has accomplished, the nightmares she has overcome, the strength that she has shown clearly places her in the category of a "Thriver!" When I read this quote by Maya Angelou I think of Nicole.

"My mission in life is not merely to survive, but to thrive; and to do so with some passion, some compassion, some humor, and some style."

https://www.brainyquote.com/topics/thrive

6

The Aftermath of Mass Shootings

Introduction

Over the last several years in America we have seen a great deal of traumatic events involving shootings and stabbings, attacking innocent people in our churches, schools, and in other public places. One cannot help but think about when and where it will happen next. I have heard many times from survivors that they never thought it would happen to them.

A few years ago, I was asked to come to a community where they had a mass shooting at a school on the west coast. One young man in the school said to me, "I never thought that it would happen in our school, especially with someone that I know." This young man was in shock that his friend would bring a gun to school and use it. The reality of this problem is that we cannot fully grasp the difficulty of going through a mass shooting until you have lived through the experience.

Over the last several years I have been involved in several mass shootings in many different capacities. I was looking through some statistics recently about what it looks like in our society compared to years ago with respect to the increase of mass shootings that have occurred.

In a publication produced by the National Center for Victims of Crime, it reads, "The number of mass shootings occurring in the past ten years is 2.4x greater than the decade prior (1998 to 2007). In fact, more than half (57%) of all recorded mass shootings occurred within the past 10 years." https://ovc.ncjrs.gov/ncvrw2018/info_flyers/fact_sheets/2018NCVRW_MassCasualty_508_QC.pdf

---

Portions of this chapter are written with permission of Arlene Holmes. Portions of this chapter are written with permission of Bob Holmes. Portions of this chapter are written with permission of Kate Buffington. Portions of this chapter are written with permission of Laura Hall. Portions of this chapter are written with permission of Sarah Bush.

This particular publication I reviewed was from 2017. The article also stated that,

"There were 11 mass shootings in 2017, more than in any other year in recorded history. Of all recorded shootings occurring in 2017, there were 117 fatalities and 587 casualties. Almost 50% of all fatalities and more than 90% of casualties occurred on October 1, 2017, at a music festival in Las Vegas where a gunman opened fire on the crowd. https://ovc.ncjrs.gov/ncvrw2018/info_flyers/fact_sheets/2018NCVRW_MassCasualty_508_QC.pdf

If you look at a comparison as to how many people die each year in DUI accidents the problem seems overstated with respect to casualties. However, it does not diminish the importance of understanding why this happens and how it impacts society, the victims, their families, and the shooter and their families. I have been privileged to meet and get to know individuals on all sides of this spectrum.

This chapter is really about hearing from the survivors of mass shootings. What it is like to be told that your daughter or son have been killed in a mass shooting, and what it is like to be told that your son committed a mass shooting. We will also talk about the impact on a community after these acts of violence.

Clearly those who have pulled the trigger, or stabbed others with knives did not clearly think about the individual impact on those who were injured, their families, the shooters family, and society in general.

I am honored to share several stories with you from those that have endured the impact that a mass shooting has played in their lives. I honor them and will always be grateful for the messages derived from their heartfelt stories.

Shooting on Penn State Beaver Campus

On December 13, 2017, it was during test week at Penn State Beaver. I was on the faculty at Penn State Beaver but happened to be out of town that day attending to my consulting work on another mass killing case that I was asked to help with. The case was several years old, and I was helping with the victim's family. While I was sitting with this family, I received a text message from our emergency services through Penn State University. It reported that there was a shooting on the campus where I taught. Of course, I was shocked, even with all the work I do and the things that I have seen, I was still impacted greatly by the news because it happened on my campus.

My first thoughts were focusing on the students and staff on campus. The questions were running through my mind, was it a student? Was it one of my students? Who was shot? How many were shot? All these questions were racing through my mind.

Then I started receiving texts from students and colleagues on campus asking me if I was on campus, and if I was all right? I of course informed them that I was out of town and was not on campus. I did receive a test from a student who was on campus and in the dorm asking what they should do. Of course, I told them to stay in their room until they received an "All Clear."

I then texted my colleague who indicated they were on lockdown in one of the rooms in the student union building with other students. All I could think about is how

I should be there helping my own campus. I knew there were very capable people and administrators that could handle the situation, but still my emotions were high, and I was anxious to get back on campus and do what I could to help and support our school.

The incident that occurred would not be classified as a mass shooting, the shooter that came onto our campus had a specific target, his ex-wife. Her name was Lesli Stone. Lesli had worked on our campus for many years. Prior to the shooting she and her estranged husband William Kelly had decided to meet on campus for William to give her Christmas presents for their children.

As a practice for Lesli, she had him meet her on campus in the parking lot so there would not be any issues. That day, he had other motives and took the life of his ex-wife Lesli and then himself.

The important thing to remember is that regardless of how many are shot, and regardless of the circumstances, when a shooting like this takes place in a public domain, especially on a college campus with students who become witnesses, it affects more than just those who were shot. It affects family and friends of the victims and shooter, the campus, community, and society in general.

One of the administrators on our campus provided a quote in our school newspaper that I thought was significant and I wanted to address her comment in this chapter. Carey McDougall who is our Director of Academic Affairs said, "I think our campus has been violated in an unimaginable way, and for so many of us our campus has felt so very safe, and I think that has shifted a little bit. I think we feel more aware of what could happen," https://issuu.com/pennstatebeaver/docs/2018march-roar

Ms. McDougall is correct that anytime something like this happens it changes you. You look at the world and life a little differently. Two people were impacted physically, but we also had students who witnessed the murder/suicide, and those images they will never be able to get out of their minds. The staff that knew Lesli will always remember what happened to their colleague and every time they leave for the night; they will remember what happened just outside their work area. Those types of images and thoughts are difficult to completely erase from your memory.

In the coming months after the shooting on our campus, I conducted focus group discussions in my courses. I am on the faculty, teaching in the Administration of Justice Department. I teach many classes including Criminology, Victimology, Serial and Mass Murderers, and several other courses. As we met, it was interesting what many of these students had to say. To protect the identity of these students I will just refer to them anonymously.

I first tried to establish a position of trust with my students, helping them see the value of our group and feeling free to share their thoughts about what they are now thinking a month after the shooting on campus. One student shared with us that since the shooting she does not want to be alone on campus and only goes outside her dorm when she has someone with her. Another student said he couldn't come on campus, or eat in our "Bistro," without thinking about what they experienced that day.

One male student of mine was in the parking lot when the shooting occurred. He quickly went over to Lesli to check on her and realized that she was probably dead at that point. He was in shock and said that he is having a hard time sleeping because of the incident.

Currently it has been about a year and a half since the shooting. A student last recently came to me and said that he has had a very difficult time since the incident, and he believes that it has been impacting his education. I went back through the last few semesters and he is correct. Since the shooting his grades have dropped, and he has turned in less papers. I of course recommended that he go and speak with our student counselor. This is another indication of the impact that the shooting has had in the lives of our students here on campus after the shooting.

What We Learn From the Penn State Beaver Shooting

Regardless of the circumstances behind a shooting at any community venue, there is one thing that is for sure; trauma will always be part of the tragedy. There are many students that to this day have a difficult time on campus. Penn State has not ignored their responsibility to the safe keeping of their students, faculty, and staff.

I have been impressed with the way our administration has treated this shooting on our campus. Since the shooting we have made other major changes to security and have also utilized our staff and faculty to have several events on campus. This includes scenarios on what to do in the event of an active shooter situation, and also events to talk about how to sustain ourselves when faced with trauma or other incidents on campus that create anxiety and stress.

As I sat with my classes in a circle after the shooting, we had some amazing discussions in our class where we created trust in our group, talked about our feelings after the shooting, and how we can work together as a university to improve our ability to help and sustain each other in a tragic event.

This past semester, the Chancellor from Penn State Beaver, Jennifer Cushman, and Director of Academic Affairs, Carey McDougall, began sponsoring events on campus focusing on healing and wellness as a direct result of the shooting. Several times a semester they would host a different event to talk about healing from trauma. It was a very effective tool in reaching out to students and staff and helping all of us to heal from this event. I applaud our campus administration for their efforts after this shooting on our campus. https://beaver.psu.edu/event/hope-healing

I was so impressed with our campus that even almost two years later, they are still offering events for students and staff to help them in navigating a world where we now have to worry about the increasing chance of our communities being subject to a traumatic event.

We may as a campus not be able to control every event that may happen, but what we can do is work together to minimize the harm caused by the selfless acts of others. We have an amazing opportunity in our community to work together to bring hope in a difficult and confusing world we live in. I am grateful that I had the opportunity to use some of the skills I have learned to help my own campus where I deeply care about each of these students I work with and an amazing faculty and staff. We truly are blessed here at Penn State. "We are . . . . . . Penn State!!!!"

April 20, 1999—Tragedy at Columbine High School

On April 20, 1999, according to the media, the mass shooting that took place that day was considered to date the worst school shooting in American history. For more than four hours students were held up in the school and for about 20 minutes were terrorized by Dylan Kelbold and Eric Harris. Both of these students charged through the school and when they had finished their Mayhem they killed 12 students, a teacher, and injured 20 more people within the school. The two teens then turned their guns on themselves. https://www.history.com/topics/1990s/columbine-high-school-shootings

I believe that it is appropriate to honor those who lost their lives at Columbine that day. When speaking their names I believe we all need to take a moment of pause and pay our respects to the beautiful children who lost their lives that day and their brave teacher. I would like to honor them by sharing their names in my book. Cassie Bernall, 17, Steven Curnow, 14, Corey DePooter, 17, Kelly Fleming, 16, Matthew Kechter, 16, Daniel Mauser, 15, Daniel Rohrbough, 15, William "Dave" Sanders, 47, Rachel Scott, 17, Isaiah Shoels, 18, John Tomlin, 16, Lauren Townsend, 18, and Kyle Velasquez, 16. May God continue to strengthen those who lost their loved ones and friends that day.

Over the last few years I have been privileged to get to know some of the survivors of the Columbine Shooting in Littleton, Colorado. Words are inadequate as to how much I have appreciated getting to know some of the students who were just teenagers when this happened. I have also been privileged to meet with some of the teachers from Columbine High School as well.

I would like to share what that day was like for them in their words and what they have done since then to find their path of healing and learning to move forward in their lives. I was touched and humbled by the attitude of these individuals who have accomplished so much since that fateful day in Littleton, Colorado.

Over the course of the next several pages, I will share these stories that have forever changed my life after interviewing each of these survivors. I cannot imagine what that would have been like to be there that day, and have those thoughts running through your head as you run through your school as the students were being attacked and killed right in front of you. Pipe bombs going off, bullets piercing through the school, creating terror and taking the lives of innocent children and one brave teacher, who up until the time he was fatally wounded, was doing everything he could to save the children's lives.

You cannot go through this type of an event without it forever changing your outlook on life and leaving them never feeling safe again in the halls of their school. A place that is meant to be a positive time in their lives for learning, growing, having fun, associating with each other in creating their paths for the rest of their lives, and leaving fond memories to sustain and cultivate their friendships.

I have been privileged to work with professionally and through my acquaintances, those who have experienced trauma. I have seen how they have created this path of resilience through sharing their stories with all of us. One amazing observation about these individuals that I have observed is that many of them have followed that path of helping others and finding strength to make a difference in the world around them through the professions and the activities they have been involved with in their lives. It is inspiring to listen to them and to get to know them.

We must find ways in our society to touch the human spirit of each other as we all at sometime will face troubled times and we must recognize that we all have the power within ourselves to not let violence and fear control our lives.

The resilience of these warriors of strength will forever remind me that we can all overcome the trials of life, regardless of what the trial looks like.

Kate Rebrovic Buffington: Living Every Day to the Fullest!

From the moment I met Kate, I knew that I was in the company of a survivor! Kate and her husband Marc are the parents of three children, including twins. Amazingly, she still finds time to be a schoolteacher for special education students in the school district where she is employed. Her attitude is inspiring. She shared with me many times that this experience at Columbine High School has helped her to see the positive path in front of her and reach out to those around her. She truly radiates a positive outlook on life, and by the way, is a great cook!

Kate shared with me that her way of surviving is to remain positive and see the good in life and the good in people. I sensed no cynicism nor anger for what she went through, but just a sweet, simple plan of happiness that she has instilled within her life to be the best that she can be and help those around her feel important and loved.

Kate Rebrovic Buffington left the refuge of her family home on April 20, 1999 to attend school at Columbine High in Littleton, Colorado. Kate, nor her family had any idea of what the next several hours would be like for all of them. She was a freshman at her high school. I asked her if it would be okay if she told her story in her own words. I would like to share what Kate wrote soon after the events of the day her school and their lives changed forever. Remember that she was 15 years old when she wrote this amazing view of that day at Columbine.

"After my math class we casually walked downstairs into the cafeteria. We grabbed a chair and sat down with our friends. My friends and I always sit by the Rebel Corner, where food can be purchased, which is also the closest table to the student exit. I sat with Laura and other friends as we ate our lunches carrying on normal conversation.

Travis, one of my friends, always waits until the line for food at the Rebel Corner goes down then he gets his food. Travis never gets pop to drink, but today he thought he'd get a Dr. Pepper instead of the usual lemonade. He was carrying back his food when all of a sudden we heard loud popping sounds; it seemed to me like a fireworks show or something. People started running out the doors yelling, "fight, fight," but there wasn't a fight.

I stood up trying to see what was going on, but all I could hear was loud booms. Students were running back inside saying, "Someone has a gun, and two people were shot."

Then teachers and faculty were running by telling everyone to get down. I sat down under my table with my arm around Laura, my friend. Travis was still standing up. I heard the whole lunchroom filled with terror and fear, except we knew not what our fear was for. The chairs sliding across the room is a vivid sound that I still hear at times. Travis was trying to look outside; he said two guys were dressed in all black, with black hats. He got down, spilling his pop, which he never took one sip of. At the same time, I looked around my table and the table next to me where my best friend was. She was there under her table. Then all of a sudden a teacher ran by saying "Run, run there inside."

I slowly got up and turned really fast to see the end of the world. Students were running all over. A huge crowd of students ran up the stairs. It was such a weird thing to see; I will never forget the sound of people's shoes clicking on the stairs as they ran as fast as lightning. I noticed that my best friend, Elaine, ran the opposite way as me, down the foreign language hall. I didn't really think much of it so I ran out the student exit with other friends.

We ran in our parking lot, down a hill to some nearby houses. I saw my Cross-Country coach, breathing so hard; I squeezed out the words, "Capra what's going on?" He quickly replied, "Kate, just run, run as fast as you can!!"

I ran with all my friends, which they went to a nearby house of strangers. Travis Jones lived close by, so he invited me, Isiah, and Dave to his house. As we were slowly walking from being out of breath, we could hear loud booms and we thought they were bombs or something. As we continued to walk, I saw a girl about our age in her PJ's. Looking over her fence, which backed up to the school. I yelled to her, "Hey, what's going on?" She ran down telling me and my friends that two guys shot people and they were lying on the ground. She told us today she did not feel good and stayed home from school.

We left her house as the four of us continued our journey to Travis's house. A car approached us; it was two girls from Columbine. They asked us if we needed a ride. We all piled into her old beat up car. None of us knew her but she was kind enough to take us to Travis's house as we all called our parents once we got inside.

About 10 minutes later, we turned on the news and they were already talking about the Columbine High School Shooting. I called my dad who was in a meeting but later he received my message. I called him a little later on his car phone and told him about the shooting and that people were dead.

He really did not know what to think, so he called my mom and told her that everything was fine. Later my friend Isiah's mom came and picked us up to take me home. They stopped at the middle school to pick up a sibling of Isiah. I wanted to see my sister Nadine. Nadine was 12 and was in the 7th Grade. I did get to see her and we waived at each other but I was not allowed to take her home, because my name was not on the list to pick her up. We just cried and waved good-bye to each other.

When I got home, I could still hear the helicopters and the loud screaming sirens. That night I watched the news and called my friends. My phone rang off the hook until the next week. I attended many memorial services and attended my first three funerals.

This tragic event is still so overwhelming to me. It seems that my worst nightmares have come true. Now whenever I enter my school that is all that I can think about and when I sit at lunch it will always be on my mind. There is nothing else to say but, "We are . . . . . . Columbine!!!!!!"

- Signed Kate Rebrovic

Copyright © Kate Buffington. Reprinted by permission.

It was an honor to read the words of Kate. I have seen a lot of trauma in my career but I can't even imagine the fear and confused feelings in the lives of those young people. They are truly heroes to me. I am in awe every time I meet someone who has been through trauma and can smile. Kate was no exception; her attitude then and now is exemplary.

So many times, in my conversations with Kate, she has mentioned family and how important family has been to her throughout her life. Kate came from a very loving and supportive family, who have always been there for each other.

I had the privilege of meeting Kate's father, Steve Rebrovic. I was so impressed with Steve, I unfortunately did not have a chance to meet with Kate's mother Linda, but the thing that impressed me about their family is the environment that her parents created in their home to help Kate cope with the emotions of the shooting.

Steve shared with me that on April 20, 1999; it was a very difficult time for them. The anxiety of what happened to their daughter was very difficult and emotional. Not knowing for some time what happened was excruciating to experience for him and his wife. As a parent and how I feel about my own children, I can try to imagine what it might have been like, but to actually have gone through that experience, no one will even know that anguish except a parent of child that is faced with such an enormity of emotion and trauma.

After meeting Kate and her father, it was clear that Kate's parents provided a home where she trusted her parents and knew she would be okay. Growing up in a religious home Kate learned very young to rely on God and each other as a family when experiencing difficulties.

Right after the shooting, Kate's parents assured her that everything was going to be okay, that it is okay to ask for help or just to talk if she needed someone to talk to. However, her parents also recognized that she needed her friends and needed to know they supported her in what she felt would help her overcome the anxiety of what happened.

Kate shared with me that for quite some time after the shooting that she felt safer sleeping in her parent's room on the floor. There is much we can learn from the trust and security that she felt from her parents. It is clearly evidence of the characteristics of the Rebrovic home where she felt safe. This is probably one of the most important aspects of helping young people cope with trauma.

Recently I was reading an article that was sharing information for parents on how to help their children cope with traumatic events. The article in part read:

> Older children and adolescents exposed to trauma also benefit from comfort and affection offered by trusted adults, reassurance of their safety, and the opportunity to talk about their experiences and worries when ready. https://www.childtrends .org/publications/supporting-children-parents-affected-trauma-separation

This article was concentrating on older children and adolescents. It is important that children feel safe talking to their parent or an adult, however, as parents and adults we also need to understand that they need their space. Kate's family truly understood this concept by the way they supported her going to many events with her peers, and with her church. She told me that she was with her friends a great deal after the shooting and her parents made sure that she got to those events that helped her so much in her healing. They assured her that whatever she needed they were there to help. It is comforting to children to know that they are understood. Kate's parents were so in tune with what their children needed, especially with Kate at this time of difficulty that she was experiencing. Kate said that she never doubted for one minute where she could get support and help.

For several weeks they did not go to school, but on May 2, 1999, they went back to school at Chatfield High School. Youth from Columbine went to school every day afternoon, and the other high school went to school in the morning. She remembers the first day going back that the other students from Chatfield High School lined the sidewalks and welcomed them back to school.

When they went back to school, Kate shared that it was not going back to school that helped her, but more of being with her friends. She shared that she does not remember learning a great deal, but they had activities for them every day. For example, she remembers going to one of her classes and they said today we are going to do music therapy. It was more about helping them moving forward and creating a safe place for them to gather.

Going back to Columbine High School in July to get her belongings from the school, she felt very nervous. They went back to school and retrieved their backpacks and any of their personal property. She said that when she entered the school you could see bullet holes in the walls, and debris everywhere. It was almost like they had not completed any cleaning or remodeling of the school. It was difficult, but she felt it was necessary for her.

When they all returned to school at Columbine in the fall, the teachers and parents had lined the sidewalks to the school to pay respect and cheer the youth as they went back to school. Kate shared that it felt good to be with her friends. They also had a big pep rally and people were clapping, the bands were playing, and she felt much better that day as she went back to school.

We know that these are the impressionable years and that our bodies and brains are still developing in our teenage years and for this type of tragedy to be etched into the minds of these sweet kids, it truly makes you sit back and reflect how devastating this was to so many in so many different ways.

I could sense some emotion in her thoughts and feelings about that day 20 years ago. However, she was composed, confident, and committed to the path of a positive outlook in her life. As a special education teacher in Colorado, Kate is now giving back to the schools and to these special needs children. I can't think of a more important job or calling in life than helping these sweet children who struggle for normality in their lives.

Kate was sharing with me that since Columbine, every time that there is a shooting, her heart sinks and it takes her back to that day at Columbine.

Kate noted that when the incident started that she and her friend's first thoughts were that this was some kind of a senior prank. Though she personally did not see Dylan and Eric, who had come into the cafeteria, she definitely heard the effects of their rampage with the explosions, screaming, and chaos, as she frantically ran from the school not knowing what was happening or why this was happening.

When she was explaining to me where she was sitting, which was very close to the student entrance to the school, she and her other friends did not know that two tables away that Dylan and Eric had left two duffle bags with propane tank bombs that had been set to explode automatically with a timer. When the bombs did not go off, they moved into the cafeteria to shoot bullets into the duffle bags to get them to ignite. A frightening thought became clear in my mind as I spoke with Kate. Kate acknowledged that if those bombs had gone off, she would have more than likely been seriously injured or had been killed.

That thought alone helps me to see the absolute miracle of Kate's life and those that were close to her. It helps me to see that Kate had an important purpose and that now that she is not only a wife and mother, but she is a schoolteacher to a very special group of students. She provides much more than her time to the people in her life, she provides them a safe environment to learn and grow and to feel loved and accepted. I cannot think of a higher purpose in this life and clearly Kate was persevered from chance in this tragedy to make a difference in her service to others.

Kate did know Danny Rohrbaugh and Steven Curnow who were both killed at Columbine. It is hard for Kate to see so many of her friends and their family members that will never be able to forget what happened on April 20, 1999, and only hopes that they find solace in knowing that her journey of taking the higher road, and to look at life optimistically, that it can help you through any tragedy that may come your way.

Kate said to me this beautiful statement, "Since Columbine I am fortunate to have my life and my family and friends. The things we went through it kept us together and it has always meant so much to me to have that kind of a support system."

Many of Kate's friends have kept in touch with her. They have started organizations to help others cope with tragedy, they often get together and continue to support and love each other. Each of them can relate to one another with their experiences. It has bonded them together and given them a purpose, to bring people together that have been through tragedy and recognize that strength comes through serving each other and being open to sharing the good times and the bad.

Kate also mentioned that going through this experience gave her a different lens of life and she took and continues to take advantage of this change in her life, to be kind to all people and live every day to the fullest. Kate acknowledges that even though you have rough days, overall she said that she has taken a positive outlook on life and will remain positive throughout her life.

I learned a wonderful lesson from Kate. No tragedy is ever asked for, but as I have spoken to Kate, she has clearly not allowed the tragedy of April 20, 1999, to limit her ability to reach out to others, to be more positive, and to find the good in life, and the good in others. I only hope that our society can learn a big lesson from Kate, "Live Life to the Fullest!"

Laura and Sarah—Survivors at Columbine High School, More Importantly, Sisters

I have had the privilege to get to know Laura Green Hall and Sarah Green Bush, who came from a very loving and supportive home. When I first heard their stories, I happened to come across a website, "Resilient Hope." http://www.resilienthope .org/. This website was created by the survivors of the Columbine High School

Shooting. As I went to the video section of their website, Laura and Sarah's video caught my attention because they are sisters and were both at the high school during the Columbine mass shooting.

After getting to know both of them, I can say with confidence that they are inspiring and motivating. Their outlook on life is representative to their commitment to healing and finding the strength to face the difficult times in their life with positive goals and making the choice to encircle their lives around their own families and finding meaning through the relationships they have established.

Both Laura and Sarah are married. Laura and her husband John have four children and Sarah and her husband Jonathan have five children. After talking with each of them, it is obvious that they have focused their lives around their families. They live within one mile from each other in Utah County, Utah. As I think about the relationship, they have with one another, it has personally helped me to appreciate the love that I have for my own siblings even though I live a great distance from them.

I cannot even imagine those feelings, running from my school, having no idea what is happening to my sibling? I can imagine I would have thoughts rushing through my mind, "Did I say I loved her today? Was I mean to her? Does she know I love her?" Then I can imagine my thoughts would then go to my parents, "Did I say I loved them? Did I tell them how much I appreciate them? I think it is possible that those were thoughts that many students, staff, and families felt that day.

I would hope that through reading their stories we all gain a better appreciation for the love we have around us and always make sure our loved ones know how special they are to us. We never know when our circumstances can change, and we will no longer have them around us. I hope and pray that we will each learn from the experiences of these brave women the importance of living to the best of our ability with no regrets.

Sarah's Journey April 20, 1999 at Columbine High School

Of course, Sarah and Laura had no idea what that day had in store for them. From my own experience in high school I remember getting stuck in the "Groundhog Day" mentality that all the days seem the same and run together. When you look back over your high school days there are specific things I remember in high school, but much of my time in school was a blur.

Sarah was 16 years old and a sophomore at Columbine High School. Sarah shared with me how that day 20 years ago changed her life forever. April 20, 1999 started out a typical Tuesday morning at school. She remembers they were taking a big math test that day. At approximately 11:20 am they suddenly heard two large explosions.

They looked around at each other wondering if it was a school prank. It was at the end of the year and so they thought that seniors might be playing a joke. As they were sitting there getting ready to take the test, the baseball coach Robin Ortiz, in a panic, swung the door open yelling, "Get the hell out, someone has a gun and is shooting!"

As Sarah and the other students ran down the hallway, she was not sure where to run, but instinctively ran down the stairs exiting the east side of the school. They ran away from the school onto a very busy road. To Sarah, it looked like they were probably some of the first students out of the school. As they ran across the street, cars were honking at them and wondering why they were running frantically across the street. At this point the public did not even know about the shooting.

As they got to the softball field across the street, they then turned around looking back toward the school. They watched as the SWAT team formed a line behind their armored vehicle and started moving slowly toward the entrance of the school, with their armored vehicle as cover.

At this moment, the students including Sarah heard gunfire being exchanged between the SWAT team and the shooters inside the school. The students started screaming and they ran away from the school, jumped a fence into the yard of a neighboring house to the field. They burst into the neighbor's home and told the women in the house what was happening.

When they got into the house, the women was kind enough to let these students just stay there. There were about 15 students that burst through the door of this home. They were watching the TV and we were getting more and more scared by what they were seeing and hearing.

The women whose house they were in, thought it would be best if they went to the meeting place, which was a local elementary school. They all loaded into the van and she took them to Leawood Elementary School.

When we got to the elementary school, they had all the students get up on the stage in the gymnasium and they called out their names and then had them go and meet their parents on the gymnasium floor. Sarah said that this is how they reunited students with their families.

Sarah said that no one really had cell phones in 1999, some of the parents did, but it made getting in touch with loved ones difficult. That is why there was a meeting place established. Buses kept coming to the school with more and more students from the high school.

Sarah described that scene at the school. She said, "It was almost like we were being auctioned off, it was a surreal, bizarre, unorganized chaotic moment." Sarah's parents and grandparents were frantically looking for their children and grandchildren. They decided to split up to the two areas where the students were being brought. Sarah's grandfather went to the school and eventually Sarah was able to connect with her grandpa at the school. They then had to walk about a mile to the library where her mother was.

When they got to the public library, she looked through the door and saw her mother that she had not had the opportunity to talk to at that point. At first they would not let her into the library to see her mother. They were holding them back. At that point Sarah burst through the door and ran to her mother and held her tight and just cried with her.

Then the waiting game began with knowing what was happening with her sister Laura. The officials would read lists of students who were being brought to the library and the school. She said, "We waited and waited to hear my sister's name, but with each list and not hearing her name we began to start feeling desperate."

About 4½ or 5 hours later, we got word that she had been evacuated and that she was at the elementary school. They rushed over to the school and were able to pick her up. I cannot even imagine what that reunion was like for them and for so many others. Unfortunately, by the end of the night when all the youth that were in the school that could make it to the schools was accounted for, there were 12 students missing, which were tragically the 12 students killed that day. The family of Mr. Dave Sanders, the only teacher killed was also waiting for information about their loved one. Many of the families were not able to confirm that their loved one had been killed until the next day.

The agony of not knowing was unconceivable to Sarah. She cannot even imagine what it must have been like for Laura that day.

Laura's Journey April 20, 1999 at Columbine High School

On the morning of the Columbine mass shooting, Laura came to school driving with her older sister Sarah. Laura was 14 and a freshman at Columbine High School. Laura remembers thinking to herself on the way to school that it was going to be a good day.

She went through her normal schedule in the morning and then at approximately 11:20 am as they were sitting in the cafeteria eating their pizza, a janitor yelled to get under their desks and that someone was shooting. For a brief moment Laura and her friends got under their lunch table. Laura was clinging to her friend under the table until they heard loud noises sounding like gunshots. At that moment they began to panic and left underneath the table and ran for the stairs. Laura was in a dress that day and for some reason she felt that she had to go over the railing of the stairs, which being in a dress slowed her down.

When she got to the top of the stairs she was reunited with her friend. They both burst into the choir room and yelled that someone is shooting. There were about 40 students in the room. Being directed by one of the seniors they ran into a closet in the choir room and barricaded the door with chairs, filing cabinet, whatever they could. The only light in the room was from a window about 1 foot by 2 feet in the door of the closet. It was mostly dark in the closet, hot, claustrophobic, and the tension among the students was very high.

As they sat in there not making a noise, outside they heard laughing by the shooters, yelling from the shooters telling everyone that they are all going to die. They heard gunfire and pipe bombs being ignited. They then heard the shooters enter the choir room, but fortunately they left as quickly as they came in because they saw no one and it was quiet. Laura and her friend and the senior young man that directed all the students into the choir closet saved their lives.

At one point, one of the female students who did have a cell phone, called 911. They told her to have everyone stay there until help came to them. She hung up the phone and then for the most part all the students kept vey silent for almost if not longer than four and a half hours. The 911 caller admonished the students not to use the cell phone, however some of the students wanted to call their parents and many of them spoke with their parents as if they were not going to see them again.

Laura was crying uncontrollably and could not stop. Many students were comforting her trying to help her relax. They even lifted her up so that she was close to the ceiling away from the group so that she did not feel so enclosed. She is grateful for students in that closet who remained patient with her and even tried to help her by raising her out of the crowd of people to get some better air. Laura talked about at one point that she needed to go to the bathroom really bad and they found a large cup that belonged to the choir director and she was able to go to the bathroom in that cup.

On a lighter note, the next week, Laura bought a new cup for the director and put a bow on it and gave it to him and thanked him for letting her use his cup. I learned very quickly from both Laura and Sarah what kind hearts they have and how much they care for others. This was a simple act by Laura to show the grace that she possesses.

The shooting, yelling, and sound of pipe bombs in the hallway lasted about 15 minutes and then it stopped. However, they were told by the 911 dispatcher to stay put until help arrived, so they stayed there for an additional four hours until they heard SWAT members coming into the choir room. They began to call out for the students and were telling them that it was the police and that it was safe to come out. I can't imagine how law enforcement felt as they witnessed approximately 40 students emerge from that small room, with not one of them injured.

At this moment they were told by the police that they were all suspects and to follow their directions exactly. They were told to grab the belt loops of the person in front of them with both of their hands until they had left the school. The students all complied with the requests of the police.

As they made their way down the stairs, they went into a portion of the cafeteria. When they entered the cafeteria, they were ankle deep in water from the sprinkling system. Laura noted that there were backpacks floating in the water with food, and other debris. They walked out the student entrance to the cafeteria and walked by the bodies of two students who were shot outside, Rachel Scott and Daniel Rohrbough. I can't even imagine what it was like for these students to walk through this mayhem.

When they were outside, they were told to run to a designated location with their hands on their head. So Laura and those 40 students ran to the designated spot in the student parking lot where they were accounted for and got onto the buses and were taken to the elementary school.

When they got to the school, they got off the bus and were able to locate their families. Laura at this point was finally, after approximately five hours, reunited with her family and her big sister Sarah. They had all been waiting, frantic for any news as this young 14-year-old and approximately 40 other students waited for over four hours to leave their confined closet in the choir room that saved all of their lives. Though I don't have the name of the student who protected these kids, I thank him for his quick thinking that saved the lives of 40 children that day.

Coping with the Aftermath for Laura and Sarah

That night and many nights after the Columbine shooting, Laura had a very difficult time sleeping alone. Many of those nights she found herself in bed with either her mother or her sister Sarah. Their father at the time was out of town in Montana on business. Sarah said that those nights she did not mind sleeping with her sister. Even though she did not say it, she really was grateful when Laura would come and sleep with her.

Laura said that things did not change much for all four years of high school with respect to sleeping with her parents or Sarah. She felt a great deal of comfort sleeping with them. Again, Sarah acknowledged the healing effect of being with her sister many nights during high school sleeping together. Being close to my own siblings, I can say that the bond that develops between siblings, especially during difficult times is a powerful coping mechanism to tragedy.

After the shooting, there were many days that Sarah and Laura gathered with other youth at their church that had been at the high school that day. That first night after the shooting they all gathered at the church and the adults and their church leaders wanted to make sure that they were all safe and accounted for. They then had a discussion about that day and just supported each other. No one talked about what happened to them that day, but just about how they were feeling.

They remember that one day during those weeks following the shooting that they sat in a circle and many shared what had happened to them and it really helped them to come together as youth and to know that they all experienced similar trauma.

They also gathered many times at parks, churches, and with friends. They found it comforting many times when they "Just hung out together." They also found by doing acts of service for others helped in keeping their minds occupied by serving others. Both Laura and Sarah talk about doing those acts of service and gathering together as key components in coping with what they had been through.

The students did not go back to Columbine High School for the rest of that year. They all went to Chatfield High School. They split the day up so Chatfield would go in the morning and Columbine students would go in the afternoon. Both Laura and Sarah acknowledged that they were all numb and that they felt like they were going to school just to fill the hours and there was not a lot of expectation of rigorous schoolwork required of them. They felt that it was a healing time for all of them to be together.

Being with others helped them to distract their minds from dwelling too much on what had happened. Both Laura and Sarah felt that it was not the right time to process what had happened, but just to feel support for each other and slowly find a safe place to deal with what they had been through.

Many times, they would be together and not say anything that would generate emotion, but it was more about hanging out and feeling support for one another.

Laura said that during the summer there was a day that they wanted all the kids to come and get their property out of the school, including their backpacks. Laura and Sarah both acknowledged that the school did not prepare them for that moment as they entered the school. The school still looked like a crime scene and it was hard to go back in there and see similar scenes they experienced the day of the shooting.

This was hard for them, but hand in hand with each other and their mother they were able to do that. It was a big moment for both and they feel it was a good experience for both of them to go back to the school.

Returning to Columbine High School in 2000

Both Laura and Sarah acknowledged that going back to school for the next year when they were a sophomore and a junior was a big deal. Not so much for Sarah, but Laura did not want to go back to the high school. She begged and begged her parents not to have to go back to Columbine. She said she would rather go to Littleton High School or Chatfield, but she did not want to ever set foot in Columbine again.

Many victims experience what we refer to as Post Traumatic Stress Disorder (PTSD) when they experience similar behavior that caused their initial trauma or are reminded through triggers as to what they experienced the day of their trauma.

PTSD is "A mental health condition that's triggered by a terrifying event — either experiencing it or witnessing it. Symptoms may include flashbacks, nightmares and severe anxiety, as well as uncontrollable thoughts about the event." https://www.mayoclinic.org/diseases-conditions/post-traumatic-stress-disorder/symptoms-causes/syc-20355967

That was why Laura was experiencing a great deal of anxiety going back to school. Eventually Sarah and her parents helped her prepare and both of them attended their first day back in school at Columbine.

The parents and the school administrators and teachers made it a very special day. They lined the school sidewalk going into the school and as the students walked into the school they cheered and acknowledged every student walking into the school.

Both Laura and Sarah shared how this helped them so much in facing that day and realizing that they can do it and that they will be just fine. Sarah indicated that they all agreed that they were going to do this mainly because they were not going to let the shooters "win." It was a very powerful moment for all the students to walk into the school that day. They all wore T-Shirts that said, "We are Columbine!" It helped us all acknowledge that we could go forward and tackle this fear.

Beyond Columbine: How Sarah and Laura Now Cope

Sarah decided during high school that she was going to be a positive person and count her blessings and be grateful for each day she had. To be thankful for her parents, for her friends, for all that she had. This was a big turning point in her life when she made that decision.

Both Sarah and Laura acknowledged that the day of their graduation respectively, they were so grateful to be through with high school and realize that they never had to go back there and go to school again. It was a big accomplishment to graduate from that school.

Both Sarah and Laura have both found different ways to cope with the trauma they experienced 20 years ago. Each of them have healed in their own ways and both acknowledged that they each have had to take their own journey, but that they have always been there for each other to encourage and help each other along the way.

For Laura, she felt that it would help her to serve a mission for her church. To lose herself in the service of others. She served a mission for her church in California.

Laura acknowledged that she did not really deal with the PTSD prior to serving her mission for her church and so she had a great deal of unresolved emotions that she was harboring within herself. She did not realize how much she had bottled that emotion and found herself really struggling to stay in California. She missed being close to her sister and parents and she also had a great deal of time to think about those thoughts and feelings and it was causing her a great distress to stay focused in serving her mission. She had left her safe place at home and felt completely alone, trying to deal with her emotional scars caused by the trauma she experienced at Columbine.

She had seen several psychologists and social workers and realized that she had a great deal of these issues that she had not dealt with appropriately for herself and she ended up leaving her mission earlier than what was anticipated. They had put her on five different medications, and she realized that she needed to leave her mission and go home and deal with what she was going through.

Laura moved to Utah to live with her sister Sarah. This was a great relief for her. She could now be close to the emotional support of her family but could now deal with the emotions that she had bottled up.

In Utah she made contact with her church leader who put in her touch with a counselor that helped her understand more clearly what she had been through and how to manage the trauma she had experienced so that she could live more productively.

Laura found the right person to help her deal with her emotions. This was six years after the Columbine shooting before she realized that she needed this kind of help in her life.

She remembers one day she was very upset about something; she could not put a finger on what was bothering her that day, but her counselor thought it would be good for her to watch a video scene from Columbine. So, he put the video on and she watched it on her own.

Laura shared how it was liberating for her and helped her in seeing that she can do these things, that she can do hard things and that she is going to find strength knowing she is stronger than she thought she was. This was a pivotal time in Laura's life in finding her new normal.

Each year Laura and Sarah get together on the anniversary of Columbine and together they decide that they are going to have a good day and do something together. If they cannot be together then they talk on the phone and acknowledge each other that day. They really like going and having a "Spa Day."

Within the last few years Sarah and Laura have been asked to speak on many occasions. The first time that Laura spoke with Sarah, there had been a stabbing in the school of the youth the day before they were supposed to speak. We felt that it was meant to be. Speaking that day provided them, as well as the students at the school, a great deal of comfort having gone through similar experiences. They wanted to show them that you could survive these events. They have found that it is such a milestone for each of us to help others.

Laura has felt comfort knowing that she has a sister that knows what she is going through. Both of them acknowledge that their grieving process is so different and that each went through it differently.

Laura also shared with me that when she was in high school after the shooting, that whenever they would have a fire alarm drill or anything like that, she would have to go home afterwards. It upset her that she felt that she was the only one who was experiencing that. She would say to herself, "What is wrong with all of you? Does this not bother you?"

After many years of counseling and finding her inner strength, she recognized that each person goes through their own healing process, that no two survivors are the same. This was a huge piece in her realizing what she was going through was normal and necessary for herself to heal.

Both Sarah and Laura want others to know that it is okay to be broken, to feel trauma, and that it is important to deal with these emotions, but to recognize that we must all go through these difficult times and to support each other. Even though both of them have been through this experience together, they both recognize that they have had to follow their own path of healing but being there for each other has been so therapeutic to both of them.

Where the Paths of Sarah and Laura Have Met

I would like to end with a metaphor. Though Sarah and Laura have had to find their own individual path to healing, one thing that they have found that has helped both of them and has pushed them beyond their comfort zone is running.

This is a beautiful metaphor. Even though they are on their own paths that they feel they must follow in order to heal, at some point one soul relates to another soul and two paths meet and come together to make one path.

Sarah and Laura have come to the "Y" in the road. They are now physically running the same path together in their road to healing after going through the tragic events of the Columbine shooting. Their paths met in Boston, Massachusetts at the Boston Marathon on April 15, 2019, and five days short of 20 years since the tragedy at Columbine.

Together these two amazing sisters ran the Boston Marathon together and crossed the finish line together. Several major newspapers and ESPN did a story on them. However, the highlight of the event for them was crossing that finish line together.

Sarah has been such a strength to Laura, but I can honestly say that neither one of them would be where they are today if it were not for each other and for their families. Both of these women truly have learned to address their emotional trauma that they suffered 20 years ago. They have recognized that when you can find the strength to overcome your trials, you can then experience a happy and fulfilled life.

I think one of the biggest lessons I have learned from Sarah and Laura is that each person must find their own pathway to cope with their trials. We then have the important responsibility to share that with each other so that we can then support one another in our individual journeys.

If others know what we are going through, then they can always be there to support us in our most difficult days. No one is exempt from trials, but through sharing our stories with one another, we not only learn from them, we bond with each other and help each other navigate through the difficulties we face. I offer this advice to all of us; Strength is found as we intertwine the lessons, we have learned through the difficulties in our lives with each other. It creates a woven cord of emotional strength that tells us we do not walk alone.

As I share these stories, I have often tried to put myself in the shoes of the survivor and have a sense of what that must have felt like emotionally and physically, but until we actually experience it ourselves it is hard to imagine the trauma, fear, and anxiety that is felt.

What I can say about getting to know these survivors is that they have a special purpose in this life, which I believe is to help bring us all together. To never forget nor take for granted those in our lives that provide us with a sense of safety and security, and more importantly, that we are loved.

Aurora Theater Shooting

Before I continue with this chapter, I would like to pay deep respect and condolences to the families of those who lost their lives and the countless others who were injured physically and emotionally.

On July 20, 2012, there were many that attended the Aurora Theater for the premiere of the Batman movie, *The Dark Knight Rises,* with no idea of the trauma that they would experience later that night.

I happened to be in Colorado that night in the Aurora area. I was in a hotel very close to the theater. I was in my hotel room, getting ready for bed when I heard on the news of the theater shooting. My heart started racing and I felt the need to leave the hotel and go over to the theater.

My concern for going over there was not about curiosity but being able to render my support with my professional experience. Though the scene was chaotic and overwhelming to see. As the events of that night unfolded, over the next several hours many people started to gather on a grassy knoll behind the theater, including people who were in the theater, family members, media, and many others.

The following day as mourners, family members, and others gathered on the grassy knoll behind the theater, they put up 12 little wooden crosses acknowledging those who lost their lives the night before. I found myself walking amongst those that had gathered for volunteer opportunities to reach out to those who were suffering to offer my support during this difficult time. I had some very personal experiences with several who were inside the theater, who were not injured, but emotionally exhausted and numb from what they experienced. I also talked with family members of those injured and in the theater that night.

Though I will not go into detail on most of my conversations, there is one in particular that I would like to share. I approached a mother who was crying and sitting by herself in the dark as others were walking around holding each other, holding candles, and talking.

This mother I went up to and sat on the grass next to her. I asked her if she wanted to talk. She just burst into tears and I sat next to her, put my arm around her, and just acknowledged her pain with my time and attention. She told me that her teenage children were in the theater and exclaimed that she was ashamed as a mother. She went on to say, "I let my kids go to the movie last night, why did I do that?" She then said, "I should have never let them go to the movie!"

My first thoughts were to say, "It is okay, it is not your fault," but I knew from experience that was not what she needed to hear. Rather than assume at that moment that I could say anything that would comfort her was probably not possible, but the important thing we can do for victims of violent crime is just listen.

So, I just listened to her for almost an hour. We had an amazing conversation and through our conversation she realized on her own accord that she could start to see some important lessons that she learned and acknowledged, that she truly had a lot to be thankful for.

Our conversation transitioned from her expression that she was a bad mother to a conversation that her children were now safe and that she is still with them. The second thing I experienced with this wonderful mother is her expression to me after our conversation that it is okay to still go out and experience life, that our lives or our participating in community events does not have to end when we are faced with tragedy.

As I left this sweet mother, she hugged me and said thank you for just listening. I cannot tell you how many like conversations I experienced and was honored to be part of that day. Just being there, nothing sanctioned, just having a rare opportunity to listen and experience with these survivors of this horrific event.

I would be amiss if I did not pay my deepest respect for the victims who lost their lives that day or the countless others who were injured both physically and emotionally. Though I have never at this point had an opportunity to directly speak to the families of those who were murdered that night, I have read about each one extensively and my heart goes out to their family members. I can only pray for their healing and understanding that a new normal is possible and that there are avenues possible for them to find answers to many difficult questions that have never been answered. There are resources and opportunities and I hope that they can find avenues to help in their healing.

My door is always open to victims to help them deal with the aftermath of their traumatic and unnecessary loss.

With that, I would like to list each victim. As you read their names, please take a moment to experience within yourself a moment of silence and respect for each one and their families. They are truly casualties to indescribable loss, and they deserve our affirmation through a moment of silence in your heart for each of these brave souls.

Those who lost their lives that night, Jonathan Blunk, 26, Alexander J. Boik, 18, Jesse Childress, 29, Gordon Cowden, 51, Jessica Ghawi (also known as Jessica Redfield), 24, John Larimer, 27, Matt McQuinn, 27, Micayla Medek, 23, Veronica Moser-Sullivan, 6, Alex Sullivan, 27, Alexander C. Teves, 24, and Rebecca Wingo, 31.

Victim Impact on the Family of a Mass Shooter

I work with survivor families all over the nation in helping them find answers to their questions about their loved ones being murdered at the hands of the offenders. As you can imagine, the questions are personal and necessary for the victims to receive some solace with what they have been through. There are many victims that I have worked with that have asked questions that I would have never imagined would have been important to them. I remember one mother who lost her daughter once asked, "Can you find out what the last five minutes of my daughter's life was like?"

I was taken back by that question. I thought to myself, I am not sure I would want to know the answer to that question. The more I thought about it, I recognized that it is not my place to judge why that victim needs that answer, but to do all I can to find the answers for them.

Once we had found an answer to that question, this young girl's mother said, "I have been looking for the answer to that questions for years, thank you, thank you!" It created understanding and helped that mother find another obstacle to overcome in her journey in moving forward in her healing.

Therefore, we should never judge or question the motives of a victim to ask the questions. As we address the needs of the families who have dealt with loss at levels that many of us will never understand, we must also consider the questions coming from others impacted by these crimes. I believe it is our obligation as professionals to support them and help them find answers, regardless of how crime has affected their lives. Though we hold vigils and hold counseling sessions, there are many unanswered questions and feelings that come months if not years after they have been impacted by a crime.

Therefore, I would like to now address another group of individuals that we cannot forget when tragedy strikes our communities and individuals in mass shootings.

I would like to discuss the needs of the family members of those who commit mass shootings. I have had the privilege to get to know several families of those who have committed these crimes. Though my message is not one of finding a reason to justify the actions of those who commit these crimes or minimize the horrific acts of violence they have committed, it is about understanding how others hurt and experience trauma as well.

One family that I met within the last few years is the parents of James Holmes, who murdered 12 people and injured 70 others. I could not even begin to imagine what those individuals went through that night in the theater.

Early in the morning, around 5:30-5:40 am, Bob and Arlene received the news about what had happened over the phone from a news reporter. The reporter asked them if James Holmes was their son and began to tell them that their son had just killed 12 people and injured 70 others in Aurora, Colorado in a movie theater.

The Holmes were of course confused, traumatized, visibly and emotionally shaken. There is no way that any one of us could fully appreciate, or even imagine what they must have felt like to receive that news that their son had killed so many people and created such mayhem.

For the next few years, the Holmes' have experienced an unimaginable emotional rollercoaster that to this day continues to surface. These emotions consist of a deep sense of loss and sadness trying to understand all the reasons why this happened and at the same time, mourn the loss of the 12 victims. They try to imagine what it was like to survive and live with what happened in that theater seven years ago for so many people, and on top of that, reconcile the acts committed by their own son.

I will not begin to try to fully understand what that must feel like for Bob and Arlene. All that I can do is listen, try to understand, and help to create opportunities for all of us to have community conversations and discuss how we can de-escalate a problem that is occurring more and more within our society.

Even today as I write this portion of the book, we just heard on the news that at the STEM school at Ridgeline and Plaza in Highland Ranch, Colorado that there was again another mass school shooting in the state of Colorado. There were at least seven people injured and one student who gave his life trying to protect his classmates. There is no telling the trauma that occurred within that school.

Today I took time and reached out to each person within this chapter to let them know that I am thinking of them as they have to re-live their own tragedy. Whenever there is another shooting, all of these families and individuals share with me how they re-live the day that *they* were impacted by a mass shooting.

Within the past several years I have had the privilege to speak with the Holmes at several conferences about the need to better understand the precursors to mental illness and find a way to support and help those that suffer from the debilitating effects of mental illnesses that can lead to so many different problems. These problems include, suicide, drug use, non-violent crime, and serious acts of violence that end in tragedy and impact so many lives.

There are many misconceptions about the problems with mental illness, which is one of the reasons why the Holmes are going out and speaking on this topic. They by all means have never excused their son's behavior, nor minimized his role, but have offered a better understanding of his life and the warning signs of problems that they missed as his parents and that the schools missed leading up to the Aurora Theater Shooting. One of the misconceptions is that those with mental illness will become mass shooters. Actually, the majority of those suffering from mental illness will never become violent but may have many other factors that create debilitating effects on one's life.

Recently I read a peer reviewed article titled, "Mass Shootings and Mental Illness," by James L. Knoll IV, M.D. and George D. Annas, M.D., M.P.H. The article is clear about the problems with understanding many of the reasons behind mass shootings. What they did find through their research and understanding of the correlation between mass shooting and mental illness is this:

> The recent phenomenon of mass shootings in the United States is likely a result of a combination of factors, including sociocultural ones that must be better understood if these tragedies are to be prevented. Mental health clinicians will best serve patients at risk of harm to themselves and/or others by crafting a risk management plan at clinically relevant or critical times. (Knoll 2009; Swanson 2008; Webster et al. 2013). https://psychiatryonline.org/doi/pdf/10.5555/appi.books.9781615371099

Basically, these experts are discussing the importance of better understanding human behavior and all the potential factors that must be addressed if we are to fully understand and appreciate the complexity of identifying those that are at risk of committing mass shootings. The combination of factors is a clear message that the Holmes have been sharing to better understand the precursor factors to those who commit these acts of violence.

A couple of years ago at Penn State University – Beaver Campus, we held a symposium. The Holmes spoke at this symposium and shared with the audiences their story of what their family has been through, but more importantly, addressed the impact their son's mental illness had on his behavior that led to the death of 12 innocent people, and affected so many others lives both physically and emotionally. It is hard to have a clear understanding of the impact one active shooter situation may have on a community, a nation, or globally, unless we talk about it as a society.

The following was through an interview that I did with the Holmes. This was such an honor to have them attend our symposium, to spend some time one-on-one with them and just chat was truly one of the highlights of the week. Since then, I have had the opportunity to get to know Bob and Arlene and speak at additional conferences together. Getting to know them has helped me appreciate the affect their son's behavior has had on their lives and how they work every day to help others understand what they went through to avoid others from having to go through the same experience.

Interview with Bob and Arlene Holmes

I wanted to again emphasize the importance of those who are affected by crime to be able to share their stories. From my experience in meeting and working with those who have experienced trauma, there seems to be a great deal of empowerment to press forward when people in general share their story. Recently, when interviewing Bob and Arlene for this book, I asked them how it felt to speak at these different symposiums and opportunities at universities to share their story. Both of them stated the positive experiences they have experienced in sharing their story. They have felt that by the comments they receive afterwards that it has had a great deal of impact in their lives, and helps them feel that they are doing something positive and important in disseminating information that will help all of us look at ways of preventing these tragedies.

It is hard for them to still believe that seven years ago their son took the lives of 12 innocent human beings and injured 70 more individuals. Not to mention, their families, and the nation who have also been impacted by what happened that day in Aurora.

It is hard for them to imagine the pain and injury both emotionally and physically that many have had to suffer. Their son James who they call Jimmy, will now be serving a prison sentence the rest of his life with no possibility of parole.

As I was talking with them, they both acknowledge that they still pray for the victims and survivors every day. Arlene said, "We mourn the loss of 12 lives, and we feel horrible about the severe injuries and trauma still plaguing those involved in the shooting."

Arlene shared a quote with me that I believe really is the essence of why the Holmes are sharing their message. The quote was attributed to Martin Luther King, Jr. He said, "Never be afraid to do what's right, especially if the well-being of a person or animal is at stake. Society's punishments are small compared to the wounds we inflict on our soul when we look the other way." https://www.mic.com/articles/132655/5-martin-luther-king-jr-quotes-people-think-he-said-but-actually-didn-t

The Holmes shared with me that their son's story encompasses early warning signs of serious problems that were not properly identified and addressed earlier in his life that needed more intense intervention. In many situations, even his own parents admitted that they really did not understand the gravity of the issues he was facing mentally. Unfortunately, many of those feelings and behavior were hidden in the depth of his mental illness that even James himself, many times did not fully understand. The Holmes made it clear that they would never blame others for their son's action, but what is important for us to realize is that we all need to take an active part to look out for one another and if something does not feel right, it probably is not.

The Holmes describe their son as one who did not break the rules, was not hitting himself, talking to himself, hallucinating, or anything odd enough for anyone to approach him or perceive that anything was wrong. Arlene said that he did not fit into anyone's preconceived thoughts that he possibly had a mental illness. The schools, and many others including themselves, just left him alone and his mental illness was not properly identified or addressed.

What has always impressed me about the Holmes is that they take responsibility too for what happened to their son. They said to me, "We do take responsibility for leaving him alone too much. He was self-sufficient, he never asked for much, he talked very little and he seemed to want to be alone." They continued by saying, "We realize now that we did not truly know him nor what he was thinking."

Clearly the Holmes learned from this experience that there are so many who do not know how to deal with the internal struggles of those with mental illness. They also learned that sharing with others is important in order for us to truly look out for one another, especially in our own families and identify the warning signs that someone is struggling with their own identity.

Though we may never be able to stop all the problems that can occur from internal struggling, we should always do our best to help and do our part to make a difference in other's lives.

Arlene was sharing with me that she went to a friend's home one time and she read a plaque on the wall that said, "A healthy family is one where family members are sensitive to each other's needs." The Holmes admitted that reading that statement, by definition, they felt that they were unhealthy as a family. Arlene shared that while growing up she was taught to be strong, be self-sufficient, and not complain. Arlene admits that she developed that same culture in her own family. Bob shared with me that his family culture emphasized avoiding confrontation.

Throughout my interview with the Holmes and in developing a relationship with them, I can tell you that they never have nor will they ever in my opinion, sidestep responsibility for their actions as parents. However, they also recognize that no matter what our shortcomings may be as individuals and parents, we have to remember that individuals still will make choices contrary to societal expectations and acceptable behavior. For that reason, in my opinion, you cannot blame others solely for the choices carried out by another.

Ever since the Holmes were told that their son had committed this crime they have been giving of their time and energy to do all they can to educate the public and professionals about the absolute need to educate and diagnose a person much earlier who is exhibiting signs of a mental disorder.

In my discussion with them, the Holmes referred to a study conducted by the National Institute of Mental Health (NIMH) around 50% of adolescents experience symptoms of mental illness between 13-17 years of age. Their website quotes that, "An estimated 49.5% of adolescents had any mental disorder. Of adolescents with any mental disorder, an estimated 22.2% had severe impairment. DSM-IV based criteria were used to determine impairment level." https://www.nimh.nih.gov/health/statistics/mental-illness.shtml

The Holmes acknowledge and firmly believe that if we are going to have any hope at identifying and helping those individuals who act out in many ways, we need to intervene much earlier in their lives before they become an adult.

This next section, Bob and Arlene talk about their son's life prior to the shooting.

James Holmes Before the Shooting

James was born in San Diego, California and lived in California up until the time he went to graduate school in Denver, Colorado.

The Holmes shared with me that their son had unwanted thoughts around the age of 10-years-old. However, he hid those thoughts from his parents and others. Those thoughts included wanting to destroy mankind.

James was considered a quiet child by his parents and the school system. He always did very well in school and enjoyed playing soccer and basketball. James was very obedient, always completed his tasks around the house, and had plenty of friends at school and in his neighborhood when he was in elementary school.

The Holmes informed me that James never showed any interest in guns and his family never owned any guns nor did their family ever hunt or target practice.

When James was young, their family moved to another city. Arlene indicated that when they moved, they noticed that he would exhibit behavioral changes signaling that he was having a very difficult time with moving. Most of his anger they believe stemmed from having to leave his friends and the school he was attending. He would become irritable and sad, which the Holmes did see as a change to his personality.

They could see this was becoming an issue and quickly started attending family counseling together to address the impact on individual family members and the family in general.

The social worker that was meeting with their family told them that their son had an "Adjustment Disorder." The social worker reported to them that this resulted in him being sad and wanting to punish them for the family's move. Arlene admitted that this really did not help, in fact she started blaming herself for the unhappiness within their home. However, she also admits trying to, what she referred to as "Happy Up" the family by planning better vacations and cooking better meals; thinking this would cure the unhappiness in their family. She explained that she had turned her focus on herself and her external environment, rather than trying to see what her son was thinking and feeling.

As time passed, he did seem to settle in better and made friends that he was able to eat with during lunch at school. She did say that he did not bring friends home and became more isolated the older he became. They noticed that his ability to interact with other people was diminishing and he was not improving.

Some of the physical signs of distress would be that James would pull out his hair to relieve his stress, Arlene and Bob did not know he was doing this. He would hide the areas of his head where he would pull his hair out which prevented them noticing the hair missing.

The Holmes learned at his trial that one of his high school coaches noticed that he was having a very difficult time being around other students. In addition, this coach did not share anything with the school counselor or with them as his parents. She only asked students to keep an eye on him. Finding out about this 10 years later in court was very upsetting to the Holmes, especially since the coach did not speak to them.

Arlene and Bob noted that one of his teachers in trial testified that he felt James looked like he just wanted to be alone, so he indicated that he just left him alone.

The Holmes ascribed his shyness as being an introvert by nature. Arlene noted that everyone in their family is known for quietness. They thought he was exhibiting typical teenage behavior by not expressing his thoughts. He spent a lot of time playing video games, but still did very well in school, played soccer, and helped with household chores.

At this time in James' life, the Holmes' admit that they did not know that the scantiness of his speech could be a sign of schizophrenia. According to Arlene, James said that he was never bullied.

Every year James would play recreational soccer from the 2nd to the 12th grade. He also worked in the summer as a teenager bagging groceries at the local supermarket. The Holmes said that he never caused any real problems, but frequently he looked tired both at work and at home. They said that when he was at home, he did not seem to display any extreme anxiety, but he was very irritable when he was disrupted or when he was stressed. Arlene also said that he played with his sister Chris, who is five years younger when they were young. As the children got older, they did not do things together. Arlene said that growing up they never really got into major fights, but they would quarrel from time to time as siblings.

James wanted to be a neuroscientist since he was 14 years old. As soon as he graduated from high school, he started attending college at the University of California Riverside where he completed his bachelor's degree in Neuroscience.

After he finished his undergraduate degree, he did move home for a while before leaving for Colorado to continue on with his formal education and complete a PhD program. While he was at home, they noticed that he was sleeping a lot more, he was very quiet, and would mostly just play video games.

Arlene shared with me that on one occasion she got quite upset with him and told him he needed to go out and find a job, which he did right away without arguing with her. Arlene pointed out that even James did not realize his lack of motivation and lack of emotions was an indicator of "negative symptoms" of schizophrenia. They did not realize how ill he was.

The Holmes admit that they were not educated nor knew the techniques for helping people talk about mental health. Arlene shared with me some basic concepts from the LEAP method developed by clinical psychologist Dr. Xavier Amador. I looked into this method and found that there are definitely these techniques available for families and individuals who have mental illness in their families. Many times, according to an article by Dr. Amador, the patients have no clue that they are mentally ill, and many times do not believe those that tell them so. https://lfrp.org/about-leap

We take for granted our ability to manage our time and our thought process, when there is so many that truly lack the ability to manage even the simplest of tasks because of mental illness.

James Holmes then left for graduate school in Colorado. He attended the University of Colorado, where he continued his studies in Neuroscience. The Holmes found out the reason he wanted to obtain this degree was to understand his own brain better.

According to his parents, once he left for college in Colorado, they did not see him very often. Arlene said that he took care of himself very well, managing his own finances, and doing his homework on his own without help. He was also a very good driver, never got into any car accidents and in most ways seemed to be very responsible for himself.

However, James quickly found that graduate school required a great deal of interaction with labs and other students and he was having a difficult time interacting with other students. They shared how James always did well in school but was really struggling in graduate school. All during this time, James did not share with his family his struggles that he was having in school.

It was not too long into graduate school that he moved from the "negative symptoms," to the "positive symptoms," of schizophrenia.

There are many articles written on the negative and positive symptoms of schizophrenia. One particular article that I looked at defined the positive symptoms to be "hallucinations and delusions," and the negative symptoms such as "Emotional withdrawal and lack of spontaneity and flow of conversation." (Coping with Positive and Negative Symptoms of Schizophrenia, by Angela L. Rollins, Gary R. Bond, Paul H. Lysaker, John H. McGrew, Michelle P. Salyers, Indiana University Purdue University Indianapolis, American Journal of Psychiatric Rehabilitation, 13: 208–223, 2010, Copyright # Taylor & Francis Group, LLC) http://web.a.ebscohost.com.ezaccess .libraries.psu.edu/ehost/pdfviewer/pdfviewer?vid=1&sid=69dc6628-118c-4b14-a1e2 -a7bb0882e8da%40sdc-v-sessmgr03

In Colorado, James' negative symptoms became the positive symptoms. He was starting to have hallucinations, anger, and delusions. According to Arlene fellow students testified in court that he did not seem to be functioning well in school and in his interactions with other students. They testified that they did not tell a school counselor or another teacher of their concerns.

The Holmes indicated that James also told his girlfriend that he had thoughts of killing people. She also did not tell anyone. James also texted a friend and told him that he had "dysphoric mania." Again, she chose not to tell anyone about what he was saying to her. To clarify the definition of dysphoric mania, there is an article from the Health Line web page. In part this article stated, "Dysphoric mania is an older term for bipolar disorder with mixed features. Some mental health professionals who treat people using psychoanalysis may still refer to the condition by this term." https://www .healthline.com/health/bipolar-disorder/dysphoric-mania

Clearly James did not have a full understanding of the mental illness that he had. However, because of the problems he was having he did go and see a psychiatrist in Colorado in the spring prior to the shooting. The psychiatrist started him on Sertraline (Zoloft), an antidepressant, and Clonazepam, which is an anti-anxiety medication.

According to Arlene, the psychiatrist testified in court that she thought that he was becoming psychotic and she offered him an antipsychotic medication, but he refused. She did not hospitalize him involuntarily or voluntarily. Despite his statements to the doctor that he wanted to shoot people and thought about it many times, she never told James' parents and kept it in his confidential notes during his counseling session.

Arlene shared that an expert on SSRI antidepressants stated that James would not have committed the shooting if he had not taken Sertraline (Zoloft), which has a warning label on the prescription that says that in could include suicidal and homicidal thoughts, particularly in young people. Again, Arlene found out in court that James had shared with the court-ordered psychiatrist that taking Zoloft caused him to "lose fear of consequences."

To give you another example of the problems that he was having when he was taking his oral exams at the end of the school year, he was asked to describe how the brain processes sound and the necessary neural circuits. He then proceeded to draw a large picture of the outside of an ear and talked awkwardly which alarmed the professors, however they never reported his odd behavior to anyone.

The Holmes shared with me that when he dropped out of school in Colorado that the psychiatrist that he was seeing called them and asked them if they were notified by James that he had dropped out of school. They suspected he would and told her that in May he had informed them that he was having a hard time with his oral presentations.

Arlene said that not once did she mention anything to them about the fact that he was stating to her that he was going to kill people. She did not say anything to them about any of her suspicions of psychosis or schizophrenia and did not say anything about the prescriptions that she had given him. Also he was not offered any stress reduction or therapy during the school year, and no follow up was arranged after he quit school. Basically, he was on his own with medication that may have caused suicidal and homicidal thoughts.

The Holmes had planned a trip to see their son in Denver and had purchased airline tickets to see him on August 9, 2012. They anguish over the thought that they were too late and did not go to Denver before the shooting on July 20th.

The Holmes heard testimony at his death penalty trial by two different psychiatrists. One for the defense and one for the prosecution. Accordingly, he was diagnosed with varying diagnoses along the spectrum of schizophrenia, schizoaffective disorder, and schizotypal disorder. He was experiencing delusions during this time just prior to the shooting.

Also, it was noted at trial that James has a medical condition that was diagnosed with an MRI of his brain. This image showed that the areas of his brain involved in impulse control and empathy were not normal. There were many signs and calls for help not only from his parents but from James himself. James called the number for the university behavior health unit just before he entered the theater to shoot people. Arlene called the psychiatrist to get further information on James, but she did not call back.

The Holmes said to me that "De-stigmatization is essential to getting help. The National Alliance on Mental Illness issued a statement saying 70 to 90% of people with a mental health diagnosis can have significant reduction of symptoms with a combination of medication and psychosocial support."

Arlene said that people have asked her why she could not see that her son was ill. Arlene said this,

> "I asked five nurses from different disciplines, except behavioral health nurses, if they had heard of negative and positive symptoms of schizophrenia. No one had heard of these terms. I went to nursing school in the early 70s, and education has changed a lot since then. I never worked in a behavioral health unit or clinic. And I think that I am so used to seeing very sick patients, that I could not see that subtle signs can be early warnings."

How the Shooting Has Impacted Their Lives

In my interview, Bob and Arlene have shared some insight that has helped them cope with the pain of what their son did, but also not being with their son and the emotional toll that has taken on their lives as well.

They shared with me that tragedy changes a person in every way. Arlene reported that they have experienced loss of sleep, inability to think clearly, consistent nightmares, and fearfulness for others. She said to me that they have experienced all of them.

They talked about the different type of coping strategies that have helped them. These coping strategies have included exercising, journaling, getting support from family and friends, and their church.

Also, they went to see a psychologist who has helped them out a great deal. She has helped them develop strategies to support them and provide them the methods to use so that they will not think about the shooting all the time.

Arlene said she has learned the terms, "stop, refocus, and self-forgiveness." Arlene said that these strategies have helped them find their road to healing. I think that this quote of Arlene's is very powerful. She said to me,

> "Every day we think about the victims of the shooting. We have a new attitude about TV and movies. In the movies, people are shot and fall down dead. In real life, a shooting may kill someone or leave someone paralyzed, severely wounded, disabled, in chronic pain, and traumatized."

Bob and Arlene want to be more involved politically. They believe that everyday people can empower themselves through letters, calls, and emails to their federal, state, and local representatives. They have written letters to the newspapers, posted blogs, and spoke to many groups.

I asked them recently to speak to my classes at Penn State University through media technology where they can be in real time with my students talking to them and the students asking questions. It has been such a wonderful opportunity not only for the Holmes, but for the students as well.

One of my students told me that they cannot believe that they were able to talk to the Holmes and how helpful it was to them. I had countless people come to me during our symposiums that we have spoken to, that they have been beyond words on how appreciative they are for the honesty and integrity that the Holmes so eloquently provide to those they come in contact with.

They have not only felt personal satisfaction for the opportunities that they have had to speak, but have often found at the events they have spoken at that they have a message for those who have been in similar situations as with their family. They said that they have found that the key to helping others would be that they need to feel that they are not alone.

Bob and Arlene shared that they used to be more judgmental about how others' adult children turned out. Now, Arlene shared with me that she has gained a lot of understanding about human development, and how parents are not in control of everything their children do. They also gave some additional advice. They explained the need to be more careful when we are bragging about accomplishments because you never know how it is affecting others. They also said we need to be careful not to brag about a child's achievements in a fashion that would embarrass others because we do not know what another parent is dealing with. She also said, "Don't assume that your adult children will not become depressed or have a mental illness."

Arlene said that she has always opposed the death penalty, but now she voices her opposition more openly. *"I let people know the immorality, the futility, and the lengthy process needed to obtain a death sentence."*

Arlene also volunteers at events for the National Alliance of Mental Illness.

Lessons Learned From the Holmes Family

Being able to get to know Bob and Arlene Holmes for the last several years has opened my eyes to several lessons that need to be shared with our communities and nation. I would like to discuss these lessons that I have learned.

The first lesson I have learned from Bob and Arlene is that we as a society cannot be naïve to think that it is one thing that leads to every individual becoming a mass shooter, or that the person who did this is a monster. We often hear in the media that these individuals are monsters, that they do not care about others, and thanks to social media we read abrasive statements that truly have no basis other than horrific emotional outbursts caused by senseless acts of violence.

Though we can all relate to frustration, anger, and outbursts due to trauma, the truth is that if we are going to be successful in having any impact on decreasing the incidents of mass shootings that we must not make unsuitable comments that blame one another and judge one another. We must work to understand what and how that pathway is created in a person's life that leads to these tragic events that have become more commonplace in our society.

We owe it to each other to educate ourselves on what troubled individuals are going through and recognize the warning signs and stand shoulder to shoulder with them to help them to discover alternatives to a potential pathway of mayhem.

Though there may be similarities in the shooter's lives, the pathway is different for each individual. The one thing that we do know is that these are people who come to a critical point in their manic state that demonstrates their inability to control their thoughts and emotions and for many reasons they continue obsessing with those thoughts or actions, which slowly will eliminate their options from acting out.

Do we see displays of irrational behavior by these individuals that many times show no compassion? Absolutely! However, most of the time we have no way of knowing the depth of their difficulties or what is compelling them to act out. We are learning that we must as a society understand what is causing these outbursts and do our best to intervene much earlier in their lives, so that they do not get to that critical point when all their options have been eliminated and they act out.

For example, prior to James Holmes entering the Aurora Theater, while he was putting the gear on inside his car to enter the theater, according to an interview conducted by a psychologist, James called the mental health hotline one last time. James claims that he could not hear anything on the other end of the phone call. The psychologist asked James in the interview why he did that, and he said, "Just one last chance to see if I should turn back or not." (Rocky Mountain *PBS* - segment from the Rocky Mountain *PBS* production *"Insight with John Ferrugia: Imminent Danger,"* which premieres April 26, 2018) https://www.youtube.com/watch?v=TjKae2rNjmg&t=1363s

Could that phone call have stopped James from acting out? Obviously, we will never know, but we do know they act out because of many reasons. It could be the need for acceptance, or they are suffering from a mental illness, a serious brain injury, all different types of abuse, and even social conditioning. These issues or a combination thereof may have led a particular offender to the point in their life that they run out of options and act out.

No one knows for sure unless we look deeply into each person's life to determine a possible path that led to such destructive behavior. Unfortunately, as Arlene and Bob shared, James was suffering from the debilitating effects of schizophrenia including increased homicidal thoughts. The combination of the mental illness, medication, and lack of options in his mind, clearly led him to act out.

The second lesson I learned from the Holmes was that no matter how much you love your children and try to support them, that it may not always prevent a child from acting out and becoming a mass shooter.

As you read from Bob and Arlene, they were doing the best they could and there were definitely things that were happening that had been misinterpreted by the Holmes, schools, counselors, and therapists.

As we know the therapist in Colorado chose not to share the information with them, possibly due to the Health Insurance Portability and Accountability Act of 1996 ("HIPAA"). The act in essence was created by congress to protect personal information from improper dissemination. Below is the definition or goal of the HIPPA act.

> A major goal of the Privacy Rule is to assure that individuals' health information is properly protected while allowing the flow of health information needed to provide and promote high quality health care and to protect the public's health and wellbeing. The Rule strikes a balance that permits important uses of information, while protecting the privacy of people who seek care and healing. Given that the health care marketplace is diverse, the Rule is designed to be flexible and comprehensive to cover the variety of uses and disclosures that need to be addressed.

https://www.hhs.gov/hipaa/for-professionals/privacy/laws-regulations/index.html

I find it interesting that on July 26, 2018 a letter was sent to Health and Human Services Secretary Azar by congress with their strong support in providing training and education for the Compassionate Communication provisions be implemented to assist healthcare workers in implementing the changes to Subtitle C, Title XI, Section 11004 of the 21st Century Cures Act and to request an update on the status of implementing this provision, which was enacted by Congress in 2016. In part, this was a portion of the letter written that requested training in the implementation.

> HIPAA regulations allow health professionals to share information with a patient's loved ones in emergency or dangerous situations. However, widespread misunderstandings persist and create obstacles to family support that is crucial to the proper care and treatment of persons experiencing a crisis. To enhance the quality of behavioral health and medical/surgical services, we believe it is essential that model programs and training materials be developed for health care professionals regarding permitted uses and disclosures of Protected Health Information through HIPAA.

https://schiff.house.gov/imo/media/doc/%5bFinal%5d%20Letter%20to%20HHS%20re%20Compassionate%20Communication%20on%20HIPAA%20July%202018.pdf

Many of the workers under HIPPA were unsure when to use and not to use this provision so congress wanted to make sure that it was vital that The Department of Health and Human Services implement training. Here is another excerpt from the letter that states:

> Unfortunately, many health providers either misinterpret or do not understand what HIPAA actually permits them to say. As long as misconceptions or ignorance of the rights and responsibilities associated with the privacy rule persist, HIPAA may continue to hinder necessary communication with significant implications for patient care and public safety in circumstances in which providers are legally allowed to share information. https://schiff.house.gov/imo/media/doc/%5bFinal%5d%20Letter%20to%20HHS%20re%20Compassionate%20Communication%20on%20HIPAA%20July%202018.pdf

We hopefully will see a great deal more training and understanding of this provision that will allow health care providers the opportunity to share information with family members that will help in protecting the patient and the communities.

The reporter with *PBS*, John Ferrugia, asked Bob and Arlene if they would have known he was having those thoughts, would they have been able to help prevent him from shooting those at the Aurora Theater?

Arlene said to the reporter, "We could fly back there and ensure that he was hospitalized. You are asking such a hypothetical question, who could say 100% that we could have prevented it, but we sure as hell would have tried." Arlene went on to say this, "It's our fault for not being educated. If you're going to have a baby, you need to understand mental health. And you need to start looking for things and making sure that your kid has no mental health issues." https://www.pbs.org/newshour/show/how-red-flag-laws-could-help-families-grappling-with-guns-and-mental-illness

I don't think anyone will ever know the agony, hurt, or sadness that the Holmes go through everyday living with what happened to their son and their family.

I appreciate Bob and Arlene being willing to share their story, for being so genuine and kind. They have become good friends and I will always honor them for not being afraid to share some very personal things in their lives about their family and being so vulnerable.

I would like to share a moment during one of our speaking engagements that has touched my heart like no other event that I have been privileged to be part of.

As we started the event at Penn State Beaver that involved the Holmes sharing about their lives and the life of James, prior to their presentation, we paid honor and respect to the victims who lost their lives at the Aurora Theater.

As the video presentation was being played, I glanced over and Bob and Arlene, and what I saw was the most compelling act of respect that I have ever seen. I saw it in their faces and in their hearts, the anguish that they feel for what happened in Aurora, Colorado, to the 12 people who lost their lives, for the 70 others who were injured and for their unmistakable grief knowing that their son committed this act. After getting to know the Holmes and what is in their heart there is no way that I could ever deny the compassion and grief they feel for all those who have been affected. I have a deeper respect and understanding of how crime affects society as I have been privileged to work with Bob and Arlene Holmes.

Though much of the professional work I do involves victim-centered outreach for those whose lives have been impacted by crime, I feel very strongly that in general, crime does not discriminate—it affects us all. There is no way to know how violent crime has impacted individuals and our communities unless we begin to listen with our hearts to everyone, demonstrate compassion through our service to one another, and show respect to every person who has suffered from these acts of violence.

We are capable of this, the question is, are we willing to put forth the effort to interact with each other and have those critical conversations? When we do, relief will be realized, and we will begin to create a pathway of healing for everyone.

In talking with the Holmes and through my involvement in these cases and working with those that have committed homicide and mass shootings, it is imperative that in our schools and organizations we create a safe environment for our children. Creating threat assessment teams and talking about mental illness and making sure that we have open and frank conversations is so important. The Holmes have taught me so much and have helped me understand what the family of a shooter goes through.

Thoughts From Dr. Peter Langman, Ph.D

Recently I was watching a documentary on the Columbine High School Shooting. Dr. Peter Langman shared important insight in this video that is worth repeating. He said, "The more we can do to keep kids who are so full of rage that they want to kill, or so depressed that they want to die then we are moving in the right direction." http://www .rmpbs.org/blogs/news/former-columbine-student-reflects-on-killers-red-flags/

I recently reached out to Dr. Langman and shared with him the contents of my book and content of this chapter on mass shootings. I would like to refer to some work of Dr. Langman with respect to understanding the offenders.

Before I provide Dr. Langman's discussion with respect to the three offender types in mass shooters, I wanted to provide the readers with an understanding of why this is important to victims.

Many victims that I have spoken and worked with and subsequently helped in finding answers to their questions, have primarily been questions that have to do with behavior of the offender and why their loved ones were targeted. It has been my experience that many victims have harbored questions ever since their loved one was murdered, and many times go unanswered for years if not indefinitely.

As one who has talked with hundreds of victims, I can tell you that we must listen, and do all we can to meet the needs of the victim survivors by listening and providing assistance based upon their individual needs. Since many victims want to understand why their loved ones were targeted, I wanted to end with this explanation of the types of offenders from Dr. Langman.

In his article titled, "The Bio-Psycho-Social Model of School Shooters," Dr. Langman said this as a generalized statement about identifying the type of offenders and why they became a mass shooter. He said in his article,

"There is no one cause of school shootings. Despite efforts to pin the blame on a single cause such as bullying, video games, or conventional ideas about masculinity, what these simplistic explanations fail to account for is that the overwhelming majority of people who are picked on, or play video games, or are faced with developing masculine identities (e.g., the male half of the population) do not commit mass violence. The critical question to answer is: why these particular individuals?" https://schoolshooters.info/sites/default/files/bio_psycho_social_1.0.pdf

So for us to fully appreciate the complexity of helping the victims understand why their loved ones were targeted we must conduct extensive interviews with offenders to better understand their upbringing and their social skills. It is also imperative that we conduct testing to see if and what physical or physiological ailment they may have. The difficult dilemma that many victims face with respect to the offender is that it may takes months or years to fully realize the extent of their behavior and why this crime occurred. Though many of the offenders may die during their assault, by learning more about the offenders who do live, we help all victims of mass shootings understand and appreciate the complexity of answering the question of *"why?"*

To further shed light on this question of "why," I again refer to this article by Dr. Langman. He discusses the Bio-Psycho-Social model as an explanation to the complexity of the fact that as we discussed, it is difficult to pin on an individual why they acted out in committing a school shooting. Dr. Langman explained his theory on these three concepts in this description.

Mass violence is a complex phenomenon that defies simplistic explanations. This article proposes a bio-psycho-social model to account for the many factors that contribute to rampage school shootings. Biological factors include those related to health, appearance, and ability. The psychological domain includes three types of perpetrators: psychopathic, psychotic, and traumatized. The social factors include family patterns, multiple types of failures, and external influences. In addition, there are issues that cut across the bio-psycho-social domains, such as masculine identity. The sense of damaged masculinity is common to many shooters and often involves failures and inadequacies in more than one domain.

Dr. Langman points out that we now have enough information to begin forming our discussions around these areas of focus to better understand the shooter and where their intentions are coming from. We hear in the news all the time either from public officials or from the victim survivors that the person who committed the crime is a monster and has no care for human life.

Generally, we can lump those comments as unadulterated emotion and lack of fully understanding or appreciating the complexity of knowing why an individual acts out and traumatizes others.

Even more important for all of us to understand is that many, if not all of the shooters, generally do not appreciate the complexity of their own issues and until they are educated, medicated, and held responsible for their actions, with time they may begin to understand more clearly why they committed this crime and better articulate an answer to a victim's question as to why their loved one was killed.

I have been involved in several victim-offender dialogues. During these restorative justice sessions we bring the offender and the victim's family members together and the victims learn from the offender why they were involved in the crime, and in many if not all of the dialogues that I have worked with, the offender many times is able to answer the questions of the victims and better explain why they got involved in this crime.

I have witnessed tears, laughter, affirmation, and forgiveness in these sessions. In Chapter 9 I will more fully discuss restorative justice, but I believe it is important to shed some understanding on this concept as part of this chapter of mass shootings. I have been involved in dialogue with mass shooting cases and the victims have been able to better understand why their offender committed this heinous crime.

In conclusion, taking into consideration the extensive knowledge and expertise of Dr. Langman, the last dialogue that I was involved with, the victim in a mass shooting was able to learn about the mental illness that the offender had, the extensive physical abuse he suffered, and his poor decision making skills centered on his lack of fully appreciating the extent of his actions because of his paranoid schizophrenia.

It is imperative that I make it clear that finding the reasons why an offender commits these crimes and helping the victims to get their answers does not excuse or minimize the harm that he has caused. This process of understanding the offender and finding the answers for the victims is only a remedy to provide answers for the victims and increase the chances that all who were impacted by this crime may experience an affirmation that through understanding comes healing.

As I conclude this chapter, I would like to share some insight from a colleague of mine. Recently I have had some lengthy conversations with Tony Guy, the current Sheriff for Beaver County, in Pennsylvania. Sheriff Guy and I have become good friends. He recently attended a symposium that we hosted at Pennsylvania State University – Beaver Campus. Sheriff Guy shared a letter with me that I wanted to share with you. I appreciated his insight and his understanding of this issue.

Sheriff Guy was a member of the State Police and retired several years ago. He has worked with offenders his whole career. He truly has a sense of understanding of the issues centered on why people commit crime. In conclusion, I have included his letter to me after attending this event on better understanding the precursor behavior of a mass shooter.

Beaver County Sheriff's Office

TONY GUY, *SHERIFF*

• *CRIMINAL DIVISION* •
(724) 770-4602
Fax (724) 728-5080

• *CIVIL DIVISION* •
(724) 770-4612
Fax (724) 728-2412

November 14, 2017

Mr. LaVarr M. McBride
Pennsylvania State University – Beaver
Administration of Justice
100 University Drive
Monaca, PA 15061

Re: Mental Health Symposium
       October 9th & 10th, 2017

Dear LaVarr,

First of all I wanted to thank you for inviting Chief Deputy Dean Michael and I to your recent Mental Health Symposium. As career law enforcement officers, having over sixty years experience between the two of us, we found this program to be exceptional. I am not aware of any similar program or any researcher/practitioner addressing this issue from a similar perspective. Your work, and the benefit of it, both from a treatment standpoint as well as the possibility of using it as potentially preventative data is truly changing lives already.

From a purely personal standpoint we simply can't imagine the courage it took for the families on your panel to publically speak about their heart wrenching experiences. Their willingness to discuss the mental health issues endured by their loved ones as well as the tragic effect on their families is very commendable. As the fathers of children ourselves we can think of no greater nightmare, other than potentially losing a child due to accident or illness, which a parent could possibly experience. These horrific events have inevitably left these families with issues that they will be forced to deal with for the rest of their lives. Without question, the actions of their loved ones have left them as victims as well.

This symposium was extremely worthwhile and important to Chief Michael and me for a couple of reasons. Not only did it educate us concerning the problems that can and do happen as a result of untreated or improperly treated mental health issues, but more importantly it was a perspective quite frankly that we had rarely experienced first-hand in our careers. As investigators with our previous agencies, the Pennsylvania State Police and the U.S. Marshals Service, we routinely were able to observe the devastation that had been caused to the direct victims of a crime and their families. We rarely, if ever, gave much consideration to the indirect trauma that was caused to the families of the perpetrators. This certainly created a gap in our overall perspective in dealing with violent criminal incidents and is something which, now recognized, we will strive to have greater awareness of in the future.

Please express our sincerest gratitude to the members of your panel for their courage and willingness to talk about these life changing events. Their participation in the symposium you arranged, while most likely stressful and uncomfortable, was undoubtedly beneficial to everyone who attended and hopefully contributed to their understanding and healing. It would be our hope that they continue to speak out and educate others about mental health issues. They may not realize it yet, but much can be learned from their experiences.

Sincerely,

Tony Guy, Sheriff
Beaver County Sheriff's Office

Copyright © Tony Guy. Reprinted by permission.

In mass shootings we cannot just look at how we help victim survivors, we must look at the way we deal with the offender, the offender's family, and most importantly society in general. Though we never want to make excuses for the offender, we must understand more clearly how these events become a reality to the shooter and find a way of working to identify these characteristics earlier and helping the offender before he commits the crime. Can we predict future behavior? No. Can we have influence on those who are having difficulties in their lives and turn the tide on their movement towards committing these acts? Certainly, it is possible. The real question is, are we willing to fully understand and appreciate the need of prevention versus dealing with the aftermath of a mass shooting. I believe prevention is better served by a society that sits down at the table and looks at what must be done to identify these traits early so we can intervene and save lives. That should be our goal, but it takes each of us to be willing to sit together in counsel and understand that it is not just one reason, just one method that ends in a tragedy that affects every one of us. We need, we must, come together.

7

Suspending Life—Cold Case Impact on Victim Survivors

Just for a moment I would like you to imagine losing a spouse, child, or sibling to a murder. Think about what that must feel like. Then let us say they never find the person who murdered your loved one. How do you feel now? There are many who to this day in criminal cases never know how, why, or by who their loved one was murdered. I cannot even imagine that type of pain and anguish.

I have never or will I ever try to put myself in their shoes and say that I know how that must feel, it is not possible because we do not know how they feel. I have said this many times throughout this book that the best way for us to work with victim survivors is to remember to listen and understand through their eyes what they have experienced, and that will in turn help us to know more clearly how to interact and support them.

I still cannot even imagine the difficulty it must be to live everyday not having the complete story of how your loved one was murdered by a senseless act of violence. I am humbled by the attitude of many of these victims and their ability to see through the difficulty of not knowing and then moving forward in their lives.

Recently I was watching a documentary on Gary Ridgeway, better known as the Green River Serial Killer. Gary Ridgeway was convicted of killing over 40 young girls and women and could be as high as 70 murders. He committed these murders from the 1980s and 1990s and was not discovered and convicted until 2001. https://www .youtube.com/watch?v=QQfjbq5jZoM

The families of the young girls and women that were killed waited as long as 20 years to finally have resolution in the case. During the investigation law enforcement

Portions of this chapter are written with permission of Andy J. Gall. Portions of this chapter are written with permission of Barbara (name changed to protect identity). Portions of this chapter are written with permission of Pamela A. Olmstead. Portions of this chapter are written with contributions by Tim Nielsen. Portions of this chapter are written with permission of Vera Lucero.

had hours and hours of interviews with Gary. During all those interviews and confessions, not once did he ever show emotion. The only time that he ever showed emotion was when one of the victim's family members was giving their statement during the sentencing hearing and forgave Gary for the murder of their loved one. In the video you can see Mr. Ridgeway show emotion. According to the documentary and from statements from law enforcement, it is the first time that Gary ever showed emotion for all of the women that he had murdered.

Now there were other victims in this same hearing that of course showed anger and emotion, but regardless of the their motivation for their statement, the fact that Mr. Ridgeway was hearing this and the importance of the victims being able to share their pain is significant in the resolution of the cases involving the murder of a loved one. In cold cases this resolution never happens, which leaves the victims many times wondering and grieving for years because they have no one or no opportunity to face the offender. https://www.youtube.com/watch?v=QQfjbq5jZoM

This emotional breakdown of Gary Ridgeway is the same behavior that I have seen many times when victims of violent crime have the opportunity to confront the accuser. From my experience in working with both victims and offenders, that forced organic relationship between the victim and the offender is complex, but confrontation is important for their to be opportunity for understanding, and though there is not always forgiveness, hearing how the crime has impacted a victim survivor seems to impact the offender. I do believe that in order for an offender to understand true accountability they need that experience to face their victims.

When you have a cold case there is no opportunity for the offender to have to face their victims or victim's family, which I believe is the only way they will truly understand accountability.

The reason I share this is because the victims who are the survivors in cold cases never have the opportunity to confront the offender. Though many victims like I said learn to live with what has happened, there are always the questions left unanswered and for many is difficult to live with.

Recently, I spoke with Andy Gall the District Attorney Chief Detective for Beaver County, PA. He shared with me that many victims in cold cases call law enforcement and want to know why they have not solved a crime yet. Chief Gall shared that there are many reasons why a case may take longer to solve, but in some cases there is not enough evidence that leads to an arrest of a suspect and that is what can be very frustrating to victim survivors.

Chief Gall points out that there have been times that they have had to explain to victims that if we rush the case and we are not getting all of the evidence we need, then we are not doing anyone any good by rushing an investigation. I know Chief Gall and he is extremely caring of others and especially of victims. Though it can be very difficult for victim survivors, the majority of those working these cases genuinely care about the family members and try to bring those who committed the crime to justice for what they have done.

So when there is not a great deal of evidence it really puts the pressure on law enforcement. Chief Gall shared with me that the victims of cold cases are very important to their work and that the hardest thing for detectives is not to have information for families in these cold cases.

Detective Gall shared that victim's in cold cases are constantly feeling emotional over not having the answers. He said that it honestly makes him feel awful and it bothers him not being able to give them more information. He understands and tries to be helpful whenever they call to assure them that they are doing their best. I will share more about Chief Gall and a detective's perspective during one of the stories in this chapter.

Through the remainder of the chapter I will be sharing several stories of heart-break, courage, and amazing strength of the family members of those who have been murdered, who to this day still do not have resolution to the case involving their loved one. We will discuss one case that has now been over 60 years since the murder of a four-year-old little girl who was playing outside her home in Industry, PA.

These stories are heart wrenching, but inspiring as we learn from them how they have coped all these years of not knowing who took the life of their family members. I pay honor to them through their stories.

Jennifer Kathleen (Jenna) Nielsen – Mother, Daughter, Wife

In January 2009, I was teaching at Weber State University in Ogden, Utah. It was a new semester and I was teaching my Introduction to Criminal Justice course. There were about 45 students in the course. I was sharing with the class the expectations for the course, and then I began to share with them some of my experiences in the field of criminal justice and the work that I have done with victims and offenders.

As I was sharing about my career and some of the topics that we would be addressing in class, one young man by the name of Tim Nielsen raised his hand and commented that when I was talking about victim's families in homicide and how difficult it is for them, that he could relate to what I was saying.

Tim shared with the class that in June of 2017 when he and his wife and children were living in North Carolina, his wife Jenna was murdered while delivering newspapers for USA Today. He then shared that Jenna was 8 ½ months pregnant when she was murdered and that their unborn son died as well.

You could have heard a pin drop in that classroom. I asked Tim if he wanted to share more about his wife's case. He acknowledges that he would. Tim continued sharing with the class that the police still have not identified the person or persons who killed his wife. He then talked about the impact that this has had on himself, his two small children, and the rest of their family. He then shared how he has decided to go into criminal justice to help him better understand the system and how individuals get to the point where they commit these types of crimes. That is when he decided to move back to Utah where he is originally from.

I was appreciative of his openness and was touched by his clarity and sincerity. In all my years working with victims, I have never wanted to put a victim survivor in an uncomfortable position with the things that I might say. I am very cautious about what I say just because I have witnessed how raw it can be for someone to have had a loved one murdered and then on top of that do not know who killed them.

After class, I asked him if he could stay for a few minutes and chat. I asked him how that felt to tell his story in front of strangers. He said that it felt good and that he knows that the more he talks about it the more it will help him move forward in his life. He said that if something good can come out of telling his story that he wants to do all he can to help prevent others from going through what he and his family have experienced. For 12 years Tim and I have now been friends. He had given me permission to share their story.

I am so impressed with Tim and love this guy so much. I cannot even imagine what Tim, his children, Schyler and Kaiden, Jenna's parents, and other family members must have gone through and continue to go through as they now are going on 12 years since her murder and still there is no viable suspect in the case.

Another tragic fact to this case is that Jenna was 8 ½ months pregnant and was due in three weeks from the day she was murdered. This is their story.

The Homicide of Jenna and Ethan (unborn son)

On June 14, 2007, Jenna was out delivering newspapers for US Today. She had started working as a paper carrier delivering newspapers to the bins at the convenient stores in the Raleigh, North Carolina area.

That morning in the pre-dawn hours, she was delivering papers to a secluded convenient store that at the time was closed. It appeared that Jenna was attacked by an unknown assailant/s and it appeared to law enforcement that after a struggle had pursued, her throat was cut and her jugular vein was severed. She more than likely died within minutes of her attack. A civilian found Jenna's body and law enforcement was called to the scene where Jenna and Ethan were pronounced dead at the scene soon after the county coroner arrived.

In talking with Tim, he shared with me that his wife was "In the wrong place at the wrong time." Tim was at home with his two boys while Jenna was at work that morning. There routine consisted of Jenna working pre-dawn hours and arriving back home in time for Tim to go to work.

Jenna wanted to have this job to help with their finances. Tim shared with me that after she had been murdered, he blamed himself and felt it was his fault for his wife having to go out and work. Those are real feelings from a husband, and there are so many emotions that spouses go through when their wife or husband is killed; Tim definitely experienced a great deal of what we refer to as "survivor's guilt" after the death of his sweet wife. Jenna was only 22-years-old when she was murdered.

"Survivors guilt" defined by Dr. Diana Raab states that, "Survivor's guilt begins with an endless loop of counterfactual thoughts that you could have or should have done otherwise, though in fact you did nothing wrong." Dr. Raab went on to say that this intense emotion is actually perfectly normal in someone who has experienced loss of a loved one. https://www.psychologytoday.com/us/blog/the-empowerment-diary/201801/what-everybody-should-know-about-survivors-guilt

They key to someone experiencing survivors' guilt is for them to have the support from family and sometimes someone professionally helping them to see that the choices the offender made in carrying out the act was 100% their responsibility. Though we can say that the family member or loved one must believe that within their heart and for most situations, time, love, and support from those around them will help that emotion dissipate.

Clearly Tim was experiencing a normal reaction to his wife's death, but that does not take away from the sting of her murder and how it affected himself and his family.

After the police had discovered Jenna, they found out where she lived and immediately sent officers to his home. In the meantime, Tim was getting worried, it was around 7:30 am and he could not get a hold of Jenna on her cell phone and she was not responding to any text messages. Jenna was usually home when it was time to go to work, and he was beginning to think that something had happened to her.

Tim reached out to Jenna's father, Kevin Blaine, and Tim asked him if he had heard from her and Kevin said he had not. They knew the route she would take so they quickly decided that they were going to go and see if they could find her. They thought that maybe she was in a car accident or something. Tim told me that, "You never try to think about the worst-case scenario."

Tim got his kids ready and as he opened the front door to their home to go find Jenna there were two police detectives walking up to his home. Tim's heart sank and he shared how at that moment he felt that something was wrong. Tim said that he did not expect to hear that his wife had been murdered, but he knew that something was not right.

The two detectives walked up to him and asked him if he was Jenna's husband. They told him what had happened and that she had been found with her throat cut and was deceased.

Tim described the next several days, if not weeks, as a blur. The police informed him that they had no suspects and were investigating the scene and all the evidence. They exhibited confidence in their voices that they would be able to determine who killed his wife.

However, after several weeks and having no progress in the case, on June 29, 2007, Jenna's father Kevin, Tim, and other family members, accompanied by law enforcement, called a news conference and indicated that they would be offering a $10,000 reward for any information leading to the suspects who had killed Jenna.

The only evidence or lead that they had at this point, was a person of interest in the area where Jenna had been murdered, seen by witnesses in the pre-dawn hours that day. A composite sketch was developed and then distributed all throughout the community. The flyers produced no real viable tips, leaving them feeling less hopeful with each passing day.

It is well known in a homicide investigation that generally family members, until there are other leads, can oftentimes be looked at by law enforcement as potential suspects. This case was no different. Especially with the fact that they had no real evidence to link any suspect to the crime. Tim was questioned very closely for months and Tim believes even to this day, there are probably some in that department that believe he was somehow involved in her murder.

The fact that Tim was home with his two children in the early morning hours, really leaves no doubt that Tim was not a suspect, however due to this case being a cold case, he was questioned several times over several months.

I cannot imagine my wife being dead from a murder and on top of that being a suspect in the case. He said there were some really dark days in his life trying to cope with his wife's murder and also being looked at from law enforcement as a suspect in his wife's death.

Tim shared with me that though he has a lot of respect for police officers and was in the criminal justice program at Weber State, and graduated from the police academy, Tim believes that there are some officers that have the mindset, especially in cold cases, that the husband, wife, or another family member probably had something to do with the murder.

Tim talks about how frustrating that was because they were spending so much time and effort into investigating him. He strongly believes that they were losing ground with ever finding out who really killed his Jenna. It was painful for him to watch this when he knew that he had nothing to do with his wife's death.

However, he does credit the police making it clear that their investigation and questioning him was protocol and was only necessary in eliminating him as a suspect. Though they said this and acknowledged his concern, it was still an overwhelming time in his life to be considered a suspect.

After Jenna's death, Tim fell into a very depressive state. He stayed home and found himself sleeping and drinking a lot, finding some way to make it through each day without his wife. Thankfully, he shared with me that he had his amazing in-laws who were extremely helpful to him during this time and helped him tremendously with the children and with his depressive state he was experiencing.

It was a lot for him to manage, losing his wife and baby, and also taking care of two small children. Tim went through the various stages of grief, however he definitely had some very difficult times, but with the help of others, Tim found his footing and believes that staying focused on his children helped him find that inner strength to move forward in his life.

Tim shared with me how going through the loss of his wife "Is so draining in so many different ways." He shared how others really do not know what that is like unless they have been through it themselves in coping with losing a spouse and child to a senseless act of violence, and not having any hope of resolution to the case. Tim also credits his family and their use of "tough love" in helping him recognize he cannot stay in this depressive state that he has got to keep living and taking care of his children.

During those months following Jenna's murder, the family was getting a lot of attention from the press to share her story. It is worth noting that at the same time Jenna was killed, there were other cases of pregnant women being killed so there was a lot of attention to their case. Tim now realizes that speaking to the media was not only important for the case, but important for himself to do everything he could to fight for justice for his wife and son.

There were many media outlets that were wanting to interview their family. Nancy Grace on *MSNBC* interviewed Tim and also Jenna's story was featured on *America's Most Wanted* with John Walsh, along with interviews from many local and regional news outlets in the state of North Carolina. Within the first few months it seemed to Tim that they were always interviewing and even a local band did a benefit concert to help in getting the word out about Jenna's case. Though it was difficult, it was so helpful to their healing to see so much support in their community for their family.

This event in the Nielsen's family has forever changed them. At the time of Jenna's death their son Kaiden was less than a year old. He is now starting the

7th grade next year. Tim shared that Kaiden appears to have some memory of what Tim referred to as "the idea of his mother," but he cannot remember her specifically. Tim said that this of course he believes has affected Kaiden growing up without his mother in his life.

Schyler was almost four years old when his mother was killed. He is now 16 years old. He of course has memories of his mother and again having to grow up without his mother has been challenging for all of them, but especially her children.

For quite some time after Jenna's murder, the children of course would ask where their mother was. Tim said that it was really hard, but he would just tell them that their mother was involved in an accident and would no longer be around them anymore.

As a father, and for that matter anyone who is a parent, it would be hard to fathom what that must have been like not only for Tim and his family, but for their children to reconcile that their mother was gone and would not be around any longer. For years his children have asked what happened, but unfortunately there are a lot of unanswered questions because of the fact that to this day there is no suspect in the case, nor story of what happened that day.

Tim decided that for now he would not share with them in detail what happened to their mother, but over the years, especially with Schyler he has pretty much figured out what happened to his mother. He knows at some point they will have a much deeper discussion when they are ready to talk about it.

Tim indicated that his two boys are awesome young men and he tries his best to be there for them and let them know he loves and cares for them deeply. He knows how important it is to make sure they know every day how much he cares for them. Tim continues to move forward in his life and has accomplished so much. In this next section, part of their journey was the passing of a law in North Carolina protecting unborn children that are killed in homicide cases when their mother is murdered.

With their permission I will now share the journey their family took in helping to pass this very important law that protected unborn children through the Fetal Homicide Law.

The Passage of Ethan's Law

Soon after Jenna's murder, Kevin Blaine, Jenna's father made it known that when they do find him, at the time he would not be charged with a double homicide; he would only be charged with the homicide of Jenna. The state of North Carolina at the time of Jenna's murder would not recognize their unborn son, who they named Ethan, as a human being. This really bothered Blaine and their entire family.

In a news conference, Kevin announced that he was very frustrated that the State of North Carolina would not charge a suspect with a double homicide. He was frustrated because he not only lost his daughter, but his grandson as well.

Several years ago, I met Kevin and his wife in North Carolina while I was speaking at a conference. Kevin shared with me his emotional trauma over the death of his daughter and vowed to do everything in his power to make sure that Jenna would not be forgotten. Though again, I could never understand that pain, it surely was heartfelt from Kevin what they all were going through not having justice for Jenna, but also for little Ethan, who never had a chance because of the homicide committed by the unknown assailant.

Kevin Blaine tirelessly worked on pressing the legislature in passing legislation to protect the unborn child in a homicide case involving a pregnant woman in the state of North Carolina. After many painstakingly long hours and four years, the family of Jenna Nielsen, with the support of public officials, together passed "Ethan Law."

According to Tim, on April 29, 2011 this law passed. The law was North Carolina's "Unborn Victims of Violence Act, known as Ethan's Law."

As discussed earlier, they still have not found the person responsible for Jenna's murder. However, Tim shared with me that having this law is such a tribute to his wife and their son Ethan. He is grateful for the dedication and hard work of his in-laws, especially Kevin Blaine, and all the work he did in meeting with legislators, the speaker of the house for North Carolina, and many others who helped in the passing of "Ethan's Law."

As time has passed, Tim resolved many years ago that they may never solve Jenna's case. He said that he has tried to move forward and said, "I cannot get fixated on whether or not we will have justice, but just do the best job I can to support my children. It has been a slow process, but I feel that I am now to a point where I can move forward and recognize that we may never have a resolution in the case." He also shared with me that even though he keeps Jenna in his memories every day, he has been able to find a way to not fixate on a resolution to the case, but to keep living and supporting his children.

Tim Today and his Involvement with Restorative Justice and Sharing His Story

After meeting Tim in my class, I began to recognize and admire the caliber of this man. I was so impressed with the way he looked at life and his exemplary will to progress in his ability to be a good father and a good person.

About a year after we met, I asked Tim if he would help me in a project with a program inside correctional institutions talking to inmates called, Bridges to Life. This program was developed in Texas and I will talk more about this program in Chapter 9. This program involves curriculum on faith-based principles that involves the interaction of inmates and victims of violent crime. It is not the offender's victim, but just ordinary people who have been victims of other crimes. I truly learned about the amazing man when he stood before inmates and told his story.

Similar to the beginning of the chapter, I would like you to think about what it would be like to lose your spouse to a horrific homicide and are left to raise two small children on your own. For many of us it would be unimaginable I am sure. Now you enter a correctional institution where there are inmates some of which have committed very similar crimes.

Now imagine yourself telling your story to those inmates. As hard as that would be, Tim volunteered to go into correction facilities with me and to share his story with male and female inmates.

I remember the first time he went into this facility, which was a federal halfway house. As we started the meeting, I introduced Tim and told all the inmates that he would like to share his story of how crime has impacted his life as a victim survivor of a crime. You could have heard a pin drop in that room as Tim began to share his story.

Tim shared with the inmates the story of how his wife was murdered, and then added to his story by sharing that his wife was pregnant with their unborn son who also died in the commission of this crime. The looks on the inmate's faces were obviously horrified of what happened to his wife and son, but you could see in each of their faces how it had impacted their lives. I even saw some inmates wiping tears from their eyes.

He then said some amazing things that I would like to share. Tim told them that he understands that inmates are called all kinds of defaming names including, criminal, offender, inmate, monster, dirt bag, etc. He then proceeded to share with these men and women that he is offended by those terms that have been readily used in our society when describing a person who commits a crime. He shared with them how distasteful it is to refer to human beings with those phrases. He shared how when we project labels onto people, we do not realize the impact and stereotyping that goes on, and the lack of confidence that these individuals feel when society views them with such derogatory terms.

He told these individuals that they are just like him. That we all make mistakes. He then went onto say that when he looks at them, he is looking at good people that made mistakes.

I remember looking into the eyes of the inmates and was honored to see their countenance and their lives impacted by the bravery that Tim showed in telling his story.

That is the benefit of this program is to allow victims to tell their story, but also increase the accountability and responsibility of inmates in how their crime has impacted others.

Even more exciting was that not one person moved or said anything during the 30 minutes he was sharing his story. When he was finished, the inmates gave him a standing ovation and then lined up to thank him for sharing his story and for being so open and honest.

I asked Tim later what that was like to share his story. He used the terms liberating, and helpful in seeing his road forward. It was almost like he was having an opportunity to look at and say something to the person who killed his wife and look at them as a human being and not as a monster. That was pure class on Tim's part and I could sense from Tim that it truly had transformed him to share his story with inmates.

Since that date on several occasions Tim has spoken with my classes at Weber State and Penn State University. He has such a compelling story of grief and pain, but also of triumph and respect for his fellow human beings who have committed serious crimes.

I will always be grateful to Tim for his openness and his respect for others. I asked Tim one last question in our interview. I asked him if he had a chance to talk to other victims of violent crime, what would he say to them.

Tim told me that he would let them know that it is going to be okay, that they can make it. He said that he would share with them that it may seem impossible at times but not to give up. I was impressed when he shared that the most important thing that they could ever do as a victim of a crime is to share their story. He said that he has shared his story so many times and each time he tells his story, it reiterates to him of the importance of telling your story to help you cope with what has happened and to learn to forgive one another and look at all people as a good person who has done a bad deed.

Tim shared that the last time he talked to law enforcement in North Carolina about the case was right after he had completed the Police Academy in 2011. Of course, Tim is very disappointed with the investigation of Jenna's case and feels that there were many things that the law enforcement could have done. Tim has read of new technology to use to conduct tests on evidence that are advancing the work in cold cases and believes that if they are not actively working on a case that no one is taking the initiative to do more to solve these crimes.

I would hope if I was ever placed in his shoes that I would show as much class as Tim Nielsen has shown in classes at the university, in correctional facilities, and to the media. He is not afraid to tell his story and each of us should not be afraid as well.

I truly sense from Tim a purpose that he has implemented in his life to be the very best person he can be to others and more importantly, the best father he can be. I admire Tim so very much. I cannot even try to imagine what that must have felt like to go through that tragedy. I am very proud of Tim and appreciate his openness and willingness to share his story. Tim, truly you have touched my life in many ways and for that I will always be thankful for our friendship.

Meeting Vera

Whenever I meet a survivor of a crime or a family member of a homicide victim it is a very humbling experience for me. I always try to prepare myself through creating a sense of reverence for what they must be going through before I meet with them so that I may better appreciate their grief. It is symbolic to mentally prepare to play an important game in athletics. I always involve God in my preparation and pray for guidance that I might be a conduit in doing everything I can to help these souls in one of their most difficult times of their lives.

I feel fortunate to have the honor and privilege to meet and get to know these heroic people. I call them heroes because of the insurmountable challenges that they are forced to endure, not by their choice, but by the choices of others who blatantly show disregard for the impact that their behavior causes on others.

Within a few months after the murder of Phil, I met Vera. An acquaintance of ours shared with me that there was a woman that he would like me to meet. He shared with me about what had happened to Phil, Vera's husband. I indicated to him that I would love to meet her, and we set up a meeting.

Meeting Vera has honestly blessed my life in many ways. I first met her at her work in a conference room in downtown Denver, Colorado. My first thoughts as I got to know her were centered on how impressed I was with this wonderful woman who had just been through months of probably the worst tragedy of her life.

Recently Vera talked about that fact that she not only lost her husband Phil to this senseless act of violence, but Vera also lost two other important men in her life, her older brother Robert, also to a senseless act of violence and then her father, only a year after Robert died. Though it has been many years since she lost her brother and father, it has been a difficult journey to have now lost a third important man her life. I cannot even begin to fully appreciate what Vera was going through at that time in her life when her husband was suddenly gone, with no explanation as to how he was murdered. All I could do was listen and provide her possible steps that she could take in her road to healing.

That first meeting, Vera asked me a lot of questions about how to work with or talk with law enforcement. I shared with her that it was important that she be respectful of their caseload, but that she keep on top of the case by setting up systematically her own schedule in keeping in contact with law enforcement. I shared with her the importance of the term, "the squeaky wheel gets the grease!" Meaning to keep in touch with them.

We also talked about general coping skills when someone close to you passes away tragically. Never once did I ever sense any anger from her or a sense of giving up. Vera is one of the kindest women I have ever worked with in my career. She was set on moving forward in her life and it was such an honor for me to be able to help her explore different ideas on how to accomplish her road in her healing process.

The beautiful thing about Vera was that she did most if not all of this on her own, and truly in my opinion is "a ROCK!" I have shared with many the strength of Vera and that she truly created a path for herself of succeeding at moving forward in her life but also continuing to honor the memory of her wonderful husband Phil, who she married in December of 1994. They had been together almost 20 years when he was tragically murdered in Denver, Colorado.

Vera, I pay honor and respect to you and your sweet husband Phil in sharing your story of difficulty, but your ability to move forward in your life and find your pathway to happiness.

Phil's Tragic Death

On August 24, 2014, Vera was in Florida at the graduation of her step-niece. Her husband Phil had gone to a Colorado Rockies baseball game that night with a friend and was on his way home after a late game.

Phil was traveling home and was only a few blocks away on Martin Luther King Boulevard. Police found Phil deceased within his car at approximately 2:20 am and Phil had been shot inside the car, one bullet to his chest area.

The police were responding after a neighbor where Phil was killed reported that a car was idling outside on the road in front of their home. When the police arrived, they found his car idling and no sign of anyone around, or any potential witnesses. Their investigation included any plausible explanation due to their lack of any direct evidence other than a bullet. Their investigation included looking to see if Phil could have been directly targeted by someone who knew him. Another explanation was that he could have been a victim in a random act of violence by a gang member? Phil was traveling home from a Colorado Rockies game and the area that he was passing through did have gang members so Vera's thoughts included the fact that though he was not affiliated with any gangs, he could have been randomly shot by gang members who were shooting at each other.

Vera, being in Florida had no idea until the next morning what had happened to her husband. On August 25th, while in the mall with her family eating lunch, she began getting texts from the police. They were requesting that she call them as soon as possible. Because she was having lunch with her family she decided to wait and call them after lunch.

She told me that earlier that week there was a problem with a purchase on her credit card that she did not authorize, and she thought they were calling to let her know what was happening with the unauthorized purchase on her credit card.

When she did call them back, a detective from the police department said, "Your husband was found dead in his car."

There are many circumstances or methods law enforcement use to notify family members of deceased loved ones, and no matter how they are told, it is probably one of the more difficult situations for family members to experience, and easily one of the more difficult responsibilities of law enforcement.

I can't even begin to imagine how difficult it was for Vera that day. Here she was having a good time with her family clear across the country and to get a phone call from police notifying you that your spouse had been murdered is an unimaginable traumatic experience.

Vera shared with me the minute that she was told that her husband was dead, she felt an overwhelming onset of pure horror. She began crying hysterically, and once her family realized what was happening, they all surrounded her and shielded her from the public as she was going through this indescribable painful experience. She noted to me that there was a kind person who gave her some water which helped her back to a sense of time and showed compassion toward her at a very difficult time.

Vera explained where the pain was coming from, "To know I would never see him ever again, never feel the warmth of his body, to see the smile on his face."

She also shared with me how blessed she was to be with her family at the time and that they were able to protect her from public display as she tried to regain her composure from the phone call.

Vera described the emotion she was feeling of being in a tunnel that led to her spiraling down into darkness. She was in utter shock and all she could think about was getting home. Her family tried to explain that for now it might be better for her to remain with her family in Florida. Even though it would be difficult and knowing that Phil would not be there, she felt overwhelmingly like she needed to return to her home.

She returned to her home the next day with her sister Judy. She met with police and they indicated that they did not have any leads. They explained that he was found in his car idling and there was no one around nor any witnesses that they have found.

Vera herself most logically thinks it might have been gang related due to all the gang activity in the area at that time. As previously stated, Phil never had any affiliation with gangs of course, but Vera feels that when he left his friends that evening that he possibly could have driven through an area where there was gang activity and was blindsided by the gang members in the area where he was killed.

Soon after the memorial service when friends and family returned to their homes, this is when things became very difficult for Vera. To have lost your husband and then to feel utterly alone was a very difficult time for her. Phil was everything to her. They had spent 27 years together. They had created this life together that was strong and to lose your spouse like that, Vera shared how devastating and lonely it makes her feel now.

It was not to long after the funeral that the certainty of what happened and what was ahead for her became her reality. Her husband had a studio and a lot of equipment. He was the sole owner of his company and worked as a freelancer as a TV producer.

She was so overwhelmed but with the help of Phil's best friend Clint, who knew the business and how to sell the equipment, he was able to help her and he stayed by her side a whole week away from his wife to help her sell everything in the studio and close down his business. It was a very difficult time for her to leave many memories as she was shutting his business down. She loved his work and helping him, and it was hard to see it all dissolve because of a senseless act that took the life of her husband.

After she had taken care of the business, she found that she was sinking deeper into loneliness and sorrow. She could see that she was isolating herself from others and still had no appetite. She worried about what was to become of her, alone in Denver with no family.

Vera found herself using social media to deal with her loneliness. She would post little sayings and thoughts about Phil, along with pictures of the wonderful memories that she had made with her husband. She told me how soothing it was to share these memories and really help her in dealing with the stress of loneliness that she was feeling, especially through the night.

I remember Vera's posting to her Facebook page, honoring her love and the man she married. When I would come into town, I would often just sit and listen. I have found through the years that listening is the most important thing we can do for those who have experienced the trauma of being a victim of a crime.

During those first few years after the death of her husband, Vera demonstrated the ability to see beyond trauma and recognize that as human beings, we need each other to share our stories with and to lean on for support.

Phil's family and parents remain very supportive to Vera even today, as she celebrates both of Phil's parents 90th birthday's this year.

I loved what Vera said about being alone. She said, "No one should ever be alone." I agree, we are all in need of love and support, especially when going through difficult times.

Detectives Run Out of Leads

After a few months the police were offering a reward for any leads on the case. The detectives were reaching out to the public because they had no viable leads to follow in this case.

You can imagine the frustration from family and friends when almost a year later they were no closer to solving this case then soon after it happened. To this day, they still have no practicable leads to the death of Phil.

Vera shared with me that after that first year she has never really heard from the police. She noted that if she did talk to them that it was because she had called them. This fact is very difficult for many victims of cold cases. They feel as though they have not only been left with the feeling that they will probably never have justice in their case but feel as though their loved one is unimportant. This is a very typical emotion of victims.

Though law enforcement are not required to keep families informed unless it has to do with the investigative strategies of the case, they do try to keep them up-to-date if there are any new leads on a case.

Law enforcement was contacted a year after Phil's death by a local TV station and they were asked about the status of the case. In reading one of the articles on the internet website of a CBS affiliate channel, they reported that law enforcement was continuing to look for Phil's killer, but had no leads. The police shared with the newspaper that they put a great deal of time and energy in these cases and unfortunately sometimes they do not have all the evidence necessary to fine the person responsible or any other leads in a case.

Vera's experience with the police was very difficult. She said to me, "They don't tell you anything. You always get their voicemail." She said trying to keep up with the case was very emotional and draining.

She found that year after year she has had to reconcile that she may never know what happened to her husband that night. She said that it has been probably three years since she has talked to the police.

Reconciling the Death of Phil and Honoring his Legacy

As I have through the years worked and helped victim's families in cold cases, I have found that each family is unique in their needs and their pathway to healing. We have to truly understand those needs if we as professionals are going to be effective in our outreach to these victim survivors.

One of the most important steps we can take in helping survivors is to ensure that the memories of their loved ones are kept alive and that we honor them with every chance we can for the good life that they have lived and the lives they have touched.

Phil was a very successful freelance video producer in Denver. He was revered by his colleagues. There were many articles written about Phil. A colleague of his who worked on several projects with him said that he was encouraging to others, cared about others, and really was a cornerstone to the creative media community.

Vera shared that Phil was a devoted husband and cared deeply for her and his family. To this day she remains in contact with Phil's family and visits them as well on a regular basis.

A few years ago, Vera met Patrick who has been such a strength to her. They are together and he has brought so much comfort to Vera since the passing of Phil. Vera stated that human beings were not meant to be alone and that she knows that Phil is now in a better place. She finds great comfort in knowing that he is okay and with his loved ones that have passed on.

I asked her if there are unanswered questions in her life with the fact that she may never know what happened with her husband Phil. She said to me, "Phil is no longer here, and he is with God and that he is in good hands and that is what helps me. This is my path now. The person who did this will be the one suffering. I can't change what has happened and I must accept how that awful event has changed my life and all the lives of people that were close to Phil and loved him so very much."

Vera said that they had a beautiful life together. Phil donated a lot of time to helping non-profit organizations. He donated time to the Wounded Warrior Project and the Denver Safe House for Abused Women. At the Gala for this non-profit after the death of Phil, they paid tribute to him and all that he had done for them.

Vera said, "Phil was a beautiful soul and he is now in a better place and that is what helps me to move forward with life." What happened to him was a lesson for her to not ever take anything or anyone for granted; that sometimes we don't learn that lesson until something happens and we should not live our lives that way.

Thank you, Vera, for the beautiful example you are of enduring a tragedy and standing up for the good that we can learn in this life through our challenges and experiences that have the potential to make us stronger human beings.

Vera looks at each day as another step forward in her progress and recognizes the importance of encircling her life with others, and together they overcome the obstacles created by tragedy. I am a true believer in relying on one another to make it through the difficult times. Truly I sense an amazing level of peace in Vera's life because she has chosen to be a survivor.

"There are those life lessons that constantly happen, even as I can see and feel these lessons, I still can't put my finger on it. To understand it all will be my journey forward. With every misstep, I will learn." - Vera Lucero

My Tribute to Vera

As I have interviewed victim survivors in many different types of cases I am always the one blessed by the lessons, I have learned from those who have suffered so much. I have learned from Vera that no matter the tragedy, we can endure, we can learn from these experiences to trust one another, to learn from each other, not to be afraid to share our stories, and most importantly, to never take anyone in our lives for granted.

Thank you, Vera, for the beautiful example you are of enduring a tragedy and standing up for the good that we can learn in this life through our challenges and experiences that definitely have the potential to make us stronger human beings.

Vera looks at each day as another step forward in her progress and recognizes the importance of encircling her life with others and together they overcome the obstacles created by tragedy. I am a true believer in relying on one another to make it through the difficult times. Truly I sense an amazing level of peace in Vera's life because she has chosen to be a survivor.

Cold Case: Beaver County

I had the privilege of working with the *Beaver County Times Newspaper* on a video series that was broadcast on their website and on YouTube. I was the host of this series that looked at many cold cases within Beaver County, Pennsylvania. It shocked me how many cases even in a small community go unsolved. We were looking at over 25 cases and that was not even all of them.

I was curious so I went to the Internet to see how many cold cases on average are within the United States. According to the Christian Science Monitor website I learned the following about cold cases.

> Across the country, unsolved murders are piling up on detectives' hard drives. Driven by the changing nature of crime, a lack of staffing in police departments, and burgeoning caseloads, unsolved murders are rising inexorably in many American cities. More than 250,000 cold cases have accumulated since 1980. In 1965, US detectives routinely cleared nearly 90 percent of murder cases. Today, on average, 40 percent of homicides go unsolved, according to the FBI Uniform Crime Report. https://www .csmonitor.com/USA/Justice/2019/0225/Solving-the-unsolved-How-cities-are -turning-up-heat-on-cold-cases

It is a very gloomy statistic, but a reality that faces over 250,000 families, communities, and individuals every day. You would think with the technology we have nowadays that we would be able to resolve these cases, but again, as I said earlier in the chapter it is a dilemma that plagues not only communities and individuals, but law enforcement.

This initiative that I was hosting in Beaver County was a two-year project from 2012-2014. During this time I had the privilege to meet many family members of the victims of these cold cases. I was also able to sit down with the investigators, police, coroners, and district attorneys on each of these cases.

It was heart-wrenching to hear their stories and know that for most of them, they may never have the full picture as to why their family member was murdered. Many of the victim survivors had a difficult time talking about the case. For many of them it is still too difficult to discuss even after many years since the murder.

I remember one of the cases, when I called the survivors; they politely shared with me that they would prefer not to be part of this series because they know that the case will never be solved. Every time they get their hopes up, they are shattered again by the fact that they know they will never know the truth.

One particular case that we featured was the cold case of Becky Triska. Becky was 14 years old and was last seen on September 19, 1958. Becky was out with some friends at a dance in Ambridge, Pennsylvania. She was last seen by her friends at approximately 11:30 pm. To this day she has never been found. There were a few suspects, one being a confessed killer in the area, Frank Senks. Though Frank admitted to killing others, he never admitted to killing Becky. https://whereaboutsstillunknown .wordpress.com/2017/08/23/rebecca-triska/

Though they have never found her remains, the family keeps praying and hoping that this case will be resolved. It was difficult for me to work on this case because over 60 years ago this young woman was taken from her family never to be seen again. To this day they have not solved the case, nor have they found the remains of Becky. It is one thing to have your daughter missing, but to never know what happened or who took her has to be even more devastating to a family.

The first case that I worked on with this series was the murder of Patty Patton. Through interviews with Pamela Olmstead and articles from the *Beaver Times* (https:// www.timesonline.com/article/20110319/News/303199956), I would like to share the tragic story of this beautiful little girl who never really had a chance to experience the joys in life, and how the Patton family has coped with the murder of their little sister and daughter.

I have been privileged to get to know Larry and Pam Olmstead. Pam is the youngest child born to Thomas and Bernice Patton. Over the course of the last several years, I have had the privilege to work with Larry and Pam, family friends, and Pam's brother Jim. I have truly been blessed to get to know this wonderful family.

Patty died on March 21, 1956. Pam, her little sister, was born two years later in 1958. Pam never knew her sister, but Pam has kept the memory of Patty alive all these years. I cannot imagine having to deal with all that this family has been through. I can't imagine what it was like to frantically look for a missing child, only to find her murdered within a mile of their home. I can't imagine what it has been like all these years to never have a resolution to their case. The only thing we can do is listen, respect, and acknowledge their loss. This is their family's story on the death and murder of Patty Patton.

In Memoriam of Patricia Mae Patton

On February 20, 1952, Patricia Mae Patton (Patty) was born to Thomas and Bernice Patton, in East Liverpool, Ohio. Patty was the only girl in her family at that time. Patty was the fifth out of eight children born to her parents. Patty's siblings included Tom Jr. (Passed away March 18, 2019), Jim, Dave (Passed away January 22, 2001), Ken, Jerry, and Ron, and on September 5, 1958, Pamela, their youngest child was born.

Patty was a precocious four-year-old, with brown hair and big brown eyes. Patty loved to go outside with her four older brothers to play. She especially loved to walk around in the puddles with her brother's rubber boots that were much too big for her feet.

One of their neighbors, Thelma Kelly who was the landlord for the Patton's home, loved her visits from Patty. She would stop by just to say "hi" and to get a handful of candy from Thelma. She looked forward to her visits almost on a daily routine.

Bernice, Patty's mother, was a stay at home mom. At the time of Patty's death, she had five children and had a full-time job watching their children, which she loved very much. Patty's father Tom worked as a "Plant Guard" at the Midland Works of Crucible Steel. Tom was a wonderful father according to Pam, their youngest daughter.

On March 21, 1956, this day started out like any other day at the Patton's home. By 7:00 am all four of Patty's older brothers were on their way to school. This morning Patty did not go outside to play until around 10:15 am.

That day she was wearing her brown knee-length pants under a pair of green snow pants, a blue sweater, green gloves, and the oversized galoshes owned by her brother. Bernice, Patty's mother, acknowledged that Patty would always stay in the yard and never would cross Brush Run Creek that ran behind their home.

Bernice was caring for Patty's youngest brother Ron and she could hear Patty playing in the backyard. Bernice lay down for just a minute on the couch with Ron and briefly fell asleep.

She woke up about 11:00 am and realized that she could not hear Patty outside and rushed outside and could not find Patty anywhere around their home. The three families that lived around the Patton's began to assist Bernice in looking for Patty.

Around noon, Thelma Kelly the only neighbor with a telephone, called other neighbors to see if they had seen Patty and to come and help them look for her. After continuing their search, they decided that it would be prudent to organize an official search party to continue looking for Patty.

A neighbor at work informed Patty's father Tom that their daughter Patty was missing.

Tom quickly left his work and came home and joined in the search for their missing daughter.

The family and neighbors were confident that they would find Patty. Their thoughts were that she was just hiding. The search party was looking everywhere; they even took flashlights and were looking in the basement of one of the houses where the kids would often play. Still there were no clues of Patty's whereabouts.

Around 1:30 pm they included the hill behind the Patton home for the search of Patty. Though Patty would never go up there, they were not having any success, so they extended the search to the hill.

Around 2:00 pm, Milo Adams, one of the neighbors who lived near the Patton home, found Patty's little lifeless body on a flat portion to the hill. Patty's body was lying face up under a cherry tree. She was fully clothed except for her gloves and hat that were later found on the hillside near an abandoned mine shaft. Officials also found two balloons on the hill, however the family said that they did not belong to Patty.

Pam Olmstead and Jim Patton, Patty's sister and brother shared with me about the balloons. They were red and blue. One of the suspects, Tim Seaman, had asked Jim Patton, Patty's older brother a few days prior to the murder of Patty what her favorite colors were. Her favorite color according to the family were red and blue. Pam believes that this is pretty strong evidence that Tim Seaman had something to do with the disappearance and death of her sister.

According to Pam there was not a great deal of physical evidence that she was assaulted. Therefore, some public officials and law enforcement speculated that it might have something to do with her thymus gland, which is a gland in the neck that helps the immune system in early life. However, Thomas F. Todd, who was the County Coroner, ruled out that the theory of the malfunction of the thymus gland as the cause of death. He also ruled out the theory that she may have been struck in a hit-and-run and left on the hill.

Two months later, a Beaver County Coroner's Jury heard the evidence and ruled that Patty's death was a homicide due to suffocation caused by someone's hand.

When I met with Pam and her brother Jim, I shared with them that at the time it was an election year and that the public officials wanted to delay the findings of the Coroner. Pam and Jim acknowledged that they were a poor family and had no political connections.

The Patton family felt as though the District Attorney for Beaver County was holding back with the investigation because of the fact it was an election year and they did not want to have to deal with a four-year-old being murdered.

I had the privilege of meeting Jim and he shared with me that their family was poor and that he and his brothers were in one room together, 5 boys in one room. He said that they either slept on the floor or all of them would have to sleep on a single mattress. Patty stayed in a bigger room with her mother and father.

Pam and Jim shared with me that they could not even afford to pay for the funeral of Patty when she was murdered. The funeral for Patty cost $412.00. That was a great deal of money back then and the only way they were able to pay for the funeral was donations from her father's work. They were able to get enough people to donate to pay for the funeral.

Shortly after the death of Patty, the police interviewed a 14-year-old boy who was a neighbor to the Patton's and was considered the last person to see Patty alive. His name was Jack Pumphrey. Jack was not only the last one to see her but reported that he had helped Patty up who had fallen around 10:15 that morning. He said that he helped her up and that she continued along a path behind the Patton home.

The Patton's questioned the story because Patty rarely went away from the Patton backyard and would have never walked across the creek to the hill where she had been found. It was reported that several months after the murder of Patty that Jack Pumphrey's had stolen their neighbors truck owned by the Seaman's and ran away from home to his grandparents because of the constant pressure he felt from the rumors that he had killed Patty.

He was sent to George Junior Republic Juvenile Correctional Training program, however he escaped from there and was found a few days later in Pittsburgh. Jack has always been a suspect in the death of Patty, but there has been no direct evidence to link him to the crime.

In my discussion with Jim Patton, even though Jack was considered a suspect in the case, he believes that another boy around the same age by the name of Tim Seaman was the one that killed his sister. According to Jim there were footprints leading from the area where Patty was found directly to the home of Tim Seaman's home where he was staying. The police never interviewed Tim Seaman because his mother was his alibi that day. In addition, Tim was not in school the day that Patty was murdered.

Both Jim Patton and Pam Olmstead believe that Tim Seaman was the one that murdered their sister, and that possibly Jack Pumphrey was a witness or helped Tim in the murder of Patty.

Jim and Pam also shared with me that soon after the murder of their sister that Jim went over to the Seaman home and was listening outside because they were arguing. Tim was arguing with his parents and saying he that he didn't mean too. Jim said that they stopped talking and Jim was running away from the house and Tim's mom saw him running away. She then went over to the Patton home and was acting suspicious and just inquiring on the case. They were acting very suspicious.

Jim Patton shared some very personal information about Tim Seaman. As mentioned earlier about the balloons, there were several other things that happened that clearly was evidence to the disturbed behavior of Tim Seaman. He was a bully to Jim, his brothers and others. Jim also shared with me that at one-point Tim sexually assaulted him. At the time Jim was around 10 years old. He never told anyone about the sexual assault for many years. He was threatened by Tim and worried that if he told anyone that he would kill him. This clearly was disturbing behavior that Jim experienced after the death of his sister.

The Patton family felt that the only ally for their family was Coroner Todd of Aliquippa. Coroner Todd was convinced from the very beginning that this case of Patty's death was a homicide. Coroner Todd did tell the family that he was getting a lot of pressure from officials to hold off on the ruling. This was very disturbing to the family, especially Patty's mother and father.

Many times, Tom Patton would contact officials in the state of Pennsylvania, but also from their representatives in Washington, DC asking for support and help. In every situation it was their practice to tell them that they must go through the District Attorney. It was as if no one was hearing or even caring about the emotional trauma that was being inflicted on the Patton family because of the lack of empathy due to the fact that it was months before they would even consider it a homicide and do a murder investigation.

Many of those who were working on the case, according to the Patton family, had theories that it was an accident. There were some that believed that she fell climbing over the fence that was too high for her to scale. The concern the family had with that theory was that she was wearing oversized galoshes that would have made it impossible to climb.

It was extremely frustrating for the family to hear all of these theories but pay little attention for a considerable amount of time that it was more than likely a homicide. At one point the police had a four-year-old boy try to climb over the fence that she would have had to climb, and he could not and gave up. It was determined that there was no way that she could have walked up the hill over a fence on her own. She would have had to been carried. Also, part of her injuries included bruising over her face what appeared to be caused by the hand of a young man around the age of 15 or 16 years of age.

Even years later the Coroner Todd believes that law enforcement and the District Attorney's office did not give this case the attention that they should have.

After all the pleas by Tom Patton, letters, and visits to the courthouse, the Patton family never heard from investigators unless they reached out to them. When they did reach out, they were told that there was nothing new.

Jim shared with me that when his sister was laying in the casket, he touched her hand and made a promise to her that he would find out who is responsible for her death.

For several years, nothing was ever done about the case and Jim shared with me that while he was serving in the Vietnam War that his promise to his sister was re-awakened as he watched many lives lost around him during the war. He again vowed to his sister Patty that he would continue searching when he returned from the war.

Jim kept his word to his sister that he would continue trying to find the killer. He did his own investigations and talked to whoever would listen to him. In the 1970s he approached the county detectives, but they showed little interest due to the age of the crime. Also, he contacted the FBI and they told him that they would not get involved and that he would need to continue his reaching out to county and local police for support.

Pam and Jim shared with me that both of their parents died with broken hearts. They were never able to find out who killed their sweet Patty, nor any of the circumstances behind why their daughter was murdered.

Myself as a parent, I cannot imagine what that must have been like for Tom and Bernice Patton to never have closure to how and by whom their daughter was murdered.

I recently pulled a newspaper article from the *Beaver Times*. This was an article that Pam provided to me. However, this article has since been pulled from the website of the *Beaver Times*. The article was written in March of 2001, 45 years after the murdered of Patty. It was an anniversary article that was posted by the *Beaver Times*.

The reporter had reached out to police agencies around the Industry area and no one really had any information about the case. The only ones that had anything was the Beaver County Detectives. They still had the file on Patty's case, but after the article came out in the *Beaver Times*, they did some research and found that there was no evidence found in the case. All of the evidence according to documentation had been destroyed.

It used to be that the County Coroner's Office held onto some of the evidence, but their office did not have the information. Corner Todd passed away in 2004 and since then they have not been able to find any evidence. It was determined through archives that the file and evidence burned in a fire, making it impossible to track any direct or physical evidence, or use it for further investigation.

In 2011 there was another article in the *Beaver Times* that sparked an interest from the County Detectives and the Pennsylvania State Police. They went as far as interviewing Jack Pumphrey in 2013. Mr. Pumphrey at the time was in a wheelchair and in ill health.

He was not helpful and said that he could not remember any details and acted distressed. The police were not able to extract any information from the interview that was conducted. The case at the time continued to go unsolved with really no evidence to prove or disprove who was responsible for Patty's death.

Pam Olmstead and Her Family Pursuit for Justice Continues

Looking back to 2014 when I met Pam, I have since had the privilege to get to know Pam and her husband Larry, their family, and Pam's older brother Jim who I met in 2016. The longer a case goes, the more difficult it is for the case to be resolved. The chance of ever finding who killed Patty is minimal because of the fact that the evidence is missing and the only two suspects according to the Pennsylvania State Police are deceased.

However, in getting to know Pam and her family, I can tell you that this family has not given up hope or concern for justice for their sister.

Pam shared with me that while growing up her parents never let her live a normal childhood. She remembers not ever going out to play unless her parents or brothers supervised her. Even in high school she was not allowed to go on dates or go out on her own unless she was with someone and even then, it was rare circumstances.

Pam said she resented this, but now that she is a mother and grandmother, she has a better understanding of the paranoia that was generated over 60 years ago when her sister was murdered.

Through Pam, I was able to meet Judy Yurick. I had the opportunity to interview Judy who had been a family friend before Patty was murdered. In 2014, Judy shared with me that she remembers as a very young girl going to the funeral of Patty and seeing her in her little white dress. She said that she watched this family for many years, and she saw the devastation to their family of never having answers as to what happened. Judy became a little emotional when I interviewed her and you could sense that even 60 years later it still has haunted this special family friend. Judy has since passed away, but my interview with her and feeling her kind spirit will never leave me. What a special support and help she was to Pam and her family for many years.

Since the showing of the episode of Patty's death in the series, *Cold Case Beaver County*, I have had the privilege many times to work with Pam on several initiatives in trying to share the message of the devastation of cold cases and how they impact families and communities.

I have had Pam come to Penn State University – Beaver Campus several times to share her story with students. She has also helped with the Bridges to Life program at the Beaver County Jail. This program allows victims of crime to go into a correctional facility and have the opportunity to tell their story to inmates. She has also told her family story and the death of Patty to inmates at the Mercer State Prison in Mercer, PA.

It is amazing to me to watch Pam tell her story. It is moving and sad to listen too. However, her bravery and her will to never give up trying is commendable. She said to me that as long as she is still living, she will continue to seek the truth into what really happened to her sister that she never met.

She feels cheated out of that experience of having a big sister, but also feels that because of this tragedy she has missed out a lot in activities while growing up and being with her friends. Though you can't blame her parents, it would be difficult to have everywhere you go, or who you see, scrutinized by her parents because of the fear that something might happen to her.

During the last several years I have explored ideas with Pam to possibly help in solving the crime against Patty. Pam was in touch with a psychic. This psychic came to the old homestead of the Patton's in 2015 before the house was torn down. Pam, I, and the psychic walked around the property and she shared information about the case that was encouraging to Pam. The psychic told Pam that she sees a unicorn and Patty had a unicorn stuffed animal. She said that the offender will be revealed through information shared by family members of the perpetrator. Evidence, meaning that it will be revealed through a family member of the killer contacting Pam and her family. Pam finds it interesting that just a couple of years ago she randomly met Jack Pumphrey's sister. However, when Pam asked her about it, she said that she does not know anything and did not want to talk about it.

The truth is that this is a new reality in society. We are seeing more episodes of missing children, men and women in our society. It is disheartening and tragic that we must have to worry about abductions, human trafficking, sexual assault, and homicide in our society. This is the new normal.

No one can say for surety that they will never have to worry about becoming a victim. We know that it is random, and that crime does not discriminate and that we unfortunately live in a troubled world where many can have others take advantage of them and become of victim of a crime.

Many years ago the Patton family sought help in the murder of Patty and to this day they continue that fight. Patty is lucky to have a family that has never forgotten about their sweet little sister who was murdered.

I am honored to work with Pam, and I am so impressed with the numerous times that she has shared her story with students, victims, and offenders. That is what is defined as character, perseverance, commitment, and vulnerability. Pam has been vulnerable many times and it has helped her to pave the road ahead. There is no way to measure the pain that Pam and her family have endured.

Pam is amazing and clearly understands the importance of family, healing, and self. Pam has and will never give up hope that there will be some conclusion to what happened to her sister that she has never met.

Pam's only plea to law enforcement is that they don't give up and never think that this case cannot be solved. She is hoping that somehow evidence will surface, whether it is a confession, or information from family members of the killer, or other evidence that would show who took the life of Patty Patton.

I believe after getting to know the family of Patty, that their intentions are not revenge or necessarily just to seek justice, but to know what happened that day and who would do this to Patty. I believe strongly that no case in unsolvable. I believe there is an answer somewhere and that we should never give up hope of finding out what happened to Patty Patton.

Houston Texas Cold Case - Mary Michael Calcutta

Mary Michael Calcutta was a native of Pittsburgh, Pennsylvania. In June 2019, I had the privilege to speak and meet with Mary's older sister. I also spoke with one of Mary's brothers. I met Mary's sister through Chief Andy Gall of the Detective Division for the Beaver County District Attorney's Office. Andy shared with me the difficult story of Mary's murder on August 10, 1979, in Houston, Texas.

Mary's sister has devoted her entire life to God in the service of ministering to others. She is also continuing to work towards finding justice for her younger sister, Mary. Mary's sister told me about Mary and the wonderful spirit that she always radiated. Mary was the middle child of six siblings, four brothers and her sister.

Faith is very important to the Calcutta family. They are an Italian Catholic family and have taught values and the importance of faith in God. Mary graduated from an all-girls school, St. Raphael Catholic High School in Pittsburgh, Pennsylvania.

Mary had a very close friend, Beth, with whom she would spend a lot of time with at slumber parties, watching movies, going places and doing things, and talking about all the things high school girls would talk about. They continued their relationship even after they graduated from high school. Mary attended secretarial school and started working. She held various positions at some of the finest companies in Pittsburgh. In addition, she had taken classes in cooking and cake decorating and she became proficient in baking and decorating cakes. Most times she made cakes for birthdays, anniversaries, and special occasions, but sometimes she made cakes for no reason at all but to surprise and please her family, friends, and co-workers.

Mary's sister shared with me some of the memories she has of Mary. The day Mary was born, September 8, 1951, her sister was standing at the window spotting her dad coming down the driveway. She called out to her father asking what her mother had and her dad called back, "She had a girl!"

Mary's sister was so happy, she loved her brothers, but she so wanted a sister. Mary was an extrovert with a charming personality. By her 20's she was warm, confident, and funny, and a beautiful young woman. Her short, wavy, dark brown hair and her large brown eyes made her very attractive. She had a slim figure and her straight white teeth always displayed a large smile. She loved to visit her sister in Florida because the climate was sunny and warm. She enjoyed the beach and she loved to swim. Mary had grown up and her sister said that she felt sure that she could be independent and live on her own.

Mary also loved to travel. She went to Italy with some friends of the family. While visiting Rome, she baked for the priests at the Vatican. Just months before her death she, herself, traveled all over the United States by bus. Her parents of course were concerned for her safety and asked her to check in as she reached each state. She did.

By 1979 all of her siblings were on their own. Mary had a friend in Houston whom she went to visit; it was a little vacation for her. She liked the climate there. On a whim, she looked for job opportunities. She was hired on the spot and took a job working for a large bank. Mary announced to her family that she was moving there. Though her parents were concerned, they supported her decision to move. Within weeks, Mary handed in her resignation at her Pittsburgh job and moved to Houston, Texas.

Her parents were apprehensive about her leaving Pittsburgh; however, they gave Mary their blessing as she set out for Houston knowing she would be happy in a warm place with a good job, while experiencing her independence.

In addition to her many interests, Mary loved square dancing. She made more friends while joining dancing groups and she was having fun. She also took self-defense classes for women and she belonged to a social group for young Catholic adults.

After staying with the friend, she had first visited in Houston, Mary eventually moved into her own place at the Orchard Apartments. Mary had some male friends through her group interests and dated while living there. At the time of her death, she was dating another resident of the Orchard Apartments.

Orchard Apartment Murders

On July 27, 1979, the nude body of Alys Rankin was found in her apartment. She was decapitated. There was a trail of blood from the apartment to the parking lot and it appears that the blood stopped there. This led investigators to the conclusion that whoever decapitated her took her head with them.

When this happened, Mary Michael Calcutta called her parents. She decided to leave the apartment for a while because the death of Miss. Rankin was close to where she lived, and it made Mary very frightened. She stayed with friends for the next ten days before she felt comfortable enough to return to her apartment, which was the Sunday before she was murdered.

The night before her death on August 10, 1979, she had talked with her boyfriend, according to his account. She had also talked with her best friend, Beth, in Pittsburgh that evening. That was the last that anyone had ever heard from Mary. The following day, Mary's boyfriend went to her apartment around 4:30 pm. After knocking several times and receiving no response, he found her apartment door to be unlocked. He entered the apartment and there he found her lying in her bathroom.

During the night at about 1:30 am she was stabbed multiple times in the chest and with other cuts in several locations on her body that appeared to be defensive wounds. It appeared that she struggled with her assailant, who also sexually assaulted her before the killer slashed her throat.

This past August marks 40 years since Mary was murdered and to this day there is no viable lead or suspect in the case. Unfortunately, there are many reasons why cases remain unsolved. Lack of evidence, no witnesses, no motive are some of the reasons.

However, the family has not given up hope that somehow there will be a break in this case that will lead to the discovery of what happened on that fateful night many years ago when Mary was brutally murdered, stabbed to death in her apartment in Houston.

One of the detectives on the case said that she "died harder," in other words, more violently than anyone he had ever seen while working as a homicide detective in Houston. (Houston Chronicle, August 8, 1999, S.K. Bardwell). The detectives had many murders that they were investigating and the detectives on Mary's case were definitely overworked.

It is Mary's brother's understanding from the detectives that there was a lot of disruption in the crime scene. Mary had a party for her church group the night before so the detectives could not isolate a set of fingerprints that they could track as pertinent to the case. As one could imagine, there were many fingerprints at the scene.

The detectives indicated that to their knowledge the two women murdered did not know each other and the evidence that they had was inconclusive as to whether the two murders were related. There was suspicion that her boyfriend was a suspect, however there was never enough evidence to support this lead.

During this time period there were several murders in the Houston area, however they were never able to connect Mary's murder with any other homicide in the area. It was not long after the homicide that Mary's sister shared with me that she really did not hear much from the Houston Homicide Detectives, unless she reached out to them. She indicated to me that this has been the pattern for almost 40 years now.

Early on, the family became involved in the investigation by asking questions and offering a large reward for any information about the murder. Even with all their efforts, there were no positive leads that brought them closer to a resolution in the case.

The family made some effort to reach-out to Dr. Cyril Wecht, a nationally renowned forensic pathologist who has helped with many high-profile cases in solving crimes. He was best known for his work on the Warren Commission and the Watergate Scandal. Dr. Cyril Wecht lives in the Pittsburgh area and was the Allegheny County Coroner and Medical Examiner. https://en.wikipedia.org/wiki/Cyril_Wecht Dr. Cyril Wecht was not able to assist us, as there was not enough evidence.

Mary's brother shared with me that the only person whom he felt was truly concerned about his sister's murder was Detective Jim Binford of Houston PD. He really took an interest in Mary's case and even assisted in a *Fox News* report about his involvement in the case. He was told by Binford that Mary's case was "always on his desk" and that he was truly connected to her case and wanted to do all that he could to solve the case. This has brought comfort to Mary's brother in knowing that the interest and concern was still there for his sister.

Now it has been 40 years since Mary's death. Her brother believes that over the years the case has lost interest. Some of the evidence, which clearly has an impact on the case, has been lost. Mary's brother indicated that he feels that if they would have lived closer to Houston that they might have had better attention to the case.

Investigation by Andy Gall – Detective Beaver County, Pennsylvania

While Mary's sister was living in Greensburg, prior to moving to out of state, she was watching the news and saw a news clip on a case that occurred in Beaver County, PA in September 1979, one month after Mary was murdered.

The case was the murder of Catherine Janet Walsh. Gregory Hopkins, who was a former Bridgewater, PA City Councilman, was finally brought to justice for the crime he committed in September of 1979. Detective Andy Gall, who is now the Chief of Detectives of the Beaver County Attorney's Office, at the time of the Walsh murder, was the first officer on the scene. He helped solve this cold case on the Walsh murder in January 2012.

Mary's sister saw what Andy had accomplished in the Walsh case and reached out to him to see if he could help her in the case of her sister's murder. She called his home to talk to him about the case. Andy has met with Mary's sister and two of her brothers.

I have been privileged to get to know Andy Gall and I can tell you that this man cares deeply about victims of violent crime and their families, and he works tirelessly to support and help those in Beaver County, PA. I was not surprised when I heard that Mary's sister had reached out to Andy for support and help on this case.

Andy went right to work for the Calcutta family by reaching out to detectives in Houston, Texas. Sometimes it can be awkward for a detective from one jurisdiction to call and ask about another detective's work, but Andy made it clear to Houston investigators that he was only trying to help. Andy has a great deal of compassion and expressed that to the detectives. Detective Sergeant Paul Motard of the Houston Cold Case Unit was not offended, but actually said he appreciated his assistance.

In 2012, Andy also contacted retired Detective Jim Binford, who through the years had been assigned Mary's case. Detective Gall walked through the evidence with the detectives that they had gathered since the murder. They continue to keep the file open in their cold case division. However, the detectives shared with Detective Gall that there was evidence lost in many cases because of damage due to weather related issues in the Houston area. There is a great deal of information that has been lost in the case or cannot be found.

Another one of Mary's friends had gone to Houston to live with Mary for a short period of time. During this short period of time her friend was able to get to know people with whom Mary had associated. However, there was no convincing evidence that any of her friends were involved in the crime. Mary's friend moved back to Pennsylvania prior to the homicide of Mary.

Detective Gall had talked with the Houston Homicide Division, read reports, and interviewed Mary's friend. It was Detective Gall's opinion that there is no conclusive evidence that those individuals that they had investigated were responsible for the death of Mary. In speaking with Detective Gall, I was impressed with the care that he showed in his cases. He has communicated how difficult it is to reach out to victims when they do not have anything new to share. He recognizes the importance of keeping in contact with them. I have known Andy for eight years and the concern that he has for others is an example of how all law enforcement officers should handle and care for the survivors.

Though he may not always have the answers that families of victims need or are searching for, he helps them to understand the process and that they are doing everything they can to solve each case. From my observation of watching him in action with cold cases, I can attest to the attention and respect he provides to victims. Andy is revered by many in his field for his ethics and for the care to those he serves.

After I first interviewed Andy and Mary's sister, I had the chance when I was recently in Houston to go to the police department. When I first arrived and said to the front desk clerk, that I was inquiring about the Mary Calcutta homicide case, I could sense some apprehension in his voice. A couple of weeks later, a detective with the Houston Police Department who works in cold cases contacted me. I told him that I was writing a chapter on Mary Calcutta's case and was wondering if he had some time to chat. I could sense that same hesitation in his voice and he said to me that he was anticipating that I had information on the case. This showed me that they definitely are always looking and hoping for new clues in the cold cases that they are presently tracking. It also gave me some encouragement that they are not forgetting about these cases, at least that was my perception from Houston that day.

This detective indicated that presently they have no further information on the case nor are they any closer to resolving this murder. However, they assured me that they have not forgotten the case and will continue to monitor the case. Though this kind of news can be dissatisfying to the family, it is the only type of information that can be provided at this time.

The only hope at this point in time, would be if someone who was around at the time of the murder who knew or saw something, but was too scared to come forward then, would come forward now to provide information to help in solving Mary's murder.

Tribute and Memoriam of Mary Michael Calcutta

The important message for this chapter is not necessarily about producing evidence to how or who committed the crime, but more about celebrating the life of these beautiful people who tragically had their lives taken by senseless acts of murder that have impacted many lives.

Words are inadequate to really understand what the Calcutta family went through that night and for several months, which turned into years of not really knowing what happened to Mary and why she was murdered.

In talking to Mary's brother, I asked him about the overall impact on their family with Mary's murder. He shared with me that Mary's parents and the rest of their family was never the same after the death of Mary. It has affected their extended family, close friends, and acquaintances. Their parents always kept a picture of Mary in the dining room and always kept her a part of them. Mary's brother shared that this did not affect their faith in any way. In fact, he said that going through this experience has helped them to draw closer to God and their faith.

Mary's sister shared the events of the weeks after the death of her sister. In part of her memories, she stated this about her family and what they were going through.

"We certainly felt the power of prayer. My parents were so noble in all of this. It was prayer that got us all through this ordeal. We were worried about my mother. She was truly a noble woman through all of this.

My Dad said for days and weeks after, my mom would cry a good part of the night in bed. He would try to console her.

*Once someone asked my mother if she had any daughters. She responded that God h*ad both of them. What a beautiful response she gave."

Personally, I have learned so much from Mary's family. They truly are a family of faith and trust in God. They have relied on God to see them through their tragedy. Though there are many unanswered questions, they believe Mary is happy with God and that she would want them to be happy too.

It has been my experience that families that go through trials such as this, if they continue to communicate with one another, support one another, and trust in a higher power than theirs, they generally see the way through their trial. Though life will never be the same, they find that pathway of creating the new normal in their lives, relying on the beautiful memories of their dear sister Mary and the impact that she has had on their lives.

Her friend Beth thinks about Mary often. She wanted to have Mary in her wedding as her maid of honor, but asked Mary's parents to stand in for her that day as they carried the chalice and bread to the altar during the wedding ceremony. She wanted Mary to share in her son's birth and his first day of school. But she knew that could never be.

Mary's family and friends will never know what she could have done, how many more times she would have made them smile or laugh, how many more hugs she would have given, how many more surprise cakes she might have baked and lovingly decorated for each of them.

The Trauma of Cold Cases on Victim Survivors

As we have learned from these stories, the lives that not only homicide affects, but also the never ending emotional drain of not fully understanding what happened or who committed the crime is so difficult on families. I was recently reading a blog on the Internet that really sums up the trauma to the families in cold cases. The article in part read:

"When a murderer can't be found, or a missing person doesn't appear after weeks or months, the added psychological stress on the families increases. Psychologists call this phenomenon 'complicated grief' due to the traumatic nature of the death or disappearance and the obstructions to its resolution.

By Allison Gamble. http://coldcasesquad.blogspot.com/2011/09/psychological-effects-of-cold-cases.html

I have had the opportunity to help in several cases where the identity and circumstances behind the murder may never be solved. I cannot imagine the strain added upon all the other stress that goes with a loved one being murdered.

I wrote this chapter for several reasons. First, I wanted to make sure that these souls that were lost would not be forgotten. So many times the victim's families in cold cases go unnoticed and untouched for years, if not permanently. That can be very emotional for families.

I have been asked what would be best to help these families. I have heard it from law enforcement, other professionals, and victim survivors themselves. Without question, they are all overcome by the sense of loss and the lack of information that will bring a close to this chapter of their nightmare. Victims eventually in their own due time, begin to heal without knowledge of committed the crime. Though they may learn to control those emotions, it still is impossible to fully appreciate how difficult that may be for many.

I hope that we have learned the absolute necessity of reaching out to these folks, just like we would any victim of a crime. They need to feel love and acceptance and that there are others looking out for them. It is a common emotion that we all have.

My suggestion is that we all try in our own lives not to be judgmental of others who have become victims of crime. We often hear terms being given to victims, "You need to move past what happened, we are praying for you, Let me know if there is anything I can do?" I think it behooves us to be more assertive with those who are suffering especially when their hearts are full, and we struggle with what to do. The best advice I can give, which I have given throughout this book, is to talk with them and ask them what they need.

Getting to know better these wonderful people in this chapter, it has given me a better definition for bravery. I look at their faces and I see individuals struggling with not knowing, but I also see those that they have encircling them. Family is the most important unit in our society. Regardless of the make-up of a family, it is still a family with needs, wants, and desires. It would create a pathway of healing just by doing that one simple thing, "What can I do for you?"

Never judge what or how a person should feel, just walk beside them. That will make all the difference in their world.

8

Aftermath—How Surviving Family Members of Murder Cope

On February 18, 2004, I was asleep in my home. We lived in Harpers Ferry, West Virginia, when I worked for the government in Washington DC. It was about 3:00 am when I received a phone call from my brother Brian. It is a phone call and an emotion I will never forget.

My father had surgery two weeks prior on his heart; he had a valve replacement. Apparently he had a birth defect that had not been detected and he had a choice whether to get the replacement or take a chance. He chose to have the surgery.

A few weeks later, during the night on February 18th, he slipped into a cardiac arrest. My mother and my 93-year-old grandma gave him CPR until the paramedics arrived. They were able to get a steady heartbeat, but unfortunately it was too long and it caused a great deal of brain damage. My brother was calling to let me know that he did not have long to live and to hurry to Idaho.

As you can imagine my emotions were all over the place. I was crying, I was laughing at some of the memories with my father, about everything you can imagine. I was able to get a flight at 7:00 am and was beside him before 10:30 am in Idaho. I love modern travel that can have you clear across the country in just a few hours.

I was grateful that I was able to spend 24 hours with my father, who was in a coma, but at least I was able to be with him. The next day, February 19, 2004 my father passed away with my family at his side.

The phone call I got in the middle of the night telling me that my father was going to die, was the most difficult phone call I have ever received. The memory of where I was and what my brother said will be etched in my mind for the rest of my life.

Portions of this chapter are written with permission of Rita L. Mihalik. Portions of this chapter are written with permission of Michelle Montgomery. Portions of this chapter are written with permission of Jolene (name changed to protect identity).

Naturally, because of his death it has caused distress in my life, absolutely. However, I also live with the belief that death is temporary and that one day my family and I will be re-united with my father. It is my belief system that has helped me to regain my emotional footing and recognize that we will be together again.

Though my grief was excruciating, personally I cannot imagine what it would be like to get a phone call or a visit from law enforcement or military personnel about a family member or dear friend where they had been murdered in a senseless act of violence, or in war. We all lose family members due to health or age, and generally we at least are somewhat prepared for most of those scenarios. However, when it comes to someone being a victim of a murder, it is incomprehensible to me of the added grief, in addition to trying to make sense of why your loved one is dead. Death can be difficult for anyone when you have had that type of experience. That is why it is crucial that we listen and we hear what those who are grieving are experiencing so that we may better understand what they are going through and how to assist them.

As professionals working with homicide victims, we often encourage and assist victims in finding a source for healing in counseling, groups, or other activities that help them and encourage them to seek their own path for healing.

Some victims become advocates for change, others begin nonprofit organizations dealing with trauma and homicide. It is heartwarming to see communities, neighbors and friends, rally behind these sweet families who lose loved ones to these acts of violence. It also amazes me to see these valiant individuals find their own individual path to healing and reach out and help others.

Several years ago, I was asked by an organization called, Parents of Murdered Children, Inc. to speak at one of their chapter meetings in West Virginia. One of the families at that meeting had recommended to the West Virginia Chapter to speak at one of the big annual events.

I first have to say how honored I was to speak and walk among these parents and family members of those who were murdered. Before I spoke in front of this group of about 50 people, I was taken back by my own emotions of what they must be going through and how brave they were to be there and confronting their pain and trying as a group to relieve that pain by gathering together.

When I finished speaking to this group of wonderful people, many of them came up and thanked me for speaking to them. I made it a point with each one of them to ask them to share just a brief memory of their loved one. I could see their eyes light up as they would share a brief story of their loved one. My wife and I had the privilege of embracing many of them and feeling their passion and love for their loved ones.

Sometimes there is nothing that we can do to bring them comfort other than just asking them to share a story about their loved one. That can change their world in a split second and bring a glimmer of hope and security in their moments of grief.

This organization is national with thousands of members. From my observation, "Parents of Murdered Children" is a progressive organization that is constantly looking at new ideas and support for those who have lost their children to senseless acts of murder.

Those that find their path create an ability to manage the pain and anguish that they feel. It takes work, courage, and support from those around them in order for their confidence and strength to gain footing and create the way forward in their lives.

A Love Story Ends in Tragedy

On one occasion, I was assigned a DUI negligent homicide case. I was conducting a presentence investigation for the sentencing of the offender. A presentence report is all of the information about the individual concerning the crime that occurred and his social history. Basically, everything about his life to the point where he committed the crime. This report is then used by the court to learn as much as the judge can about the individual that is being sentenced, including a recommendation from our office as to what we would recommend as an appropriate sentence based on the severity of the crime and his past.

This case is still vivid in my mind. It was a tragic story of a two young people who had fallen in love and were planning to get married. The names and some of the details have been changed and I will refer to them as Dan and Lisa.

Dan and Lisa had known each other since high school. They truly loved and cared for each other and as time passed, it was obvious to both of their families that it was a matter of time before Dan proposed to Lisa.

They went to a special place to the both of them in the city where they lived. When he finally "popped" the question, she threw her arms around him and said, "Yes." It was an exciting time for them, and they were excited to tell her parents about their engagement.

In the meantime, in a city north of where they were, there was another young man, who I will refer to as John. John was 21-years-old and working as a bartender in a hotel bar. He had finished his shift and decided to have a few drinks before heading home to meet some friends. At the time, he did not realize how intoxicated he was when he left the bar. He was traveling on the interstate.

In the meantime, Dan and Lisa had got into their car, full of life and so excited to tell their parents that they were now engaged. They proceeded outside the city and were traveling on the interstate heading north.

On the interstate, John was traveling south and claimed that he was trying to change the channel on his radio, was not looking at the road, drove down into the median and up on the other side into oncoming traffic. When he came up into oncoming traffic he went head-on with Dan and Lisa's car. Each car they estimated was going around 60 miles an hour.

It was a devastating collision that destroyed both cars. Dan and Lisa's car ended up in the median upside down. When Lisa had come back to consciousness, Dan was having difficult time breathing. Cars were beginning to stop, and first responders were on their way. Lisa pulled herself over to Dan and held him close to her. It was very cold, and she could see their breath as they talked.

Dan's breathing became shallower, and Lisa was crying, telling him to hold on, that help was on its way. Dan with all the strength he had, assured her that she was going to be okay and said he loved her as he died in her arms in a demolished car upside down in the middle of the interstate.

John received minor injuries and was arrested for Negligent DUI Homicide. This is a felony and he was arrested.

Lisa was injured quite badly as well and took months for recovery. The love of her life was taken from her and his family by the negligence of John, who made a devastating choice to drink and drive, which resulted in the death of Dan, on the day he asked his fiancé to marry him.

I met with Lisa months after the accident. My heart ached for this young woman whose dreams of marrying Dan were extinguished that night. So aside from losing her fiancé, her own health problems associated with the accident that were very serious was a very slow recovery for her.

I then had the privilege of meeting Dan's family and finding out the impact of their son's tragic homicide and how they were dealing with the loss of their son. I called his parents and asked if I could come and visit with them. They agreed with enthusiasm to finally have an opportunity to share how this had impacted their lives. They asked if it would be okay if some of their family came to the meeting as well. I said, "Sure."

I did not know what that meant when they asked if family could come, but when I arrived at their home I was greeted by Dan's mother and father and when we went into the living room the room was completely full with aunts and uncles, cousins, and close friends. I estimate there were around 35 people in this room. It was not a shock, but surely it put some pressure on me to find a way to answer their questions and to investigate for the court how this crime had affected their family.

I shared with the group what was currently happening in the case, that he had pleaded guilty to a felony negligent homicide and was looking at serving a lengthy prison sentence. This was positive news to some of the family and to other family members they were wondering if there was some alternatives to incarceration.

The mother of Dan said that she would at some point like to meet his parents. She talked about how much they are probably hurting as well because of what their son had done. She showed real empathy for their offender and his family.

I asked her if he was here right now, what she would say to him. She sat there for a moment and then said with confidence, "I would take him in my arms and I would tell him that I forgive him and that he needs to learn to forgive himself." She showed this offender John true compassion in her words.

Dan's mother barely got this out, when Dan's brother shared with his mother his concern with his mother's feelings. He was not happy and felt very frustrated. You could have heard a pin drop in that room.

Dan's mother with all her grace and unconditional love for others looked at her son who said that and told him that she loved him, but that he was not Dan's mother and that she cannot live in hate for John, nor can she not forgive him. She told her son and all that were there, that no one can know what each other feels, the only way we can help each other through this is to listen and respect each other for how they feel.

There was not a dry eye in the room, including me. We are supposed to be strong and be objective, but listening to Dan's mother and the love she had for others and the need for sharing her path of healing, was inspiring to everyone in that room.

I kept in contact with that family for several years. I learned a lot from this family. I was still fairly new in my career and to see the healing process with this family and the definite difference in not only their coping skills, but how they perceived this case, provided me with the understanding that every victim and survivor is different and that their healing and what they need to see them through can look very different.

It has definitely been my experience in the hundreds of cases that I have worked on that each victim survivor is different and deserves our respect, regardless of how they feel about the individual who committed the crime and how our system dealt with the case.

I think our system and those who work in the system have become cynical in many ways to the understanding that we need to treat each victim with respect and listen and learn, rather than think just because we are a professional does not mean that we know what they need. We need to listen as I have said many times and not judge them for their path of healing, whether it is forgiveness or not forgiving them and wanting them to suffer for their crime.

A Victim Survivor's Road: Mourning and Coping in Murder Cases

Dan and Lisa's story is tragic. It created so many different paths for the family members and friends. Again, let me emphasize that we must learn from them what they need. Our advice should be based on what they share as to their individual needs.

For example, the mother of the deceased young man really wanted to meet the young man that took the life of her son. Not to chastise him, but to let him know that she had forgiven him and that she hopes he has a full life ahead of him.

Of course, some of the family members would have been upset because of the unconditional love she showed toward the individual who killed her son. However, we have to be able to respect that each person grieves and handles these deaths in different ways. Again, respect is vital and understanding what they have been through is crucial.

Continuing down this same thought, a person's experience with trauma can have a very positive effect. Challenges that we face are not by design to bring us down, but to learn from these experiences as we face the challenges of this world. As we triumph over our difficulties, it strengthens our belief system in a power higher than ours to help us and see through any tragedy.

Working with Victim Survivors of Homicide

I have now been working with offenders and victims of violent crime for over 30 years. Since 2006 I have been honored to work with families in homicide cases all over the country. Sometimes I wonder how I have been so lucky to have this rare look at crime from the perspective of those most impacted by these meaningless acts.

With each new case I am assigned it is obviously difficult to see these families having to endure the horror of a friend or family member being killed. I have learned that there is really nothing I can do personally to diminish the sting of this type of death, but once again I can surely listen to their needs and provide them with resources to fulfill those needs.

For the remainder of this chapter, I will address two separate families who faced the odds of having a loved one murdered and have found their path in their journey, which is truly incredible to watch.

I want to thank them for their willingness to once again share their story. They are powerful examples and I am so grateful for their support. I only hope that I have assisted them in their journey since their loved one was murdered. Thank you so much for the opportunity to work with your amazing families.

Tragedy at Cliffside Restaurant and Bar in Harpers Ferry, West Virginia

If you have ever visited Harpers Ferry, West Virginia, you know how beautiful this national park is in the summer and really throughout the year. It is peaceful and one of those places on earth that I have honestly felt tranquility and I call it my "utopia effect." I love to walk on the trails and around the rivers of the Shenandoah and Potomac Rivers.

While working in Washington, DC, our family lived in Harpers Ferry and truly not only enjoyed living in a surreal environment, but also got to know and love many dear friends who we still visit today. I will never forget about our time in Harpers Ferry.

December 2, 2006 was an ordinary night at the Cliffside Inn, located on Route 340, in Harpers Ferry, West Virginia. Michael Mihalik had gone to work for his evening shift.

At around 10:00 pm, James Robert Jones who at the time was 25-years-old, walked into the Cliffside Inn Restaurant and bar and open fired. He killed Michael and injured two other patrons of the bar that night. Michael was shot in the chest. He was pronounced dead at Jefferson Memorial Hospital. The other victims who were shot, both sustained injuries to their legs.

The police learned from witnesses that James Jones entered the bar, shot six times with a 9mm. One of the amazing facts about this case is that before he could shoot any additional rounds, patrons at the bar tackled him and held him down until police arrived.

A Mother's Worst Nightmare

Rita, Michael's mother was home that evening on December 2, 2006. She received a phone call from a neighbor who happened to be listening to the police scanner. Her neighbor knew that Michael worked at the Cliffside and she heard that there had been a shooting and there were three people who were shot.

Frantically, Rita inquired if she heard any names of the victims and was told that no names were mentioned. She then started calling Michael's cell phone but he was not answering. She then called the Cliffside. No one was picking up, but finally someone did answer. They finally shared with Rita that Michael had been shot and that he was being transported to the local hospital.

Rita quickly left in a panic to the hospital in Charles Town, West Virginia, a small town next to Harpers Ferry. When she and her other children arrived at the hospital they were informed by hospital personnel that Michael had died from his gunshot wounds.

Rita indicated that she felt numb and that it all seemed surreal. She was asking to see Michael, but due to the type of death, it was quite some time before they let them see Michael.

Rita indicated that the man that killed her son came into the bar in a black trench coat and had been on drugs when he open-fired on those in the restaurant.

Michael was loved by those in the community. He had many friends and was very close to his siblings Michelle and Matthew. I was honored to spend several days with Michael's family after the homicide. My heart truly ached for this sweet family who is a very close family and clearly they had a great deal of love and respect for one another.

The funeral was one of the most beautiful funerals that I have ever attended. There were close to 600 people at his funeral and clearly the love that was shown to their family was overwhelmingly representative of the caliber of this family and those that dearly loved and respected them.

There were a lot of tears and I asked Rita what really helped her as she dealt with the loss of her son. She said something that I have shared many times with others. Rita indicated that instead of being angry and sad about what had happened to their family with the loss of Michael that she is grateful, and content with the fact that she was honored to be his Mother during his short 26 years of life. She said remembering the good times of his life and recognizing the privilege it was to be his mother is what has really sustained her these 13 years since his death.

Obviously she dearly misses her son, but she also knows that this is not the end, that she will someday be reunited with her son and her other children and that God truly is looking out for their family.

The Court Process and the Impact on the Mihalik Family

One of the most difficult things that I have witnessed with families in homicide cases is the hours and hours of court hearings leading up to and including a murder trial. I have sat through hundreds of hours of court hearings with these families and I can tell you first hand from an observation position only, how difficult it is for the family to not only see the person who murdered their loved one, but to hear motion hearings and testimony from many and trying to reconcile their loved ones death at the same time. It is in my professional, as well as my personal position, that the court process is one of the most difficult processes that we put these families through.

I attended many court hearings with Michael's family. I could see the looks on their faces when the defendant would enter the courtroom, I could hear it in their voices when they discussed the case pre and post hearing conversations.

One of the things that impressed me the most about their family is that though of course they were upset and frustrated as to why Mr. Jones shot and killed their son and brother, I also noticed a desire for them to understand why this person killed their loved one. A lot of the questions that they asked the prosecutor and myself is why did this happen and is he mentally ill and just a lot of questions centered on the person who took Michael's life.

Though at the time they were not able to get all the answers, they did learn that he was suffering from a mental illness and was using drugs. That information alone helped them to understand some of why he acted out and killed Michael.

Rather than go through a lengthy trial, the prosecutor in the case after having a discussion with the family worked with the defense attorney to reach and agree to a plea agreement rather than a trial.

I sensed from their family a relief that they would not have to go through a lengthy trial and that he would admit and plead guilty to killing Michael.

When a defendant pleads guilty in a case, especially a homicide case, it provides to the families one step closer to finding their path to healing by not having to worry about the case any longer and start to focus on themselves and their healing.

Even with a plea agreement it was still over a year before he finally entered a plea and was sentenced to a minimum of 25 years to life in prison.

Attending the sentencing of a guilty murderer is of course challenging to the victim's family. Though very agonizing to watch, being the survivor I am sure is much more emotional than I could ever perceive. However, watching them and many other families go through this process helps me to appreciate the magnitude of difficulty that it is for them to endure.

I could sense from them a relief when the court proceedings had ended and they were able to share with not only the court but with the defendant what they had experienced as a family.

Victim Impact for the Mihalik's

There is always a great deal of anxiety at the sentencing hearings. This one was no different. Michelle, Michael's sister, and Rita both provided statements to the court at the time of the sentencing and also had the chance to read their statements in open court so that the defendant and the court could hear from them the impact this crime had on them.

Rita shared with the court first the impact of Michael's death on her and her families lives. Rita shared with me that one of the questions that the prosecutor asked her and her family is how the crime has affected all of their family. Rita shared with me that, "Our hearts are broken! We have shed many tears. We will never hear his voice or get a hug and kiss again. All we have left is photographs, personal items, and our memories. Our lives will never be the same."

When you hear those words from a grieving mother you cannot help but begin to at least sense how it must feel to lose a loved one.

In my courses at Penn State, when talking about victims of crime, I will often put them through a scenario. I share with them a case and talk about the brutal facts of a homicide and the impact on victim's family members.

Many who see crime in the comforts of their own home on television, whether it is on the news or a crime show, such as *Criminal Minds*, have a somewhat distorted view of how it truly impacts family members of homicide victims.

I will have victim advocates come to my class and act like victims and the students will have to work through with the advocate how to deal with emotional trauma, anger, the court process, and many other difficult scenarios for victims. It is generally an "eye opener" for students to participate and to actually have to respond to the questions and emotions of the victims.

Even with all the cases I have worked on, it still does not prepare you for some of the raw emotion that happens in the victim survivor's home and in court.

Rita went through with me the struggles that they all went through. Rita and Michelle shared with me that Michael was Michelle's best friend. They always confided in each other and had a very close bond. Similarly, Matthew, Michael's younger brother was also very close to Michael. It was of course very difficult on Matthew as well.

At one point after Michael's murder and before the court process was complete, I had the honor to meet with Rita and her family, extended family, and friends of Michael. We all got together and had a session about grieving and really gave all of them an opportunity to process and share how they were feeling.

Those experiences are always amazing to me, but I could see that this opportunity for Michael's family and friends was exciting to see them processing and sharing their thoughts and feelings openly. It is good to vent and I believe it helped them out so much to be able to get together and just talk about what happened and how it affected their lives.

I shared with Rita and her family the importance of talking and processing. I shared with them my experiences of seeing how positive this can affect their lives, especially after a homicide.

As it became clear that he would being pleading guilty, I shared with them the importance of their victim impact statements and how beneficial and impactful their statements can be in the courtroom.

I shared with them that making their pain and emotions transparent, though it can be difficult to discuss, can have an amazing impact on others who hear their stories and feel their spirits. As they prepared their statements we talked many times and I always shared with them the importance of these statements being their own words and from their hearts.

I would like to share with you their statements word for word. I believe it is impactful to hear the beautiful words of Michelle, Michael's sister, and Rita, Michael's mother.

Victim Impact Statements for Court of Rita and Michelle

As you read their statements put yourself in their shoes and what that must have felt like to share those feelings in a courtroom of people and having the defendant in the room.

Rita had an interesting observation. She told me many times that she wanted to make sure and have Mr. Jones looking at her when she made her statement. She felt it would be important for him to show that he is really listening to the impact that he has had on their family and on Michael. Not once during the reading of both Michelle and Rita's statements did he look up.

After the hearing I explained to them that many of these individuals have so much shame and discontent with their lives that they really have no way of fully understanding and coping with the emotions that they have to face.

It has been my experience that for most of these individuals, it takes years of incarceration and maturity for them to begin to recognize what they have done and the countless lives that they have impacted by their behavior. Many have told me that it is too sensitive to talk about or think about. Clearly they know that they must experience that level of pain and shame in order for them to find their own path to healing.

The following are their statements, verbatim.

Rita's Statement

My son, Michael Glenn Mihalik was murdered on 12/02/2006 while bartending at the Cliffside Bar & Grill. My family has gone through a great deal of pain and adjustments.

Michael's physical absence has been very hard to deal with for all of us. Michael was a grandson, son, brother, cousin, nephew, boyfriend, student, Latter-day Saint, and a friend to many. Our hearts are broken! We have shed many tears. We will never hear his voice or get a hug and kiss again. All we have left is photographs, personal items, and our memories. Our lives will never be the same.

My daughter Michelle has been very angry and depressed while grieving. Michael was her brother and best friend. They spoke every day. Michelle has a wall up around her.

My son Matthew has been very angry and depressed while grieving. Michael was his big brother and mentor. They were sharing a residence. Matthew has kept everything bottled-up inside. He cannot deal with the loss of his brother.

Myself, I have been very depressed while grieving. I have lost 25 pounds and have not been able to sleep very well. I am taking Prozac and attending counseling. I have also joined the support group, Parents of Murdered Children (POMC). I never knew of this organization until my counselor told me. It is unbelievable what we don't know about until something happens to you. Many things remind me of Michael and bring back the tears again and again. My faith in God gives me strength to keep going on.

I am not angry with Michael's death. In my heart, I know and feel Michael is in the spirit world. Michael is in a place of peace and joy. I feel a sense of gratitude. I am grateful to have been chosen by God to be his mother and spend twenty-six years with him. I have experienced so much love as a parent. I know I will be with Michael again.

Today, I have a stronger sense of family, increased faith, and hope and want to be more charitable and serve others. I have promptings to help other parents who have lost their children (something I'm supposed to do). I have inner peace and joy!

Copyright © Rita L. Mihalik. Reprinted by permission.

Rita introduced me to the Parents of Murdered Children. As I stated in the beginning of the chapter, this is an amazing organization that truly cares for those who have lost their children to homicide. Coping with tragedy is not meant to be endured alone. Rita clearly has set a pattern in her life of helping others and allowing others to help her.

As I stated previously, I have had the rare privilege to get to know Michelle and Matthew, Michael's siblings. My life has been blessed knowing them. They have amazing strength and though they have suffered sadness many days, they have relied a great deal on each other. Sometimes siblings of murder are emotionless because of their trauma and that is why it is critical for them to share their feelings and not be afraid to talk about this topic.

I am proud of both of them so much and appreciate their willingness to share not only their family story of tragedy, but healing as well.

I asked Michelle if it would be okay to put her statement she read in court in my book. She said that would be fine. Both Rita and Michelle have said that if they can help others who have gone through this or help others understand how difficult it is, it would bring much joy and satisfaction to them to know that they helped others through their own experiences of trauma.

Below is the statement that Michelle read in open court to the defendant. No one truly understands how difficult it is to go through a tragedy like this. Michelle is amazing to me. She is grounded in life, has a strong sense of self, and is also a mother and wife. She provided a beautiful and descriptive statement. You could sense the emotions that she felt listening to her in the courtroom. I could sense a great deal of personal healing by the way she shared her story in court. Thank you, Michelle, for letting me print your story in my book.

Michelle's Statement

On the night of December 2nd, 2006, I received a phone call from my mom saying that there had been a shooting at the Cliffside. At first, we thought maybe there had been a fight at the hotel, or maybe in the bar. We certainly didn't think it had anything to do with Michael. When I had talked to him an hour and fifteen minutes before, he said it was a slow night. He was starting to clean up and was going to call it an early night. Even so, I still wanted to make sure. After 20 or so frantic phone calls to his cell phone with no answer, I got extremely worried. I wish more than anything that he could have gotten out of there sooner.

That night you walked into that bar in which you were a regular customer, shot and killed Michael, and then tried to kill three other innocent people. Michael didn't even have a chance to say hello or ask how you were, which he always did to anyone who walked through those doors.

Mike was kind and gentle. He was a generous and caring person. He never judged anyone. Mike had little money, but was very wealthy in friends because of these attributes. You knew Michael for many years and were often the recipient of his generosity. He gave you free drinks, let you run tabs when you had no money, and went without many tips because he knew you were having tough times. Michael would give you and anyone else he knew the shirt off his back or the last dollar to his name if you needed it.

And how did you repay his kindness? You shot him in cold blood. You robbed us of a son, a brother, a friend. You took my big brother and my best friend. You have ruined Thanksgiving, Christmas, and Birthdays for my family as well as yours. Now, two families will know the sorrow of a missing son at family gatherings. You have cut short Michael's promising life and wasted your own. And for what? Because you thought he had stolen from you? The 7-11 incident which was rumored as a possible source of your anger was in fact a case of mistaken identity that involved neither Michael nor our brother Matthew. Knowing Michael all these years, you should have known better.

Throughout this process, you have shown no remorse, no sign that this was a mistake, but I know in my heart that Michael would forgive you for doing this to him. I'm not sure that I ever can. Michael will never be a husband or a father. I experienced the joy of having Michael at my wedding. This is something Matthew will never have. Michael will never know his brother's children. He will never know my children. For these things, I will have a hard time forgiving you. For the tears, the sorrow, the anger, the grief, I will have a hard time forgiving you.

I understand that you have been picked on, have been an outsider, and have gone through some traumatic experiences in your life. I do feel sorry for you that you've had such a hard life. If you only walk away with one thing from this, know that Michael was in no way responsible for your troubles, but only treated you with kindness. It is likely that you could be in prison for the rest of your life. Those years will be very difficult for you, but they will be difficult for all of us as well. Each day that you are there is another day that we will not have Michael to brighten our lives. May God show you forgiveness.

Copyright © Michelle Montgomery. Reprinted by permission.

Rita felt like there was no connection when she was making her statement. She was disappointed that he did not make a statement, but realizes with his situation and mental illness it may have not been the right time to make a statement.

One of the things that concerned me was the lack of attention given to them by the Victim Advocate for that area. Rita shared with me that they did not reach out to them except to let them know when court was and generally it was in the form of a letter.

This is a major issue, especially in smaller jurisdictions. Many have reported this lack of attention or concern for their cases. It is critical that we always involve survivors in the process. They need information, which is what helps relieve the tension and stress that they are going through. The best way to manage this difficult part of working with victims is to involve them, get their opinion, and allow them to share how they are feeling. These are simple but powerful messages to the survivors that they matter, when we involve them in the process.

Rita shared with me that she still carries with her a sense of sadness of not having her son with her. She shared that she feels like Michael is her guardian angel and he is watching over her.

Rita is now retired from her full-time job and she has found that what has really helped her, it is helping others. She volunteers and helps seniors in submitting their taxes and volunteers at other organizations. She loves to let other people know that there are others out there to help them. Truly Rita has recognized the positive ways in which she can cope with losing her son to a senseless act of murder. She has provided me with a better understanding that tragedy does not have to define your future. She truly is a wonderful example of someone who has not let tragedy control her life, or affect her ability to serve others.

Rita and her family are like thousands of other families who have lost loved ones to murder. It is comforting to family members to not feel alone. That is why for Rita, being involved with an organization that supports families who have lost loved ones, not only helps family members not feel alone, but provides each person the necessary tools to continue on in their journey.

I appreciate again so much for being allowed to share their story. Rita and her family will always have a special place in my heart. They are genuine people who not only show love to each other, but are an example of how tragedy does not define a family, it strengthens the family. That is what Michael would want.

Necessity of Self-Care for Homicide Victim's Family

This final story for this chapter has to do with the struggles of a mother of a teenager who was murdered 20 years ago in a senseless act of a young man who took the life of several people while they were at work.

Jenny was 16-years-old when she was murdered. To honor the request of the family for anonymity, I will change some of the details of this case in order to protect them.

Like so many other victims I have written about in this book, I want to respect their wishes and be able to tell their stories. The words of the emotions and what they went through is not altered, only the details of the case.

I want to thank this sweet family for allowing me to share their story about their beautiful daughter who was taken from this world at such a young age. They have been amazing to work with. I have spent many hours with them and I can tell you that there are no words to describe my respect and admiration for Jenny's family.

I have learned many valuable lessons in working with homicide and other violent crime victims and their families. I have learned that each has a unique set of circumstances that creates many difficult moments in their lives in so many different ways. I have also learned that they each grieve and process the death of their loved one differently.

When Jenny was murdered, her mother Jolene was completely in shock and truly had no idea the sense of loss that has plagued her and her family's lives at that horrific event several years ago.

Jenny grew up on the east coast in a large city. Jenny loved high school and was a cheerleader and was in choir. She was an extremely talented singer. Jenny had obtained her first job working at a retail store where she had been working for a few months.

On the day she was killed, Jenny and her co-workers were closing the store when the gunman rushed in from the street to rob the business. He told the employees that no one dies if they give him the money. The employees were complying, but apparently changed his mind and as he took the money he open fired and shot multiple employees, including Jenny. Jenny, pleading for her life, was shot in the head and she died on the way to the hospital.

Her mother was watching TV waiting for her phone call from Jenny to come to get her from work. She heard the news that there had been a shooting at the store where her daughter worked. She quickly headed down to her work and was told that her daughter had been transported to the hospital and that she should go there.

So Jolene and her husband James and one of their children Daniel went to the hospital. When they arrived they were escorted to a room. A minister was there and the doctor looked at Jolene and then looked at the ceiling. He said to her and Jenny's family, "For all practical purposes your daughter is dead." She asked him what he meant and he said the same thing. She then looked at the minister and asked him where her soul was and he said she was with God.

Jenny at this point was what we refer to as brain dead, but they did not explain it to Jolene very well and she did not understand what the doctor was saying, not only because they did not explain it very well, but she was feeling numb and unresponsive because her daughter had just been shot. At the time, she could see her breathing with the tube and they still had her heart beating and breathing, but they never explained it to their family. Jolene learned a valuable lesson from this experience that hospitals need to explain what being brain dead means.

The hospital personnel asked if they could harvest her organs and noted that she had put on her driver's license that she wanted to donate her organs. Jolene shared with me that there was a woman that needed kidneys to live and was able to use Jenny's kidneys. Also, there were two men who can now see because of Jenny.

What a beautiful way for the family to know that there is part of their daughter that lives in others and has given them an opportunity to enjoy life because of her self-less act of donating her organs.

Coping with the Aftermath of Jenny's Death

I remember that day I met Jolene. She shared with me pictures of Jenny, not just a few, but many pictures of her growing up and up until the time of her death.

What a beautiful girl Jenny was. You could see her energy in her pictures and the fun that she had with her family and friends. Jenny was well loved by her family and friends and truly had the prospects of a wonderful life until that tragic day.

Jolene shared with me that a couple of years before her death that her daughter went through a time where she was not really focused on the right goals. She had made some choices that had created some difficulty with her parents in controlling her behavior and it became difficult to manage their daughter's life.

Jolene calls it a very trying time in their lives. She shared with me that she decided after speaking with a counselor that she had to instill in her daughter some understanding of accountability and truly felt that her use of tough love changed the course of her daughter for the remaining year of her life.

She remembered that during the last year before Jenny died as one of the happiest years of her life. They did things together; they talked and truly transformed their relationship. She remembers before Jenny had made the changes in her life, one day Jolene was so frustrated that she even wished some very negative thoughts about any future for her daughter.

For many years after her death, Jolene even felt survivor's that maybe she should not have had those type of thoughts. However, I shared with Jolene that there are many parents who have those thoughts and that it is perfectly normal to have doubts about our children's paths that they take.

No one understands those emotions unless you have had a daughter or son murdered. When a victim feels those negative thoughts, it is important as we previously discussed with the article from the US News and World Report that we must talk to someone about our emotions and what we are feeling.

She indicated that it was at least six months after the murder that she was in a trance and would not really be listening to others when they were talking to her. She lost focus at work and did not know how to help at her job. She said that at her work she was really good at helping others with their ideas and after the homicide, she said that she would not be able to help them.

The great thing about Jolene is she took several opportunities to vent with her dear sisters and friends. They helped her process some of her emotions and find a path in her journey that has helped her take control of her life and be very successful in understanding that her daughter is okay and that she knows that she will be with her again someday.

Jolene shared with me how after the murder, for at least a couple of years, she just shook inside. People would ask her how she was doing and she would take advantage of those opportunities to open up and share her deepest feelings.

As part of her thoughts about her daughter and where she was after she was killed, she found herself becoming obsessed with death and the afterlife. She wanted to know all about what happens after you die. Many conversations she had with her family and friends were focused on what they thought about death and what happens to you when you die. She truly described it as an obsession and had a difficult time thinking of anything else at the time.

She shared with me that she read Christian and near-death experience books on the topic. She remembers one Christian book she read, it was about a man who had two daughters killed in an airplane crash and he wanted a sign to know they were okay. Jolene told me a story from one of the books about this man who reached into the ocean and asked God for a sign. When he pulled his hand from the ocean he had a shell in his hand and then he put his hand back into the ocean and then there were two shells. This was a sign to him that both of his daughters were okay.

On one occasion when she was grieving, she asked God for a sign. Jenny really liked red cars and a red car came by Jolene's car and she noticed written in the dust on the car was her daughter's name, "Jenny." That was so comforting to her at the time.

On another occasion when Jolene was watching TV, the doorbell rang and she went to answer the door and no one was there. She went back and began watching TV again and had the strongest impression that it was her daughter Jenny just reminding her that she is not far away.

It is Jolene's belief that when you go into terrible shock when something bad happens, she believes that it is God's spirit that surrounds you like a blanket to protect you. She said to me, "I was shaking so hard but I do feel that God protected me so I could help my son and others."

Jolene shared a very personal story about when she read her daughters schoolwork after the murder, Jenny had written in her schoolwork just before she died. After Jenny's backpack was returned to Jolene, because the police had taken it for evidence, she shared with me what she read in her homework. In their health class she was asked the question if you were pregnant what would you do? In her journal she wrote, "My mom and I used to not get along but now she is my best friend so I would go to her first and we would figure out what to do." She wrote so many good things about our relationship that year before her death. She would say things in her journal like, "She is so slender and beautiful!" She was describing her mother the day she remarried.

Jolene also shared with me what really sustained her those months after her murder were her friends and family. She said to me, "Looking back I can't begin to tell you how much it saved me when they surrounded me with love, but now that I look back at that experience, it saved my life."

It has been my experience in working with these families that many of them truly have been sustained not by anyone solving their problems, just by being there and available is what helped her most.

She also shared with me that after the murder it was not really a concern of what would happen to the man who killed her daughter, it was more about Jenny and wanting to know she was okay. She said, "All I cared about is where she was and was she at peace and was she all right?" She said that when others die she did not think about much where they went, but when her own daughter died, it became an obsession with knowing where she was.

Again, Jolene shared another very intimate moment in her grief. She remembers going into Jenny's room and praying. She felt completely hopeless not fully understanding what it would be like for Jenny when she died. She also said that if God had the power to control where Jenny went, that she wanted God to take Jenny's sins and give them to her and let Jenny be at total peace. Jolene shared with me that when your own child dies that the afterlife becomes extremely important.

Jolene remembers before Jenny was murdered, she went to her work to pick her up. Jenny would be cleaning up and Jolene would come into her work and just watch her clean and just hang out and talk to her and her friends. One of those times that she was there, Jenny put her arm around her mother and said to a co-worker, "I want you to meet the only person I know that is as nice as you are." It was her friend Ann. That meant so much to Jolene to have her daughter say that about her. She said that it made her feel so important in her life.

An interesting fact about the night she was murdered, her mother generally would be there sitting there watching her daughter close up the business for the night, but about a week before she died, Jenny told her mother that she does not have to come early and just sit around and wait. She told her that next time to just stay home until she calls her on her cell phone. Jolene knows that her daughters request is what saved her own life. She felt that if she had followed her routine, she too would have more than likely been shot that night of the murders.

Jolene did not go the entire trial of her daughter's murderer. She said she went to about 80 percent of the trial. It was two years after the murder that the trial took place. She was still numb and really had no emotions for the killer. She said at the trial that she went numb, that it was so surreal thinking that she was sitting at the trial of the man who killed her daughter. She said that she would get emotionally disoriented and could not focus.

After Jenny died, as I had previously mentioned, Jolene lost her focus at her job and it was so hard for her. She stayed there for another year and then had to change jobs. She had a great job, but had lost all interest in her job in sales. She had a longing to work with the elderly and knew she had to move on and so she did. This job with the elderly was what she really needed. Concentrating on helping others really helped her to keep her focus on them and not on what had happened to Jenny.

Working with the elderly she feels it is what saved her soul. She called it a "calling" to work with them. "I had to do it and it helped me so much in dealing with my daughter's death. After six months of working there it helped me so much." Even her family noticed the difference in her when she started working with the elderly.

She fell in love with those people and that is when she turned around and began to find herself again and live. It was her saving grace where she was working. She said, "When I started helping other people is when I started to experience peace within my soul."

Working with Families in the Aftermath of a Murder

I don't believe that any of us are prepared for those kinds of phone calls no matter what the circumstances. However, in my observations those who have lost loved ones to a murder, there is another element to their death that unless you experience those emotions first hand, it is difficult to fully appreciate the increased devastation of the senseless way in which your loved one was killed.

As professionals working with these types of cases in the role of victim advocacy and reaching out, it is vital that we all understand that no one truly knows what it is like and I will emphasize this again and again, all we can really do is listen, try to understand where they are coming from, and help them in their road to finding a path that will help them see that they can survive and that in many situations, make a difference through the memory of their loved ones.

The Need for True Advocacy for Homicide Victim Survivors

We live in a world where homicide seems to be happening more often all over our country. The reasons individuals have murdered others is exhaustive. I have talked to many offenders who have committed homicide, I have heard about every reason why they committed the murder. Many of them have a difficult time accepting full responsibility for what they have done. In the next chapter I will discuss more in-depth the importance of helping these offenders with accountability and responsibility.

However for now, I want to address the side of victim survivors and the need for professionals working with victims to look at more progressive ways for us to attend to the needs of victims of violent crime and specifically murder within this chapter.

Many victims feel persuaded by prosecutors and victim advocates that it is not prudent to learn about the person who committed the crime. If they have questions about the offender, many times those victims are told that it doesn't matter, he killed their loved one and they need to be punished. I have heard horror stories from victims about some of their experiences going through the criminal justice process. It does not matter what side we are taking, controlling how a victim reacts or cope with a case must be by their choice and not part of an agenda for prosecution or defense.

With that said, I had a victim once tell me that law enforcement and the prosecutor showed them a video of the actual murder of their son that was caught on a close circuit television at the business where he was murdered. They showed the video to the family just after the murder, not even a week after the funeral, and then commented that he is an animal and they are going to "fry him until his eyeballs pop out!" They told the victims he is a "mad dog" and "needs to be put down like a dog."

Though the crime that was committed was horrible and this individual must be accountable for what he did, it does not excuse prosecution or defense to use the emotions of a victim to bring what is referred to as justice to a family of a murdered victim.

If you were to ask victims to define justice, you would get many different versions or definitions of justice. It is important to understand where a victim is coming from before we try to help them cope with the horrific court process and the aftermath of a homicide.

Another very pointed example is a defense attorney trying to influence the victim survivor in a homicide case by openly trying to manipulate a victim into believing that somehow they will be responsible of committing another murder if the person is executed.

An example of this was a case I had where the defense attorney told the victim after the victim agreed to meet with them that the defendant has a family and if he is executed it will mean another murder, you don't want that to happen do you?

This example is totally inappropriate and should never be used on a victim survivor of a homicide or for that matter, any violent crime.

So what is it that clearly helps victims through this process, to begin with, we don't know what they need or want so we listen. Then when possible, we should do everything we can to accommodate these individuals who have lost their loved one to this senseless act.

Another aspect of victim advocacy is to acknowledge and validate their fears, their feelings, and the requests to the best of our ability. If we can't, then we need to not only explain to them why we cannot meet that need, but work with them on helping them to understand and to reconcile with them so that justice can be served, but also that they understand and feel that the system is listening to them.

The Importance of Validation to Victim Survivors

Along with being careful not to define justice for victims, another aspect of advocacy is acknowledging their position and helping them to feel validated, but also educate them on the process and the parameters that the system must follow.

For example, a judge should always validate a victim in the court process all the way through the sentencing of an individual. Some judges have made it clear in their courtroom that victim statements are important and will not only be listened to but used as part of the sentencing process. Other judges, even in open court have made it known that they realize victims need to make their statement, but that their statement does not matter with respect to the sentencing process.

Recently, I was reading an article where a couple in England was making a statement at a parole hearing on the man that stabbed their son to death. He was looking at receiving a parole date and the family was speaking to the parole board via video technology, sharing with the parole judges their feelings about the offender being transferred to a less secure facility for transition to the streets. They of course were distraught that this man who brutally stabbed their son would potentially be released, however what the parole judge said was just as devastating to them.

When the victims had finished their statement, the judge thanked them and he thought that the audio feed to them had been disconnected, but it was still live to the victims. The judge said to those in attendance at the hearing, thinking that the family was not listening. He said, that someone should tell the families that their statements really have no bearing on his decision. Can you imagine being the victim survivor of your son being brutally attacked and stabbed to death, and the judge telling those in attendance at the hearing that their statement makes no difference in their case?

In addition, the parole judges according to the article, only to use the behavior of the offender while he is incarcerated as behavior that will decide whether or not they are moved to a less secure facility or release from prison all together.

Though this may be a true statement for some courts, it should never be said to a victim. There statement does matter. I have heard judges in the middle of a sentencing after they had heard a victim statement, say in open court that after the victim's statement they are changing their sentencing and imposing a more punitive sentence on the individual, solely based on the testimony by the victim or victim survivor in a sentencing for a violent crime.

I am convinced after sitting through hundreds of hours of court proceedings that the most important thing we can do for victims is to listen to their needs, accommodate them when we can, and if we cannot, then we are honest and not only explain why, but help them by receiving feedback. Though they may not always agree with the results of the adjudication of a person who commits a crime, they will at least feel listened to and understood.

I believe it is our duty and sincere obligation to do all we can to make right a wrong and show human kindness in the process.

I truly hope that our system will continue to do their part to bring justice to all cases to protect society first, and then to meet the needs of the victim survivors, and respect for the laws of our land. I still believe that is possible.

9

Restorative Justice—A Path of Healing

My Roots to Restorative Justice

Back in the late 80s and 90s when I was most active as a state and federal probation officer, I was always stepping outside my comfort zone and trying to think of ways to help men and women who have committed crime to better understand accountability and responsibility by having them answer questions to me as to the reasons they committed their crime against their victims. Just having them complete the conditions of their probation did not seem like enough to accept accountability for their actions. They needed to talk about it and recognize what went wrong and why they acted out.

Though we had them in counseling and they would address some of those issues in treatment, still they never really talked about the impact their behavior had on others to the extent that it changed their thinking to be more cognizant of how their decision making affects others. I would have long conversations with them about why and sometimes it was very enlightening to me and difficult for the offender to specifically talk about the way they treated others. I really wanted to help them own their behavior.

So, my goals became more focused on accountability and responsibility. I was really motivated with my caseload to do all I could to help them not only successfully complete parole or probation, but to be accountable to society and show responsibility to their victims.

Portions of this chapter are written with permission of Richard Burr. Portions of this chapter are written with permission of Howard Zehr. Portions of this chapter are written with permission of Ellen Halbert. Portions of this chapter are written with permission of Robert Autobee. Portions of this chapter are written with permission of Lola Autobee. Portions of this chapter are written with permission of Scott Autobee. Portions of this chapter are written with permission of Mia Gallippi. Portions of this chapter are written with permission of John Sage.

We clearly want all parties in criminal offenses, whether they are juvenile offenders or adult, to be more accountable to themselves, their families, victims, and society. The only way we can do that is to provide opportunities for them to confront some of those emotions and to talk about it freely so they know it is okay to talk about and that their behavior does not have to define them for the rest of their lives. The goal is to help them to see the good within themselves.

It was and always has been important for me to develop trust before I ask offenders difficult questions about their crime, but I found it interesting that the majority of those I supervised were upfront with me and to my surprise, many of them thought it would be important to say they are sorry to their victims. Of course there is always a few that do not want to participate with my discussions about their victims, but those that do, I feel it truly helps them in realizing how their behavior affected the victims and their families, the offender's family, and society in general.

As a probation and parole officer, I would then contact the victims in many of the cases and I would ask them what I could do for them? Do they need answers to questions, do they feel safe with the offender on the street? Those were questions I would always ask. I of course got many answers from those and other questions, but what I found most intriguing is that many of them wanted to know more about the person who committed the crime and of course would always ask me if they honestly were sorry for what they did.

There were many cases that I would facilitate meetings with their victims. Mostly cases of a family or friend who had committed a criminal act against a family member, however there were other cases as well.

For many years when I was a federal probation officer, I did not even realize I was participating in restorative justice, and it was not until around 2005 that I realized I was already doing that with many of my cases. I saw this process change many lives by better understanding the details as to why they committed the act against their victims. Many of my cases I would have them write letters to their victims, but there were many as well that met together with their victims.

I remember many of my cases that when I would share with the victim that they could have this information about the man/women who committed the crime, they were curious and then became ecstatic when they found answers to their questions that only the offender could answer. It was empowering for those who participated in this process.

I remember in 2000 I was facilitating a meeting between a father and his daughter who he had sexually abused. As I interviewed his daughter who at the time, he committed the offense was 14 years old, she had many questions for her father. Now in her early twenties she wanted the chance to meet with her father and ask him questions. Once we had it approved by all parties, including the therapists, we had a meeting and I facilitated the discussion.

It was an amazing meeting! The daughter asked very detailed and blunt questions to her father and without hesitation he answered all her questions and expressed that he understands if she never wants to see him again.

The results of this meeting have been life changing for this family. They now are visiting on a regular basis. She is now married and has a child of her own. However, now that she has a child, she does require that her father live according to their boundaries but will always allow him to be around her son. She said that since their session, she has forgiven him and that she feels like she loves him again and his accountability has completely changed her outlook on what she had previously felt, before she knew about this process. Many victims just want to know that first and foremost, they are sorry, and secondly, that they have learned to control their behavior and that they will own it the rest of their lives.

The offender in that case shared with me that what has and continues to impact him the greatest is the understanding from his daughter as to how devasting the behavior was. It helped him accept and understand accountability at a level he would have never understood if he had not gone through the victim/offender dialogue. He now has gone 20 years without reoffending.

As I look back over my career, it is interesting to note that I had been involved in restorative justice for many years but did not even realize that is what they called it. I first was introduced to the concept of restorative justice in Washington, DC, when I worked for the Administrative Office of the United States Courts.

My first assignment in Washington, DC was working as a training specialist in the Training Branch for the Federal Defender Services Division of the Administrative Office of the United States Courts. My responsibilities were to manage all of the Habeas Corpus Death Penalty Training that was sponsored by the United States Courts.

It was during this time that I was privileged to meet several attorneys. One of those attorneys was Richard "Dick" Burr from Houston, Texas. Dick was one of the attorneys for Timothy McVeigh, who was convicted for his part in the Oklahoma City Bombing. Dick was Timothy's attorney during the appeals process of his case. I was intrigued by the work that he was doing in the defense community called Defense Initiated Victim Outreach. He was working with Tammy Krause, who was at the time working in Harrisonburg, Virginia at Eastern Mennonite University with Howard Zehr, who is internationally known for his work with restorative justice.

It was all three of these individuals that have impacted my life and provided me a foundation of understanding more clearly the power of restorative justice within our criminal justice system. For years experts have said that it won't work, but I have seen it work every day since getting involved in 2005. It is the most influential process to facilitate change that I have ever participated within the field of Criminal Justice.

Concept of Restorative Justice Defined

I want to at this point of the chapter discuss the definition of restorative justice, and the importance of this work within our criminal justice system.

Howard Zehr as I previously mentioned has been a huge influence in my life. I have a great deal of respect and admiration for Howard. I have spoken at conferences with Howard and I have also been schooled by him at Eastern Mennonite University several years ago when I was trained in the program, "Defense Initiated Victim Outreach." Howard is one of the calmest men I have ever met. His insight is amazing, and I could listen to him speak all day. I considered Howard to have been one of my main mentors in working with crime victims and restorative justice.

Recently I was reading on his website, Zehr Institute of Restorative Justice. I wanted to share a brief biography of Howard and his amazing career and the thousands of people that he has influenced in the work of restorative justice.

> Widely known as "the grandfather of restorative justice," Zehr began as a practitioner and theorist in restorative justice in the late 1970s at the foundational stage of the field. He has led hundreds of events in more than 25 countries and 35 states, including trainings and consultations on restorative justice, victim-offender conferencing, judicial reform, and other criminal justice matters. His impact has been especially significant in the United States, Brazil, Japan, Jamaica, Northern Ireland, Britain, the Ukraine, and New Zealand, a country that has restructured its juvenile justice system into a family-focused, restorative approach.
>
> A prolific writer and editor, speaker, educator, and photojournalist, Zehr actively mentors' other leaders in the field. More than 1,000 people have taken Zehr-taught courses and intensive workshops in restorative justice, many of whom lead their own restorative justice-focused organizations.
>
> Zehr was an early advocate of making the needs of victims central to the practice of restorative justice. A core theme in his work is respect for the dignity of all peoples.
>
> From 2008-2011 he served on the Victims Advisory Group of the U.S. Sentencing Commission. He serves on various other advisory boards.
>
> In 2013, Zehr stepped away from active classroom teaching and became co-director, with Dr. Carl Stauffer, of the new Zehr Institute for Restorative Justice. http://zehr-institute.org/staff/howard-zehr/
>
> *Copyright © Howard Zehr. Reprinted by permission.*

One of the things that intrigues me about the work of Howard is the fact that he looks at the big picture and does not choose sides on who needs help and assistance. He believes that all parties, including the community need assistance in the healing process that have been victims of violent crime.

I think in order to truly understand what restorative justice means; we need to turn to Howard Zehr for a definition of restorative justice. This definition of restorative justice is found on his website. Clearly restorative justice is healing and a necessary part of our criminal justice system that creates fairness and responsiveness to crime. Restorative justice according to Howard Zehr is defined this way.

> Do a Google search for the phrase "restorative justice" and you will get over a million "hits" – and this for a term that was virtually non-existent 30 years ago. Ask what it means, and you may get a variety of answers.
>
> For many, it implies a meeting between victims of crime and those who have committed those crimes. A family meets with the teenagers who burglarized their home, expressing their feelings and negotiating a plan for repayment. Parents meet with the man who murdered their daughter to tell him the impact and get answers to their questions. A school principal and his family meet with the boys who exploded a pipe bomb in their front yard, narrowly missing the principal and his infant child.

The family's and the neighbors' fears of a recurrence are put to rest and the boys for the first time understand the enormity of what they have done.

Restorative justice does include encounter programs for victims and offenders; today there are thousands of such programs all over the world. But restorative justice is more than an encounter, and its scope reaches far beyond the criminal justice system. Increasingly schools are implementing restorative disciplinary processes, religious bodies are using restorative approaches to deal with wrongdoing – including clergy sexual abuse – and whole societies are considering restorative approaches to address wrongs done on a mass scale. Of growing popularity are restorative conferences or circle processes that bring groups of people together to share perspectives and concerns and collaboratively find solutions to the problems facing their families and communities.

Restorative justice emerged in the 1970s as an effort to correct some of the weaknesses of the western legal system while building on its strengths. An area of special concern has been the neglect of victims and their needs; legal justice is largely about what to do with offenders. It has also been driven by a desire to hold offenders truly accountable. Recognizing that punishment is often ineffective, restorative justice aims at helping offenders to recognize the harm they have caused and encouraging them to repair the harm, to the extent it is possible. Rather than obsessing about whether offenders get what they deserve, restorative justice focuses on repairing the harm of crime and engaging individuals and community members in the process.

It is basically common sense – the kind of lessons our parents and fore-parents taught – and that has led some to call it a way of life. When a wrong has been done, it needs to be named and acknowledged. Those who have been harmed need to be able to grieve their losses, to be able to tell their stories, to have their questions answered – that is, to have the harms and needs caused by the offense addressed. They – and we – need to have those who have done wrong accept their responsibility and take steps to repair the harm to the extent it is possible.

As you might imagine with so many Google references, the usage of the term varies widely. Sometimes it is used in ways that are rather far removed from what those in the field have intended. So, when you see the term, you might ask yourself these questions: Are the wrongs being acknowledged? Are the needs of those who were harmed being addressed? Is the one who committed the harm being encouraged to understand the damage and accept his or her obligation to make right the wrong? Are those involved in or affected by this being invited to be part of the "solution?" Is concern being shown for everyone involved? If the answers to these questions are "no," then even though it may have restorative elements, it isn't restorative justice. – Howard Zehr http://zehr-institute.org/what-is-rj/

Copyright © Howard Zehr. Reprinted by permission.

We learn from Dr. Zehr that restorative justice is simply working with the different entities within our system to help in repairing the harm caused by crime, bullying at school, and many other activities that call for some type of action in order for us to restore socially acceptable behavior and hold guilty parties accountable. Howard Zehr made it very clear that repairing harm and gathering people together will assist us in solving community problems.

Through the years I have felt honored to work for the state and federal government in my various capacities. Overall, I still believe we have a good system that is clearly there to protect our communities, individuals, and their families. However, I also believe that one area that we have drastically fallen short with is the way we perceive those that commit criminal acts. There is no doubt that when a person commits a crime, they have offended all of us at some level and they must pay their debt to society and be accountable and responsible for their actions. When we think about the phrase debt to society, what does that mean?

Does that mean they need to spend years in prison to be punished? We often hear members in our society saying, "He is scum and needs to go to prison for a long time!" What does that mean? Is that productive, especially since he will be getting out of prison at some point, and do we want them to get out of prison feeling worse about themselves and then becoming our neighbors? I would hope we can truly conceptualize what that means to throw away human beings and consider them to be too reprehensible to have them in our communities. Who are we to judge that individual?

I want to make it clear that I am not saying that those who commit heinous crimes should be considered for less severe consequences for their actions, but what I am saying is we need to be more proficient at reviewing cases and using the different tools we have to help an offender be accountable. Rather than thinking that punishment through a long prison sentence is always the answer to changing a person's life and steering them away from crime.

There have been many offenders who have committed homicide and sexual assault that should do significant time in prison, but what we have not completely solved yet is how we take a man that will be incarcerated and help them on their road to be a better human being, so when they get out they will be productive members of society. Yes, some are successful, but as we know there are many who have not learned their lesson through punishment and need other forms of accountability to ensure that they understand the importance of full responsibility for their actions. By holding them more accountable to society and their victims, we will have a better chance of assisting individuals to be successful in navigating the criminal justice system and changing their lives.

We know from statistics that the recidivism rates in America are high. The challenge is really not about how much time, but what do they do with their time and how can we as a system hold them more accountable and accept responsibility for their behavior.

Frankly, I would like to see professionals in the field of social sciences assist in being better at educating our communities why people commit crime and work together with them in discussions where we can talk about these topics and when appropriate, find solutions rather than continuing to punish and throw away individuals and somehow think we are doing a good thing.

Those who commit crime really need to think about what they want in life. How do these offenders feel about the crime they committed; does it make them feel awful about themselves? Many times, they do not see the road ahead and all they are trying to do is survive each day.

Individuals that have given up hope and have lost their way, have a difficult time recovering, regardless of the amount of punishment you can inflict.

The better route for us to serve and work with the offenders is to help them recognize first their accountability to themselves, then to their victims, families, and the community in general. The community truly should be our number one concern and helping these offenders recognize their worth and the road ahead is clearly a better option than treating them like a "scum bag."

We judge people so harshly who commit crime or are homeless on the streets. We tend to not recognize the fact that they have children, are brothers, sisters, and veterans who have fought in wars. We also tend to look at those who commit crimes as a throw-away, or a monster, or a loser, and many more inappropriate pronouns.

We need a society that starts to believe in human beings again and recognize just because a person goes to jail, has been in jail, or is called a monster, that does not define them as a human being. I can think of so many reasons why people become offenders and it is beyond our full understanding.

In addition, there are many offenders who have been victims themselves or experienced trauma that has severely altered their ability to understand the importance of making good choices. This is never an excuse but helps us to understand where they are coming from and how we can help them.

For example, I was talking with a warden of a prison. He informed me that in the processing of each inmate they ask them if they have been a victim of abuse. I asked him what they do with the information. He informed me that it was for statistics and that they really did not do anything other than keep the data on the inmate. What? That does not even make sense to me and he agreed. We have taken the caring aspect out of the equation and are slowly turning away from truly understanding why people become criminals.

Defense Initiated Victim Outreach, Is That an Oxymoron?

While working in Washington, DC, I asked Dick Burr and Tammy Krause about the program that Dick initiated called, "Defense Initiated Victim Outreach," and the purpose for victim specialists reaching out to victim survivors? They shared with me that the services for these specialists were requested by defense attorneys handling death penalty and other violent crime cases nationally. I was confused because that is generally not a position that defense attorney's take in reaching out to victims of crime. It sounded like a conflict of interest.

Myself, being in probation and parole, I was generally focused on prosecutorial responsibilities and did not have much to do with defense attorneys, other than working with both parties in plea negotiations on violations of parole and probation. I was intrigued, but cautious about Defense Initiated Victim Outreach.

Once I listened to several presentations at the death penalty conferences, I managed with the US Courts, and after talking with Dick Burr, Tammy Krause, and Howard Zehr; I was excited about this program. It truly gave victims more information in the case involving their loved one and allowed them to ask questions to defense attorneys. I have now been involved in this service to victims for almost 14 years.

I would like to tell you about Dick Burr and his background. I recently interviewed him for my book. I was so grateful when he took the time to speak with me and I would like to share with you some of his insight into restorative justice and why he, Howard Zehr and Tammy Krause, began supporting Defense Initiated Victim Outreach. Just a little about Dick, he is now mainly working with Post-Conviction Relief in death penalty cases. For the benefit of the reader who is not familiar with the term Post-Conviction, I have provided the following definition.

> Post-Conviction Relief is a general term related to appeals of criminal convictions, which may include release, new trial, modification of sentence, and such other relief as may be proper and just. The court may also make supplementary orders to the relief granted, concerning such matters as re-arraignment, retrial, custody and release on security. https://definitions.uslegal.com/p/post-conviction-relief/

This is extremely important work, for we know that there have been many reasons some have been treated unfairly by the system. An attorney who participates in this type of criminal defense, they are assuring that their constitutional rights have not been violated by reviewing all the information on the case and finding any information that could share new light on a case. I cannot think of anyone more qualified that Dick Burr in doing this type of criminal law. Recently, as I was reviewing documents on the Internet, I found an article about Dick Burr. In 2000 Dick was named the "Best Lawyer of the Year" in Houston, Texas, with the years of service to the indigent who cannot afford to defend themselves in capital murder cases. https://www.houstonpress.com/best-of/2000/people-and-places/best-lawyer-6603719

I asked Dick why our system seems to struggle using restorative justice in adult criminal cases. He shared with me that for many years restorative justice has been a big part of the juvenile justice system but has struggled with the adult system due to the banner of retribution in our adult system. I share Dick's belief in this problem within our adult system. There are many people who do not fully understand restorative justice, so many within our adult system automatically think that restorative justice is about getting the offender a less punitive sentence or letting them off all together if they say they are sorry.

Of course, my experience in restorative justice is quite contrary to less punitive. Restorative justice in the adult system holds the offender more accountable, for they now have to answer to the justice system and to their victims, and to the community. So, Mr. Burr believes with time and a clearer picture with what restorative justice is all about, we will make it easier to introduce concepts of restorative justice into our courtrooms on a regular basis. We are seeing this with Drug Courts, Veterans Court, and Mental Health Courts. We are recognizing the need for a deeper look into why crime is happening and how we help our communities to heal from these tragedies.

My next question to Dick had to do with the Defense Initiated Victim Outreach. I asked him if he could share with me how he came up with the concept and share a little history behind the roots of the program.

Dick shared with me that when he was representing Timothy McVeigh; he was overwhelmed by the amount of impact to the victims and their families in the Alfred P. Murrah Federal Building bombing in Oklahoma City. Altogether, 168 people were killed, including 19 children that were in a daycare center. There were over 650 people injured and millions of dollars of damage to the area. https://www.history.com/topics/1990s/oklahoma-city-bombing

Dick shared with me that this was overwhelming to think about how to serve the needs of his client Tim, and yet show compassion for the families and those affected by the bombing. He indicated that he felt that in order to be compassionate they must be proactive in reaching out to the victims and allowing them to ask questions, and he felt it was important to help them realize that even though they had an important role in protecting the constitutional rights of their client, it did not blind them to the devastation that their client caused. Most importantly, Dick wanted them to feel that they were being listened too.

The problem was he did not know how to reach out to them and for them to feel that he was being genuine in his approach with the victims and their families. This is when Dick called Howard Zehr and asked him if he could help in reaching out to the victims in the Oklahoma Bombing.

So, Howard and Tammy Krause, who was working with Howard at the time at Eastern Mennonite University, met with Dick and his defense team representing Timothy McVeigh.

Dick and his defense team met for four days, learning about restorative justice and how their team could use the principles of restorative justice into the case and reach out to the survivors in the Oklahoma City Bombing.

They reached out to many of the victims who had submitted from the victim impact list. "We got in touch with them through a letter and shared with them that the intentions of reaching out to them was to allow them to ask questions to the defense team specifically related to Timothy's case."

The letter that they sent to the victims first and foremost shared their sympathy for what happened and assured them that their work had not lessened their concern for the families and their suffering.

Tammy was tasked with reaching out to all the victims and following up with them. She ended up talking to about half the victims that they had reached out to. None of them at the time really wanted to meet at that time.

However, about a year after Timothy McVeigh's trial ended, Dick and his team were able to meet with some of the victims and were able to answer their questions. They met for one full day of questions and answers. It was an amazing experience for his team and for Tammy to meet with them and hear their concerns and questions.

Since that time, Defense Initiated Victim Outreach has continued to gain traction in our adult system. I have worked on many cases and later in the chapter I will share the story of some of the victim survivors and their experience with victim outreach and restorative justice practices.

In the last few years I have had the privilege of working some non-capital murder cases as well as death penalty cases in Defense Initiated Victim Outreach. It has been an amazing journey and has been extremely helpful in the cases that I have been asked to help with.

I asked Dick what he felt some of the benefits in his eyes are with respect to the defendant's involvement in answering questions from the victims. Dick indicated that if the client is involved in the process he will begin to start understanding the emotion of what happened and eventually breaks down the wall of the defendant and gives him a chance to hold himself accountable through what he has learned from hearing the direct questions from the families of the murdered victim. Dick also indicated that it provides them a chance of transformation in their lives. He said that if these individuals face up to the harm, they caused it would help them understand what real remorse feels like and help them turn their lives around and do what is right.

I asked Dick what his impressions are as to the validity of the work of a Defense Victim Specialist, with respect to the benefit to the victims.

I really liked what Dick said; he put it this way, "When a crime happens, there is a relationship that comes into play. An organic relationship is developed, and the victims need to have attention paid to it." They may have a lot of questions for the defendant and Dick believes that the only way for them to truly get an honest answer is to reach out to the defense team and for the victim to have the opportunity to ask the questions. This is a service that prosecutors cannot provide to victims, nor the advocates that work in their offices.

Dick said that the victims generally need an opportunity to express how they feel and release that anger and frustration that they often feel. What a better opportunity for a victim that participates in this service and can share how they feel directly with the defense attorneys and their client who murdered the victim survivors loved one.

Dick believes that Defense Initiated Victim Outreach is the only way to allow the victim and offender to participate in this process and not get in the way of litigation. He believes that it is a necessary part of healing for victims and that if they want to participate, they should have every right to and not feel awkward because the questions are to the defense attorneys.

As I shared earlier, I have now been involved in this process for many years. I can say without hesitation it is the most powerful service I have ever seen for victims. It has helped so many victims. I have had many victims agree to speak in my classes at Penn State who have participated in this process. Many of them have said that this opportunity of restorative justice has literally changed and saved their lives.

I was originally trained at Eastern Mennonite University by Tammy Krause and Howard Zehr. At this training I was able to speak with victims who had gone through the process, prosecutors that were willing to share their feelings about this program, and after two weeks of intense training I was convinced of the importance of this work.

Many victims have questions for the defense, but our system has always directed victims away from any contact with defense attorneys. Many feel that if defense attorneys reach out to victims, they are trying to get them to see their side and express negativity towards a death sentence. Whether you are from a prosecutorial mentality or defense, we must be careful in our system not to create a tunnel vision effect on victims by keeping them concentrating and believing that supporting a certain position defines justice.

The way I look at justice may be completely different than someone else. We as a system need to honor that individuality and not try to persuade victims to feel a certain way. Present the facts and back off and let them make their own decisions.

I am not supporting the death penalty one way or another in this chapter, but what I am saying is that we must allow victims to have all the information possible from the prosecution and defense and let them decide what is most comfortable and healing for them to support. To persuade a victim one way or another is wrong and unethical. It is not our duty as a member of the criminal justice community to decide for a victim what they need for healing.

Victims also need us to be upfront with them and help them to understand that potential outcomes of a case are out of all our hands. That is why it is important for victims to have the big picture on all the possible outcomes so they can see that just because they may feel a certain way, that does not necessarily mean that is what will happen. They need to be prepared if the outcome is not what they expected or wanted. Clearly victims should understand the importance of not basing justice or relief on one particular outcome of their case.

Here is a simple way to understand what I am saying. When I go to a restaurant, they provide me with a menu. There may be others that express their opinion on what is good on the menu including canned speeches by the server on their own opinions, but ultimately it is my choice what I want to eat on the menu.

Some prosecutors tell victims that the death penalty is the only way you can get justice in this case. The prosecutor has an extremely important part in the criminal justice system. Their job is to defend the laws and expose those who violate the laws and hold them accountable. There should never be partisanship from anyone in a professional position within our system to influence a position on the death penalty. We should never ever use tactics of persuasion on victims. Present the menu and let them choose.

In addition, defense attorneys with hidden agendas in their contact with victims to solicit sympathy for their client and make them feel guilty if they support the death penalty is reprehensible, unethical, and should never be used as a tactic to put on the shoulders of a victim.

We should feel obligated to provide the evidence on both sides and let the victim decide where their healing process can be best served on their position.

Think about it this way, if we force or heavily influence a victim to feel a certain way and then later after the execution, they feel guilt and shame for having participated in a process that took another human life, the survivor may feel responsible because they supported something that they really did not believe in; we have now just added another level of trauma in their lives.

To be fair, you may also have a victim that feels compelled to support the death penalty and then the offender gets life in prison and somehow because of what they have been told, they feel like they "lost" the case. Convincing the victim's family that somehow, they lost the case because they did not get the death penalty is not true and should never be discussed. We have to be so careful in how we present information to victims so they can feel complete autonomy in their decision to support a particular position. Once they have made that decision, we should honor that.

There are so many variables and influences that can affect the death sentence, and all victims should clearly understand that and know that at any given moment during the process a death sentence can be dropped and will not be part of the menu of potential outcomes in a case. I have worked on cases personally where this has happened and if it were not for their questions and truly understanding how death penalty litigation works then they would have been devastated when the death sentence was taken off the menu of sentencing options.

I remember one case where the family had this happen. I had prepared them for the possibility of that happening. When it did, they were not shocked and upset. What they wanted to know at that point is what it would be like in prison for him and of course having the concern that he might get out of prison. So, they asked me some very pointed questions.

I contacted the Department of Corrections (DOC) and I obtained from them all the possible scenarios for the individual who killed their loved one. I presented many pages from the DOC that explained the process of deciding where an inmate will be housed and what he will be doing day-to-day in the prison. When I presented this to them, they were so appreciative and clearly saw that this inmate who committed a horrible act against their family would not have it easy in prison and his chances of being able to kill anyone else were reduced drastically. That brought them relief.

So even though the death penalty was not on their menu of options now, because we prepared them for the possibility that the death sentence will be eliminated from the sentencing options, though disappointed, they understood and it made it much easier for them to accept.

After the death penalty was eliminated from the options, I asked the family if they wanted to go inside a prison and see what it is like. They took me up on the offer and I was able to arrange for them to tour a maximum-security prison. At the end of the tour they were shocked as to how secure the facility was and they could see that there was no way he could escape where he would be housed. It brought them huge relief. That is what this work is about, is helping them to find answers to ease their pain and create a healing path for them.

Can we take away all their pain and anguish, of course not, but we sure can do our part to help them, empower them, and provide much relief by educating them and answering their questions.

I once had a victim advocate ask me a question when I was trying to explain this process to her. She said to me, "What if they ask you a question that will hurt them?" I was not sure what she meant at first. She was basically frustrated that I would answer any question they had and that it might hurt them emotionally to get an answer. I was surprised that a victim advocate would ask me such a question.

I replied back to her respectfully that if a victim asks a question, we should honor them with answering their question. We can be courteous and let them know that they may not like the answer, but ultimately, it is there choice and we should not take that choice away from them that is not our job. It would just cause more frustration in their life by not having the answers to the question that this mother had in her mind. I have had many victims ask me those difficult questions. I knew that it would be hard to hear, but she said to me, "I need to know and if I don't know, that will be worse on my soul."

That position within our judicial system is invaluable! Speaking from a practitioner position, I can share with you that I have seen this service work within many victims and survivors' lives and has brought them to a level that they would have never imagined in their healing.

Again, as I conclude, as a Defense Initiated Victim Outreach Specialist, I make it very clear to the victim survivors that my role is to answer their questions. I do not have an agenda other than allowing them to ask questions. My position is to provide them with all the information they ask for, including questions asked to defense teams or any other entity that they ask for my help. I then am privileged to stand back and let them make their own decision and not follow any hidden agendas. Many victims will tell me that one of the most challenging parts of being a survivor is hearing from others what they think the victim needs. However, these wonderful people who have been through so much shared with me that healing comes from gaining knowledge about what happened to them or their loved ones and from being believed and listened too. I think we can manage that in our system.

Ellen Halbert – Director of Victim Services, Travis County Texas (retired)

Over the course of my career I have been privileged to get to know many people in our criminal justice system that have impacted my life and have shown me that we have some really wonderful people in our system that work so hard every day to help so many. I am amazed at the strength in many of these men and women who have been a victim of a crime and have found the strength and courage to not only heal, but to become advocates for so many that suffer victimization from crime.

One such person that I have been privileged to meet, train with, and get to know is Ellen Halbert. Ellen and I met in 2005 when I went through Defense Initiated Victim Outreach training in Harrisonburg, Virginia. The thing that I was most excited about was gaining a new friend in Texas, but also that Ellen was the Director of Victim Services for the Travis County District Attorney's Office in Austin, Texas, and loved restorative justice.

As I shared, restorative justice has struggled gaining momentum in the adult system with district attorney's offices. However, Ellen was one who had a very important job to direct the work of victim advocates in one of the biggest counties in Texas. She not only supported restorative justice, but also spoke about it in meetings and conferences that I attended and has been a mentor of mine with my work in restorative justice. I have used some of her quotes about restorative justice at national conferences where I have spoken about this topic.

Ellen's work is extensive in the field of victim services. Ellen began her career in 1986 working in victim services in Travis County. During that first year of her employment she became a victim of a crime as well. She was raped, beaten, and left for dead in her own residence.

After her recovery from her victimization, she continued her work in Texas with victims. In 1991 she was appointed by Governor Ann Richards to the Texas Board of Criminal Justice. This is where she was introduced to the inner workings of restorative justice. During the course of her work in Travis County, she subsequently became the Director of all Victim Services for Travis County Texas, after six years with the Texas Board of Criminal Justice. As you can imagine, that was a huge responsibility and one that she took very seriously. She had a great deal of influence and was an amazing leader until her retirement in 2013.

Because of her victimization, she also co-facilitated a working group for victims of violent crime for over ten years. Ellen has also been on many committee's on victims' services. She has had an amazing career and has influenced the lives of thousands. I have a deep respect for Ellen in all that she has been through, but mainly because of the kind of a person she is and how she cares for everyone.

She was also the editor for an award-winning publication called, "Crime Victims Report." She did this for a number of years in her support for victims of crime. She was the editor for over 12 years.

Ellen was also on the Advisory Council for Restorative Justice and Dialogue from the University of Texas in Austin. She also served for many years on the Board for the Bridges to Life program out of Houston, Texas. I will write later in the chapter on this program. She has been recognized and honored all over the United States for her work as a survivor and restorative justice practitioner.

As you can see, she has had an amazing career and has helped so many. However, Ellen went through a very difficult time in her life. What she went through is nothing short of a miracle. For many reasons, Ellen should not have survived her attacker in 1986.

In 1986 Ellen had come home from work and a drifter, 18-years-old, had broken into her residence and was hiding in the attic until the next morning. He then came out of the attic and attacked Ellen in her bathroom as she was getting ready for work.

For approximately the next two hours, this intruder brutally raped, stabbed, and beat Ellen with a hammer. Ellen was stabbed four times, twice in the back of the neck. He stabbed her in the left breast and then he hammered a knife into her skull. He then proceeded to hit her in the head many times with a hammer.

Because of the injuries to her head, they could not tell how many times he struck her with the hammer, but they are thinking that he hit her at least 8 to 10 times. Ellen explained that when he hit her in the head with the hammer, that it split the skin on her scalp into pieces.

During the many plastic surgeries, they were trying to stitch and repair the damage caused by blunt force to her head. Over the course of treating Ellen, she had over 500 stitches in her head alone.

For many months after the crime she still had a difficult time growing her hair back. At the time of trial, she wore a hat because her hair had not grown back. During the trial, the District Attorney had her take her hat off to show the jury, which you can imagine would be humiliating to any victim survivor.

Her family for quite some time thought she would not survive, and the doctor had not given her a very good chance of surviving based upon his medical experience. Ellen's survival is nothing short of a miracle.

The man that did this to Ellen went to trial soon after he committed the crime. It was about three months after the crime that the trial occurred. He was found guilty and given a life sentence. However, unless stated in the sentence, in Texas, a life sentence generally means an individual will be eligible for parole in 20 years.

Ellen has made it a point to make sure that he stays in prison due to the brutality of his crime and the potential for him to inflict that same type of crime on someone else. Ellen makes a very valid point that you can forgive someone and move forward in your healing, but it does not mean that this person should go free. She made it clear that he is a very dangerous man and needs to be in prison. There is a big misconception of restorative justice that says that restorative justice means you have to forgive, and they receive a lesser sentence. That is not necessarily the case, especially in violent crime. There are many times that an offender must stay in prison because of their mental illness or inability to control their behavior. There are many cases where restorative justice has been used, however the defendant has not received a lesser sentence due to his propensity for violence and future dangerousness to the community.

The piece of Ellen's story that is even more amazing and is clearly a reflection of her concern for all people is her act of kindness toward the man who did this to her. Very soon after Ellen's recovery, she found the strength within herself to forgive the man who raped and brutally beat her to the periphery of death.

Ellen shared that she could not be the kind of mother, daughter, or community member if she held inside her the hate and anger from being a victim of a brutal crime. She had to go through a difficult journey, but she was committed. She shared with me how the power of forgiveness has blessed her in her life. She has found that she is more compassionate and helpful to those around her because she was able to let go of that anger and see the good that came from this trial in her life.

Another important lesson that she shared is how vital it is for victims to tell their stories. She could not emphasize enough the importance of victim survivors sharing their story with others. She made it clear that she is always ready to tell her story to anyone who will listen. She also shared with me the importance it has been for her to go inside of prisons and tell her story to inmates.

Ellen shared that she loves to tell her story to either someone in the community or inmates in jails or prisons. She said that when a victim thinks they have healed, that if they tell their story again, they realize how telling their story helped them heal just a little more each time they tell their story. The forgiveness she gave was not said to him directly but was in her heart.

After her victimization she had been doing some reading on forgiveness and she knew that she had a lot of responsibility in her life and she had to forgive so she could do the things that she needed to. She spent some time helping her parents with their health problems, her full-time job, and being a mother. Having those responsibilities was part of her motivation to forgive.

When Ellen was serving on the board for criminal justice, she learned a great deal about restorative justice. She realized the powerful piece it was playing in her life by being able to move past her anger and forgive him.

Of course, the question always comes up, as a practitioner, do you bring up your own victimization to victims of crime that a person works with. Ellen indicated that for the most part she did not discuss with victims about her own victimization but concentrated on the needs of others and as a result, it also helped her to cope with her own victimization by not dwelling on it.

Ellen pointed out that as a victim advocate when she would speak with victims about forgiveness that they do not necessarily have to say it to the offender, but just within their heart so they can rid themselves of the hate and anger that festers the soul, which breeds negative emotion.

About seven years after the crime the brother of the offender called her and wanted to share with her about his brother. Ellen listened and learned a great deal about his life. She learned that he had a black father and a white mother, that the father had a mistress living with the family, and that his father was also into witchcraft.

The father had his son involved with him, who was the man that attacked Ellen. She believes that his upbringing and the way he was treated is the main reason he is the way he is today. This conversation helped her understand some of the history behind why a man would do this to another human being.

As I said earlier, she of course did not want him out, but many of the things that she learned about him helped her to understand his background. She indicated that it made her feel sorry for him and what he had to endure while growing up. To Ellen it does not excuse, but explains why a homicide or other violent crime generally occurs in a person's life. Ellen believes that one of the things we need to work on is training. Training our practitioners about the importance of being more careful and helpful to victims of crime.

Ellen wanted to do a face-to-face meeting with her offender and contacted victim services in her county. However, the offender who committed this crime did not want to meet with her. She was disappointed because she wanted to meet with him and talk about what happened, but unfortunately that has never happened to date.

Ellen has participated extensively in restorative justice in her career. Aside from her duties as the Director of Victim Services for the DA, she was trained and conducted a victim/offender dialogue, and community circles to discuss crime and its effect on others. Early on after her victimization, got involved with many aspects of restorative justice because of the healing effect it had on her ability to help herself and to help those who were victims of crime.

Restorative justice is about the journey. I loved what Ellen told me when I was getting ready to speak at a national conference. I asked her about practitioners and how we as practitioners support the autonomy of a victim in helping them find a path for healing. Ellen said to me, "People who are victims of crime heal in different ways. Some really want to put it behind them and go forward with their lives and never think about it again. But then others have many, many questions. And the only person who can answer [many] of the questions victims have is that offender."

Ellen has also participated with the Bridges to Life Program in Texas. I will discuss this program more in detail later in the chapter. Ellen would go to the prison and participate by sharing her story with inmates. This program has an element of importance that involves crime victims coming in and telling their story to inmates. It has been proven to be an effective tool in helping the offenders understand the pain and suffering they have caused, but also empowers a victim to not only sharing their story but sticking to their steps in recovery and continuing to heal.

I appreciate Ellen so much sharing her story and being such a great example to me of someone who has been through so much and found it in her heart to forgive in order for her to find her path of healing.

Again, let me emphasize that restorative justice does not require forgiveness. I have seen a great deal of survivors who have found it in their heart to forgive the person who committed the crime. It however does not mean that this person should not be held accountable within the criminal justice system.

We should be looking as a system on how we can create less trauma by allowing victims to ask the questions and participate in our criminal justice system process by making their own decisions, and practitioners doing all they can to support a victim's wishes. https://www.youtube.com/watch?v=yWyOTrdkyOg

The Autobee Family – Courageous and Forgiving

On October 18, 2002, Sargent Eric Autobee was murdered in Limon Correctional Center while working as a Corrections Officer. Eric was working in the kitchen of the prison. Prior to Eric working in the prison he was the chef at several Mexican restaurants in the Pueblo, Colorado area. He told his father, Bob Autobee, that he wanted to work in a prison to help inmates learn how to cook. He loved cooking and thought it would be great to give back to the community and work at the prison, to help inmates learn a trade so when they get out of prison they can have a more productive life.

Eric's parents Bob and Lola Autobee live in Pueblo, Colorado. Their other son Scott and his wife Liz live in Pueblo as well. Bob was a Correctional Officer for about one year when he got a job working for the city of Pueblo, where he worked until he retired a few years ago. Lola, Eric's mother, works for the City of Pueblo, Colorado. Scott, Eric's brother, works at a local hospital on their security force. He has such a wonderful little family and is the pride and joy of Bob and Lola.

Eric Autobee was born August 19, 1979. He graduated from Pueblo County High School in 1998. Eric excelled in school and was the recipient of School District 70 MINDS scholarship in 1998 while still in high school. Eric's parents shared with me that he continued in college by attending Pueblo Community College in 2000.

Eric loved big game hunting with his father, brother Scott, and family and friends. He loved turkey hunting and fishing. He was a huge Denver Broncos fan, enjoyed billiard pool, and the Colorado Avalanche hockey team. His parents shared with me that he was the proud owner of "Red," his 1964 Chevy Impala. He was also an altar server and usher for St. Joseph Catholic Church. He loved everything about life his mother Lola shared with me, and always showed his appreciation for all that Jesus Christ gave him personally. His parents shared with me that they know that he is with God and doing good things for others. Both of his parents have felt his influence many times in their lives. He is missed so much by his sweet family.

I have had the privilege to get to know the Autobee family and they have added so much joy to my life, by their example of unconditional love for others and their willingness to forgive the man that took their son's life. I am a better man because of what I have learned from the Autobee's.

I wanted to share a little about Bob and Lola Autobee. Though Bob only worked for the Colorado Department of Corrections for about one year, he has always supported the prison system and has had family members and friends who have worked for the Department of Corrections. Though he and Lola were not completely thrilled about Eric going to work inside of a prison, they supported their son.

Bob decided that it was not for him to work in a prison and so he went to work for the City of Pueblo. Bob recently retired from the city and enjoys working in his yard and going to his cabin. He and Scott are avid hunters and have been going hunting since Eric and Scott were very young. Bob remembers some great times with his two sons Eric and Scott, hunting, fishing, and camping.

Bob and Lola's lives have always been focused around their two sons and Scott's family. Bob and Lola have three wonderful grandchildren, Morghan, Hunter, and Benjamin. They are their pride and joy.

The Autobee family has always been very active in the outdoors. Bob and Lola have done a marvelous job in raising their boys. I have been in their home and seen the trophy taxidermy animals that they have caught through the years including bear, deer and elk. I love going to Bob's house in the fall because he makes fresh jerky with this jalapeño's mixture.

It would be hard to find a closer, strong, loving, and kind family than the Autobee's. I admire this sweet family so very much and am honored to know the Autobee family. I wish that I would have had a chance to get to know Eric. What an inspiration Eric is to his family, which of course has been difficult with his life cut short. However, they honor their son everyday by the kind of lives they live, serving each other and showing kindness to all of their friends and family. This is one family that would do anything for a stranger. Truly heroes to me.

End of Watch "Sargent Eric Autobee" October 18, 2002

On the morning of October 18, 2002, an inmate at the Limon Correctional Center within the Colorado State Department of Corrections, brutally attacked Eric Autobee while he was working in the Kitchen that day helping inmates learn how to cook.

Inmate Edward Montour took an industrial size soup ladle used in the prison kitchen and struck Eric over the head repeatedly until Eric was no longer moving. Just before noon, Eric was rushed to Swedish Medical Center, in Englewood, Colorado. The Autobee family was informed by the Warden at the facility that their son was at the Medical Center in Denver. When they arrived at the hospital, personnel informed them that at 12:30 pm, their oldest son Eric was pronounced dead. http://www.odmp .org/officer/16431-correctional-sergeant-eric-jason-autobee

Of course, a family of a murdered victim have many questions. The main question is always, why? Why would you kill our son? What did he do to you? Those are just a few examples of questions that family members have. The Autobee family is no different. They had many questions as to why Edward killed their son in cold blood.

The inmate who murdered Eric was Edward Montour. Edward Montour was suffering from paranoia, mental illness, and was desperate to make a statement to the prison and to inmates that he could take care of himself. Inmate Edward Montour originally went to prison for murdering his 11-month-old infant daughter.

Inside a prison, other inmates would refer to an inmate like Edward Montour, as a "Baby Killer." If inmates get a hold of a "Baby Killer," they could injure him for life, or worse kill him. Edward also became aware that others had labeled him a snitch.

Unfortunately, in his volatile and paranoid state, he acted out and took the life of Eric. In this mentally ill state, he was defending himself and showing he should not be reckoned with. That is why he killed Eric Autobee, to show the other inmates that he could handle himself. He clearly did not perceive the long-lasting effect that decision had on so many people, including the Autobee family and friends.

Inside a prison, we know that weaker inmates, or inmates with certain crimes committed are prey to other inmates who despise snitches (those that tell on other inmates) and generally any crimes against children.

Tragically, Bob Autobee shared with me that there is now some question to the validity of Edward's original case on the conviction of killing his daughter. There is evidence that the injuries she suffered falling out of his arms in a rocking chair were possibly due to a medical condition and not abuse. That case is pending. However, the fact that he took the life of Eric requires that he be accountable for the murder of Eric regardless of what happens in his other case. However, if that case is overturned, then Edward should not have been in prison in the first place. No matter how you look at this case it is tragic.

The thing that impresses me about Edward Montour, that even though he claims that he never killed his own daughter, he has never denied killing Eric Autobee and openly admitted in open court and takes full responsibility for taking his life. I witnessed Edward taking accountability for killing Eric, which brought great relief to the Autobee family.

The Aftermath of the Murder of Eric Autobee

As a father, I cannot even imagine what that would be like to get a phone call from the prison, informing me that my son was taken to a hospital in critical condition. Then arriving at the hospital with his family they are informed that their son had passed away due to injuries he sustained in an attack by an inmate in prison.

Bob shared with me that he went into a shock after Eric's death. He could not function. He was angry and depressed and felt alone. He started drinking more and even tried drugs to numb the emotions that he was feeling. This went on for quite some time.

Bob's wife Lola did all she could to help Bob. She wanted him to come back to church and not be angry with God or the person who took Eric's life. No matter what anyone said, for quite some time Bob remained in this state of disarray and anger. No matter what Lola or Scott said for quite some time, he continued his frustration and disassociation from family and friends.

Eric's mother Lola and I talked many times for many hours. She shared with me that journey of reconciling the death of her son was to be reminded that she was Eric's caregiver on earth and that now that he was back with God, God was just borrowing him to them. I thought that was so beautiful. Lola has such a kind heart and I have learned so much as a practitioner from this beautiful woman inside and out. Truly Eric and Scott were blessed with a mother of physical and spiritual strength who taught them to love and respect each other and those around them.

Lola shared with me that it was not too terribly long after Eric's death that she found the place in her heart to forgive Edward Montour. Though she has forgiven him, she feels very strongly that he should never be released from prison.

Scott's journey was like his mother Lola. Scott shared with me that after Eric's death that the only way for him to reconcile the death of his brother was to forgive the man that took his life. Though this was very difficult, he put his trust in God and moved forward. Through the years since Eric's death he has come closer to God, church, and his family.

Scott is amazing and truly inspirational to me. I was impressed of the concern he had for his father, especially after Eric's death. He is grateful that his father has taken the higher road and has made so many changes in his life.

The Lingering Court Process and Change of Heart for Bob Autobee

Soon after the death of Eric, the prosecutor for the case got in touch with Bob. He told him that he was going to pursue the death penalty. Bob shared with me that because of his frame of mind, he trusted the system and that it would do the right thing.

Bob shared with me that Edward Montour made it clear after the murder that he wanted to die and so he pleaded guilty in open court and said he wanted the death penalty. So Bob shared with me that the court granted his wishes and sentenced him to die after he pleaded guilty.

Bob shared with me that it was a few years later that he was notified by the prosecutor that the Colorado Supreme Court overturned the sentence because it was an illegal sentence. After the US Supreme Court reinstated the death penalty in the late 70s it required that a jury and not a judge must decide all death penalty cases. Therefore, the judge gave Edward Montour an illegal sentence and he now would be facing a jury trial instead of pleading guilty. The conviction was nullified in 2007 and they were required to start completely over. https://www.democracynow.org/2014/3/5/the_death_penalty_is_a_hate

Bob had found that the way his life was going he would not be able to continue with his anger and frustration. He began going back to church and found that his heart was beginning to understand that holding on to the anger and the frustration was only bringing him down and not helping him in his road to recovering after his son's death.

However, he now had to face this case all over again almost nine years later. He was overwhelmed again and could no longer continue supporting the criminal justice process. He informed the prosecutor that he wanted nothing more to do with the process. He asked them not to contact him anymore about the case.

In the meantime the new defense attorneys that would be representing Edward on the new trial contacted me and asked me if I would reach out to the Autobee family and help them though Defense Initiated Victim Outreach, the program that I was introduced to in Washington, DC.

I agreed to reach out to the Autobee family. I first contacted Lola Autobee. I was expecting a quick phone call just to inform her that I had been asked to reach out to them. She shared with me that they were aware that I would be calling them.

Lola and I spoke for several hours that night. She shared with me that difficult journey that their family had been through and her continued concern for Bob and the difficulty that he has had and that now that he is making progress, they have to start all over again. She was very nervous about this whole process and the impact that it would have on Bob.

She shared with me that he had no interest in continuing his involvement with the process and was not sure if he would talk to me. However, he agreed to meet with me after Lola had shared with him that I had talked with her for several hours. The day and time was set for us to meet.

I was invited into their beautiful home. I cannot tell you how intrigued I was with their immaculate yard and home. I told Bob that their yard looks like a country club. The inside of their home is warm and inviting. I went into their family room and it was full of memorabilia of the years of hunting and fishing with their two boys, their high school achievements, and many other invaluable air looms from their children.

As we sat down that evening after a wonderful meal from Lola, we started talking about the case, from the time of Eric's death to the present day. We spoke for probably seven or eight hours.

There were many tears shed by Bob and Lola, there was laughter talking about their experiences with their family, and some of the trips and different events in their lives. I wanted to get to know Eric before we really started talking about the case, so that evening was about getting to know each other and to talk about their family. Toward the end of the evening we began our discussion about the case.

I let them know right at the beginning that I am only there to listen. I am not involved in this case to solicit a good deal for the defendant, but that this work is about defense attorneys answering questions that victim's in these types of cases have. I also shared with them that I would do all I could to help support them in any request that they had. Little did I know at that time what remarkable things I would witness from the Autobee family.

Bob and Lola shared with me that evening some very intimate emotions about what they had been through with the case and that they were entering their 10th year of dealing with the case and that they would prefer it to end. Bob shared with me at first, he really wanted the death penalty and now he has had a change of heart. He realizes that the death penalty will do nothing to help him. He recognizes that the death penalty to him is about hate and killing people. He indicated that he does not want to be part of any process that allows the state to kill people. They shared with me that they know that their son Eric would not want the death penalty and Bob stated that he does not want another man put to death because of his son's case.

When we finished our conversation after 1:00 am, they asked me to stay with them in their home. That generally is not the protocol in these cases I have been asked to support, but they insisted.

Lola escorted me down to a bedroom. She shared with me that this was their son Eric's room and that they would like me to stay in his room. I was overcome by such an honor. I had a wonderful night's sleep and the next day we continued our discussion. It was a pleasure spending that time with Bob and Lola.

Lola shared with me that she believed the best thing for her husband Bob is to be able to share how he feels. Bob agreed and indicated that he wants to get his message out there to stay away from hate and proceeding with the death penalty.

He asked if I thought we could get him on radio and TV about his concerns for the length of time the case is going and his position on the death penalty. It was amazing to listen to and watch Bob. Many folks that Bob has talked to through the years are amazed that he is the father of a victim of a murder, and yet he has forgiven him and is doing all he can to fight the death penalty.

Soon after we first met, Bob was thinking of all the things that he could do. Thankfully, we had connections in the area and soon he was speaking on *Democracy Now*, a show on *CNN*, several newspapers, and he was asked to speak on a panel about the death penalty with Sister Helen Prejean, the author of "Dead Man Walking," which was also made into a motion picture. It was amazing what events and opportunities Bob was able to participate in.

During this same period, the prosecutor contacted Bob and his family and indicated to them they were going to have to move forward with another trial and wanted to know if we would support that. Bob said that he is tired of this process and going to court. It had been over ten years and he just wanted it over with. He asked the prosecutor not to contact him and that he would not be in the courtroom.

Bob indicated to me that he did not want anything to do with another trial. The prosecutor changed with a new election year and the new prosecutor asked to come to see him and Lola at their home. There were about eight or nine of them that came to his home and met with Bob and Lola. Bob asked me to be there as well.

Bob shared with them that he was not going to support the death penalty and asked them to take it "off the table." They of course said that they were not going to take it off the table. They said that he was not the only victim, that the state was a victim, that the department of corrections was a victim. This frustrated Bob more, but he was cordial to them throughout the meeting.

Meeting Edward: Victim/Offender Dialogue

As the trial was getting closer, Bob asked me if it would be possible to meet Edward Montour, the man who killed his son. I said that generally that is something that happens after a sentence. Bob asked me to try.

So, I contacted the attorneys for Edward Montour. They informed me that it was not only possible, but they would see what they could do to make it happen. After a few days they notified me that they had received permission from the court to have a meeting in the courthouse with Bob Autobee and Edward Montour, the man who killed Eric.

I reached out to a colleague of mine in Colorado, Peggy Evans. Peggy agreed to do the Victim/Offender Dialogue. She met with Bob and his wife Lola and then she met with Edward Montour. She was making sure that they were ready for such an encounter.

After she had met with them for several visits it was all arranged. In December of 2014, Bob Autobee and his son Scott met with Edward Montour. I witnessed this meeting and it was one of the highlights of my career. I have completed several of these types of meetings, but it is always an amazing experience that you will never forget.

I personally witnessed Edward Montour apologize to Bob and his son Scott and told them how sorry he was and that he will always keep that in his heart so he will not forget the pain he caused the Autobee family. It was a very emotional to watch the exchange between them. We all left that meeting that day with a better appreciation for what it means to forgive someone who offends you.

You hear about family members, loved ones, and friends that offend each other over insignificant matters and never speak to each other again, or maybe years before they reconcile. I watched a man who sat and talked with the man who killed his son and all I heard was forgiveness, respect, and apologies. It is the most amazing part about my consulting work, to see this interaction and to see healing from both the victim and the offender. You cannot go through an experience like that and not recognize that there are truly decent people in this world who deserve our respect by not judging them but listening to them.

Bob had a chance to listen to the words that Edward shared with him about how and why he killed his son. Some will ask me, was he sincere? That is a difficult question, but I cannot see him or any other person being subjected to that process if they did not feel remorse and compelled to make it right with those that they have deeply offended.

It is difficult for anyone to face their accusers or for those they have offended. Many will do all in their power not to ever have to face that reality. It is interesting to note that many offenders have no problem going to prison for their crimes, but when you ask them to meet with their victims and be accountable to them for what they have done, they honestly are more afraid of that then they are going to prison. It is not easy to face that part of their crime. By having them participate in this process they are participating in restorative justice. I have heard some offenders say that the restorative justice process was more difficult to go through than going to prison. That says a lot about the fact that some believe that restorative justice makes it easier on the offender.

Another interesting observation for me was watching Bob's son Scott. At first Scott shared with me that he would prefer to stay over in the jury box in the courtroom instead of sitting at the table with the man who killed his brother.

However, during the interaction between Bob and Edward, he had an opportunity to speak. His father asked him if there was anything that he would like to say. He told Edward that he has forgiven him and that he has given it to God. He also said that maybe someday they will meet in Heaven. There was not a dry eye in the room.

During the break in the meeting, Scott came over and sat with us at the table for the remaining of the meeting. He shared with me that it felt more comfortable sitting with Edward. It was an event that clearly changed lives and helped all of us understand a little better what it means to heal from a tragedy.

Bob has come with me multiple times to events all over the country where he has shared his journey from the beginning when he was so full of hate and anger, to where he is today. He is currently planning his third meeting with Edward.

Bob, Lola, and their son Scott are true examples to me of those who have been through so many traumas, and been on a roller-coaster journey that has brought them to the point in their lives where they have been able to forgive Edward and continue on their path of healing. The healing process is considered a path that a victim survivor experiences the rest of their life. Bob said, "I just could not live with all that hate, I had to forgive Edward for myself and for my family."

Bob realized that there was no way they were going to honor their request to not have the death penalty. Bob told them that if they proceed with the trial that he will attend court, but he will not be inside, he will be outside picketing the courthouse.

When Bob said this, I was taken back, I had never in my life seen or heard of anyone picketing outside a courthouse during the trial of the man who killed their loved one. The thing I learned about Bob is there is no way of stopping him. Once this wonderful man has made up his mind he will not stop.

So, when the trial started for Edward Montour, Bob did exactly what he said he would do and he started picketing the courthouse where his son's murderer was on trial. No sooner did this jury selection start that Bob and several other victims of homicide joined him in protest to the death penalty. It was a rare sight indeed, to see a victim's family member outside picketing a trial of a murderer.

They were very passionate about life and they wanted to make sure that those in Colorado and the world for that matter knew that they were not supporting a process where someone else dies.

At this time, Bob was contacted by an attorney who said they would represent Bob. The attorney could see that the courts were not listening to him. He had also requested that at the time of sentencing he have an opportunity in open court to talk about his position on the death penalty. He was told that he cannot do this.

The attorney Iris Eytan, an attorney in Denver, Colorado, represented Bob and his family. She was protecting Bob so he could picket the courthouse and so he could testify at the trial in the sentencing phase if he is convicted. He wanted to testify as to why he is opposed to the death penalty. The prosecution was doing everything in their power to stop Bob Autobee from testifying in court. Just before the trial started, the judge did rule that he could not testify at the hearing. Bob shared with me that this was very frustrating to him.

He was shocked as was his attorney on the fact that the prosecution was completely ignoring Bob and his concerns about this case. The prosecution was opposed to everything that Bob was trying to do.

As the jury was being selected, the prosecution finally conceded and said that they would accept a plea of Life without Parole in lieu of the death penalty. Though there was clear indication that much of the prosecution's decision was based on the possibility that his first offense of murdering his daughter may be overturned. This was one point the prosecution was relying on to show a history of violence and that he had already killed one person. I personally believe that it was a combination of that, but the insistence of Bob not having the death penalty, picketing the courthouse, and wanting to testify in court.

Bob shared with me how much he has appreciated those that have supported him in his life. One of those individuals is Carla Turner. Carla recently passed away with a valiant battle with cancer, but she was the president of the organization called Coloradians for Alternatives to the Death Penalty. She was extremely supportive to the Autobee family, especially Bob. She was instrumental in getting Bob involved in supporting five death penalties that subsequently were resolved without the death penalty being imposed. He misses Carla very much and her passion for helping to abolish the death penalty in Colorado.

For years Bob supported the death penalty, but for him, in his opinion the death penalty does nothing for our system, in fact he considers it to be a hate crime. He referred to it as domestic terrorism and having a bad influence on our children, by teaching them to hate. He said, "It promotes hate, racism and apathy, which promotes violence."

You can see the power that comes through a victim feeling personal empowerment to do everything in their power to heal the way that will help them most. Bob clearly was not letting anyone tell him how to heal. He knew what he needed to do and he did it. No one can fault Bob Autobee for his persistence in doing what he felt was the right thing to do.

Should Every Victim Meet their Offender?

Now it is important that all survivors of crime know that if they do not want to meet with an offender that no one should put any guilt on them or make them feel that it is wrong that they do not want to meet with them or not forgive them. True advocacy to victims of crime requires listening skills in order to better understand and not telling them what they need for healing.

The journey of a victim is very personal, and no one should ever judge someone for participating in a process that you may not want to participate in yourself. There are many victim survivors that may never feel the need or want to know any details about the crime or ask the person who committed the crime any questions. We should also honor victims regardless of their pathway.

In restorative justice it is not about what the system thinks the victim, offender, and community need, it is about meeting the needs of those who have been most impacted and hold accountable those that have wronged someone else by having them answer to those they have offended. As I said earlier in the chapter, restorative justice may include the ultimate punishment of the death penalty. Restorative justice does not necessarily take away the punishment. There is still a requirement of accountability to the law of our land that we cannot ignore. We may not agree and if not we need to work together to come up with solutions that best fit our community and what helps those who are impacted. Having critical conversations with each other is important to restorative justice.

How that happens is the question and what prompts discussion with the interested parties as to how we can best meet the needs of the victim, offender, and community. The only way we find out is by having the critical conversation about restorative justice.

I was speaking with a victim survivor not too long ago and she was sharing with me that her offender is deceased and died the day he victimized her and her classmates. The shooter took his own life. She heard some of the things that can happen with restorative justice.

She shared with me that there is a big part of her that wishes that the perpetrator was still alive so she could ask him questions about why and how. I cannot tell you how many victims I have worked with that have asked those same questions.

Bridges to Life – A Journey for Offenders to Understand Accountability and Responsibility

The last section of this chapter is concerning a program that is centered on the principles of restorative justice. Bridges to Life is a faith-based program that requires the offender to appreciate the importance of being accountable to those they have offended, including God.

The program is a 14-week program where victims have an opportunity to meet with inmates and share their stories with the inmates to help them better appreciate what they have been through. It also allows the inmates to share their story with victim survivors and volunteers. The wonderful thing about this program is that you do not have to necessarily be a Christian in order to participate in this program. It is a program for all faiths and all religions, because the program is built around principles of faith including accountability and responsibility.

To better appreciate how this program obtained its roots, I sat down with John Sage the founder of the program. We have known each other for 11 years and I have grown to respect John so much. I cannot say enough about the compassion that John has for others. He inspires me and has been so helpful to me in so many ways. It is a privilege and honor to know John Sage. He has shared some insight that clearly has helped me in my journey to participate and manage the Bridges to Life Program in Utah and in Pennsylvania.

I went to their website that is very informative and provides a great deal of information about this program. The website Bridgestolife.org does a very good job explaining the history behind this program. In part on the website it reads:

> Bridges to Life Bridges to Life (BTL) is a faith-based restorative justice program for incarcerated men and women that provides a platform for life-changing transformation. Starting in one prison in Richmond, Texas, with 41 inmate graduates in 1999, over 50,000 men and women have graduated from the BTL program in 167 prisons and alternative facilities.
>
> Founded by native Houstonian John Sage in 1998, BTL was born out of an unspeakable tragedy: the murder of John's sister Marilyn in 1993. In the wake of this devastating event, John realized the terrible toll it had taken, not only on his family's lives, but also on those of his sister's friends, co-workers, and community.
>
> As he searched for spiritual answers to his grief and pain, John began volunteering for a prison ministry where crime victims shared their stories with offenders and saw compassion born in them as they awakened to the impact of their actions. After experiencing the powerful restorative effect of this process on both the offenders and victim volunteers alike, and wanting to expand it to others, John developed the Bridges To Life program.
>
> Based on the principles of restorative justice, the mission of Bridges To Life is to connect communities to prisons to reduce the recidivism rate (particularly that of violent crimes), reduce the number of crime victims, and enhance public safety. The spiritual mission of Bridges To Life is to minister to victims and offenders in an effort to show them the transforming power of God's love and forgiveness. https://www.bridgestolife.org/history-and-mission
>
> *From* Restoring Peace *by Kirk Blackard. Copyright © 2010 by Bridges To Life. Reprinted by permission.*

I had the opportunity earlier this year to sit down with John. Soon after his sister was killed in 1993, he was working in a real estate business. His sister was killed in her apartment by two 19-year-olds, a man and a woman. They later received the death penalty for killing her sister. When his sister was murdered there was a great deal of anger and frustration as you can imagine, and he was having a very difficult time concentrating on his work. That next year John suffered from serious depression.

Because of his depression he started working part-time and was on a temporary disability because he could not concentrate on his job.

John then went through what he called his own personal spiritual journey, did a lot of reading, and began feeling much better. He had a lot of ideas on what to do to continue on a better path and ended up volunteering for a Prison Fellowship program called the Sycamore Tree. The fundamental principles of this program were similar to Bridges To Life. However, because of the passion he felt in this program and wanting to adjust the program, he began writing his own curriculum and even was able to get it inside the prison and use the curriculum as a test.

Soon after finishing the curriculum and seeing the success of the program, he was able to get final approval from the Department of Corrections in Texas and has continued to expand, and improve the program that has been extremely successful and is available in several states and internationally.

This insert is from their website that talks about the success of this program. Bridges To Life is an evidence-based program that has had amazing results. Here is a piece from their website about the success of Bridges to Life.

> Bridges To Life changes lives. Recidivism studies reveal that over 85% of BTL graduates do not return to prison within 3 years after release! When offenders develop compassion and take responsibility for their actions, fewer return to lives of crime after leaving prison, crime rates are lowered, and communities are made safer. BTL volunteers report higher levels of fulfillment, forgiveness, and hope in their own lives after participating in the program.
>
> The following comments are from evaluations completed by recent BTL graduates at the Hutchins Unit in Dallas, when asked: What did you receive from the BTL program?
>
> - "I learned to accept my past, learn from my mistakes, and realize there is hope for a change."
> - "I was forced to be honest with myself and take accountability for my actions."
> - "A reflection on self, revealing what I must do to stay free, and peace of mind."
> - "It will help me stay home with my family and do the right thing when I am released."
> - "It showed me my mistakes are in the past to learn from, but the future can still be great."
> - "I learned to think of others and to listen before I react to situations."
> - "I turned from anger to patience and self-control."
> - "I developed empathy and now can feel the pain of the victims of my crimes."
> - "If God can turn me around, He can turn anyone around."
> - "I changed my thinking . . . that I never realized needed to change!"
>
> *From* Restoring Peace *by Kirk Blackard. Copyright © 2010 by Bridges To Life. Reprinted by permission.*

Several years ago, at Penn State University, I applied for a grant to support the possibility of using Bridges to Life with students in our program. I was approved for the grant and was able to take several students to Indiana to receive four days of training and to go inside of prisons and participate with this program.

We then came back to Pennsylvania and we now use this program with our students who would like to volunteer and receive credit for participating. It is great because it gives them experience, including credit to go towards obtaining their degree.

I have had several students who have assisted me with this program, but in the last four years we have used around 30 students to support this program here in Western Pennsylvania, who are all students at Penn State University.

I asked one of our students who provided logistic support and has been a volunteer many times in the program if she would share a little about her experience in the prisons and with this program.

Mia Gallippi has been working with Bridges to Life for about three years. She just graduated from Penn State University in our Administration of Justice Program. I asked her if she would share her experience as a volunteer in this program. Mia Gallippi states:

> From personal experience, I think it is so important to keep this program going and have it in many more facilities. In the prisons, it really seems to make a difference with the inmates which is the intent of the program. I believe the victim speaker part in the beginning of the night is very crucial and important to have. The inmates really relate and connect to these speakers. Even though these are victims of crime and not offenders of crime, all the feelings and emotions are still the same as previously mentioned.

> There are just so many aspects to this program that I think are so advantageous and contribute positively to society and the Criminal Justice System. This program has changed my view on life and has been a very eye-opening experience. I have learned how to understand people more and give them second chances. People always judge my opinion on that, but I think if they actually went through this program with the inmates, their perceptions would alter too. I also learned that inmates are not "animals" as society has perceived them to be. Some of them really could not help how their situation went. Some inmates lacked parental guidance growing up, some had bad living situations, and so on. These inmates could not control some of these factors, and more than likely would not have ended up in prison if it wasn't for those uncontrollable situations. I am not saying this applies to all of the inmates, but it definitely applies to some. I have noticed a major change in these inmates that followed through with the program; and by change, I mean a very positive one.

Copyright © Mia Gallippi. Reprinted by permission.

Mia was a very big part of the success of getting our program started in Pennsylvania. Mia assisted me with some of the research for my book and for the work in getting Bridges to Life started in this area. Her aspirations are to work in the federal system working with offenders and trying to help them finding their paths to a life without crime. I have no doubt that Mia will be very successful in her career and I am grateful that she and so many other students have had the opportunity to participate in this program and to learn and to experience the field at the same time. Thank you, Mia, for your assistance with my book and also for being a big part of the success of this program Bridges to life.

I have been privileged to work with many students from Weber State University and Penn State University – Beaver, Shenango, and New Kensington campuses in facilitating this program. These students have volunteered the time, own transportation traveling many hours to participate in this program. Thank you for your service to our communities to victims and the inmates.

Sister Helen Prejean (My Mentor, My Friend)

In 2010 I was working on a very important case of a prison murder. It was a case of a Correctional Officer in a federal prison who was murdered by two inmates.

My goal in this case was to help the victim's family by getting answers to their questions and to support them as their family went through the death penalty trial. This was a difficult time for this family. The attorneys that I was working with said that they have a contact that could possibly help us in contacting Sister Helen Prejean, a Nun in the Catholic Church, who is also the author of the award-winning book and motion picture called, "Dead Man Walking."

The reason I was so intrigued about meeting her is that she had always been one of my mentors with the work that she does. I believe that men and women in prison must be accountable to God and to the laws of this land. We must do all in our power to make sure that not one person loses their identity going through the process, however it does not mean that they should not be accountable for what they have done.

As a result of my involvement on this case, we scheduled and flew to New Orleans, LA and met with Sister Helen Prejean. Sister Helen is one of the kindest, gentlest, compassionate women that I have ever met. She reminds me of my dear mother. While there I sneezed, and Sister Helen said to me that I must be catching a cold. She took me in her kitchen and gave me some really strong vitamins and a cup of hot herbal tea.

Through the years, the lessons that I have learned from Sister Helen have impacted the work that I have done, helping victims and offenders. There are many who do not fully appreciate restorative justice. Sister Helen is an advocate for the abolishment of the death penalty, but also works very closely with the victim's family members.

The case that we reached out to Sister Helen was a case where I was working with the victim's family. This family did want the death penalty, and Sister Helen gave them the same respect that she would have if they were against the death penalty. She is there to support and help those who go through our system. Sister Helen values human life and I will always appreciate her compassion and her passion to help others.

Whenever I think of my time with Sister Helen and what I have learned from her I cannot help thinking about Mother Teresa and all the work that she did. Sister Helen is selfless in the time and energy that she gives to so many in helping them in their times of need.

With all the wonderful people she has met, in my observations of Sister Helen, she always finds a way to make you feel like you are the most important person in the world and gives her undivided attention. Thank you Sister Helen for your dedication to others and to the countless hours you spend loving those and helping those around you.

Final Thoughts on Restorative Justice

Throughout my career I have had the opportunity to do so many things. It has been such an honor in all the work I have done and yet to do in this field. Out of all the work and people I have met and worked with, I would have to say that the work I have done in restorative justice has changed my life. I will never look at crime the same way.

We as members of our society must take an active interest in how we treat victims, how we treat offenders, and how we treat each other. Today I was watching a YouTube video about an argument between two motorists in a parking lot. They of course were fighting over a parking spot. They were yelling at each other and using horrific profanity. One was a woman and one was a man. I was repulsed by the terms they were using to each other and more disturbed when the man shoved the woman into her car. I could not believe what I was seeing.

I live by the opinion that we must look out for each other. Regardless of what we might think about the death penalty or punishment in general, what we think about people who commit horrific acts on each other, we have to find a way to understand why this is happening and what is needed to rectify the problem. Instead of complaining about those types of people that cause these problems and refer to them as "monsters and horrible people," maybe we have to remember that from a restorative point of view, we are no better than anyone else. Are there individuals who make terrible choices, hurt, and offend others? Of course, but honestly, do we know why? Do we care? I would hope so.

10

Resilience of a Survivor—A Journey of Hope

Resilient Hope

Several months ago, I was searching the Internet for a video that I could play for my class about victim survivors and their path of healing. As I was perusing different videos, I came across a website called *Resilient Hope*. I was fascinated by the title of the organization, so I read the home page about their purpose for their organization. I was even more intrigued with the fact that the individuals who started this website and this organization were all victim survivors of the Columbine High School shooting in Littleton, Colorado on April 20, 1999.

I watched several videos and that is where I was introduced to several survivors that I can now call my friends. These individuals are inspiring to me and I am grateful and honored to be able to have them tell their stories in this book and to partner on other projects spreading a message of hope for those who have been through trauma and do our best to prevent these tragedies from occurring.

I was curious after reading about the fruition of *Resilient Hope* and so of course I wanted to reach out to Kathy Carlston who founded this organization and lives in Salt Lake City, Utah.

Within a few days I was honored to spend some time with Kathy. She is an amazing human being with such passion for those who have been through difficult times in their lives. Of course, her story of what happened at Columbine could not be left out of my book.

I want to share a few inserts from their website that I believe are significant in representing the reason why I wanted to write this book in the first place. I soon realized after speaking with Kathy and several other victim survivors from Columbine that our paths were meant to cross.

Portions of this chapter are written with permission of Katherine M. Carlston. Portions of this chapter are written with permission of Jennifer A. Taylor. Portions of this chapter are written with permission of Nikki (name changed to protect identity). Portions of this chapter are written with permission of Carter (name changed to protect identity).

Many times, we hear that when members of our society go through difficult times, there are many that never recover physically or emotionally. I also know from my experience in working with survivors that there are many that do recover. I would not pass up the experiences I have had in my life to lend support and help to so many brave individuals.

We know that tragedy at any level is difficult to bear in our lives. Sometimes we feel there is no escaping the darkness in our lives that we feel from a traumatic experience. Many victims of crime are in a daze for many days, months, and years not being able to fully grasp what has happened to them. Many survivors describe it as a "fog" or "dream like."

As I have talked about, these events in our lives are not there to break us down. These experiences are a journey that will help us learn to overcome and to build our own journey of hope for peace and happiness.

On Many occasions, I have heard victim survivors saying that it is not fair, why did this happen to me? Many will question their safety, their belief in God or a higher power. Some will feel lost and alone, while some will internalize their emotions and not properly deal with what they have been through.

We must see the value of reaching out to one another, helping each other, not judging, but understanding what is happening to us and around us. Tragically, there is a loss of civility in our world and when tragedy strikes, it is my opinion that we have been given an opportunity from God to find our path of healing and gain the strength when we are faced with adversity.

When we go through tragedy, we can either give up or find a way to survive. On *Resilient Hope's* home page as you read the words of why Kathy started this non-profit, keep in mind the hope to survive, to find happiness, and to rid us of darkness.

> . . . Resilient Hope provides survivors with a safe, private space where they can take refuge, feel understood, and find resources to help them heal. When these viewers feel ready, Resilient Hope invites them to share their own experiences of resilience. Having a place to share their journey toward healing, survivors will be able to turn their darkest times into beacons of hope for others. https://www .resilienthope.org/

Copyright © Katherine M. Carlston. Reprinted by permission.

I think it is interesting how Kathy shared on her website that survivors will be able to "turn their darkest times into beacons of hope for others." I could not agree more, by having survivors tell their stories, we create a refuge for others, born by our experiences that help to create a pathway for others in finding their own new normal.

I was privileged to sit down and speak with Kathy about her story. As with the other stories in my book her story was compelling and gripping to say the least. Kathy took one of her darkest hours in her life and she has literally transformed her story into an eyewitness account of the strength one must achieve in order to overcome the challenges we face.

Kathy is a great example of courage and faith for a better day. Kathy was generous with sharing her story of what happened that day and subsequent days and years to follow.

Kathy Carlston's Journey of Resilient Hope

Kathy has an amazing career thus far in her life. On the *Resilient Hope* website, I wanted to share a couple of paragraphs that help us get to know Kathy and her accomplishments. On the website it reads:

> Thirsting for healing amidst horror and grief, Kathy and her classmates began to walk down an uncharted course. When they were most uncertain of what healing could look like, Gerda Weissmann Klein, a holocaust survivor, visited the students of Columbine and shared her story with them. Through the power of Gerda's story, Kathy and others were able to see a spark of light. Perhaps healing and living a happy life was not as impossible as they had feared. They now had a real, tangible example of hope for a bright future in Gerda's resilient story – a template that inspired them to keep going.
>
> Since Kathy's experiences at Columbine in 1999, she graduated from film school and became a filmmaker, working on several movies, including The Avengers, Oz: The Great and Powerful, Captain America, and more. After hearing of tragedies all over the world, she decided to use her talents as a filmmaker to work toward building a library of multimedia resources for survivors of mass violence. http://www.resilienthope.org/

Copyright © Katherine M. Carlston. Reprinted by permission.

Kathy has done some amazing things but being a survivor of Columbine High School clearly was a challenge that neither Kathy nor anyone signed up for that spring day on April 20, 1999. Kathy's day started out like any other day. Kathy loved Tuesday in the cafeteria; it was free cookie day on Tuesday's at Columbine High School.

Kathy remembers getting her lunch tray and going and sitting with her normal friends at a table inside the cafeteria. As they started to eat their lunch and talk about typical high school conversations, Coach Dave Sanders stood up and yelled for everyone to get on the ground under the lunch tables.

At first Kathy thought it was a prank, so she even joked about it with her friend Nicole, but they both and other students realized it was not a joke. We then heard a popping noise outside the exterior doors to the cafeteria. At that point everyone started to panic and run. Most of the students ran up the stairs to where the cafeteria was due to the noise on the exterior of the cafeteria.

Everyone around Kathy began to run up the stairs, so she followed the crowd and began to realize that it was not a joke or a prank. There were a few in her group that were running, and they ran to the science hallway.

They ran past the first door and tried to open the second door, but it was locked. They ran to the third door, which was opened. They burst into the classroom and the teacher had them all against the wall that could not be seen by the glass in the door to the room.

Everyone was still, no one made a sound. All they could hear was the shooters, Eric and Dylan running down the hallway yelling and laughing. She could hear weapons being shot and could hear the pipe bombs, which physically she could feel through the linoleum floors. At this same time, Coach Sanders entered the room Kathy and her friends had entered.

The horrifying sounds of gunshot, laughing, and pipe bombs seemed like it lasted an eternity for Kathy, but realistically it was about 15 minutes into the terror that all the shooting ceased and they could not hear anything after that. It appeared to be over to them, but they were told by emergency personnel to stay in the room and that they will be found and escorted out by the police.

She said that she could tell that Coach Sanders had been shot. She remembers him having a blue shirt and red all over his face. She remembers that when they did finally come and rescue them that his shirt was soaked in blood and his face was white. That is not a significant notation, but just what was seen through the eyes of a victim survivor. When she was leaving after it was over, Coach Sanders was barely alive, but what she remembers most about that scene when they were leaving was that his shirt was red, and his face was pale.

During the several hours they were in the room, she remembers the students were talking to emergency services trying to get them to rescue Coach Sanders because of his injuries. However, due to safety concerns they took precautions and just worked with students who were trying to stop or slow down the bleeding. Kathy remembers many students taking their shirts off and using their shirts as bandages to attempt to slow the bleeding down by keeping pressure on his wounds. There were apparently two boys that were Eagle Scouts and had just finished the first aid merit badge and were able to assist Coach Sanders. Tragically, Coach Sanders passed away due to his injuries after being shot by Eric and Dylan.

For the duration of the time that they were in the science room, there were twenty to thirty students in the room. Most of the time there was little talking except toward the conclusion of the event when the SWAT team members came in and escorted them out of the school.

Kathy remembers walking back down the stairs to the cafeteria. She remembers seeing one of the teachers Ms. Wyatt holding hands with some of the students helping them through the debris and mayhem in the cafeteria. Kathy remembers at one-point Ms. Wyatt picked up one of the female students and carried her so her feet would not get wet from the sprinklers in the cafeteria. She just remembered feeling a little safer knowing there were others to support them and help them during this time. She remembers walking out of the school and seeing Rachel Scott and Daniel Rohrbough, who were both lying down not moving. They had been shot on the school grounds eating their lunch outside the school.

When they got out of the school, they quickly got into a police car and were escorted out of the area. They were dropped off by a holding area and there were lots of people and media she said. She walked from there to the library.

She remembers walking into the library and seeing her father. She ran into his arms and she just stayed in his arms feeling safe from that day's experience.

On a lighter note, after they left the library, he took her to McDonalds. Her father knew how much she loved Dr. Pepper. He bought her the largest Dr. Pepper and she shared with me how good that tasted after being in lock down for more than four hours with no food or drink.

In the days following the shooting, Kathy felt that each day was a little easier to bare. Though it would be years before she would feel like she was progressing, she remembers feeling safer with her friends and peers. She remembers going to the group activities with other students and the night of the shooting her church met in their chapel to talk about the day and had them share anything that they were feeling. It was just being together and drawing off the safety of being with each other that stood out in her mind as comforting that night.

One of the things that she was struggling with was leaving Coach Sanders in the room, knowing that later he died; she felt the survivor's guilt and was having a difficult time processing her feelings that somehow, she was responsible for him not making it.

She remembers one of the experiences she had that helped her in processing what happened. One of her cousins, a nurse at the time, was talking to Kathy and shared with her that due to his injuries, unless he would have had surgery immediately, he would have never recovered.

She also remembers the night this happened that she cried so hard that there were no tears left. She cried the next day as well and similar the next several days. However, about a week after, she woke up and did not cry that day and realized that she can make it, that she can move forward in her life and that all will eventually improve with time.

Another emotional time for her was going back to school. At first it was very difficult, especially when they returned to school just after the shooting. They attended Chatfield High School and just to be there with her friends brought her comfort, knowing that she was not alone.

Being able to talk about her emotions and know that her fellow students would say, "Me Too," was comforting to her to recognize she was never alone going through this difficult time in her life. One of the things that Kathy remembers and appreciated so much were the comfort quilts they were given. Just those little gestures were so helpful to Kathy and her friends. What Kathy is sharing goes right in line with the importance of listening and providing little gestures to survivors that they matter, that we are there to help them.

Columbine High School, the school district, parents, and the community provided the students at Columbine with a great deal of support through activities, acknowledgement of their need to talk, to be with each other, giving them space when they needed it, and most importantly listing to their needs. After interviewing several students from Columbine, considering that there was no precedence for this type of outreach, Columbine High School was amazing in the aftermath of the shooting. Were they perfect? No, but being together, they drew off of each other's strengths.

Kathy recalled how her sister Liz, who was a junior in high school, five years later, wrote a book about her experience and the experience of other students. She was able to draw the illustrations for the book and Kathy shared how much that meant to her, but also how it helped her in her healing.

Some of the difficulties for Kathy have been safety. Not knowing if they would be safe in school and even after high school. She remembers in college even feeling vulnerable and would now consider herself hyper-vigilant. She also believes that even today she is always cognizant of potential dangers around her. She said she always sits in a restaurant where she can see the exits. After the shooting she received a great deal of counseling and different types of therapy during the first ten years after the shooting. She told me that it was very helpful with several episodes of depression that she sustained.

The first ten years were the most difficult for her. There are times even today that she thinks about it and the trauma that these sweet, innocent kids had to endure that day, which are reminders to her to stay vigilant. She said she is always aware of her surroundings at any public establishment, making sure that she knows where all of the exits are.

Though things have become progressively better in Kathy's life, it does not mean that she has totally overcome those emotions. That is difficult for any trauma victim to totally recover. I don't think any person has ever totally recovered from trauma. However, survivors can become more adaptive to their new normal and can use those things that have happened to the betterment in their lives and not only become stronger themselves, but help others along the way.

That is one thing that I have admired so much about Kathy is her will to improve in her own life with the resilience she has shared in her life, but also because of her voracious desire to help others.

Prior to the Aurora Theater Shooting in July of 2012, Kathy knew that she wanted to do something to help others who had been through trauma or difficult times. She had started to formulate her thoughts on a non-profit to help others in telling their story and helping others through that story.

After the Aurora Theater shooting that is when she started to not only put serious thought into such an organization, but she actually put it together. Through the help of others she had stayed on this path of creating a website that not only helps the survivors in telling their stories, but is also a resource to others who have been through difficult times that there is hope for gaining strength and resilience in your life after you have experienced trauma.

She has spent many hours tirelessly setting up a non-profit that she was inspired to call, "Resilient Hope." A non-profit geared toward building stronger individuals, families, and communities for those who have experienced trauma in their lives.

The stories were developed to give not only a voice but a face to the brave men and women who have shared their difficult trials through story telling on video. I have watched every video and it has inspired me beyond words. Every story is difficult to listen to, but at the same time is wonderful to listen to. To hear first-hand accounts of their traumatic experiences and the aftermath is compelling and truly shows their resilience and their desire to help others through their own story.

Without exception, every story on their website shared their road to recovery and how they navigated those difficult days. How many times have we reached out to someone who has been through an experience, health problem, or even something simple like, "how did you build your shed in your back yard?"

We learn from hearing others stories, which in turn help us to navigate our own difficulties. If I can lessen the burden on another person through sharing with them what I have learned in my life, then I feel that my experience, regardless of how difficult, may help someone else in their own trauma and difficulties they have faced.

There are many that are hesitant in telling their story, but the power that is given and shared is well worth the effort we make when we are ready to tell our story. Not all who experience trauma are comfortable in telling their story. We need to make sure and honor all who are not ready to tell their story. That is why websites like *Resilient Hope* are so important because they provide that example to victims who have a difficult time telling their own story. With time, they will learn to share their story even if it is to a family member or themselves. Never underestimate the power of acknowledging to yourself the tragedy that you have endured.

Acknowledging to yourself is the first step in getting help. I want to thank Kathy for her personal resilience and for her willingness to share her story and help us see the importance of storytelling. Her passion and love for others is apparent in this project. She has taken her skill in technology and can now use it for helping others. Kathy thank you for your example, thank you for having the insight and knowledge to organize and provide opportunities for so many to find help and guidance. Kathy, you truly are inspiring and a blessing to so many.

Jenny Taylor's Story of Courage and Hope

I met Jenny Taylor through Kathy Carlston. Jenny has been a major contributor in helping with Resilient Hope. I was so intrigued with Jenny's story that I wanted to share it in this last chapter with the theme of resiliency.

It is fascinating to me as I have put this book together to see how the pieces have fit together within the different chapters. What Kathy and Jenny have done with this non-profit has captured the importance of victim survivors telling their stories.

Jenny shared with me that she has been more focused on helping Resilient Hope achieve its footing than telling her story. I loved how she feels that helping to launch this website and non-profit has helped her in continuing her journey in recovery from that fateful day. Jenny shared with me how inspiring it has been to hear other's stories through the website and she is so grateful to be part of this.

Jenny has developed a wonderful career in teaching and instructional design. I went to her LinkedIn account and I read a little section she put on her page with respect to her philosophy about her career.

It reads, *"I have always had an inherent sense of curiosity and ambition to solve problems—qualities that led me to instructional design. I believe training should be about solving problems and asking, "What change do we want to see?" "What do people need to do to reach their goal?" and "How can I help people practice doing the things they need to do?" https://www.linkedin.com/in/jennifer-taylor-35980590/*

Copyright © Jennifer A. Taylor. Reprinted by permission.

I really was impressed with her personal statement about her philosophy. Getting to know Jenny I can see in her the quality of helping others selflessly and trying to solve or help others who are either having difficulty or needing to solve a problem. She has inspired me and I am grateful to be able to get to know her and tell her story. My time with Jenny and hearing her story was such an inspiring experience for me—Thank you Jenny.

Jenny's story took a similar path as Laura Hall from Chapter 5. Jenny was with Laura the entire time while they were in the school in the choir room and choir room office.

Jenny's sister Anna was a senior. Anna was in the choir room, but she went to the bathroom right when the shooting started and was able to get out right away. She did not see her sister until later that afternoon/evening. What a reunion it was for her to see her and to know that they were both okay. I cannot imagine what it would have been like to be in their shoes not knowing whether your sister or brother was okay.

That day as she was sitting among the same friends Laura was sitting with, she remembers a wave of students running away from the cafeteria windows towards them. Some students flooded the stairway, others ran out the doors. Jenny followed some of her classmates up the stairs.

For a moment Jenny lost track of Laura when everyone was running up the stairs. Jenny did not realize that she was running up the stairs ahead of Laura. While running up the stairs, she lost her shoe and turned around and was running back down the stairs, when she ran into Laura. She grabbed hold of Laura and pulled her into the choir room with her.

Jenny remembers being shuffled into the choir office by a one of the senior students. She remembers that for the first few hours there was minimal talking between the students. If they did talk it was in a whisper. Toward the end of their time, which was about four hours in the choir office, SWAT team members escorted them out. When the law enforcement officers came to the room, the students thought it was the shooters. The senior boys guarding the door yelled and asked who was in the room. Those that had entered the room yelled that it was the SWAT team. It was such a relief to Jenny to know it was the police instead.

Jenny, along with the other students were told to get in a line and hook their fingers through the pant belt buckle of the student ahead of them. They were led through the auditorium and out the back door of the cafeteria (the door that led to the soccer fields where Daniel and Rachel were lying. They waited at the top of the hill outside the school for the police. When the police came around, they jumped into the police car and were taken to Clement Park, where they got on a bus that took them to Leawood Elementary School.

When Jenny got to the school she was in a daze and was not sure what would happen next. That is when she spotted a familiar face and she then found herself running across the stage into the arms of her neighbor, John Schwindt. She hugged him tight and for the first time in hours she felt safe.

I cannot imagine being a parent of the children leaving the school that day. On this day Jenny's father, Michael, was on a business trip in California when he heard the news of what happened in Colorado. As a father myself, I cannot imagine what that feeling was like being so far from your family and your daughters who were under attack at the school.

Jenny's mother was working in the yard when Brooks Brown showed up, told her that something was happening at the school, and asked to use the phone. Her mother contacted their neighbors Mike and Sue Nyland, Trudy and Todd Thacker, and John and Denise Schwindt. All these families helped Jenny's family in making sure that all the children were safe in the four families. Jenny will never forget the help of her neighbors with their family that day. She did not see her father until the evening. She said that it was such a relief for her to see her parents after the event of that day.

One thing that I have learned from these victims in these cases is that many of them have expressed that the deep love for their family members is what helped them throughout this traumatic experience. They felt safe with their family. It is beautiful listening to their stories of reunion with their families and how much it meant to see them.

Through life experiences, we oftentimes take advantage of our relationships with our families and we don't realize how quickly it can all end. As I have said, these experiences truly handled correctly create a bond between individuals that establish a shield and a protection from the trauma that we have experienced. We should always do our best to preserve those precious relationships in our families.

Jenny remembers for months after the shooting having night terrors. In one of her terrors she would be blow drying her hair. She would bend over and when she would flip her head up in the mirror she would see a black shadow behind her with a trench coat and it was frightening her to the point of having a panic attack.

Jenny also has a recurring dream that she even experiences today, that she is kneeling in a circle of people that are standing around her. She is in the middle of this group of people and a man in a trench coat will walk up to her, put a gun to her head and pull the trigger. She will wake up screaming as though she is truly being shot.

Jenny shared with me something very intimate, yet wanted me to share it within this book. She said that she has a difficult time to this day in trusting people. She said that she lives with a sense of fear all the time.

Many of her friends went through counseling after Columbine, but she never completed any long-term counseling. Jenny did share with me that on one occasion she did go to a counselor. The counselor, after Jenny had shared her story, told Jenny that she understood what she was feeling. Jenny said to her, "No you have no idea what I'm feeling." She then walked out of her session. Jenny shared with me that this experience turned her off from counseling and she never went back. She however can see there were several times in her life when she could have benefited from talking it through with a therapist.

Though she feels that fear can be detrimental, it can also be good because it teaches us to survive and adapt. She remembers doing simple things like singing a religious hymn, trying to change her thoughts that were causing disruption and more fear. She said by diverting those emotions in singing, it helped bring her comfort many times.

She remembers crying over the smallest things and had a really hard time just finding joy. She said what really helped her was being around her friends and sharing with each other the experiences they had been through, which in turn helped them cope with their feelings.

She shared with me how hanging out with Laura Hall helped her out tremendously because Laura went through a similar experience and it helped her to relate to Laura and trust that Laura knew what she was going through.

Another thing that really helped her was that there was a non-profit organization that was called the Linus Project. This project would supply blankets for comfort to crime victims. She loved her blanket and remembers many times crawling up in her blanket and finding great comfort in the warmth of the blanket.

After high school Jenny went to college and found herself really enjoying her college education. She felt that she enjoyed school so much that her social life began to suffer. She went to that school because that is where her sister was, but once her sister graduated, she was not enjoying the rigid rules of the university and decided to return to Colorado where she attended school in Boulder.

Over the course of time since the shooting there have been many times where she has wondered if God had forgotten her, felt distant from God, and felt abandoned. As she has matured, she now recognizes the important role that God has played in her life and the fact that he had not abandoned her, but was with her the whole time and saw her through many dark days.

Jenny indicated that even today she still has a difficult time trusting people and feels that is the reason that she has not been able to have a serious relationship or get married. She believes with time that this will subside, but clearly, she recognizes this and is trying to do her best to continue healing the best way she can.

I believe that is why she has been involved in helping others is that she is healing by being with and hearing the many stories from others by assisting Kathy with this website. I asked Jenny to tell of an experience that she remembers that was difficult to deal with at such a young age of having to deal with that kind of trauma. She then told me about sitting in a science class at Chatfield High School just after the shooting because their school had been shut down for the rest of the year.

As she was sitting in her science class, she remembers putting her hand on the black shining surfaces of a science lab and her body heat did not leave any moisture from putting her hand on a shiny surface. She thought at that moment that she was dead and that she had no body heat.

It was then that she realized that she must work to overcome her fear and to be successful in her recovery. She literally thought that she was emotionally dead. She said, "It was a moment that I realized I was processing my feelings. It was a visual representation of how I was feeling. All those feelings were materializing, and I was not leaving an imprint." She recognizes now the imprint that experience made on her life and is now part of her life story.

As I conclude this section, Jenny shared some insight with me that I would like to share with you. Again, one of the reasons that Jenny wanted to help with this website and non-profit was because of this beautiful statement where she said, "I am trying to capture the stories so those within our communities can understand how to heal and how people can go through difficulties and learn from each other."

My experience interviewing and getting to know Jenny has given me amazing insight into the will of the human spirit to cope with human tragedy and to find a pathway of healing through our own experiences and will to survive.

Nikki—Finding Resiliency Through Her Journey

Several years ago, I was speaking at a conference with my wife Carol. We were speaking on the topic of the impact of sexual abuse on victims. After the presentation, a woman by the name of Nikki came up to Carol and I and thanked us for our presentation and then shared with us that she had also been a victim of sexual abuse, but so much more.

She shared with us a little about her life and how her childhood was altered because of the licentious attitude of sexuality in her home and the lack of parental support and guidance that led to experimentation and eventually to her involvement with drugs, alcohol, and within the sex industry as a female dancer, prostitute, and drug addict.

The chilling part about her story is that in the work that I have done in my life, her social upbringing and what she was exposed to in the home, was a façade to what was really taking place.

Many things that happened in their home were hidden and not discussed with individuals outside their family. When Nikki would experience behaviors that were inappropriate for any adolescent or young adult, it made her feel unsafe or not comfortable. She could not share a great deal with either her mother or grandmother for two reason. One, she did not fully understand it herself and thought that many things she was experiencing were normal for any home.

Secondly, she was constantly being told by adults about what was happening in their home should not be told to or seen by children. Those conversations about adult interactions would be confusing to any young child, yet no one in her home seemed to be concerned about what they were exposing her to.

For example, her mother was very young when Nikki was born. In many ways her mother was still a teenager. So much that Nikki's grandmother did not trust her daughter to raise her own child. Nikki's mother was concerned about her friends she was associating with and going out with them and not being responsible.

We will discuss many of the aspects of what I have addressed in the first part of this Chapter as I share Nikki's story. I first want to say how proud I am of Nikki and all that she has accomplished in her life. She has never given up fighting her past, fighting for her children and her husband, and overcoming odds that were not in her favor for many years.

Nikki's mother was 18 years old when she was born. As I mentioned, her mother was so young when she had Nikki and for many years, her grandmother raised her. Nikki shared with me that when she was an adolescent there were many challenges and confusing times in her life, but she also has fond memories of living with her grandparents.

For example, things that stood out to her included making cookies with grandma or mowing the lawn with her grandpa. She said she remembers Easter egg hunts, and just doing things that were not materialistic, just doing things together. A lot of the fond memories were centered on the things they did as a family that created those sweet memories of a family.

Nikki lived in many places while growing up but spent most of her childhood with her maternal grandparents. In her own words, Nikki shared some sweet memories while living with her grandparents.

"My grandma's house was cozy and filled with warmth. Grandma packed the house full with all her trinkets and treasures, things she ordered from television. She collected all sorts of knick knacks. Grandma had figurines of birds, Hummels, and Norman Rockwell statues with sweet images of family and children. I especially loved her porcelain deer.

I wanted to grow up and get married, and have a family. I fantasized about being a mom and having my own family one day. Grandma was an amazing housekeeper, and she showed me the best way to make a bed and how to make sure there wasn't one wrinkle left in the sheets. She taught me how to do laundry, and I loved to iron Grandpa's work shirts and fold the towels.

I enjoyed being outside running around and playing while my grandfather worked in the yard. There was a concrete walkway that ran from the street down to the front porch. It felt hidden and safe with the hedge all around. The walkway had pinkish-red paint that was peeling off, and I could pick off the layers of paint and see the color that was underneath. I would get a chip of paint under my fingernail and it would hurt, but that never stopped me from picking at the paint...

I was around six years old when my grandpa took my training wheels off on the driveway. I still feel choked up when I think that he cared enough about me to teach me how to ride a bike. He was holding onto the back of the bike with both hands and telling me what I needed to do, and it was a special moment for us. When he let go, I wobbled back and forth, pedaling and balancing. After a few moments, I was able to push myself forward and go. It was a huge deal, being able to balance on two wheels. After that, there was no stopping me. I had places to go and I didn't have to wait for anybody anymore."

I loved to cook with Grandma. At Christmas time we made cookies and Jell-O salads. My aunt and cousins would join us and spend the day together laughing and cooking. It was a joyful time for our family. We made fudge and divinity, jam thumbprint cookies, and Russian teacakes.

My grandma and great grandma would bake homemade bread and cinnamon rolls. There would be a loaf rising in the kitchen with a towel over it, and I could smell the yeast in the air. In the summer, we had bread and apricot jam with hot green tea, with milk and lots of teaspoons of sugar. Great Grandma loved to drink tea any time. She would say, "Should we have us a cup of tea?" And then we would put the kettle on, and I could smell the bread or cinnamon rolls baking, and it felt so homey and cozy."

Nikki said that her grandmother and mother would always talk to her about adult things, problems they were having, and if there was one thing she would have wished as a child, it would have been that they would not have exposed her to so many of their adult conversations.

Another issue that Nikki shared with me that was confusing to her was the fact that her family hid a lot from those outside her home. She said to me, "Our family was very focused on our appearance. We made sure we weren't overweight, our shoes were not scuffed, and our clothes and hair looked nice. My grandma loved to go shopping with me and buy me beautiful things."

From my experience, there are many times in families that when there is a great deal of focus on appearance there tends to be a lot of secrets and dysfunctional behavior that sends very mixed messages to children and they are confused about what a normal family looks like. They see one way and feel another because of the fact that appearance sets precedence on what people outside the home see.

Tragically, things were not always good in her home growing up. She recalled some very dark memories that shadowed the fond memories she had with her grandparents. In her own words she said:

"Those days of fun and carefree times with my grandparents and family were there as an anchor. They helped to endure the storms of chaos brought on by alcoholism and addiction that plagued many of my family members. Mental illness would change the ones I loved, into faces I did not recognize. Behaviors so confusing and contradicting I was living with a different family entirely. Sweetness and peace evaporated instantly in a moment. Fighting, yelling, rage, and violence became a normal occurrence."

Nikki's mother had many struggles. Nikki did not get along with her mother while she was growing up. There was a lot of tension, distrust, and confusion experienced with her mother. In Nikki's own words she will talk about her mother and the problems she faced in her adolescence and as a youth.

"My mother was in and out of my life. She was hospitalized with suicide attempts. I was with her during her black out drinking bouts and attempts to take her own life. She slit her wrists when I was very young, maybe four-years-old. I heard crying and screaming and opened the bathroom door to see the bathroom sink filled to the top with blood. She had taken a razor and made a cut across her wrists. I was shocked at the images I saw. My mother, her face stained with tears and pain, the bathroom filled with blood, towels wrapped around the wound as my grandfather escorted her into the car. I stood on the front porch as she drove away shocked and afraid.

Outside looked no different, the plants were still beautiful, the sun was still shining, but I had witnessed an event that had changed my view of the sweetness and innocence of childhood. It was unfortunately one of what would be many images of darkness I saw because of my mother's self-destructive behavior.

She battled with alcoholism. Her drinking was never done in a social way. Our family religion did not allow any drinking at all so it was done in rebellion and hiding. She put it in secret places, putting the bottle in her purse and going into the bathroom to sneak it. I learned to not trust my mom because she made many promises that she broke to me swearing she was done drinking only to start again. I took this personally as if she did not care about me. I wanted to be put up for adoption or allowed to stay with the several family members that took me in when things got rough.

I lived at grandmas, my aunt's house, sometimes neighbors of mom, anything was better than the fear I felt when being alone with my mom. I remember the pink ribbon that kept the top of the vodka bottle closed in her purse and the disappointment I felt when I found it in her things. There were all sorts of places that she hid her alcohol; her dresser drawer, her purse, in the back corner of the cupboard where the pots and pans were. I gained self-worth from my ability to find it. I believed I was magical and gifted. It took great talent to know where she hid her bottle while she was telling me nothing was wrong. I had developed an ability to know if it was a drinking time just by walking near my house. I believed maybe I was psychic or divinely inspired by God. In my thoughts I told myself that God sent me to my mom because I was so strong. Even though at times I felt angry at God and wanted him to rethink my placement on earth with the family I was brought into, I endured believing it was my purpose knowing I had no other option. When I found her bottle it was a signal for me to put on my armor. I needed to take matters into my own hands to stop her from drinking. I tried pouring out her liquor and filling it with water. Crying, yelling, and pleading with her to not drink, making her promise she would not do it again. She let me down over and over again, our frail connection to each other eroded with each painful experience we shared.

When I was very young she was hospitalized and taken away from me, for periods of time. Sometimes a week or two. The longest separation we experienced was when she moved to Los Angeles to take a job at my uncle's carpet store. I liked it when she was out of my life, things were calmer and I could sleep better at night.

My mother would get up in the night when she had been drinking and cook food on the stove. I lay in bed cuddled next to my grandma listening for danger. Pots clanking while moms intoxicated body bumped into the doors as she walked by. I felt afraid not knowing what could happen. I worried the stove would be left on and a fire would start or maybe mom would burn herself while trying to cook. I knew that when she drank she was not as clear and aware as a sober person. Alcohol changed mom into a very angry person. She would say things that were scary to me about my grandpa and how much she hated him. She yelled at him and they would get into violent fights, trying to hit him or throw things at him.

Over the years I learned from my mom that she believed she was sexually abused by my grandfather. I went over the stories of her childhood with her. Trying as best I could to help her sort out her confusion and pain. My very life depended on my mom getting well and I spent a lot of time trying to figure out how to make that happen. She used me to process the memories she carried. She was confused as to why her mother put her in bed with my grandfather when her baby sister was born. She was only two years old. She told me that my grandma did not want any more kids and that grandma was unable to cope with the stresses that haunted her marriage and her own personal life. She believed that her mother rejected her like a dog rejects the runt of the litter and she was forced to cling to my grandfather.

I did not know what to do with the information that my mom entrusted me with. I was confused and my mind tried to solve the mystery of her sexual abuse. It was not something that I could see and no one was ever telling the truth around me, I was not sure who and what to believe. My mom told me I was an old soul and filled with wisdom. I was somehow helping just by listening to her. I could tell that she got some relief so I continued to be her counselor and confidant.

When mom was not drinking she slept a lot. There were days that she stayed in bed all day. I dreaded it when she told me she was going to lay down for a little nap because it often turned into the entire day. I felt lonely and depressed when I was with my mom. I turned to music as a way of expressing the loneliness I felt inside. I cried a lot and spent time praying and asking God why. I noticed other people's lives and the calm and stability they had that I longed desperately for.

My mom desperately wanted to do better. She would talk to me about how sorry she was that she had hurt me. She told me how much she loved me all the time and that everything she was doing in life was so that we could have a better life.

She sent me to stay with family and wanted the best for me. There was tension between us often and I would get so angry at her that I tore my room apart screaming and raging. I cried a lot. I grew tired of feeling sad. I felt the sadness was so great and endless that it would swallow me whole. Tears flooded me and there seemed to be no stopping them or a solution. I would distract myself after exhaustion from crying by looking at my reflection in the mirror. I would stare into my own eyes and I would notice the change in the color of them. I felt they looked pretty turquoise blue. It was a way of making the sadness a bit more bearable. Distracting me for a moment. But mostly I allowed myself to feel anger. It was more productive and I needed the power that it gave me. I heard the words she told me but could not understand the struggle she had. The promises were broken and I did not want to hear how much she loved me anymore. She tried to start a better life for us many times by going back to school at a junior college to study, she went to counseling and doctors to help her with her depression. She was in and out of recovery groups separating from her family that seemed to bring out nothing but painful memories for her.

But happiness eluded her. She could not grasp life. She was emotionally unstable and volatile. She always struggled with making ends meet. We were on welfare and assistance for food. We got handouts from our local church.

Her last major suicide attempt was when I was 10 years old. We were alone together on Thanksgiving. She was cooking a turkey we had been given by the church. It was just the two of us. There was a feeling of sadness that hung in the air and I sensed something off. I went into my usual mode of becoming a detective. Interrogating my mom and trying to get information to protect myself. I knew that something seemed off with her. I sensed she had begun drinking again. My heart fell grief and heaviness in my chest. My throat felt full with emotion.

But there was something else happening and I had an overwhelming intuition to find the phone book and call my mother's therapist. I knew her name and looked it up. I picked up the phone and called letting her know that something strange was happening with my mom. I could not put my finger on what it was but I knew it was not just drinking. My mom's doctor told me to hang up immediately and call 911. I did as she told and within minutes the ambulance arrived. My mother had passed out and was unconscious. She had taken an entire bottle of antidepressants along with drinking. She had a heart attack and was very close to dying.

I went downstairs to stay with the neighbors. I felt so uncomfortable with them. Their house was dark and they drank alcohol out in the open. I was friends with the little girl, but I did not know them, and I wanted to be with someone I could feel safe with. My mom was gone for a period of time maybe a week and then we went back to life as we knew it. There was no discussion about what had happened. I never went to counseling or processed the event. It was something that happened and that was all there was to it.

I filed it away with another one of the disappointments I felt about my mom. A stronger wedge to be between us and my anger and rage grew larger and larger. Looking back now I realize that my mom's behavior and her love for me were two entirely different things. As a child I could not understand how she could love me and then do the things she did. What I know today is that it had nothing to do with her love for me. My mom was not well and her inability to get better and my rejection of her has caused us a lifetime of pain and turmoil. We have not been able to mend our relationship. I continue to work on learning compassion and forgiveness and her struggles continue to trigger me back into the same pattern."

Copyright © Nikki (name changed to protect identity). Reprinted by permission.

I would now like to share some of the paths that Nikki endured as a child, as a young woman, and as an adult, and how all of this really started by the confusion and disruption that she experienced in her youth. We oftentimes hear that upbringing in the home is critical and that if there is dysfunction there are better chances for chaotic and confusing experiences that a child is forced to endure.

As I mentioned earlier, Nikki's grandma took over as her mother for her mom. She talked about how her bonding with her mother was not there because her grandma did not trust her mother because of her behavior and choices. She was born in the 60's and was conceived by a teenager her mother met at a party. Nikki said, "My mother was dealing with her own pain of sexual abuse and shame. She also felt a great deal of shame of being an unwed mother in the 60s." Nikki represented shame to her mother because she was conceived at a party.

Nikki believed in marriage and wanted to be married but growing up was confusing for her and caused a lot of mixed emotions about what a family is. There were many inappropriate boundaries that were not followed in her family. Nikki had two uncles on her mother's side that were sex addicts and both of her uncles forced her mother into having sex. She was raped by both of her uncles, one that resulted in a gang rape with her uncle and his friend. She never told on them, but did tell Nikki. Many times, Nikki's mother told her things that were happening to her and that had happened to her in the past. This put a great deal of pressure on Nikki, and many times she felt as you read her statement about her mother that she found herself trying to figure out how to help her mother survive. That is too much for any child to have to endure, trying to help her mother survive. This created resentment towards her mother and also opened the door to a lot of unsupervised behavior as an adolescent and youth.

While growing up Nikki felt she had no boundaries. As a small girl around the age of five she remembers watching her older cousin abuse her younger cousin. She then at age of seven was abused by a neighbor boy and forced her to give him oral sex. She also recalls several encounters with other children acting out in sexual ways. There were no boundaries and many times she never understood if what she was doing was normal or okay, but she had no one to talk to about them because her mother was dealing with her own problems. Many times at this age she would call her aunt to come and get her because her mother was so drunk she could not wake her.

Around this same time period she also witnessed her mother having sex with a man who was married to someone else. This of course caused even more confusion about sexuality, and she was only seven years old. She also remembers playing "nudist colony," with her cousins where they would walk around and crawl around naked. Again, no supervision so they could basically do whatever they wanted.

When Nikki was eight years old, she was involved with several other children her age who were acting out sexually. Between all these encounters with her cousins, neighbors, watching her mother have sex with a man, it was causing a great deal of confusion on her attitude and knowing what sex was. She had no idea what it meant to have healthy boundaries, or experience adequate supervision from adults.

By the time she was 10, her understanding of appropriate behavior was so confusing. Her behavior started to worsen with respect to how she felt about herself. She would play spin the bottle, demand gifts from boys, and they began to use her in what she referred to as her "flirting power."

At age 13 her mother met a man we will call John. He came to their house and began having sex with Nikki's mother. Nikki was lying on the couch trying to sleep, but with them having sex she could not sleep. She remembers that he started flirting with her too at the age of 13. She told him that she wanted to me a model like Brooke Shields and he started taking pictures of her with her shirt off.

Also around this same time period, she was forced into a house by a bunch of boys and they were forcing her to kiss them, she was able to escape but she was scared, angry, and confused by all these things that were happening to her.

When she was around 14 years old, she was over at a friend's house and was introduced to alcohol, drugs, and pornography. Her friend's mother even bought pornography for them.

By the age of 15 things were not getting any better. She had a new boyfriend. They were actively engaged in sex and she got pregnant. Nikki moved in with his family but had an abortion after four months of being pregnant.

By now she was using drugs, alcohol, and also binge eating and purging herself. She wanted to be thin and was becoming bulimic. When Nikki turned 17-years-old she dropped out of high school and went to continuation school.

She met a new boyfriend who was into heavy drugs. This enabled her to continuing using drugs. By now she was using marijuana, cocaine, methamphetamines, and alcohol. She also continued with her anorexia and bulimia, and began cutting and burning herself. With little communication with her family, Nikki was having to deal with life's challenges on her own.

Her new boyfriend cheated on her and during this whole time when she was living with him and his family. She also got pregnant twice and had abortions. He was abusive and hit her and even pulled her hair, but she was obsessed with him. What was really hard for her is while she was having the abortions he would ignore her and she found out he was having sex with her friend.

Nikki began stealing checks from her grandparents to be accepted in with her new friends that were into drugs. She was also binging and purging herself five times a day to keep skinny. She remembers one time being so drunk at the age of 18 that she jumped out of a fast-moving RV on the road to the beach. She had a head injury, but never sought treatment. Her life was completely out of control with her sexual addictions and drug and alcohol usage.

When Nikki turned 20 she moved to Los Angeles and answered an advertisement for modeling. She answered the advertisement but found out it was an escort service.

During this same time period she auditioned and became a dancer at a nude dance club. To get the job she was forced to sit on the boss's lap while he would put his hands all over her while she whispered in his ear.

From age 20 to 25 she worked in various adult clubs in Hollywood and also moved back in with her abusive boyfriend. She used drugs and alcohol, and practiced her eating disorder daily. She also prostituted with men for $1,000 a time.

Nikki knew that no one knew where she was, and she thought she would be murdered. She feared her life was ending. She had to just tolerate this lifestyle. She recalls having to beat up an old man who was trying to take advantage of her.

During this time she also worked in an adult book store in their peep show booths. She was in the booth behind glass and had to talk on the phone. Nikki talks about how awful it was to watch them and perform in front of them. She said to me, "Every experience was traumatizing, and I went home and sobbed every night."

During this time, she also made some adult videos as well. Her life was in a spiral and she felt no escape from this lifestyle. She was strung out on methamphetamine and became psychotic and paranoid. She said at this time in her life she even tried to make a deal with the devil to take her soul for money.

In this lifestyle she was in, men would take advantage of her and she ended up on two occasions being raped after she had passed out from drugs and alcohol. She became homeless and would live in rundown hotels. She at one point moved in with a man who had gone to prison. He put some pills in her drink and she woke up with him and his friends raping her.

She was stealing drugs from dealers and had to leave town. She moved to Sacramento; moved in with a guy and his parents she had met. She was able to get a real job and tried to get out of the sex industry. This guy she met abandoned her at his parents' house and never came back. While she was staying at his parents, their nephew choked Nikki and forced her to have sex with him.

Finally, when Nikki was 25 years old she did go to a rehab center and admitted that she cannot continue on doing what she had been involved in. Unfortunately, she leaves and goes right back to drugs because she had "gained weight," which was one of her triggers for using drugs. She spent months again on drugs, got to the point where she was not caring anymore, and cut her face with a Bic razor. Finally after going to a homeless shelter, she checked back into the rehab center.

After she finished with the rehab center at 26-years-old, she moved back to San Jose with her grandparents and began a serious attempt at sobriety.

At this point she met her husband-to-be and she indicated that they were sexual right away. They were having problems based on his problems with pornography that started when he was a young man. Nikki said that she could not live with those magazines in the house.

He agreed to go to counseling with Nikki and they decided to get married and start attending church again. She indicated that he was a very devout believer and promised her he would no longer look at porn. Truly at this point in her life she was unaware of the addictive side of pornography and thought that all men looked at porn.

They did get married. The first job that Nikki received after they got married required her to go out of town for training. She received a phone call from her husband

and he told her that he was calling phone sex lines while she was out of town. Nikki said that this traumatized her with all of the memories of her past, working in the strip clubs. She stated at this point in her life that she hated sex and just felt it was a woman's duty to make a man happy.

When Nikki was 28 years old she had her first daughter, who was the love of her life. She loved being a mother, however she felt very inadequate and put so much into being a wife and mother that she became depressed and suicidal and again cut her face with a razor. She said, "I was having severe anxiety and depression, and I started counseling. I cried a lot, and I thought there was something wrong with me."

By the time she was 29 or 30, she was pregnant with their second daughter. There was a lot of fighting with her mother. She tried to cut off ties with her, and she began swallowing shards of broken glass. She felt very strongly that she needed to go into the hospital, and during this same time her step-grandmother committed suicide by hanging herself. Nikki was trying to save her family to make up for all the bad she felt she had done.

Nikki and her husband moved in with her husband's mother after she was diagnosed with ALS. She died one year later. Nikki helped care for her and as a result of the lifestyle change, she started to gain weight. This bothered her and she occasionally was purging again, and experiencing marital problems and constant fighting. Nikki was also worried that her children would be sexually abused.

All of these feelings were a result of the many different things that Nikki went through in her life. She started seeing a psychiatrist who was helping her with her depression, and sexual anorexia, which is loss of interest in sexuality. At the age of 35 she checked herself into an eating disorder treatment center. It was in that facility that she was diagnosed with Post Traumatic Stress Disorder (PTSD). She went to a psychiatrist who prescribed her medication for severe anxiety. She eventually went the homeopathic route and got back into counseling.

Since that time, Nikki and her husband continue to move forward. Though they will always be working to overcome their sexual addictions, they have made steady and sustainable progress. They are finding peace through their spirituality and raising their children. She now teaches as a lead kindergarten teacher and has found a great deal of satisfaction working with children trying to help them as they are growing and developing.

Nikki has been through so much in her life and you can see that much of her path that she had chosen involved being introduced to behavior very young that was difficult for her to comprehend. She was confused and truly lost her innocence as a small child by having to deal with adult situations at a very young age. She was making poor choices and was afraid to talk about what was happening in her life and became depressed. She thought that the only way that she could survive is do what she saw in her life and that was for women to be objectified and to please men with her sexuality.

Though it has not been easy, Nikki has not given up on her marriage, her children, and the new lifestyle that she has chosen and been following for many years now. I admire Nikki so much for going through the experiences she went through, having the addictions that she had developed, and still was able to move forward finding her new normal, recognizing she has this in her past but that it does not define her.

I want to say that Nikki is one of my modern-day heroes. Working in this industry and being trapped with multiple forms of addiction, she never gave up, she hung in there and showed not only and most importantly herself, but she showed those around her that you can be in your darkest moments in life and still through your choices make changes that will bring you joy and happiness the rest of your life.

Nikki does not let her past define who she is. She has chosen the higher road in her recovery and how she feels about herself. She is an awesome mother and is so supportive to her children and her husband.

Now what she can do is use it for her betterment. Through sharing her story in this book and talking to me, creates a path for her that shows her vulnerability by not being afraid to share a very personal and embarrassing time in her life. However, she is not afraid to talk about it and to do everything in her power to facilitate change in herself and help others. If I were in Kindergarten, I would want Nikki to be my teacher, hands down!!!

Carter's Story: "He Was Our Friend"

In this last chapter, it is about finding resilience and hope in a world where we are constantly being challenged with so many difficult situations. Along the same theme of violent crime, when a child is traumatized, many times they do not recognize trauma until years later.

When they reflect on their lives, they realize that their trauma that they have been dealing with since their abuse is generally in the forms of not trusting men, or adults, or having a low self-esteem or confidence.

For Carter, she did not realize how non-trusting she had become of men until she pieced it together after hearing a story of a victim in one of her classes at Penn State University – Beaver Campus.

I remember that day, I remember when Carter came up to me and said that she wanted to chat for a minute. We had just had a guest speaker talk about her trauma and I could tell by the look on Carter's face that she had a deep question for me.

She started to ask me a question which really turned into a statement of, "I think I was a victim of a crime?" She also said it was a family friend and he did not touch me, so it wasn't that bad."

I cannot tell you how many times I have heard a similar reply to abuse. Though an offender may have not raped a person, their behavior has crossed the line and caused trauma, discomfort, and confusion.

Carter's story is a perfect example of what happens when you are groomed by a family friend and innocently the victim and their family become intrigued, mesmerized, or groomed by a perpetrator so that they may take advantage of a sweet innocent child.

When Carter was seven years old, she was living with her parents and her older brother and just enjoyed being a "kid." She was very active and has always been active throughout her life in sports. She learned from her father to be a speed skater and loved to skate with her family. Her father was a speed skater when he was younger and skated until he got married.

Carters father knew Jim very well. They met and became friends when he was 20 years old when they both were into speed skating. When these incidents occurred, he was around 50 or 60 so they knew each other for over 30 years when the crime occurred.

Again, when Carter was seven, Jim began coming to the their house on the weekends. He would arrive at their home and spend the day with them, and then he would go back to the town where he lived at the end of the day, which was an hour drive. He would then come back the very next day. He eventually started to spend the night during the weekends, downstairs on the couch in the family room.

Carter's bedroom was through the family room, up the stairs, and was the door directly at the top, just to the left was her parents' room. Her brothers room was downstairs – past the living room and past the kitchen on the left hand side.

Jim got very close to their family over the course of the next two years. It seemed to her that he was coming around more and more and would even come to their family gatherings, and parties they had at the house. He would also go to events for skating with their family and even helped Carter as she was getting to be more familiar with the sport.

Jim continued to grow closer to both Carter and her brother. Carter shared how he would buy them gifts, candy, and would bring her little bags of chips to the house. She also remembers him buying a new set of wheels for her skates and basically anything she wanted.

He would tell her what she was getting for Christmas and what she wasn't getting. He would find out from my parents and then tell Carter what she was getting. He especially got close to Carter. She found it odd that when she and her brother would fight that he would always take her side regardless if she was right or wrong. If she was sad he would cheer her up, if she had been in an argument with her parents, he would in a round-about way bad mouth them agreeing with her.

Another thing he would do is he would always drive my brother and I around anywhere we needed to go. Carter shared with me that in a way he became like a second parent or like a nanny to us. He spent a lot of time with us and we trusted him.

The important thing to remember what I talked about in Chapter 3 is that grooming is not just for the child, but also for the parents. He has to gain their trust. I remember one time interviewing an offender and he said that gaining the trust of the parents is as important or more important than gaining the trust with the child that they had planned to abuse.

As things became progressively more personal, she noticed things that made her start to feel uncomfortable. On a few occasions he would have his hands in his pants at weird times, like when her brother and her were in the car.

Then on one occasion Jim was sitting on the floor leaning against the couch watching television in family room with Carter. She was lying on her stomach facing the television at an angle. On the other side of the coffee table from where he was sitting, she laid her head down and tilted it to the left and she could see under the coffee table. That is when she noticed that he placed his hand up into the bottom of his shorts out stretching his penis down his right pant leg and was massaging himself. At the time she did not know what to do and tried to ignore that it happened.

The occurrences started to get worse. On another occasion she was folding clothes downstairs in their basement. He then came into the room to give her some company. He sat off to the right of Carter's point of view. She was picking clothes up from the basket behind her and setting them off to her left. He again in front of her, put his hands in his pants and began moving his hands. Then after a few minutes he pulled his pants down to his mid-thigh and completely exposed his penis to Carter and began masturbating.

As you can imagine Carter at this point, was extremely confused and nervous. They never said a word that she can remember, he might have asked her how my day was, or other insignificant small talk given what was happening. When she finished folding clothes, she went upstairs and never told her parents.

Carter was not sure how she would explain to her parents what was going on. Her parents trusted him, and everything to her felt so dirty and she didn't want them to know what she had seen.

At eight or nine years old, she was worried about how she could explain to her parents that this man that was part of their family was showing Carter his penis, masturbating in front of her, and making her feel repulsive. She said, "I would just try to get through the moment and then I'd tell myself that it would all be over soon, and I could forget about it."

These are appalling positions that these offenders put their victims in, especially the ones that are small and really have no clue how to handle that type of behavior. It basically creates a pathway of non-trust in relationships and misconceptions about human intimacy.

The last occurrence where Jim acted out was in June when Carter was eight years old. She was getting ready for Nationals in Nebraska, the national speed skating competition that she qualified month's prior.

It was a warm, sunny day and Jim was over at our house again. She remembers that it was later in the day and she was about to get in their hot tub. Most summers she said that they had a pool but that year they did not, so her mom would fill the hot tub with cold water, put bubbles in, and turn on the jets.

Her parents were downstairs in the basement, and her brother and his friend were in his room and she was outside with Jim standing next to the pool of water. Carter was standing in her swimsuit when Jim said he wanted to take a picture of her to show his mother. He supposedly lived with his mother. Carter and her mother later discussed the fact that neither of them had ever met his mother and they questioned her existence. So, she stood there and let him take a picture of her and then proceeded to get in the bubbly pool.

He got into the pool with her and they were just small talking. He then took his trunks off and then he floated to the top of the water exposing his genitals to her and played it off and commented about his fat belly. She was very close to him in the hot tub and at this point she clearly did not know what to do.

At that moment she heard the back door in the basement open and her father came outside and saw for a brief second what he was doing and told Carter to go upstairs. He then questioned him about what she saw? Her father was very upset and told him to get his things and to leave and never come back to their home.

The Aftermath

Carter's parents came and sat her down and asked her what she saw. There was some indication from her that maybe it was his thumb. She knew that it was not, but did not know what would happen if she told the truth.

Her parents called the police. They came to their home and her father told them what he saw and then they questioned Carter. She told them that she was not sure what she saw. The police based on the information she shared with them, decided not to prosecute him for what he did. Carter said that he never came back to her house again. A few years ago, he tried to contact her through Facebook, but she would not accept his friend request.

For years now Carter has basically suppressed what happened and never told her parents about what happened on the three different incidents. Clearly Jim was on his road to progressing to the point where he would have tried to sexually assault her. It was bad enough what he had done, but he had not quite acted out by physically abusing her yet. He was grooming her and her parents and each time he was getting closer to acting out.

About a year ago in my class when she came up and told me her story, I was so impressed with her candid nature and the fact that she was not afraid to talk about it, especially when she realized that she too was a victim of his actions.

Since that day she approached me, she has taken it upon herself to get some help in counseling, and to share her story with other students, and she has even helped in the program Bridges to Life that we talked about in Chapter 9. She is truly an amazing young woman who recognized that what he did was wrong and that he took advantage of her innocence and thank God that her father came out the back door at that time. He had not come out of the house; she very well could have been on her road to the next level of grooming which is to actually commit the act of sexual abuse. He had been working on her and her family for two years or so.

When we talk about resilience, so much of it has to do with attitude. Though I have seen Carter shed some tears and has had to go into the dark side of what happened to her in counseling, she shines as a beacon to all young ladies who this has happened to, that it does not define you or is not your fault.

In July I took Carter and some other victims of violent crime to speak at the National Conference for Victim Assistance. For the first time since this happened, Carter was able to stand up and tell her story to over 600 people. That is astounding and clearly a sign of resilience and determination to succeed.

Carter is continuing on her education and I have no doubt that this young lady will achieve many things in her life and that because she has come forward at a young age, she will have many opportunities to tell her story and to help others. I for one am a better person because of her example of stamina and perseverance. Carter clearly shows resilience through her commitment to change and never allowed that incident to define her or control her emotions. Carter I am proud of you!!!!

Closing Remarks to My Book

I clearly did not appreciate the journey this project was going to take me through. Even with all the encounters I have had working with victim survivors, it did not prepare me for the important lessons I learned from each one of the survivors within this book.

I will always recognize them as true warriors of strength in a world that has thrown at them difficult challenges that have created their pathway towards resilience and healing.

There are many that know me, and I realize that I can get very emotional when I talk about the tragic experiences that others have suffered. I see in their faces the strenuous affect that trauma has had on them. I have heard it in their stories, sitting with them when they have had to re-live their trauma and watching the agony on their faces when I have accompanied them to the court hearings. I am truly amazed at the resilience of those I have been privileged to get to know and who have been willing to tell their stories.

I want to conclude this book by sharing some thoughts about resilience and the importance of our ability to create a way where we can find the inner strength to face the difficulties in our path and recognize that we are not defined by the difficult or bad things that happen to us. There are many victims as we have heard that internalize their victimization and find themselves confused, shamed, upset, and having many other emotions.

I love this quote about resilience, it reads, "We all face difficulties, challenges, and setbacks, but resilience is what determines whether we fight through it and grow, or whether we cave in and let those challenges defeat us." https://hackspirit.com/resilience-quotes/

All these victims chose to face their challenges and recognize the importance of not giving up and not letting their victimization seize their ability to succeed personally in their lives. Our challenges in my opinion were not meant to bring us down, but to give us an opportunity to build self-reliance, self-worth, and resilience.

I remember a young lady calling me in the middle of the night, terrified of what happened to her and reliving the experience over and over in her mind, trying to determine her level of responsibility for what happened to her. She was taking on a great deal of the responsibility because she let this man into her apartment.

This really sheds light on the importance of our work. We have got to understand that each survivor of a crime must work very hard to achieve resilience in their lives after being a victim. It is a very difficult challenge. Most victims at some point, even have feelings of completely giving up because it seems the harder, they try the more challenges they face and there does not seem to be any light at the end of the tunnel for them. They have a difficult time seeing the light within themselves.

We each have a light within us. It is the light within our spirit that gives us the will to meet our challenges and to face our fears and realize that we have that ability to overcome. In Christian belief there is the light of Christ that is within us and they truly believe that Christ's influence and enduring the crucifixion gave us the power to overcome our trials and be forgiven of our sins through Christ's Atonement.

Even if you do not believe in God or Jesus Christ, most people believe that there is a higher power that gives us the strength to face our fears and our pains and know that we will be okay. It definitely is not easy, but succeeding and finding strength is worth those struggles because they show us our ability to see the light at the end of the tunnel of our trials.

Through my experience with my family and with victim survivors and their families I can attest that each family and individual I have worked with, which is in the hundreds if not more, involve the belief in a power higher than theirs that gives them strength to endure.

Endurance is one of the most important characteristics of a victim survivor. They must envision if they cannot see light at the end of the tunnel and recognize that strength to endure is mostly centered around family and friends. We as the family and friends of victims, as I have said before, must be willing to sacrifice our time and develop patience when working with our friends and loved ones who have been victims of crime.

As I have said many times, just listen with your heart as you approach working with victim survivors. I really like this quote, "Resilience is accepting your new reality, even if it's less good than the one you had before. You can fight it, you can do nothing but scream about what you've lost, or you can accept that and try to put together something that's good." – Elizabeth Edwards. https://hackspirit.com/resilience-quotes/

I can say without hesitation that the survivors who have shared their story are clearly in the group of those who have learned to accept their new reality and see the good that has come from their trials in their lives. I not only believe, but I know that they will succeed.

I have laughed with them, cried with them, and watched them from a distance as they faced many challenges. I cannot do it for them, each person must travel their own road, but I can tell you that at the end of a marathon race, I am the one with the cowbell making all the noise yelling with excitement as they merge out of the tunnel and into the light of self-respect, self-esteem, and self-confidence.

I will end my thoughts with one of the most salient quotes that I found in my research to coincide with my book.

> "We took the path that led others nowhere and only we saw the light at the end of the tunnel. They warned us about the monsters we would encounter, the odds that we would meet. And they laughed when we got the scars while fighting the dragons on our way. When we came back out of the tunnel, holding the sword that they always craved for tightly in our hand. Bleeding and the sun shining on our face. We became the tales they wanted to be. We became the reflections of what they always wanted to see themselves through. We became the warriors they had always imagined of."—Akshay Vasu

https://www.goodreads.com/quotes/tag/tunnel

Those of you that have suffered, those of you who still suffer from being a victim of a crime, I pay my deepest respect to you this day. I pray that you always know that you are capable, you are strong, and you can and will emerge from "Standing in the Dark."

CPSIA information can be obtained
at www.ICGtesting.com
Printed in the USA
BVHW070741010721
610936BV00006B/106